Hartmann, George Wilfried, 1904-

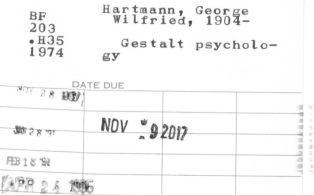

Gestalt psychology

GESTALT PSYCHOLOGY

A SURVEY OF FACTS AND PRINCIPLES

By

GEORGE W. HARTMANN, PH.D.

ASSOCIATE PROFESSOR OF EDUCATIONAL PSYCHOLOGY, TEACHERS COLLEGE, COLUMBIA UNIVERSITY. SOMETIME SOCIAL SCIENCE RESEARCH COUNCIL FELLOW AT THE UNIVERSITY OF BERLIN

PSYCHOLOGY SERIES

ALBERT T. POFFENBERGER, PH.D., *Editor*

Professor of Psychology, Columbia University

GREENWOOD PRESS, PUBLISHERS

WESTPORT, CONNECTICUT

Library of Congress Cataloging in Publication Data

Hartmann, George Wilfried, 1904-
Gestalt psychology; a survey of facts and principles.

Reprint of the 1935 ed. published by Ronald Press Co., New York, in series: Psychology series.
Includes bibliographies.
1. Gestalt psychology. I. Title.
BF203.H35 1974 150'.19'82 73-16649
ISBN 0-8371-7213-6

Originally published in 1935 by Ronald Press Company, New York

Reprinted in 1974 by Greenwood Press
A division of Congressional Information Service
88 Post Road West, Westport, Connecticut 06881

Library of Congress catalog card number 73-16649
ISBN 0-8371-7213-6

Printed in the United States of America

10 9 8 7 6 5 4 3 2

TO

ROBERT S. WOODWORTH

PREFACE

Within the last decade American psychological circles have witnessed a recession of interest in the behaviorist movement and a steady growth of critical investigations centering about the doctrine of *Gestalt*. Although historically the two theoretical positions developed contemporaneously, a number of influences conspired to delay the vogue of configurationism. First of all, as a product of German thought, it was couched in an alien tongue with all the difficulties of translation and interpretation which that implies, particularly in a highly technical field. Second, the war and its consequences interposed a brief but huge obstacle to professional contacts. Third, Gestalt psychology is pitched in a rather high intellectual key and consequently offers more resistance to popularization than behaviorism, whose positivistic and materialistic features represent an extension of a familiar tradition to all phases of mental life. And last, the leaders of the movement have been so busy pursuing an ambitious research program, proselytizing, and engaging in polemics that a really adequate synthetic treatment from their own hands constitutes one of the biggest gaps in contemporary psychological literature.

German scientific writing is proverbially famous for its obscurity and there is much in the sheer phraseology of Gestalt which repels one by its vagueness. Precise definitions are conspicuous by their absence. Nevertheless, the difficulties which even well-trained psychologists with different experimental backgrounds experience in comprehending the basic contributions of configurationism lie largely in the intentional and violent break which it makes with the past. It is like some sudden forward leap disturbing the continuity of scientific development. The revolution which has occurred in physics within the last quarter-century presents an analogous situation, for few laymen, and perhaps few physicists, are fully at home in the new realm of relativity.

This volume is an attempt to bring together in convenient form all the material necessary for a more than superficial understanding of the subject with which it deals. It is intended to be read with profit by any one who has had a first course in elementary psychology. Essentially, I have aimed to give a sympathetic picture of the Gestalt system from the standpoint of a non-configurationist, although I must confess that an examination of the evidence has left me more favorably disposed toward the theory than I had originally anticipated. My major task has been that of an expositor and interpreter and only secondarily that of a critic. Had my equipment and resources been adequate, I should have preferred to make this work a complete reference handbook, but external limitations compel me to rest satisfied with a less pretentious, but I hope equally serviceable, summary and orientation.

Many passages derived from important scattered sources appear here in English for the first time; and while I realize that the manner in which they have been woven together leaves much to be desired, the busy reader and student should find here the gist of the most significant documents in this field, which should give a background that will make possible an intelligent reading of the new material constantly being prepared and issued under Gestalt influence. Economy and pithiness of expression have been sought throughout, and in an effort to attain the maximum of compactness, liberal use has been made of quotations, both direct and condensed. More sources than actually appear in the references have been examined with an eye to inclusion in some way or other. As implied above, the necessity for brevity has always been regarded, otherwise the volume would have inevitably expanded into a digest of psychology in general, for it is very easy to cross the loose boundaries of the Gestalt domain. The experimental mass may seem a bit unwieldy but in emphasizing the laboratory products of research motivated by the Gestalt principle I am stressing what I am persuaded will prove the most permanent contribution of all. Minor inaccuracies and inconsistencies probably still remain, but a genuine effort has been made to reduce them to a minimum.

I am indebted to the Social Science Research Council for the fellowship award which made it possible for me to spend the academic year 1930-1931 in the very citadel of Gestalt psychology, participating in characteristic investigations and profiting from the personal contacts and library facilities then available at the *Psychologisches Institut* of the University of Berlin.

Permission to quote text material and to reproduce figures has been generously granted by the numerous publishers, authors and editors whose works are referred to in the present volume.

GEORGE W. HARTMANN

State College, Pa.
April 25, 1935

CONTENTS

Part I—Historical

Part II—Theoretical

ILLUSTRATIONS

TABLES

GESTALT PSYCHOLOGY

PART I—HISTORICAL

CHAPTER 1

THE ANTECEDENTS AND DEVELOPMENT OF THE DOCTRINE

Wertheimer's Experiment: The Problem of Origin

That type of scientific research in the field of psychology which is identified by the name of "Gestalt" seems to have been first definitely introduced by Max Wertheimer in a famous experimental paper [1] on the "Perception of Apparent Movement" which appeared in 1912. This hundred-page study (to which frequent and detailed reference will be made during the course of this volume) is a meticulous and thorough investigation of a specific laboratory problem, but apart from the consequences to which it led, it contains little to distinguish it from countless other researches so representative of German scholarship. Even its main finding—that an object *seems* to move from one position to another when it is merely presented twice in two different places with an appropriate short time interval between both exposures—was well known to earlier specialists in sensory physiology and is now familiar to many amateur attendants at motion picture performances. Evidently the *fact* with which Wertheimer's monograph dealt cannot be responsible for its importance; it is rather the new *explanation* of the phenomenon which he offered which lends significance to his work.

What was this interpretation? It is not easy to give a simple answer without anticipating much of the material which must come later. Briefly, Wertheimer demonstrated that the various

1 "Experimentelle Studien über das Sehen von Bewegung," *Zeitschrift für Psychologie*, vol. 60; also reprinted in *Drei Abhandlungen zur Gestalttheorie*, Erlangen, 1925.

conventional theories offered at the time were inadequate to explain the occurrence of the event under *all* conditions, and that a wholly new interpretation was necessary. Traditional notions of retinal and brain action during visual perception were rejected and a preferred substitute sketched (but not fully developed!) by assuming the existence of cerebral "cross-processes" as the correlate of the psychic relations which seemed to be just as "original" in the experience as the fundaments upon which they were previously supposed to depend. The attachment of

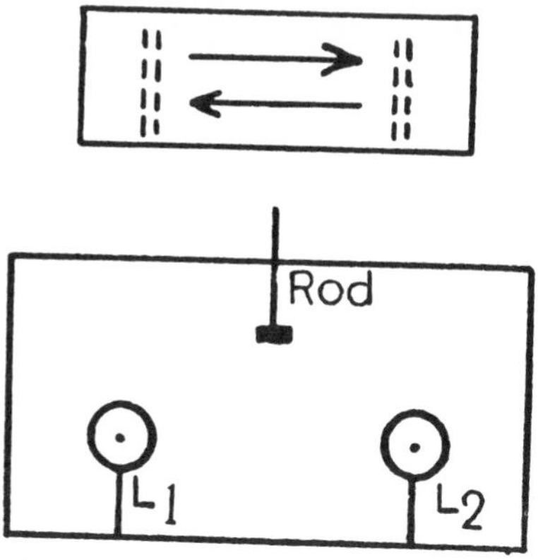

Figure 1. A Simple Device for Showing the Phi-Phenomenon

When two light bulbs are illuminated in rapid succession the resulting shadows cast by the steel rod appear to jump back and forth.

clarity and richer meaning to this statement hinges upon the development of the concept in the following pages.

Wertheimer's method of investigating the movement phenomenon can be readily reproduced with the aid of two electric bulbs and a metal upright.[2] Place two lights along the edge of a table separated by a few feet; between them and the wall of the room stand a thin rod. If one now rhythmically switches the two lamps on and off, the shadow cast by the rod will move back and forth in lively style between two positions, provided the optimal time interval (about 60 milliseconds) is used. If the time

[2] See Higginson's article on "A Simple Class Demonstration of Apparent Movement" in *J. Exper. Psychol.*, 1927, *10*, 67–68. The essentials of this experience may be seen in the flashing of fireflies on a warm summer evening, in the sparks of the fireplace log, and in the change of traffic lights when the red ball seems to be converted into a green one.

between the two light exposures is too short (say 30 milliseconds), the two shadows of the rod will appear simultaneously; if the interval is too long (in the neighborhood of 200 milliseconds or one-fifth of a second) mere "quiet" succession is noted. Under favorable conditions, apparent movement possesses all the phenomenal characteristics of objective motion.

Naturally, no one who has ever observed this event disputes its subjective nature: the real conflict appears when opposing theoretical accounts are examined. One plausible view held by Wundt maintained that kinaesthetic sensations produced by the "jump" movement of the eyeballs were the determining factors.

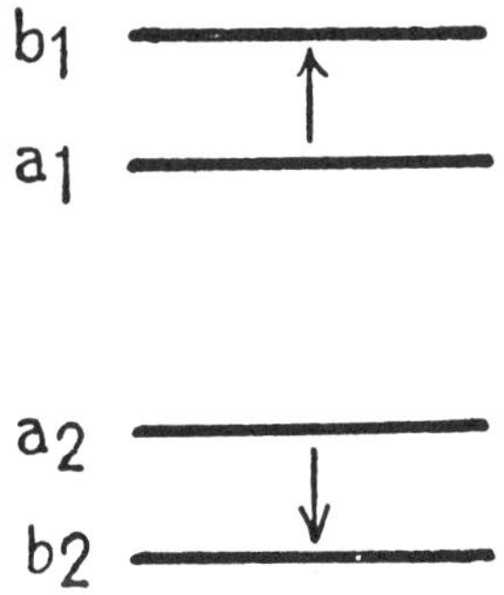

Figure 2. Schema Indicating Wertheimer's Method of Disproving the Eye-Movement Explanation of the Phi-Phenomenon

With constant fixation the simultaneous but opposed displacement of two lines can be observed.

However, Wertheimer obtained the phenomenon when he arranged his tachistoscopic exposures so that the total presentation time for the first object plus the time-interval plus the exposure period for the second object did not exceed one-tenth of a second; since the minimal time for eyeball reactions is somewhat greater (around 130 milliseconds), this explanation must be excluded. Furthermore, the movement readily occurs even with rigid fixation of a definite point in the visual field. An even more decisive elimination of the eye-movement hypothesis was accomplished by the simultaneous production of two antagonistic apparent movements, so that a_1 appeared to shift to b_1

and a_2 to b_2, as in Figure 2. Obviously the eyeball cannot move in two opposed directions at the same time, with the result that the explanation of the event must be sought in some other mechanism.

Marbe's theory that after-images of the first object accounted for the apparent shift was equally well excluded by the following procedure: Before the apparent movement was produced, a strong after-image was created by gazing at a small, bright cross or a lamp filament. This was now projected upon a definite spot within the exposition field on the screen. Again, the phenomenon was witnessed despite the stationary holding of the after-image. Wertheimer proposed calling this concrete observation of apparent motion the *phi-phenomenon,* the Φ standing for whatever occurred between *a,* the first exposure, and *b,* the second. Under special conditions, "pure" phi was obtainable; i.e., the observer saw neither *a* nor *b* nor the movement, but simply "something in motion." This is a genuine "dynamic" occurrence which on neither *a priori* nor other grounds requires to be traced to a "static" base. The curious reversal of revolution in a spoked wheel often noted while watching a moving automobile may thus be explained.

Wertheimer's physiological hypothesis is built upon the existence of central "diagonal functions" (*Querfunktionen* in the original) or "between-processes." Whenever a central locus in the brain is excited a concentric neural spread of a certain magnitude occurs around it. If two such spots are aroused, two excitation rings are formed which predispose the areas they embrace to further excitation. If now, point *a* is stimulated, and shortly thereafter an adjoining point *b,* some kind of physiological "short-circuit" occurs between *a* and *b,* and a specific excitation occurs over the intervening distance. If the concentric overflow from *a* is at its maximum and similar excitation rings now come from *b,* the direction of the neural process is determined by the fact that *a* was first there. The nearer the two points *a* and *b,* the more favorable are the conditions for the arousal of the phi-process, which in itself is an extensive specific whole.

Since Wertheimer claims that as far as the personal experience goes there is no difference whatsoever between the perception of *real* and *illusory* movements, he is implicitly proposing that *wherever two identical phenomena are found, it is necessary to assume that the corresponding brain-processes are identical.* The Talbot-Plateau law, which comes to mind readily in this connection, would then have to be interpreted as follows: A uniform grey disc and one constructed out of any variety of sectors which produce an equivalent visual experience when rotated must arouse the *same* brain-process.[3]

The main reason why Wertheimer may be considered the founder of Gestalt psychology rather than many other eminent predecessors and contemporaries—whose general attitudes and whose specific claims were often amazingly like his own—is that he, or the small group of brilliant young *Dozenten* who attached themselves to his standard at the very beginning, gave a militant or reformist turn to the movement.[4] He and his disciples—Köhler and Koffka were his subjects in the above experiment—became the ultra-radicals of the day, abandoning practically all the axioms and postulates of established psychology with the exception of the naturalistic standpoint and the appeal to experiment; whereas most psychologists, even though they shared many of the views and furnished much of the supporting material for the opposition's most trenchant criticisms, protested against such extremism and clung to the "grand tradition." The non-Gestalt or anti-Gestalt theorists were motivated by a desire to patch and repair the imperfections implicit in the conceptual structure of the older experimental psychology; the school of energetic disciples which centered around Wertheimer, on the other hand, was more interested in making

[3] This thesis is developed with a high level of technical perfection in the later experiments of Cermak and Koffka. See their article on "Untersuchungen über Bewegungs-und Verschmelzungsphänomene," *Psychol. Forsch.*, 1922, *1*, 66–130.

[4] The breadth of application of the idea of Gestalt soon made it overflow the rather narrow boundaries of psychology. This implicit universality seems to have been felt by its adherents almost from the beginning and is in part accountable for the boastful and superior air with which it has been expounded. That the configurationists do not think meanly of their discovery is apparent from Koffka's assertion, "The term Gestalt is a short name for a category of thought comparable to other general categories like substance, causality, function. But Gestalt may be considered more than simply an addition to pre-existing conceptual principles; its generality is so great that one may ask whether causality itself or substance does not fall legitimately under it." See his article on Gestalt in the *Encyclopedia of the Social Sciences.*

an absolutely new start. So faithfully have the configurationists adhered to this initial program that a deficient sense of historical continuity is occasionally painfully evident in their published works, which seem to imply that scientific psychology did not exist before 1912!

It is an intricate and unrewarding task for an examiner of documentary evidence to reach a decision on the debatable question of priority, especially, as in this case, where the methodological viewpoint and procedure is more significant than the concrete and immediate experimental accomplishment.[5] The situation has a strange and illuminating parallel in the rise of behaviorism, an attitude now internationally designated by this American neologism. Watson undoubtedly is the father of the behaviorist movement because in 1911 he vigorously championed the cause and compelled even the most unsympathetic psychologists to attend to it. His program was too audacious to be disregarded or even quietly assimilated. But one could wage a pretty war of words concerning the intellectual ancestry of Watson's ideas. Disregarding the direct influence of the functional philosophy of the Chicago school ultimately derived from William James, or even the broader effects of an enlightened materialism, there was a strong "anti-consciousness" trend among German biologists of the 'nineties (Bethe, Beer, von Uexküll, and in some respects, Loeb.) The physiological and neurological beliefs of Pavlov and Bekhterev had begun to permeate foreign thought in the first decade of this century. Even in English writings the atmosphere had been altered by the new emphasis given to the word "behavior" by McDougall, Max Meyer, and others. So far as the paper record of dates goes, one could easily justify a charge of "unoriginality" against both Watson and Wertheimer—but the same device would deny that Darwin initiated the modern theory of evolution. From the historical point of view, all that leaders of any

[5] As early as 1894, Exner had written: "The total impression aroused by a picture which moves across the retina is made up of excitations from a great many functionally dissimilar fibers. That we should, nevertheless, have a unitary experience, in which the part-sensations are unnoticed, is caused by what I shall term the principle of central confluence." What difference there may be between the "short-circuit" of Wertheimer and the "confluence principle" of Exner is still uncertain. See *Entwurf zu einer physiologischen Erklärung der psychischen Erscheinungen*, Vienna. 1894.

great intellectual change do is integrate the scattered ideas already existent on any scientific problem, adding impetus and direction to the inarticulate or uncoördinated trends.[6] The supporting evidence for this view is presented in sections below.

Mach and Ehrenfels

The man who first made the problem of Gestalt a controversial issue in modern psychology was Ehrenfels, an Austrian philosopher, who wrote a discussion on "Gestaltqualitäten" in 1890 for an obscure and relatively inaccessible journal.[7] Ehrenfels' point of departure was Mach's notable "Analysis of Sensations" which first appeared in 1886 and passed through many editions during the life of the author.[8] Mach was interested in a question of descriptive psychology: what are intrinsically those mental presentations which we call "spatial forms" (like a square upon paper) or "melodies"? Are they a mere *composition* of elements, or are they something new, accompanying the aggregation, but nevertheless *distinguishable* therefrom? It is evident from the phraseology of his inquiry and the whole tenor of his discussion that Mach looked upon a gestalt not as a mere composite of elements but instead as something (in contradistinction to the elements upon which it rests) novel and to

[6] The writer's point of view on this topic is better expressed by Boring's claim that "The progress of thought is gradual, and the enunciation of a 'new' crucial principle in science is never more than an event that follows naturally upon its antecedents and leads presently to unforeseen consequences." Cf. the rest of his clever critical article on "Gestalt Psychology and the Gestalt Movement," *American J. Psychol.*, 1930, *42*, 308–315. If, however, a saltatory theory of intellectual progress be correct—and the Gestalt idea of insight applied to human history would seem to support it—then the judgment of the chronicler would need to be different.

[7] Christian Ehrenfels, "Ueber Gestaltqualitäten," *Vierteljahrschrift für wissenschaftliche Philosophie*, 1890. Also reprinted with some later comments in a curious post-war monograph entitled, *Das Primzahlengesetz entwickelt und dargestellt auf Grund der Gestalttheorie*, Leipzig, 1922. There is little point in tracing the faint hints of a doctrine championing the primacy of the whole throughout the entire history of European thought. To do so in this connection would merely be a display of uneconomical scholarly effort. Our understanding of the present situation is not greatly advanced by knowing that Aristotle's *Metaphysics* contained a philosophical lexicon on the dependent relations of parts-wholes or that Kant has an obscure passage on the same theme in his *Critique of Judgment*. Probably the first historical record of reflection upon this theme is found in the remark of the Chinese sage Lao-Tse (B.C. 600) in his Tao-te-King, 39th saying, "The sum of the parts is not the whole!" In this volume, however, we are concerned with the immediate and not the *remote* origin of the Gestalt concept.

[8] E. Mach, *Die Analyse der Empfindungen*, 9th ed., Jena, 1922. In it we find, "The tree with its hard, rough gray trunk, its numberless branches swayed by the wind, its smooth soft shining leaves, appears to us at first a *single indivisible whole*." From the context, however, we learn that this naïve impression must be succeeded by scientific analysis if the experience (and the thing experienced) is really to be understood. The distinction between a pre-analytical and post-analytical datum appears to be of importance here and in all other Gestalt discussion.

a certain extent independent. Descriptively, he was a sensationalist of the most extreme sort, emphasizing the elements and neglecting the superstructure. Bühler, in fact, claims that he was "gestalt-blind." There is plenty of ambiguity in Mach's position and he probably would have leaned more toward the interpretation later made by the Graz school (see page 43) than that adopted by the adherents of Wertheimer; nevertheless, he had touched ever so lightly the problem of *organization* in mental life, an issue which continues to dog the footsteps of the theorist and experimentalist alike.

Ehrenfels saw that this point was of paramount importance and proceeded to develop it. Like many Germans with a strong musical background, he was fascinated by the patterns displayed in tonal sequences, and offered a most persuasive account of one's auditory experiences. "In order to apprehend a melody, it is not enough to have an impression of the momentarily sounding tone in consciousness, but—where the tone is not the first one—it is necessary to have at least a few of the preceding tones simultaneously presented in memory" (page 11 of Ehrenfels' article). Isolated reception of the individual sensation certainly does not occur in this situation.

He then raises the question whether the experience is more than the sum of the separate "local determinants" or whether in the total presentation more can be found than appears in the component sensations. With what now appears unnecessary academic sublety, Ehrenfels asks us to conceive the difference between separate tonal sensations brought together in a single consciousness on the one hand, and distributed among *n* conscious units on the other; and decides—introspectively, of course—that "more" is present in the first instance than in the latter.

Better, or at any rate more comprehensible, evidence is offered by another classic illustration. Consider a measure of any simple melody with which you are familiar. If it be played in a given key, identical notes will recur with a certain frequency. Now change the key in which the melody is played. It will then contain not a single one of the tones out of which it was constructed in the first case; nevertheless, the similarity is *immediately* recognized without reflection by any one with a minimum of musical sensitivity. Return next to our original key and play the melody again and follow this by another repetition, *retaining the same rhythm, but changing the tonal sequence so that exactly the same number of identical tones appear as before but in different order;* i.e., if the original sequence was *e g f a g g f e c e d,* make up another permutation which like it contains three *e's,* three *g's,* two *f's,* one *a,* one *c,* and one *d.* With the exception of the preserved rhythm, no one will notice any similarity to the original melody, unless an artificial analysis leads to a comparison and counting of individual notes (Ehrenfels, page 16).

Ehrenfels concludes that the resemblance between spatial and tonal patterns rests upon something other than a similarity of their accompanying elements. The totals themselves, then, must be different entities than the sums of their parts. Added evidence is offered by the fact that a person when asked to reproduce a melody in other than the original pitch (which, because of the differences among voices, he usually *must* do), does not reproduce the sum of the original single impressions, but a wholly different complex, which has the sole resembling attribute that its members stand in an analogous connection to each other as do those of the previously experienced complex. In other words, the "Gestaltqualität" (= form quality) or *whole* has been reproduced: the elements or *parts* have not.[9]

Beyond the rather banal distinction between temporal and non-temporal form-qualities—the latter being considered simpler—that is all of pertinence in Ehrenfels' original article. But it was enough to set many wheels a-going. In an appendix which was issued long after the first publication, the author tried to deal with some of the problems which had grown out of the initial discussion, particularly the perennial one concerned with the distinction of "relation" and "form-quality." He maintains that the melody can be *heard* and the square *seen,* but not the similarity or difference of two tones or of two spatial points, i.e., the former (*Gestaltqualität*)[10] can be directly sensed

[9] Some writers have remarked that the phrase, "He can't see the forest for the trees," is a popular expression for the failure of the form quality to appear.

[10] Köhler has made a terminological clarification which should be of service from this point on. "In the German language—at least since the time of Goethe, and especially in

or perceived, while the latter (= the relation) lacks this self-regulatory character and cannot occur without our own contribution or without the peculiar activity of the process of comparison. This involved logical analysis became even more complicated in the hands of some fellow epistemologists.

In accordance with his philosophic temperament, Ehrenfels tried to exhaust the broader implications of the idea which he had developed. Whoever has reached the conviction that all combinations of psychic elements yield something unique will inevitably attach to them (i.e., the "combinations") a much greater importance than if they are simply seen as displacements of eternally recurring constituents. These psychic combinations never repeat themselves with complete exactness—a principle which finds its best expression in the field of aesthetics. Just as some colors are more colorful than others, so some patterns are more "figured" than others. A heap of sand or a lump of earth has less *form* than a tulip or a swallow. This is what Ehrenfels terms "height" or "degree" of Gestalt—a feature which increases with the product of the constituents, their unity, and the multiplicity of parts. In fact, it is suggested that what we call beauty is none other than "degree" of Gestalt!—If it is rather difficult for us to accompany von Ehrenfels into the higher realms of speculative fancy, it should be even plainer that we must part company with him as soon as he maintains that the cosmological principle of the universe is the bringing forth of new patterns. It is not our concern to test the validity of these deductive outcomes of preoccupation with the Gestalt doctrine; it is enough to show that much of the ground later to be traversed by the experimentalist had already been surveyed from the theorist's armchair.[11]

his own papers on natural science—the noun 'gestalt' has two meanings: besides the connotation of 'shape' or 'form' as a property of things, it has the meaning of a concrete individual and characteristic entity, existing as something detached and having a shape or form as one of its attributes. Following this tradition, in Gestalt theory, the word 'gestalt' means any segregated whole, and the consideration of *Gestaltqualitäten* has become a more special side of the gestalt problem, the prevailing idea being that the same general type of dynamical process which leads to the formation and segregation of extended wholes will also explain their specific properties." *Gestalt Psychology*, New York, 1929.

In this work, Gestalt (capitalized as in the original German) will be used in contexts where the theory or viewpoint of an existing school of writers is involved, and the internationalized lower-case form, gestalt, for which there is already good precedent, will be employed in discussions of the concrete pattern phenomena so labeled.

[11] In 1891 appeared Husserl's "Philosophy of Arithmetic" in which he suggested the use of the term "figural moment" to designate the "peculiar unitary analogies among various sense-qualities." This is the same as Ehrenfels' *Gestaltqualität* and appears to have been independently developed.

The Contribution of Wilhelm Dilthey

From its very inception, the idea of Gestalt was most hospitably received by those "tender-minded" individuals who saw in it the inevitable reaction of the human spirit to its own dissection as practiced by the "new" experimental psychology of the day. The dominant school of Wundt with its "brass instrument" technique and physiological bias exemplified a trend toward minute analysis of mental activities, which even many friendly critics felt was forfeiting the substance of mind for the thin shadow of acceptable scientific form. Psychology in its early decades undoubtedly fed upon the crumbs which fell from the richly laden tables of physics and biology, and those who held a higher conception of its mission demanded that it cease playing the rôle of an auxiliary science. One man who was destined to play a prominent part in German intellectual life—Wilhelm Dilthey—set his energies to the task of saving psychology from its own barren futility in a remarkable paper[12] which appeared in 1894, wherein he presented his ideas on the difference between a "descriptive" and an "analytical" type of psychology;—a distinction now often represented by the contrast between the terms "understanding" and "explanation." What these designations imply may be gathered from the discussion below.

Dilthey postulated a fundamental difference between the spirit and method of the "natural sciences" and the contrasted *"Geisteswissenschaften"* — an idiomatic compound approximately rendered by an older nineteenth-century label, "mental and moral sciences." In fact, the German term seems to have arisen as a translation of this phrase in John Stuart Mill's writings. It includes not only that which we have recently learned to embrace in the description "social science" but also linguistics, the humanities, and the philosophical disciplines. From our contemporary vantage point, it is plain that Dilthey was battling with the dual nature of psychology—a dualism which is conveniently but probably not permanently expressed by the saying that psychology serves as the apex of the biological

[12] "Ideen über eine beschreibende und zergliedernde Psychologie," *Gesammelte Schriften*, V, 1, pp. 139–240, Leipzig, 1924. This is a reprint of the original 1894 article.

sciences and the foundation of the social sciences; or, as Weiss has condensed it, by the term *biosocial.*

Basically, Dilthey questioned the legitimacy of applying the procedures and hypotheses of the anorganic sciences to the problems of mental life. It was his contention that the causal interconnections employed by the natural sciences are *derived* in character, while in the *Geisteswissenschaften* they are *original,* i.e., comprised within the datum. "By *descriptive* psychology I understand the representation of the components and connections of each mature human mind as they are united in a single tie, which is not added by reflection or deduction, but is directly experienced. This psychology is a description and analysis of a relation which is as primitively and directly given as life itself" (Dilthey, p. 152). This new position was opposed to the older scheme of explanatory psychology by which all mental phenomena were constructed from a limited number of definitely determined elements—a point of view brilliantly championed by James Mill, Spencer, Herbart, Fechner, Helmholtz and others. The *explanations* of psychic activity offered by this approach are founded solely upon the intellectual processes; *understanding,* however, is possible only through the coöperation of all the dispositional powers (*Gemütskräfte*) in the act of apprehension (Dilthey, p. 172).

Dilthey maintains—in a passage which startles one by its premonition of the thought later crystallized in the catchword slogan, "The whole is more than the sum of its parts"—that all psychic processes are characterized by the fact that *the apprehension of the "total" is a condition precedent to the adequate interpretation of the "item."* The full import of this suggestion is not developed at length but the following citation has a programmatic ring, "In psychology all functional connections in experience are *intrinsically* given. Our knowledge of individual facts is simply a dismemberment of this union. Herein is manifested a firm structure, immediately and objectively present (page 173, Dilthey). It is in this spirit that the standpoint of "atomism" is rejected, and Faust's mockery of Wagner's attempt at a chemical synthesis of the homunculus is quoted as a fitting commentary upon the efforts of contemporary systematists.

Such a position, of course, ran counter to the enthusiastic positivism of the science of the *fin de siècle* and it is small wonder that Ebbinghaus sharply attacked this view. But a minority definitely felt the force of Dilthey's reasoning and saw that his strictures did not necessarily mean the end of all psychology. He had merely tried to create a "useful" psychology to serve as the basis of the moral sciences in the same way that mathematics affords a valuable and indispensable foundation to the natural sciences. To be sure, Dilthey took a wholly different path and insisted that neither introspection nor laboratory experiments could reveal the nature of mind: that, he felt, was best sought by an examination of a man's history.[13] It is plain from the whole tenor of his writings that Dilthey needed an ancillary science of human nature just as the earlier utilitarians and the classical economists elaborated a crude one incidentally to their main concern, and just as contemporary students of social life find psychiatric views more serviceable than the orthodoxies of the experimentalists. Nevertheless, he left a ferment behind and the following highly theoretical passage later proved to be richly charged with experimental possibilities: "The psychic life process is in all cases an original unity from its simplest to its highest forms. Mental life does not grow together from parts; it does not build itself up out of elements; it is not a composite, nor a result of coöperating atoms of sensation and feeling: it is primitively and always a comprehensive unity. Out of this unity psychic functions differentiate themselves, maintaining, however, their original connections. This fact, which is expressed on the highest plane by the unity of consciousness and the unity of the personality, distinguishes mental life completely from the entire corporeal world" (Dilthey, p. 211). We shall have ample occasion to meet this recurring theme as it presents itself with numerous variations in the succeeding decades.

[13] Spranger, Dilthey's distinguished pupil, has demonstrated the rich interpretative possibilities of this standpoint for a theory of personality. See his exposition of the fundamental character types in *Lebensformen* (English translation, *Types of Men*, Halle, 1928). According to this volume, "understanding" consists in penetrating the peculiar value-constellation of an individual.

Other German Theorists of the Nineties

There is good reason for characterizing the early 'nineties as a period when the totality concept fascinated those psychologists who could not rest satisfied with the dominant sensationalism of the day. People wanted to study the organism in "long-section" as well as "cross-section." Even such diverse views as those held by Freud in his thesis of the meaningful determination of every psychic act and the doctrine of "creative synthesis" as formulated by Wundt[14] share in common the endeavor to overcome the purely aggregative character of mental life which experimentalism had apparently demonstrated. Sander (*vide infra*) in his comments upon this interesting coincidence suggests that there may be something uniquely German about the attitude, since it can be traced (under many disguises, of course) back to the national mystics of the middle ages when the concept of totality as a description of mental states first emerged. The dynamics of Leibnitz and Herbart's "apperception" were definite moves in this direction, albeit over the mistaken road of associationism. Certain it is that many German writers with all varieties of metaphysical bias were quickly attracted to the doctrine. Meinong,[15] Höfler, Husserl, Witasek, Cornelius,[16] Martius, Schumann, Stern, Avenarius,[17] to mention

[14] Ideas such as these appear frequently in his *Physiological Psychology*, especially in the section devoted to a discussion of his principle of creative resultants (vol. 3, 6th ed., pp. 755–756): "All actual psychic processes are compounds;" "The product which results from any collection of elements is more than the mere sum of those elements;" "A clang is more than the sum of its constituent tones." That Wundt meant this to be taken in a functional and not just descriptive sense is indicated by his citation of binocular vision as a case of a complex perception in which "certain elements have lost their independence." Apparently even the foremost champion of modern elementarism had caught a glimpse of complexities which lay outside the bounds of his systematic beliefs.

[15] Meinong is the hyper-logician of the Graz school whose main contribution seems to have been a terminological one. That "squareness" which Ehrenfels termed a *Gestaltqualität* is held to be related to the four sides demanded as genus to species, but Meinong prefers the phrase "funded" or "consolidated content" (*fundierter Inhalt*) to designate the new entity; of necessity, the various part-contents which merge to produce this are called the fusing or unifying contents (*fundierende Inhalte*). The derivation of the idea from the jargon of public finance is plain. As in other hypotheses concerning mental synthesis, he *presupposes something which can be synthesized*. Meinong, like most of the Grazers, is not easy reading. Cf. his most strictly psychological paper in the *Zsch. f. Psychol.*, 1891, II, 245 ff.

[16] Hans Cornelius approached the problem by working down from above in opposition to Meinong's procedure. He starts with the complex which he terms the fusion. To him the original mental structure is a total which is gradually split into sections by means of analytic attention. Before we know anything well, it is but a huge total impression. This massive whole disintegrates upon examination, as a result of which something appears to be lost. It is strange that this insight failed to lead to anything more specific, save by proxy in the person of his pupil, Felix Krueger. Cf. the interesting papers in the *Vierteljahrsschrift f. wissen. Philos.*, 1892, *16*, 404ff. and 1893, *17*, 30ff. The best single survey of this entire group of "old-timers" is still to be found in Madison Bentley's "Psychology of Mental Arrangement," *Amer. J. Psychol.*, 1902, *13*, 269–293.

[17] It has been claimed that what configurationists mean by gestalten is only a special

only a few of the prominent writers at the turn of the century—manipulated this theme in diverse ways, giving a logical or experimental turn to the doctrine as their temperaments dictated. The tachistoscopic and eye movement studies of Erdmann and Dodge (1898) in connection with reading phenomena demonstrated the presence of "higher" perceptual units, but most colleagues interpreted them as synthetic products rather than as primary realities.

Stout's Position

The English-speaking world did not lack important figures whose critical thought had led them to similar views. Ward, and especially his disciple, Stout, had discerned, even if they did not loudly proclaim, the reality and significance of the "wholeness" factor in perception. In the third chapter of his first volume on "Analytical Psychology" (1896), concerning the apprehension of form, Stout raises three fundamental questions, all of which were patently influenced by the contemporary German debate:

1. Can the form of combination remain the same or relatively the same, while the constituents vary?
2. Is it possible to apprehend all the components of a whole without apprehending their mode of connection?
3. Can the whole be apprehended without apprehension of the parts?

To the first two inquiries he returns an affirmative answer, adding the following significant comment, "We do not wish to imply that the same elements may enter into different combinations without themselves undergoing modification. *An element which is apprehended first as part of one whole, and then as part of another, is presented in two different points of view, and so far suffers transformation*" (page 71 of Stout, italics mine). The importance of this recognition for later theoretical development was probably diminished by his negative reply to the third

---

case of what Avenarius called "characters" in contrast to elements in his biological psychology.

item, in which he alleges that where there are no parts there can be no combination of parts either in fact or for thought, and that only in Wonderland can the grin be divorced from the cat. This type of reasoning illustrates beautifully the limitations of the older British school, for while unimpeachable on logical grounds, Stout's conclusion does not square with the plain results of observation. Existential reality is again confused with perceptual presence. One may know a person's face well without discerning the individual lines and curves of his cheeks.[18]

The Work of William James

The late Miss Calkins [19] has performed a special service by showing that pioneer honors for preparing the background of configurationism must be awarded to that arch-eclectic, William James. Let us examine some of his more notable dicta to see how this position is justified.

In his *Principles* (1890), James fought a bitter and steady fight against the current psychic atomism, or, as he christened it, the "mind-stuff" theory. He protested against the obscure assumption that our mental states are composite in structure, made up of smaller states conjoined. Against this view, he delivered his most telling blows in the famous chapter on "the stream of thought." Almost at the very first sentence we read, "No one ever had a simple sensation by itself" (James, page 224). Like Heraclitus of old, James was profoundly impressed by the dynamic and changing character of personal awareness as the following excerpt shows:

> It is often *convenient* to formulate the mental facts in an atomistic sort of way, and to treat the higher states of consciousness as if they were all built out of unchanging simple ideas. It is convenient often to treat curves as if they were composed of small straight lines, and electricity and nerve force as if they were fluids. But in the one case as in the other we must never forget that we are talking symbolically, and that

[18] It may be of interest to note that Stout wrote in his *Manual* that the line "*Tum pius Aeneas umeris abscondere vestem*" brought to his mind the prosaic notice, "Smoking is not allowed in the courts and grounds of the college!" This fact he holds cannot be explained by a physiological theory of stimulus and response. The *identity of the metrical form* of the two lines furnishes for him the explanation.

The writer has for some years suffered a memory confusion between "Theophrastus" and "Paracelsus," which is probably caused by the fact that they are both four-syllable names with similar distribution of accent, as well as sharing the property of being rare and "classical."

[19] Critical comments on the "Gestalt-Theorie," *Psychol. Review*, 1926, *33*, 135–158.

there is nothing in nature to answer to our words. *A permanently existing "idea" or "Vorstellung" which makes its appearance before the footlights of consciousness at periodical intervals, is as mythical an entity as the jack of spades.* (I, p. 236.)

His insistence upon the importance of "transitive" states of consciousness and of the reality of "feelings of relation" is a note which constantly reappears. No Gestalt writer has satirized sensationalism more keenly as numerous passages testify. "The traditional (!) psychology talks like one who should say a river consists of nothing but pailsful, spoonsful, quartpotsful, barrelsful, and other moulded forms of water. Even were the pails and the pots all actually standing in the stream, still between them the free water would continue to flow" (I, page 255). "Whatever things are thought in relation are thought from the outset in a unity, in a single pulse of subjectivity, a single psychosis, feeling, or state of mind" (I, p. 228). And in a footnote he preaches the doctrine of the primacy of the whole in the following terms, "In a sense a soap-bubble has parts; it is a sum of juxtaposed spherical triangles. But these triangles are not separate realities. Touch the bubble and the triangles are no more. Dismiss the thought and out go its parts. You can no more make a new thought out of 'ideas' that have once served you than you can make a new bubble out of old triangles. Each bubble, each thought, is a fresh organic unity, *sui generis*" (I, p. 279). If any further evidence be necessary to demonstrate that James was thinking very definitely along lines which were ultimately to assume clarity in the Gestalt theory, it is certainly conveyed in this positive statement, "All brain-processes are such as give rise to what we may call *figured* consciousness" (II, p. 82).

Dewey and the Biological Trend

A few years later one of James' famous disciples, John Dewey, expressed the discontent of the period in an historic paper on the reflex arc concept.[20] The big problem of that

[20] *Psychol. Review*, 1896, *3*, 357–370. The italics in the quotations are my own and are inserted to draw attention to phraseology which was to acquire a richer freightage of meaning with the coming of Gestalt. Dewey's later *Studies in Logical Theory* (University of Chicago Press, 1903) make thinking in terms of natural wholes the criterion of sound speculation.

period was to explain how a movement became adjusted to a particular sensation which released it, and in Dewey's view the two were part of the same unit, viz., the reflex circuit. He wrote, "The reflex arc idea is defective in that it assumes sensory stimulus and motor response as distinct psychical existences, while in reality they are always inside a coördination and *have their significance purely from the part played* in maintaining or reconstituting the coördination; and (secondly) in assuming that the quale of experience which precedes the 'motor' phase and that which succeeds it are two different states, instead of the last being always the first reconstituted, the motor phase coming in only for the sake of such mediation. . . . There is just a change in the *system of tensions*. . . . What the sensation will be in particular at a given time will depend entirely upon the way in which an activity is being used. It has *no fixed quality* of its own. The search for the stimulus is the search for exact conditions of action; that is, for the state of things which decides how a beginning coördination should be completed."

It should not be assumed from the fact that most of these writers possessed a heavy philosophical bent that the concept of organic unity or wholeness was a trivial speculative concern of unscientifically-minded metaphysicians,[21] for biologists in this period as well as psychologists had begun to feel uncomfortable in the presence of phenomena which did not fit the conventional scheme. In 1894, for example, cytological research had advanced far enough so that E. B. Wilson [22] could say, "I will point out one all-important point; that the cell cannot be regarded as an isolated and independent unit. The only real unity is that of the organism, and as long as its cells remain in continuity they are to be regarded, not as morphological individuals, but as specialized centers of action into which the living body resolves itself, and by means of which the physiological division of labor is effected." Conceivably this is the intellectual atmosphere out

[21] Not that this feature is wholly absent. General Smuts' recent ambitious volume on *Holism and Evolution* (New York, 1926) is robbed of potential influence by the failure of the idea to carry with it the necessary support of sufficient empirical data. His book repeats Hegel's methodological error on a smaller scale.

[22] *The Mosaic Theory of Development* (Woods Hole Biological Lectures) Boston, 1894. The neo-Aristotelian view that life is systemic organization is anticipated by Aristotle's remark that a dead finger is not a true finger because it has lost its organic relation.

of which behaviorism with its slogan of the organism-as-a-whole developed, although it is curious that the logical implications of Wilson's position which were so clear with respect to *morphological* units were not discerned with *functional* ones.

Contributions of David Katz and Karl Bühler

With all this evidence at hand indicating that many of the more fundamental doctrines of the contemporary Gestalt school had been "anticipated" a generation or more ago, why didn't the new movement become conscious of itself much earlier? Frankly, this is one of the riddles in the history of psychology.[23] One can only hazard a few guesses in explanation. Perhaps psychologists were still too prone to take their methodological cues from classical physics and had to wait until the advent of the quantum theory had rocked this complacency; possibly the great but much misunderstood work of the Würzburg school [24] in the first decade of this century was an indispensable preliminary to any new departure in the science; most likely, the professional experimenters needed the intervening years in which to adjust their laboratory practices to the new ideas born far from the workshop.

Allotting then to the proponents of *Gestaltqualität* the rôle of John the Baptist, what event shall we consider to mark the first definite appearance of the new faith? We have decided above in favor of Wertheimer's *Habilitationsschrift* of 1912; largely because this became the Scripture of a personal following, but partly because the only other possible contenders, Katz, Bühler, and Krueger, have repudiated the later developments of the theory. Without attempting for the present the intricate task of distinguishing among the several varieties of Gestalt—for to paraphrase a famous political utterance, we are all Gestaltists now—it will be profitable to examine the contributions of other distinguished psychologists to the movement.

---

23 The ordinary philosopher, like his brother psychologist, refuses to believe that the Gestalt notion contains anything significantly new, but if they are right it is curious that the dramatic consequences of the position were not effective sooner. "It's all in James" is a common way of dismissing the pretensions of configurationism. See a typical article by Commins, "Some Early Holistic Psychologists," *J. of Philos.*, 1932, *29*, 208–217.

24 Külpe's attacks upon associationism vie in thoroughness with those of Wertheimer. See his *Outlines of Psychology* (Titchener's translation), 1909, p. 189ff.

In 1909, Katz offered a most exhaustive example of the new phenomenological type of analysis in his monograph, *Erscheinungsweisen der Farben* (modes of appearance of colors). The main accomplishment of this comprehensive study with its variety of new experiments, observations, and viewpoints was the final demonstration of the absence of a one-to-one correspondence between the experience of color and the external stimulus. This fact as such had been known since Hering's elegant visual work on contrast, adaptation, pupillary action, and the influence of peripheral factors, but Katz's further descriptions compelled a new orientation toward the problem, particularly since he added a distinct set of perceptual laws and a novel terminology. For example, one of his generalizations on field magnitude states that under non-normal illumination, the color quality of objects approaches the appearance under normal lighting conditions in proportion to the increase in the area of the visual field affected by the non-normal illumination. For instance, if one views the objects on a wall through a colored or smoked glass and either recedes in person from the wall, holding the glass at a constant distance from the eye, or if one maintains a steady position and brings the glass nearer to the eye, one finds that an increasing portion of the visual plane becomes affected by the non-normal lighting. In both cases, an adjustment to the illumination occurs; e.g., a white piece of paper is seen to become whiter as the "field magnitude" grows.

Such a central adaptation to illuminating conditions occurs only in those colors which are the hues of definite *things,* i.e., which can be apprehended as qualities of the objects, as in the case of a "yellow banana." These "substantial" colors Katz called "surface colors" (*Oberflächenfarben*) and distinguished them from "plane" or "film colors" (*Flächenfarben*), which may be illustrated by the color of the blue sky, most after-images, the hues which one sees in a spectral apparatus, or which one may discern when the eye is illuminated through the closed lid. These last do not appear as the colors of definite objects, but are generally vaguely localized and have a less compact structure than the "surface colors." Such finely executed experiments gave the death-blow to the "constancy hypothesis," which was cleverly satirized by Köhler [25] a few years later as having long been bolstered up by appeal to auxiliary hypotheses such as unconscious judgment or inference, attention, experience, etc.

Meanwhile, Bühler, the assistant and intellectual executor of Külpe, had been experimenting directly in the field of form perception. The idea of the dominance of perceptual wholes over their constituent parts first began to take concrete shape in his volume on *Gestaltwahrnehmung* (1913). A sample experiment will best illustrate the nature of Bühler's contributions: He found that discrimination of linear magnitude was better when the lengths to be compared were parts of rectangular figures than when they were merely isolated.[26] The orthodox determination of psychophysical limens was seen to be markedly dependent upon the configuration employed during the measuring process.

Rubin and Experimental Phenomenology

But the one work outside their own circle which gave the initial Gestalt coterie more aid and comfort than any other was the product of the Danish psychologist Rubin, a protégé of Höffding at Copenhagen. Oddly enough, the study was performed at Göttingen where experimental phenomenology appears to have been well established about 1910 under the direction of G. E. Müller, one of the most ardent champions of the legitimacy of the sensory reduction of all mental processes. Since its findings have played such a prominent part in the development of *Gestalttheorie,* it will be rewarding to examine them in some detail.

Rubin's original problem[27] concerned the fixation and recognition of figures, but in developing this research, he had to in-

[25] "Ueber unbemerkte Empfindungen und Urteilstäuschungen," *Zsch. f. Psychol.,* 1913, *66,* 51–80. The constancy hypothesis assumed that the relation between local stimulus and sensation observed under one set of conditions held equally well under all circumstances, provided that the state of the sense-organ was unaltered.

[26] This does not mean that spatial thresholds of parts are always greater than those of wholes. If a circle is split so that two semi-circles with an intervening white space result, the gap must be considerable before it is sensed. Not all totals necessarily behave in the same fashion. The difficulty of determining what shall be considered "whole" and what "part" in any concrete situation is a recurrent one in all Gestalt literature. Dynamically, however, a part is more than a whole of smaller range.

[27] *Visuell wahrgenommene Figuren,* Copenhagen and Berlin, 1921. This is the edition commonly referred to. The original Danish monograph, which is a closed book to most scholars, appeared in 1915.

quire into the differences in the phenomenology of figure and ground. He had early noticed that if one sketched a square by means of four lines, one tended to describe it as composed of *four* elements; but if instead it were produced by complete incision of a piece of paper, one tended to describe it as a *single* figural surface, i.e., a unit or whole with parts. He examined critically his own and others' experiences in the presence of meaningless black contours on a white background, and distinguished between the "included" or positive field and the "including" or negative field: simplicity dictated calling the former "figure" and the latter "ground."

Figure 3. Rubin's Vase Figure

The black and white surfaces function alternately as figure and ground.

In one of his first experiments along this line, Rubin showed that these two aspects of the total visual field behaved differently in memory; e.g., there was a pronounced tendency (as represented by a correlation coefficient of .83) for the subjects to perceive as figure in a later test-series the same datum which had been fixated as figure originally—a fact which he labelled the "figural after-effect." This effect persisted even where the absolute magnitudes of the figures had been altered. Under special instructional conditions it appeared that if the field which had been experienced as figure (or ground) at the moment of fixation appeared as ground (or figure) in the later test it was not recognized as such. We can acquaint ourselves readily with this discovery if we look critically at the areas surrounding what are normally perceived as "figures" in a familiar rug; how often is amazement the result of identifying these new and odd contours!

The significance of this distinction for the theory of perception can hardly be overestimated. Helmholtz (*Physiological Optics,* vol. 3, p. 163, 1910 ed.) had called attention to the fact that the Zöllner or herring-bone illusion disappeared if he re-

Figure 4. Another Reversible Experience
Either a black "iron cross" or a white propeller can be perceived.

acted to the white strips as snow-covered branches on a black ground rather than making the normal reaction of seeing the black strips as the objects fixated. But no one followed this suggestive hint until Rubin brought out those distinctions which are best observed in ambiguous figures (cf. Figure 3). Normally one sees a plain vase; it is only after a period of fixation that the profiles of two faces spring forth. What was once ground becomes figure and *vice versa.* In Figure 4, the black and white crosses have a similar reciprocal relation. The important feature to note here is that *the surfaces emerge as a whole and not piecemeal.*[28] The ground (as one would expect from the designation), is generally localized *behind* the figure, is less structured or differentiated, less penetrating, less independent, less meaningful, and in a sense, less "real" and lively than the figure. The figure has "thing"-character and the ground "stuff"-character, a thing being considered as stuff plus form, as in the case of a water drop which is essentially water and a representative spherical contour.

A very interesting experiment probably inspired by Katz's procedure (*vide supra*) was performed as follows: Upon one part of a white sector of the black-white cross pattern (Figure 4), a faint shadow was cast. The subjects were asked to alternate voluntarily between the two figured patterns and to tell in which instance the shadow was more pronounced. Invariably the observers reported a more marked shadow when the black cross was seen as figure. Evidently the central factors which produce an approximation of the brightness of the shadowed part of a white field to the brightness of the remaining field are more effective when the shaded region is a part of the field which is experienced as figure than when it is a part of the field which appears as ground. The important fact to note is that whichever field acts as figure for the moment *functions as an integrated unit* in its effect upon the events. Colors, e.g., which belong to the figure in a percept are more impressive and better retained than the same ones located in the "ground."—Certain types of aphasia, again, may merely be extreme instances of the reversal of the normal figure-ground relationships. What a hideous abnormality it would be to see the ground of the Sistine Madonna[29] as figure! While it is true that generally the area responded to as ground appears on the peripheral and less sensitive portion of the retina, this fact alone does not suffice to give an adequate causal interpretation of Rubin's phenomena.

---

[28] "In some cases sensory organization seems to change without any influence being exerted upon it from without, simply because processes which remain the same for some time in the same part of the nervous system tend to alter conditions in that part and to block their own path. We know that the same thing occurs in electrolytical cells in which the current polarizes the electrodes and thereby creates forces opposed to itself." Köhler, *Gestalt Psychology*, New York, 1929, p. 185.

[29] It has long been recognized in portraiture that the field or setting in which the figure occurs is an important determinant of the artistic value of the whole.

An unpublished *Aussage* experiment conducted by the writer with four pictures gave an average error of 55% for the "figure" items and 73% for the "ground" items, revealing a definite memorial advantage in favor of the former.

The basic rule which emerges from these researches is that *a field cannot be experienced simultaneously as figure and as ground.* Another fundamental rule expressing the probability that one field will be seen as figure rather than ground is phrased by Rubin as follows: When two homogeneous, differently-colored fields exist in which one is definitely larger than the other and encloses it, the predominant probability is that the smaller enclosed field will be apprehended as figure (Rubin, p. 79). There is also a strong inclination to view as figure the lower part of the field or at least that region which stretches from below upwards. Moreover, as in the case of the double-cross pattern, it is easier to hold as figure that cross whose sectors stand vertically and horizontally, i.e., more erect. The law of precision or *Prägnanz* (not yet formulated in Rubin's day) is here beautifully illustrated. Certain colors, too, appear to outweigh others; e.g., if blue and green systems comprise the cross pattern, the blue system tends to dominate as figure. The size of the sector system is likewise influential.

Rubin draws some interesting epistemological conclusions from his investigation. The fact that the contour exercises its major formative influence on the *enclosed* rather than the *enclosing* field is a principle of fundamental importance in delimiting the boundaries of objects and thereby facilitating our knowledge of "things."[30] It is unsatisfactory and superfluous to explain the customary limits of objects to the action of attention. All that is attributed to the attentive function is better expressed by the figure-ground relation. "If the field appears as figure, the form of the field has a greater degree of clearness; but a lesser degree of clarity obtains where the field is apprehended as 'ground'" (Rubin, p. 99).

It would be surprising if the contour which separates the figure from the ground did not arouse considerable interest concerning its properties. That something unique characterizes it is clear from Meissner's "paradoxical" observation that if the hand be immersed in quicksilver no pressure sensations appear within the skin area submerged, but only on the borderline be-

[30] In the letter E one sees three black horizontal projections to the right, but not two white ones to the left. The intervening white belongs to the ground and not to the figure. In the letter O the white within is phenomenally "livelier" than the white outside.

tween the free and the immersed regions. Rubin's further analysis shows that the contour is not a separate entity but rather determined by the nature of the figured surface to which it "belongs"; e.g., in Figure 5, if the contour "belongs" to one field, it is concave, if to the other, it is convex.[31] From the con-

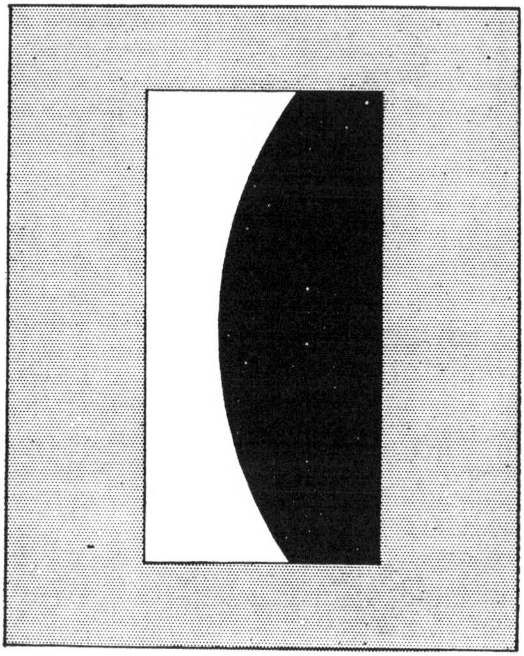

Figure 5. The Dependence of the "Quality" of the Contour upon the Nature of the Area Embracing It

The border line is convex if part of the black and concave if part of the white.

tour to the line is a natural step and here, too, it was easy to demonstrate that the "character" of a line changed with the plane figure to which it "belonged."

It would be a grave error to assume from Rubin's illustra-

[31] Compare this fact with another familiar observation: If one pours into a test-tube water, mercury, phosphorus, aniline, hexane, and gallium, six distinct liquid layers are formed. This is a stable system; if the cylinder is shaken, the layers will again separate. To the layman it is astonishing that six distinct fluids can be found, each of which furnishes so hostile an environment to the molecules of the other five that they remain largely segregated.

tions that the figure-ground relationship holds only for vision. An experiment by Wever and Truman[32] shows that it operates in audition as well and is probably a general characteristic of perceptual experience. Normally, sounds are heard against a background of relative silence but it is perfectly possible to determine the course of the auditory threshold in the presence of a tonal background provided by an organ pipe or any similar sound source. At first one has difficulty in hearing the figural-tone at all unless it is of high intensity, but an adjustment to the groundal-tone soon occurs and the figural-tone can be discriminated almost as readily as under other conditions. Correlated with this change of threshold is a change in the observer's experience, a change which is best characterized as the emergence of one tone as figure and the recession of the other to become the ground of the perception.

Rubin's work represents a type of experimental observation in which the analysis of sensory components is eliminated in favor of the more direct description of one's experiences. The attempt to build a scientific psychology upon the detailed protocols of trained introspectors is abandoned in favor of reports which aim to convey the immediate "appearance" or impression. It is, therefore, a sample of that experimental phenomenology which seems to have originated in the suggestions contained in the writings of the distinguished contemporary philosopher, Edmund Husserl. Husserl's own writings vie in obscurity with those of Kant and Avenarius, and a lengthy discussion of his neo-Cartesian logic and metaphysics would be out of place here, save that historically he unquestionably contributed something to the intellectual background from which configurationism emerged.

Gurwitsch[33] has given what are probably the most useful hints of the relation between Gestalt theory and phenomenology.

[32] *J. Exp. Psychol.*, 1928, *11*, 98–112. A study now in progress at the Berlin laboratory employs the groundal tone alone as the effective stimulus, simply raising or lowering its intensity at periodic intervals, whereby it becomes functionally a figural tone set off from the preceding and succeeding vibrations. In this way the difference limen under special conditions can be determined, whereas the absolute threshold was the main concern of Wever and Truman. Simple reaction time, too, varies inversely as the degree of differentiation between the figure and ground in the stimulus-situation.

[33] "Phänomenologie der Thematik und des reinen Ich," *Psychol. Forsch.* 1929, *12*, 278–381. Although Husserl did state that "apprehension is a singling out, every perceived object having a background," he has rejected the empirical development of this thought by Gestalt writers.

Methodologically, both approach the psychic realm from the descriptive angle: objects in the customary meaning of the word vanish, leaving only *noemata,* i.e., things which are known; the world *as it really is,* is excluded in the account and only the world *as it appears to be at the moment* is considered. In their interpretations of cognition and epistemology, Gestalt and phenomenology rest upon a common base. What the latter calls the thema or thing thought of is, of course, the "figure," and its thematic field similarly corresponds to the "ground." We cannot *think* of an inkwell without logically implying its surroundings any more than we can perceive a figure without a milieu of some kind. Just as an inkwell upon an office desk is different from one upon a piano keyboard, so a thought or idea in one setting is felt as fitting and in another as inappropriate. This method of phenomenology is substituted for the analytical procedure, and the wholes or gestalten are taken as they come, in their own right, and described, not in terms of any arbitrary set of elements, but in any manner that seems adequate to the practical situation. Whatever introspection is employed is not a perception and report of the self, but a perception of experiences affecting the organism. Throughout the methodological spirit of Gestalt one senses a tacit agreement with Bergson's claim that "the relation between the 'phenomenon' and the 'thing' is not that of appearance to reality, but merely that of the part to the whole" (*Matter and Memory,* Eng. trans., Allen & Unwin, 1919).

PART II—THEORETICAL

CHAPTER 2

THE PHYSICAL BASIS OF THE GESTALT THEORY

Köhler's Naturalism

Gestalt psychology came of age in 1921 with the appointment of Wolfgang Köhler to the chair of philosophy at the University of Berlin, vacated by the retirement of Stumpf, under whom he took his doctorate. This post carried with it the directorship of the Psychological Institute with its well-equipped laboratory and other facilities offering ample opportunity for the "new school" to justify the scientific promises it held forth. The one thing which more than any other contributed to Köhler's election as *ordinarius* was undoubtedly the timely publication of a study in natural philosophy which most friendly critics consider his *opus, viz.*, the book with the forbidding title, *Die Physischen Gestalten in Ruhe und im stationären Zustand* [1] (Static and stationary physical configurations). Since this volume has become one of the outstanding charters of the new movement—as measured by the frequency of citation from both friend and foe—it is imperative that its contents be examined for whatever they may yield to a better understanding of this distinctive approach to the problems of psychology.

The first item which catches the eye as one turns the title page is the laconic dedication of the work to Carl Stumpf. Since most of the original Gestalt coterie had been pupils of Stumpf, it is interesting to speculate upon his part in fostering the move-

[1] Braunschweig, 1920; also Erlangen, 1924. My citations are based upon the second German printing. It is a misfortune that this book never appeared in an English version, whereas many lesser ones have.

I am indebted to my former colleague, Dr. John G. Aston, Professor of Physical Chemistry at The Pennsylvania State College, for a critical perusal of this difficult chapter. If any errors remain they are due solely to my defective interpretation of the original.

ment. As far as the written record goes there is little to indicate that he was in any way responsible for the later drift of events. His own researches were largely confined to analyses of tonal experiences and his systematic papers are transitional hybrids between what one may summarily designate as Wundtianism and the phenomenology of the South-west German theorists. Stumpf has himself disclaimed any direct indoctrination, and whatever influence he may have exercised in the initial development of the Gestalt view is too vague and personal to be identified.

An unusual note is struck as soon as one observes that there are two prefaces: one for philosophers and biologists and another for physicists. In the former, Köhler begins with the statement that the "definite impression" of a visual figure, the "specific character" of a musical motif, and the "meaning" of an intelligible sentence are surely more than the sum of the respective colored points, tonal sensations and individual word-meanings. Such structures have been named gestalten and thereby subsumed under a concept which appears to be very fruitful scientifically. If psychology were the first or only empirical science, this new concept could advance by wholly different means from those which it is expected to employ, because the prevailing criteria of scientific thinking are those which have been developed by other sciences with an advantage of several centuries on their side. Chemistry, especially in its law of compounds, would seem to offer some helpful clues, but the entire basis of chemical combination is too shifting at present to aid in the determination of fundamental psychological categories.

The appeal to the biologist appears in the similarity of the physical and mental facts of organismic unity and adaptability. In his neurological and physiological hypotheses, Wertheimer had considered the brain action as a configured total process; if now, it is possible to demonstrate the existence of physical gestalten, a legitimate hope arises that the central brain processes are merely special cases thereof.[2]

[2] Köhler does not mention the point here, but it is quite obvious that the logic of Gestalt is opposed to the usual interpretation of Mendelian factors in inheritance, even though this be the proudest quantitative area of modern genetics. Genes, chromosomes, and determiners are mixed together and an organism results. But if the part is altered by an alteration of the whole this position certainly needs modification.

In the physicists' foreword, the initial idea states that physical systems reach a given state such as equilibrium only when a condition for the *entire* system is fulfilled. For the system *as a whole,* the available work energy[3] must be a minimum, the entropy a maximum; and the scalar or vector magnitudes, whose grouping constitutes the system, do not assume definite amounts and positions, but through their joint organization *relative to each other,* produce a lasting structure (Köhler, p. xvi). The simplest and perhaps ideal illustration is found in a closed electric circuit in which the current at any one point is determined by the conditions affecting all other points. On the other hand, a group of mutually isolated neighboring circuits comprise a physical complex of independent *single* systems. In the first case, the structure of the system presents an objective unity no matter how extended in space the system may be, since at no point does the local condition preserve itself unaltered; it is only in the total structure that it is maintained. In the second case, however, the parts of the physical complex are a pure summative multiplicity, depending upon arbitrary human thought as to whether they will be combined or not (Köhler, p. xvii).

If, as the foregoing has rendered likely, there are gestalten in visual space perception, basically nothing more is required to explain them than that we acknowledge that the optical sector of the nervous system possesses the properties of a physical system (Köhler, p. xix). A consideration of many striking so-called visual "illusions" lends plausibility to this view. How any object will be seen depends not only upon the particular stimulus affecting a limited receptor region but also upon the remaining stimuli which influence other regions.

The keynote having been struck in his dual introduction, Köhler proceeds to the derivation of the first physical Gestalt factor. We observe gestalten only when the spatially extended perceptual field is filled in a non-homogeneous manner. A form must touch our body surface upon some *restricted* area, the pressure must be marked off against uninfluenced or more weakly

[3] It hardly seems necessary to remind the reader that in modern theory "energy is not a physical thing, but rather what we would call a property of a system as a whole," as Bridgman remarks in his *Logic of Modern Physics,* New York, 1928.

stimulated skin, before one can speak of a tactile configuration, and it is only when color *differences* appear in the visual field that it is possible to see patterns. The implication is (although Köhler does not say so directly) that *the contrast or opposition resulting from the "figure-ground" phenomenon is fundamental to all experience.*

Having granted this postulate, Köhler next asks us to consider the sensory surfaces as part of the central nervous system, an admission easy to make, since in many respects—embryologically, chemically, and structurally—this certainly holds for the retina. The receptor surface, then, is simply part of the somatic field like the nervous system. Under normal life conditions the somatic field will be differentially excited because stimulation falls unevenly upon the sensory areas. The neural reactions which ensue are distinguishable into five distinct types of processes: (1) Complete equilibrium or rest; (2) Stationary conditions; (3) Quasi-stationary processes; (4) Periodic-stationary events; and (5) Dynamic sequences. All these varieties correspond to elementary distinctions in physics, but psychologists have yet to make them part of their thinking in practice. The *first* type is most simply represented by a body lying upon a table, whose gravitation is compensated by the elastic counterstress of the table-top. Were this same body to be falling in a vacuum, a dynamic process (*class 5*) would be involved. It could be roughly characterized as a process in which no phase of its activity showed signs of equilibrium. The fourth type is exemplified by the resonance of a membrane responding to a definitely and repeatedly given vibration. A stationary process (*class 2*) occurs whenever a system passes continually through the same procedure without altering any of its systematic properties. The best example of this is the coursing of a liquid in pipes: if as much flows away from a given point as flows toward it, the complex does not change its attributes. Constant electric currents also belong under this head. If the changes in the conditions to which the system is subject are slowly made, so that the action of the specific dynamic factors is unnoticeable, a quasi-stationary process results (*class 3*) (see discussion of this point in Köhler, pp. 4-6).

Köhler's first use of this classification is in his hypothesis that the excitation consequent upon definitely prolonged stimulation is a chemical reaction which may be dealt with as a stationary condition, or at least as a quasi-stationary process. These processes are isothermic (in the thermodynamic sense), a fact which permits the application of the law of mass action to them. Leaning at this point rather heavily upon Nernst's "Theoretical Chemistry," Köhler reaches the conclusion that a stationary reaction may be characterized as one in which the concentration (i.e., mass per unit volume) of all participating substances in the mixture is preserved constant during the process; the absolute mass as such is secondary or irrelevant. More fully stated: The excitations of somatic fields under constant external conditions are quasi-stationary chemical reactions in dilute solutions in which ions participate. Consequently, the condition of excitation is always adequately determined by the concentrations of the reacting molecular substances including the ions (Köhler, p. 13).

The meaning of all this for psychology lies in the fact that *a purely homogeneously aroused field (visual or otherwise) cannot develop anything other than a uniform stationary chemical reaction.* If, however, the sensory surface be inhomogeneously but steadily stimulated, *unequal* stationary reactions occur in different parts of the neural field involved. If, in addition (as in the case in the nervous system), ions participate in the reaction, and if in the regions of varying reaction the ionic concentration is not exactly equal (i.e., the concentration of positive ions is not equal to that of the negative ions), there arises at once along the entire boundary curve between two distinct areas *a leap of electrostatic potential* (Köhler, p. 16). Thus, a new and startling interpretation is given to the phenomenon of the contour as brought out in Rubin's figures (*vide supra*); the same interpretation, of course, holds for tactual contours like points or geometrical outlines applied to the skin. Between the subordinate parts of homogeneous fields, no differences of osmotic pressure or ionic concentration arise; hence, jumps in potential do not take place since the arousal of these electromotive forces is dependent upon excitation *differences* in *non-*

homogeneous fields. The biological significance is found in the fact that "excited" substance becomes negatively charged in comparison with its unaffected environment—a phenomenon which many have felt is the surest criterion of life itself (Köhler, p. 22). Applied to the figure-ground situation, this suggests that the figure is negatively loaded and the ground presumably is positive. In general, *wherever a gestalt is perceived, leaps of potential occur along the constituent borders within the optical field.*

Having laid this naturalistic foundation, Köhler proceeds to ask: Are the properties of the parts adequate to explain the properties of the whole? This question may be answered in the affirmative when strictly summative or additive situations exist as in the case of weight, where the weight of the total is undoubtedly identical with the sum of the weights of the separate items. But in the case of the potential difference presented above, we have a "functional" difference which appears only at the moment that the two electrical charges are brought into physical connection.[4]

It is literally false physically for one to say that the potential difference of the system arises from the potentials of the parts: on the contrary, the reversed statement would be appropriate. The word "difference" has normally misled one into thinking of the potential difference as an algebraic resultant, whereas it is actually a *primary attribute of the total system* (Köhler, p. 30). If, for example, we seek to bring the total system to a higher or lower, negative or positive "electrostatic level," the absolute potential magnitudes of both solutions may be altered at will, but the leap of potential between them remains always the same (Köhler, p. 31). Before the union of the parts, there exists no electromotive force, and the electrostatic potentials of the parts previous to the physical communication have nothing to do with the potential leap in the whole; if the system be divided into parts again, the electromotive force vanishes. Such a system is a physical gestalt and satisfies both criteria of Ehrenfels for

[4] "To be the electropositive side of such a physical system is no less a gestalt property in a definite electrochemical whole than to be the dark side is a gestalt property in a sensory pair."—Köhler, *Gestalt Psychology,* New York, 1929, p. 219.

phenomenal configurations, viz., that (1) the whole is more than the separate experiences added together and that (2) the relative displacement of the items does not affect the essential identity of the whole—this last being more commonly known as the *criterion of transposability.* The mathematical theory of Nernst shows not only that the electromotive force between two solutions can remain the same with utterly different absolute concentrations, but that this is always true in the case of equally proportionate concentrations on both sides. Transposition in the physical field occurs under exactly the same conditions as those which produce gestalten in psychology; i.e., through the maintenance of the proportions between the absolute data, as in the case of the "squarish character" of a square two inches on a side preserved in the case of a square two feet on the side. Had psychology taken its cues more from physics and less from geometry it would have seen the full import of these hints long ago.

Since the opposition of summation or addition *versus* system or gestalt [5] is prominent in the preceding discussion, Köhler finds it necessary to describe in some detail the difference between the two concepts. In sociological theory, much is made of the distinction between an *aggregation* and an *organization* and it is curious that Köhler fails to make use of the attractive illustrations which this field provides. Perhaps, since he had a very special audience in mind—as indicated by the two prefaces—he deliberately avoided such attractive but semi-speculative examples. Instead, simple cases of the differential effects of arrangement upon the essential character of the component items are presented. Six coins, for instance, may be laid upon a table so that they form the corners of a regular hexagon but this set-up does not alter their natures in any noticeable way; if half of them are removed the other three remain in exactly the same order which they had when all six were there. Similar facts lie at the bottom of the laws of the conservation of mass, of

[5] Erich Becher, in his critique of this position, holds that *system* and *gestalt* cannot be equated on all occasions. "Four-sidedness" is a true gestalt quality but color differences are founded upon systems or complexes. A shadow, again, is a physical gestalt but its parts are not causally coherent like the parts of electrical structures. See his review, "W. Köhlers physikalische Theorie der physiologischen Vorgänge," etc., *Zsch. f. Psychol.*, 1921, 87, 1–44.

electricity, and of energy, where the simple totalling of arithmetical quantities is decisive. A lack of reciprocal influence may be found in other natural distributions.[6] Three stones, one in Australia, another in Africa, and a third in the United States, constitute such a nonfunctional grouping, since each can be removed or displaced without in any way disturbing the others (Köhler, p. 47). Philosophers, of course, have argued that every element in the universe has some kind of connection with every other, but in most instances such hypothetical connections have a vanishing effect upon observed happenings. We would be much surprised if in shifting the furniture of a room the table responded with a change of shape or a shift in position to the displacement of the chair!

However, one must distinguish sharply between these instances of the arrangement of physical objects or "things" as such and the non-additive groupings which occur in physical systems. Where thermodynamic laws are applied to gases (as in Gibbs' phase rule) the principle governing the system prescribes what shall take place in the parts. The electric charge on the surface of a conductor, too, is a *structure without genuine parts.* If the real distinction between these two types is obscured, it is because our traditional logical criteria have neglected the structural feature. In the case of the electric charge as it is spread over the conducting surface, it would be more appropriate to term that which for purposes of analysis one would normally tend to call a *part* a "structural moment." A "moment," then, is that which is borne by the remaining structure and in turn supports it, the total structure itself being a *unitas multiplex.* The structure of an electrically charged hemisphere is strikingly different from the structure upon the half of a full sphere, since the hemisphere has sharp edges and it makes a big difference for the structure whether the hemisphere is solid or hollow; but hollow or solid spheres condition the same electrical structure. This structure, be it noted, is also independent of the *absolute* amount of the charge. If the charge be increased

[6] If I grasp the leg of a chair and pull, the entire chair follows but the air particles do not. There is a "dependence" in one case which is absent in the other. It is a metaphysical riddle why we see objects directly rather than the air-waves which mediate them. Cf. Fritz Heider's original essay on "Ding und Medium" in *Symposion,* 1927, *1,* 109–157

or diminished, the total structure goes through a quick dynamic process or readjustment, i.e., a change of "level" occurs throughout. Köhler thus draws the highly important inference that *electrostatic charges are transposable,* and, therefore, satisfy the second Ehrenfels criterion for gestalten.

One of the postulates of Maxwell's electromagnetic theory is that a structure cannot be fully determined without reference to its "field." This may be taken to mean that the "energy" present in a structure is configured. Science in the centuries before Faraday behaved as though the limits of a body were determined by its elastic and chemical effectiveness—a view still held by the scientifically naïve—but there is no reason why the boundaries of an object cannot be equally well-defined by the extent of its electrostatic or magnetic influence.[7] Although a definite revolution in one's thinking is requisite in order to feel at home with this new viewpoint, its scientific "respectability" is beyond question. Köhler quotes with obvious approval a neglected passage in Maxwell's[8] great work:

> We are accustomed to consider the universe as made up of parts, and mathematicians usually begin by considering a single particle, and then conceiving its relation to another particle, and so on. This has generally been supposed the most natural method. To conceive of a particle, however, requires a process of abstraction, since all our perceptions are related to extended bodies, so that the idea of the *all* that is in our consciousness at a given instant is perhaps as primitive an idea as that of any individual thing. Hence, there may be a mathematical method in which we proceed from the whole to the parts instead of from the parts to the whole. (Vol. II, pp. 176–179.)

Another more practical testimony to the reality of physical gestalten is found in the peculiar difficulty of all precise measurement.[9] It is only the novice who has not learned that the act of

---

[7] Wertheimer has also declared in an informal public lecture that "the effects of a thing belong to its innermost nature."

[8] In the preface to his first edition, Clerk Maxwell remarks with approval, "Faraday's methods resembled those in which we begin with the whole and arrive at the parts by analysis, while the ordinary mathematical methods were founded on the principle of beginning with the parts and building up the whole by synthesis." Cf. *A Treatise on Electricity and Magnetism*, 3rd ed., Oxford, 1892. The skeptic will probably be tempted to express the hope that this formal resemblance of the two approaches really implies a genuine kinship!

[9] The methodology of tapping the field in order to establish the value of the charge or potential at the separate points with the aid of a probe has characteristic difficulties. The probe begins to distort the field of the conductor being investigated, and thus also its charge structure, as soon as it is introduced into the field.

observation itself affects the character of the event observed. Many persons have assumed this to be the unique disadvantage of the introspective technique in psychology, forgetful of the fact that the "inner behavior" of the observer is influential in all scientific observation: the difference, in other words, is only a matter of degree and not of kind. The ideals of "isolation" of the datum to be investigated and "control of all essential conditions" in general scientific method have probably conduced to a neglect of existing physical gestalten—which are just as numerous as "things"—because of technical difficulties in the attack. All the numerous "corrections" which have had to be attached to the measuring procedures in every field of science are silent witnesses to the reality of configurational influences.[10]

Since simple arithmetical or algebraic operations give us a wholly incorrect picture of the nature of the physical gestalt, Köhler turns to another branch of mathematics for guidance and finds it in the theory of integral calculus and the concept of functional equations; in fact, he reaches the significant conclusion that gestalten exist wherever the integral calculus can be applied and *vice versa.* This implies that all cognized relations must ultimately be quantitative in character. Furthermore, all cases in nature where equilibria of some sort occur are found upon closer examination to possess the properties of gestalten. Specific instances which require the Laplace equation for solution, and, therefore, show that the differential calculus is also applicable to configurations, are as follows: the magnetization of bodies without residual magnetism when influenced by permanent magnets; the equilibrium of a membrane stretched with uniform tension over an even plane; the stationary heat currents in plates or three-dimensional bodies; the stationary diffusion stream of a dissolved substance in a solvent; the stationary electric current in tri-dimensional bodies; and many problems in hydrodynamics, such as the stationary movement

[10] The informed reader will undoubtedly know that this is only one of many views which physicists and psychologists have recently begun to share in common. Eddington, in discussing the consequences of the FitzGerald contraction, i.e., the fact that a rod moving in the direction of its long axis is shorter than when it is in motion along the short axis, states: "Absolute distance, not relative to some special frame, is meaningless." Such a rock-bottom physical magnitude as length is a dependent function of the gestalt of which it is a part. Cf. *The Nature of the Physical World,* New York, 1929.

of a fluid in an extended field when a rigid body of prescribed form is fixed in this field as an obstacle (Köhler, p. 119). Two famous questions in mathematical theory—the related problems of Dirichlet and Neumann—also refer directly to physical gestalten. Most of these problems are rarely investigated in experimental physics and are almost exclusively questions for mathematical physics to solve. Nevertheless, an experimental attack is by no means excluded—one has simply to determine, if, in the case of a constant conditioning form or topography, an arbitrary *local* alteration of the extended structure can be introduced *without causing the total system to react with a complete mass displacement throughout.* These clearcut cases in which a change in the part immediately affects the whole are known as "strong" gestalten; if, however, the energy of the system is unordered (as in set-ups for studying the conservation of energy), the presence of a "weak" gestalt is indicated. Even in these limiting cases, it is incorrect, or at least unwise, to speak of a "part" of a system; one remains closer to the heart of things if the term "part" is understood to mean "structural moment in an organization."

Resistance to the Gestalt brand of thinking is encountered because most Western European scientists, trained as they are in a certain variety of analytical research, are prone to see in it evidence of contamination with the vagaries of intuitive mysticism. Against such erroneous identification Köhler and his confrères strongly protest. One view of the physical world would be that nature consists of purely mechanical links (*Undverbindungen*—"and-connections" or plus-summations) between independent parts, whose additive total constitutes reality. Another opposed view would be that nature contains no independent parts, but that all conditions and events are real only in a total universal relation, all "parts" being products of abstraction. Köhler maintains that the first proposition is wholly false, but that *even the second hinders rather than furthers an understanding of the Gestalt principle.* As expressed above, it is less a result of empirical research than the emotionally-toned utterance of a human being weary of strenuous thought and readily satisfied with a romantic-philosophic construction. The "union of all with all" is probably correct in a purely formal sense, for the observer of the disintegration of a radioactive preparation cannot demonstrate that some infinitesimal influence from the fixed stars is not operative; but such an attitude would contribute little to the understanding of the specific characteristics of limited types of processes (Köhler, p. 156).

Not everything in the world can be regarded as relevant to a given system, for if that were so there could be no scientifically manageable isolated systems. If things were infinitely complex and all aspects of their interrelations were equally relevant to all purposes, nothing could be understood. Their very "togetherness" would have to be sensed by a kind of dumb mystic rapture. The existence of a scientific body of knowledge is itself evidence that natural systems can be found which are neutrally isolated from other systems. (Sidney Hook.)

Logically, the existence of indefinitely vanishing effects cannot be denied, but the "cosmic" and "particular" quantities appear to be related as the magnitudes 1 and 10^{10}. This is one among many points where Gestalt theory and the theory of relativity come into contact. Nevertheless, the greatest enemy of the fruitful and concrete consequences of the configurationist principle in psychology would be the thesis that the "immediately given" is a total state of consciousness as such. The older psychologists appreciated this dangerous cloudiness, but unfortunately leaped to the other extreme in their policy of punctate sensations. Both evils are avoided as soon as one recognizes that *the laws of science are the laws of systems,* i.e., "structures of finite extent"—a generalization applicable to both physics and psychology.

Another enemy of the true Gestalt position Köhler sees in the so-called *production theory of the Graz school* of psychologists, a theory which viewed the elements as "funding contents" and the configuration itself as a "funded content." The gestalt in their eyes is "produced" by a strictly psychic process; the physical world as such possesses no gestalten.[11] Köhler views this theory as an unprofitable compromise which is still at heart attached to purely geometrical thinking, and rejects it as a sheer psychologism, to which his opponents, one may readily suppose, would retort that his own position is tainted with "physicalism"!

Having made this long excursion into the anorganic realm, Köhler returns to consider the organism in a chapter prophetically labelled with a citation from Goethe, "Denn was innen, das ist aussen" (For that which is internal is also external.) The sensory processes underlying perception have in the past been wrongly assumed to arise from independent local peripheral stimuli, each insulated from the rest in the somatic field, and individually meaningless, acquiring significance only through the action of higher mental operations, such as association, attention, judgment, etc., upon them. To be sure, physiological contrast theories based upon the assumption of physical systems in the receptor surface (Hering) existed, but the resistance which they encountered showed how dominant the opposite ideology was. Nothing seemed clearer and more reliable than

---

[11] Spearman says the quarrel is as to whether the operation of perceiving shape is in essence binary or unitary—the Grazers, of course, being binarians and the Berliners unitarians. The Wertheimer group says that when different sensory nerves are excited simultaneously the interconnecting cortical neurones at once short-circuit the excitation, while the older school demands an extra brain level. See "The New Psychology of Shape," *Brit. J. Psychol.*, 1925, *15*, 211–225, from which these sketches are taken:

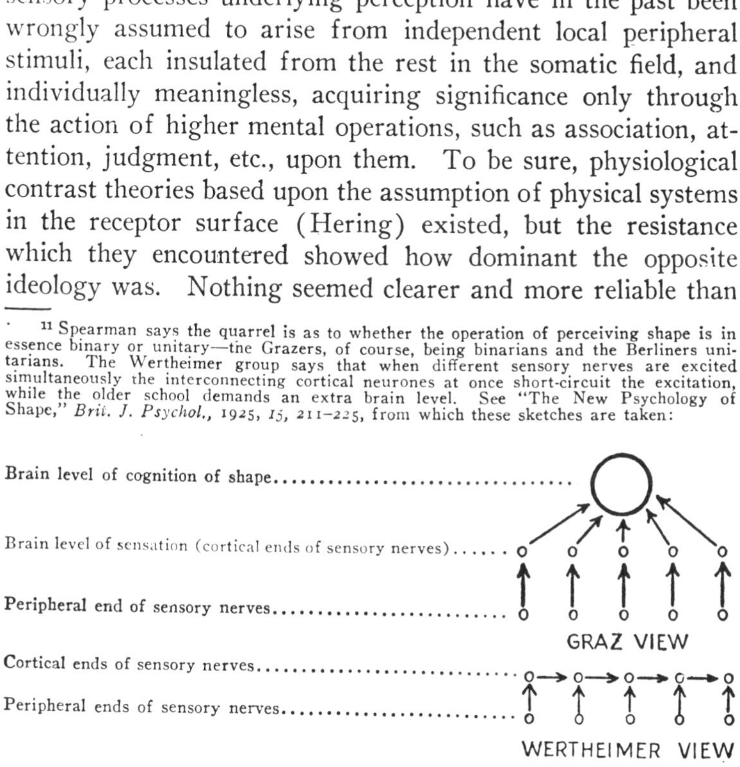

Some irreverent Yankees have called this the difference between the one-steppers and the two-steppers! Nevertheless, the Graz writers are not to be lightly dismissed, particularly since they represent an older school of configurationism. They maintain that the gestalt is by no means univocally determined, either as to form or as to structure. Thus, four dots arranged in the form of a square may be seen as two horizontal lines, two vertical lines, or two oblique lines at right angles to each other. Benussi, the ablest experimentalist who followed Meinong's theoretical position, was, therefore, not altogether unjustified in holding that *the determinant in equivocal cases must be some psychical factor which unites sensory contents into patterns.*

a correspondence between experience and reality accounted for on the basis of pure point geometry.

Nevertheless, our visual world reveals an order of a much more striking and immediate kind. A homogeneous field is seen as uniform without "points" and consequently without "relations" between them, and where gestalten in the narrow sense arise they are seen as compact closed structures lifted up from the rest of the field. When Köhler asserts that the phenomenal field has non- or trans-geometrical properties, he simply means that the sensory response is *conditioned* by, but does not exactly *correspond* to, the stimulating situation. Instead, the physiological process in the optical system has the same general properties possessed by physical spatial gestalten. Although this process may be extended in time, it acts as a complete objective unity. *The optic-somatic sector is a physical system* in more than just an analogous sense and the correlations between it and the phenomenal field are built upon the common ground of identity, i.e., the likeness between the "two worlds" is a structural one.[12] A similar equivalence for the thought processes is also claimed.[13] This factual resemblance is not just a *material* one; the *specific configurational features* are themselves preserved (Köhler, p. 193). Existing consciousness, then, is directly related to the real structural properties of psychophysical events and not arbitrarily linked to elements, which, by their very nature, are incomparable with it.[14] Physiological psychology, therefore, has been at a loss to explain how vibrations or displacements of brain molecules could produce the actual content of our mental life. But that is because the wrong physical concepts have been brought to bear upon the problem:

[12] Cf. an utterance of Wertheimer in one of his university lectures, "The *material* of sensation is indeed different from the material of the physical world, but the *structure* is the same." The thorough-going rationalism of Gestalt could hardly be better attested, for it is the very essence of rationalism to postulate symmetry, if not identity, between thought and reality.

[13] The aid afforded by the device of Euler's circles in solving syllogistic problems is an illuminating case in point. Köhler's thesis is that perceptual and thought patterns are involved in a network of physical and physiological conditions which must always be taken into account. By following this clue, the configurationists hope to bridge the gap between psychology, biology, and physics. An animal is an elaborate "machine" only if the molecule is a very simple "animate" individual.

[14] Von Frey, whose early researches in cutaneous sensitivity were a bulwark to the elementarists, later acknowledged the strength of Köhler's arguments. He says, "Progress lies in the conviction that the somatic processes corresponding to the psychical gestalten must have a similar structure." Cf. his paper, "Ueber Wandlungen der Empfindungen bei formal verschiedener Reizung einer Art von Sinnesnerven," *Psychol. Forsch.*, 1923, *3*, 209–218.

the most significant aspects of consciousness have least to do with this. If, instead, the essential structural properties were investigated, a more promising "lead" would present itself.[15] This should not be taken to imply the existence of a double consciousness with a purely summative sensory multiplicity *plus* a configured consciousness over and above this. Such a view would play into the hands of the "production-theory" which has already been rejected.

There are many facts in visual perception, especially the phenomena of color induction, which are difficult to reconcile with the older assumption that simple stationary streams course between the retina and the central areas. The difficulty is in-

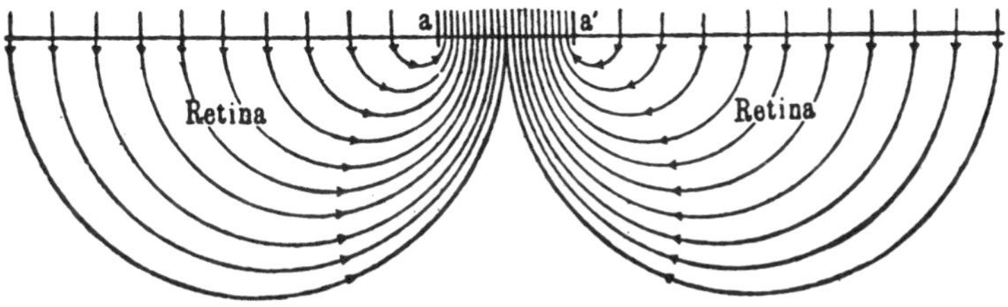

Figure 6. Optic Nerve Pathways Illustrative of the Electromotive Forces in Figure-Ground Percepts. (After Köhler)

creased by the knowledge that electromotive forces are developed during retinal functioning. Now every electrical displacement produces a magnetic field within and about itself. This must also hold for the nervous system; consequently, whenever the paths of two currents run adjacent to each other, the two streams must each cross the magnetic field of the other. A rough illustration of how this may operate is offered by the following situation:

Assume that we have before us upon a homogeneous gray ground a single white figure of limited size and simple form

[15] In a recent experiment which has aroused a good deal of acrimonious debate, Wever and Bray placed electrodes on the exposed auditory nerve of a cat and led off the nerve action currents through an amplifying system to a detecting apparatus. Sounds applied to the ear of the animal produced neural effects which corresponded to the frequency of these sounds. If confirmed, this means that *identity* and not *similarity* of wave number is involved. See their account on "The Nature of Acoustic Response" in the *J. Exp. Psychol.*, 1930, *13*, 373–387.

such as a circle. Electromotive forces arise first, at points *a* and *a′* (see Figure 6), i. e., on the border between the unevenly stimulated retinal regions; and second, between the excited areas, and the optic pathways (Köhler, p. 206). The same electrical displacement must in general ensue throughout the homogeneous surroundings of the circle as in the "retinal circular field" itself, and since the figure extends over a relatively smaller retinal surface than its differently-toned "environment," the average current *density* within its circular field is far greater than in the neighboring field. This proportion in energy density must be retained in the neural tracts as far as the central areas;[16] in so far as the configured process is electrical in nature,[17] the "figure" corresponds to a much more lively state of affairs than the broad ground. The energy in the figure or gestalt in the narrow sense is closely packed, while in the ground it is thinly spread out. Had the situation been reversed with a grey circle of the same magnitude in a white environment, the significance of the electrical current would also have been reversed, but the region of greater electrical density would still have been the "figure." Consequently, the area which will be seen as the gestalt is not dependent upon the absolute brightness or coloration, which is distinctly a secondary factor. Indeed, the color-quality of visual surfaces is itself subject to configurational influences.

A further ingenious step is taken with the application of the Gestalt principle to the historic Weber-Fechner law. In an earlier section, it was noticed that the leap of potential is independent of the absolute ionic concentrations, but dependent upon their *ratio* to each other; e.g., in determining differential brightness thresholds with two neighboring fields, one may triple the concentration on both sides and obtain entirely altered speeds of reaction, but the electromotive force is always the same—in other words, transposition in Ehrenfels' sense has occurred.

---

[16] This assumption may well run counter to the general properties of nerve. There is some reason for believing that conductivity is much lower in the longitudinal section than in the cross-section. One investigator estimates this relationship to be about 1:5. See Hermann, "Ueber die Fähigkeit des Weissen Lichtes, die Wirkungen fertiger Lichtreize zu schwächen," *Zsch. f. Sinnesphysiol.*, 1913, *47*.

[17] Becher has indicated that Köhler's exclusive reliance upon an assumed *electrical* character of the nerve impulse is more favorable to the Gestalt hypothesis than an admission of its *chemical* character (which is also real enough) would be. The latter feature can still be better understood if the transformations occur within isolated pathways.

The electrochemical formula for the dependence of the jump in potential upon the basic variables is

$$\Phi 1 - \Phi 2 = \text{const. } \log \frac{C_2}{C_1}$$

which is none other than the relation expressed by the familiar Weber-Fechner law that the intensity of sensory response increases in arithmetical series as the stimuli increase in geometrical series. This striking formal correspondence is probably more than accidental. The ill repute into which this generalization has fallen—a fashion probably set by James—is unfortunate, since it is probably the classic example of a great scientific generalization holding only within definite limiting conditions. All empirically-derived laws, when pushed to their upper and lower limits, reach zones where their validity becomes uncertain.

The problem of mental and physical parallelism with which Fechner wrestled receives another extension in Köhler's treatment of symmetrical figures. In a circle, we have the simplest and most perfect example of symmetry. It is alleged that the phenomenal symmetry of the seen circle permits us to conclude that the psychophysical event in the region of the "figure" must likewise be symmetrical. However, this implies a *functional* resemblance between the two and not a geometrical one. The only possible way—unless we postulate pre-established harmony—by which a geometrical symmetry in the stimulus pattern can give rise to a symmetrical form-perception is *via* a psychological process which itself possesses dynamic and functional symmetry. Lotze's "local sign" theory with its auxiliary physiological index may, therefore, be dismissed as superfluous.

This is a parallelism of a wholly different sort from that regnant a half-century ago, which postulated an exact relation between brain processes and states of consciousness with utter incomparability of both. But the universe is not as devoid of meaning as that and the parallelism of Gestalt insists that the highest psychic activities are literally, concretely, and in every case *specifically* related through their configurational properties to the somatic structures[18] (Köhler, p. 234). The dependence

[18] This is possible because *physiologically a gestalt consists of the afferent, central, and efferent portions of the nervous system functioning as a unit:* there are no isolated paths, no single point excitations connected by strands; the *form* of the excitation and its spread are here of importance.

of many forms of human thinking upon spatial gestalten has often been noted.[19]

On a simpler level, the kinship of tactile and visual gestalten—a kinship not to be explained by associationist constructions—and the re-discovery of certain "optical illusions" (e.g., apparent movement) upon the skin furnish interesting supporting evidence. It is evident that a doctrine which many persons felt was a disguised "vitalism" is merely positivism of a subtler kind. Driesch and other vitalists overlook the universality of that type of organization just demonstrated as existing in anorganic structures.

The concluding chapter of this closely written work lays the groundwork for the law of *Prägnanz*—a term which may best be translated by "precision," although "eidotropy," a word earlier used by G. E. Müller to designate the tendency of an image to become "typical," would have some advantages. This theme is developed by noting that a physical gestalt results from a grouping of certain forces which operate upon a given form and only cease to transform it when the form has become stable. In all processes which terminate in such an end-state, the diffusion takes a direction which tends toward a minimum of structural energy. The question is raised, "How do gestalten look which correspond to smallest possible energy values?" One of the well-known laws of electrodynamic displacement states that two currents which originally form an angle together tend to run parallel and in the same direction. Numerous electromagnetic illustrations could be adduced to show that these transformations occur in the direction of heightened uniformity, simplicity, and symmetry. Another favorite instance, worthy of recording because of its dramatic persuasiveness, seems to indicate that the principle of *Prägnanz* represents a tendency present in all natural events. If one produces a soap film upon

[19] Köhler insists strenuously upon the special type of parallelism which this implies. "When some one experiences that flash by which a new idea or the solution of a problem comes to him, he will suddenly interrupt his walking or abruptly strike his head. Here both his inner experience and his outer aspect will exhibit the same interruption of continuity. For similar reasons the activity of a man as it is seen by us will often show an organization which corresponds to the organization of his doing and planning, as experienced subjectively." *Gestalt Psychology*, New York, 1929, pp. 249–250.

a wire frame and then carefully places a small amorphous closed loop of thread upon it, nothing occurs at first to either film or thread; but if one pricks the membrane inside the outline of the loop, the thread *immediately assumes a circular shape.* Bursting the inner film subjects the thread to the exclusive control of the surface tension forces of the outer film which seek to enclose the greatest possible surface within the smallest possible space.[20] Small wonder that Köhler quotes with enthusiastic approval a saying of P. Curie, "Asymmetry produces the course of nature. The absence of symmetrical elements is necessary for the occurrence of every natural event."

That a strong tendency toward simplicity and regularity of gestalten exists can be demonstrated by a great many disparate facts in psychology.[21] At the Göttingen Congress of Experimental Psychology in 1914, Gelb reported that if three light points were briefly flashed successively in a straight line, they were seen as a *symmetrical* group, even when the two intervals had an objective ratio of 10 to 30 cms. This pressure toward symmetry of gestalt was especially marked if the time intervals from points 1 to 2 and 2 to 3 were equal or appeared to be equal. Moreover, a neat observation of Bourdon indicates that if three, four, five, or six points are arranged evenly about a center, phenomenally a triangle, square, pentagon, or hexagon result; eight points, however, no longer compulsively result in an octagon, but yield instead a circle. Goethe in his color researches had long ago noticed that the after-images of square originals quickly became blunt at the corners and terminated in smaller rounded images,—evidently because the circle is a more "prägnant" or precise gestalt than the rectangle.[22]

With this theme the most profound single volume in the field of Gestalt psychology is brought to a close. Even if metaphysicians succeed in the usually easy task of demolishing Köhler's

---

[20] Mach in his "Science of Mechanics" was the first to popularize this interesting observation. Cf. page 386 of the English translation (1893).

[21] It is curious that there are only six unsymmetrical large letters in the entire Latin alphabet—F, G, J, L, P, Q, R. Similarly, the animals which Polonius saw in the cloud may be interpreted as an effort to "structurate" an amorphous mass.

[22] It is interesting to note how much of our language has meaning only with reference to the description of gestalten and not elements. "Straight" is significant only with respect to an implied structure; similarly with "sharp," "round," "simple," "symmetrical," and many other adjectives.

philosophical conclusions, the extraordinary value of the work in stimulating new forms of investigation remains unaltered.[23]

Gestalt and Relativity

When the cessation of the war permitted German scholars to visit foreign shores again, they brought with them two scientific theories which a future historian may well consider the outstanding intellectual triumphs of the first quarter of this century —the theory of Einstein and the principle of Gestalt. As befits the dignity of an elder brother the physical version of the new mode of thinking about nature won a popular hearing some years before the psychological approach was expounded, but when it did arrive keen minds everywhere recognized the kinship between the two. It would be false to assert that configurationism is simply a diluted application of the concepts of relativity to mental life. Since the two arose together within the same span of years (1905-1920) and shared the same milieu (German university institute life), there is much reason for suspecting that the contact was a one-way affair, for psychologists ever since Weber's day have been taking many hints from the physicists without the compliment being returned. We do know that Einstein and Köhler were both students of Planck and it is altogether likely that they absorbed related ideas from a common speculative atmosphere.

Wherein does the similarity of the two views lie? Primarily in the opposition of both systems to the summative and additive treatment of data. Einstein's declaration that the theorem of the addition of velocities employed in classical mechanics can no longer be maintained is matched by Wertheimer's assertion that the component members of a psychic structure are really interdependent, each of them being what it is by virtue of its place in the whole! Similarly, the former's claim that the sole dynamical datum in two or more bodies moving relatively to each other is matched by the configurationist's denial of the reality of a single isolated sensation and insistence upon the

---

[23] Many persons are inclined to think that Köhler's physical data are purely gratuitous, but he himself would object to viewing them as mere analogies.

primacy of the patterned perception. Humphrey[24] has shown these relations more clearly than any one else as the following quotation indicates:

The teaching of Einstein is that absolute rest and motion are meaningless for physical science and that motion can signify only the changing position of bodies relatively to each other. Thus, to take the simplest possible case, all that we can observe is a change in distance in the two bodies in mutual relation. We have then a dynamic whole process, with respect to which it would be distorting the facts to claim, for the purpose of calculation or description that either of the reference bodies is unique as compared with each other. . . .

Between these two theories, that of the German physicist and of the German psychologist, there stands out an immediate parallel. Each strikes at the discreteness of the cosmos, at the local autonomy respectively of the physical and the psychic. Each begins with a negative, distinctive attack,—sensations are not independent, velocities and spaces and times are not absolute. True, the notion of cosmic interdependence was not new. Thus, while we have Newton claiming the gravitational interdependence of physical matter, we find also a school of philosophers declaring an associational interdependence of psychic material, and indeed the parallel between these two modes of thought was brought out by Hume in a famous passage (Treatise on Human Nature, Pt. I, sec. 1), "Here is a kind of attraction which in the mental field will be found to have as extraordinary effects as in the natural."

Reiser[25] has recently shown in even more detail the common ground shared by physical relativity and psychical relativity. In dealing with solutions with different ionic concentrations the answer to the question of whether a given solution is "electropositive" or "electronegative" depends on the relation of this given solution to the other solutions with which it is being compared. This is matched in the phenomenon of simultaneous color contrast where the chromatic properties of the perceived pattern are not "absolute" but are "relative" to the total situation. In some phenomena it is often impossible to disentangle one form of relativity from another. The Doppler effect, e.g., occurs in astronomical observations with a displacement of the Fraunhofer lines toward the red or the violet ends of the spectrum, depending upon whether a star is receding or approaching

[24] "The Theory of Einstein and the Gestalt Psychology: a Parallel," *Amer. J. Psychol.*, 1924, *35*, 353–359.

[25] "Physical Relativity and Psychical Relativity," *Psychol. Rev.*, 1930, *37*, 257–263.

the observer, but the same relation also obtains in sound transmission. "We are all familiar with the experience of hearing the pitch of a bell at a railroad crossing change as the train we are in approaches, overtakes, and passes the ringing bell. When the train is approaching the crossing the source of the sound is moving (relatively) toward us. Accordingly, we overtake a greater number of sound waves per unit interval of time, and hence, the pitch appears to be higher; as we recede from the bell fewer waves strike our ear per unit interval of time and the pitch of the sound appears to be lower. *A variation in the relative velocities of the observer and the thing observed produces the same effect as an objective variation of the stimulus when the observer is at rest with respect to the source of the stimulus.*"

Whether this remarkable datum is to be treated by the physicist or the psychologist separately or in conjunction is a matter of indifference as long as one recognizes the community of law and standpoint involved in both approaches.

CHAPTER 3

THE PHYSIOLOGICAL FOUNDATIONS

The physiological data in support of the Gestalt hypothesis are drawn largely from the newer researches in the field of cerebral localization, the genetic development of reflexes, and that division of biology which is concerned with "regulation" as expressed by the facts of coördination in organic functions, regeneration of members, etc. It is not at all difficult to see why the configurationists should be deeply interested in the implications of such phenomena, since in all these instances the question of the dominance of the organized whole over its members comes to the fore. Traditionally, neurologists have accepted special anatomical topography as the only explanation for order—a restricted machine concept with monotonous elementary currents conducted compulsively from a point of stimulation to a point of reaction, for which Gestalt wishes to substitute the principle of dynamical self-distribution.

A glance at the history of cerebral localization since the days of Gall and the phrenological controversy shows a peculiar cyclical oscillation of opinion between the view that the brain is a complex mechanism subdivided into definite areas with restricted functions (Broca, Munk, Wernicke, Ferrier, Sherrington) and the opposing position that the cortex at least operates as a unit (Flourens, Goltz, Loeb, Franz, Lashley, Head). The problem to-day remains one of the biggest issues in science. The orthodox physiological psychology (perhaps best represented by Ladd and Woodworth and Herrick's manual) upon which most contemporary American psychologists have been reared, sponsored a fairly precise sensori-motor localization, although acknowledging that the greater part of the cerebrum consisted of "silent areas" whose rôle was largely conjectural. Neurology has always been influenced by psychological systems —witness the name "association fibers"—and the "neo-phrenology" of a generation ago was perfectly adapted to the piecemeal description of mental life then current. The early animal work of Franz, indicating that habits were lost after extirpation of certain regions but that they could be re-learned after recovery from the insult, first threw doubt upon the adequacy of the rigid doctrine of "centers" as typified by Broca's area. The resulting theories of *substitute function* and *equipotentiality,* and the clinical successes of re-education in aphasia emphasize the limitations of the strict specificity approach, and fit in nicely with the Gestalt theory which *conceives the nervous system as highly permeable and without isolated segments functioning independently of the rest.*

Lashley's Cerebral Studies

A pretty illustration of the inevitable drift of events may be found in following the sequence of Lashley's publications in this sphere of research. When he began his investigations about 1916, his approach was that of an uncompromising behaviorist, fully persuaded that the conditioned response and the reflex arc would provide an adequate account of the adaptive conduct of organisms. Barely a decade later, the logic of his own findings had forced him into the opposite camp. In the volume [1] which best expresses this change of heart, the conclusions offer definite aid and comfort to none but the Gestalt theorist and to Spearman's "g" factor hypothesis. What was the evidence which compelled this new allegiance?

By means of a thermocautery, varying amounts and different parts of the cortex in a large group of rats were destroyed and their learning records made after recovery from the operation (10-30 days) compared with those of normal animals in such tasks as maze-running, brightness discrimination, etc. Comparing the records for the two groups according to errors, time, and number of trials, Lashley found that in general the cerebral lesions were attended by an increase in the amount of practice necessary to solve the problems, but that *the degree of deterioration in learning ability and retentiveness was proportional to*

[1] *Brain Mechanisms and Intelligence,* University of Chicago Press, 1929.

the amount of brain tissue injured and independent of the area of the cortex affected. "Equal injuries in different cortical areas produce equal amounts of retardation. . . . The *magnitude* of the injury is important; the *locus* is not" (Lashley, pp. 58-60). The gap between the normal and operated rats varied with the nature of the problem to be learned; in the case of brightness discrimination, the operated animals were even superior to the normals! Previous study had indicated another peculiarity of the visual function. "If the animals are first trained and then subjected to operation, the habit is abolished by any extensive lesion within the occipital third of the cerebrum, and the amount of practice necessary for re-learning is closely proportional to the extent of the injury. . . . Destruction of any other than the occipital region does not affect the retention of the habit. If the destruction is made before training, it has no effect upon the later formation of the brightness habit, even though the entire occipital third of the cortex is extirpated. Thus, the habit, once formed, is definitely localized, in the sense that it is dependent upon a definite part of the cortex for performance. Its initial formation, on the contrary, is not conditioned by the presence of any part of the cortex; the learning process is not localized, in the foregoing sense" (Lashley, p. 86).

Another startling experiment showed that even the kinaesthetic cues—which Watson had earlier apparently demonstrated to be the basis of the rats' maze-learning—were not only negligible but conceivably irrelevant factors in explaining the performance. Since Lashley's language is so precise on this point, one can do no better than cite the appropriate passage, "The ability to perform the maze habit was unaffected by complete transsection of the fasciculus gracilis and fasciculus cuneatus at the third cervical level, although marked disturbances of kinaesthetic sensitivity resulted. Section of all ascending tracts in the lateral columns of the cord likewise produced no disturbance in maze-running. After such lesions the animals ran the maze accurately in darkness when all other directive sensory cues seemed ruled out. . . . All of this evidence opposes the view that reduced learning ability for the maze or the loss of the maze habit after operation is the result of sensory defect as such.

The habits are not lost after destruction of the peripheral sensory mechanisms, and this lack of effect of sense privation is not due to shift in the use of other sensory directive cues. The habit is lost after destruction of the visual cortex in animals which were blind during learning, which indicates that the loss is due to some other than the sensory function of this area" (Lashley, pp. 114-115).

As if this conclusion alone were not enough to shock the schema of a conservative neurology, Lashley proceeds to demonstrate the indifference of effect where the efferent pathways are interrupted as well as the afferent. To quote again, "In one set of animals, the pyramidal tracts were completely cut; in another, the rubrospinal; and, in the final series of cases, all possible descending tracts were interrupted. All these animals ran the maze in retention tests without errors. They showed marked incoördinations, greater difficulty in negotiating the turns of the maze than did any of the cases with cerebral lesions, but absolutely no disturbance of orientation in the maze. This shows the ability of the rat to perform the maze habit after destruction of any of the organized descending tracts of the cord" (Lashley, p. 115).

It does not require more than an elementary knowledge of general psychology to see that such findings, if verified, pronounce the death knell of the standard theories of the reflex arc, synaptic changes, etc. Lashley, himself, is fully aware of these implications, although his phraseology occasionally betrays a reluctance to admit the utter incompatibility of these two positions. Notice how the following passage supports Koffka's earlier contention, even to the extent of employing a similar illustration: "With the eye fixed and a pattern moved across the field of the macula, the same reaction (e.g., naming the object) may be elicited at any one of a thousand points, no two of which involve excitation of exactly the same retinal cells. To say that a specific habit has been formed for each of the possible positions is preposterous for the pattern may be one never before experienced. The alternative is that the response is determined by the proportions of the pattern and within the limits of visual acuity, is independent of the particular cells excited."

This means that, not only on the retina, but also in the central projection on the cortex, there is a constant flux of stimulation such that the same cells are rarely, if ever, twice excited by the same stimulus, yet a constant reaction is produced. The activity of the visual cortex must resemble that of one of the electric signs in which a pattern of letters passes rapidly across a stationary group of lamps. The structural pattern is fixed, but the functional pattern plays over it without limitation to specific elements. . . .

Neurologically, these relationships must be in the nature of ratios of excitation, patterns without a fixed anatomical substratum, since the sensory and motor elements of a situation may change fundamentally without altering its logical significance. We seem forced to the conclusion that a final common path may be somehow sensitized to a pattern of excitation so that it will respond to this pattern in whatsoever part of the nervous tissue it may occur. In the simplest cases, the relationships forming the basis of reaction seem expressible as ratios of intensity of excitation; in others, as ratios of spatial extent or temporal distribution. The relationships involved in insight are more difficult to analyze, but there is in some instances sufficient similarity to cases of sensory discrimination to suggest that the basic mechanism must be fundamentally the same.

The problem of reaction to ratio thus seems to underlie all phases of behavior to such a degree that we might be justified in saying that the unit of neural organization is not the reflex arc or the system of reciprocal innervation but is the mechanism, whatever be its nature, by which reaction to a ratio is produced (pp. 158–159–160–161).

Did ever avowed behaviorist speak the dialect of Gestalt more plainly?

A brief excursus into the field of educational psychology will help to indicate some of the practical influences which a belated but inevitable recognition of the material presented above must exert. The familiar Thorndikian position (known to teachers throughout the length and breadth of the American continent) maintains that *if* learning is restricted to particular synapses, there can be no influence of training upon other activities than those actually practiced; any improvement in unpracticed functions must be the result of nervous connections which they have in common with the practiced activities.[2] The rejection of the

[2] Although transfer effects may be small they are real enough. Arabic numbers traced with the finger-tip upon any part of the body are easily identified, but it is hard to imagine what the "common elements" responsible for this overlapping can be. Even if the subject must convert the tactile-motor impressions into a visual image, how has he learned to do this?

older doctrines of "formal discipline" and "transfer of training," leading indirectly to a great variety of curricular changes, seems to have been based as much upon the plausibility of such reasoning as upon any convincing experimental evidence. However—and here is where one experiences most vividly the consequences of an ever-changing body of scientific facts—it is very doubtful if the same neurons or synapses are involved even in two similar reactions to the same stimulus. "Our data seem to prove that the structural elements are relatively unimportant for integration and that the common elements must be some sort of dynamic patterns, determined by the relations or ratios among the parts of the system and not by the specific neurons activated. If this be true, we cannot, on the basis of our present knowledge of the nervous system, set any limit to the kinds or amount of transfer possible or to the sort of relations which may be directly recognized" (Lashley, p. 173).

But these animal experiments of Lashley are not the only ones which lend a most convincing touch to the correctness of the Gestalt hypothesis in the field of physiology and neurology. The manner in which grammatical forms function in speech is hard to reconcile with the classic assumption of confined pathways. One of the great riddles of syntactical expression, so far as the neurologist is concerned, is that once we learn a new word, we use it in correct grammatical relations in limitless combinations with other words, without having to form new associations for each setting. How is this possible? In his Presidential address[3] before the Ninth International Congress of Psychology—the full import of which has not as yet been appreciated—Lashley offers a tentative explanation in terms which fit neatly into a configurationist context:

> Unity of action seems to be more deeply rooted than even structural organization. In working with animals and human beings, I have been more and more impressed by the absence of the chaotic behavior which we might expect from the extent and irregular form of the lesions. There may be great losses of sensory or of motor capacities, amnesias, emotional deterioration, dementia—but the residual behavior is still carried out in an orderly fashion. It may be grotesque, a caricature of

[3] Karl Lashley, "Basic Neural Mechanisms in Behavior," *Psychol. Review*, 1930, *37*, 1–24.

normal behavior, but it is not unorganized. . . . Even dementia is not wholly unintelligent. It involves reduction in the range of comprehension, in the complexity of the relations which may be perceived, but what falls within the patient's range is still dealt with in an orderly and intelligible fashion. . . .

Such phenomena suggest that the nervous system is capable of a self-regulation which gives a coherent logical character to its functioning, no matter how its anatomical constituents may be disturbed. If we could slice off the cerebral cortex, turn it about, and replace it hindside before, getting a random connection of the severed fibers, what would be the consequences for behavior? From current theories, we could predict only chaos. From the point of view which I am suggesting we might expect to find very little disturbance of behavior. Our subject might have to be re-educated, perhaps not even this, for we do not know the locus or character of habit organization—but in the course of his re-education he might well show a normal capacity for apprehending relationships and for the rational manipulation of his world of experience.

This may sound like a plunge into mysticism, but an example from another field will show that such self-regulation is a normal property of living things. Wilson and later Child have crushed the tissues of sponges and hydroids, sifted the cells through sieves of bolting cloth and observed their later behavior. The cells are at first suspended independently in the water, but may be brought into aggregates by settling or centrifuging. Starting as flat sheets, they round up into spherical masses and begin differentiation. Embryonic stages may be simulated and eventually adult individuals with characteristic structures, mouth, hypostome, tentacles, and stalk in normal relative positions are produced. In spite of the abnormal conditions to which it is subjected, the formless mass of cells assumes the structure characteristic of the species. Of course, many abnormal forms appear, but even these follow the characteristic scheme of organization (pp. 19–20).

Driesch's Embryological Experiments

The famous growth studies of Driesch bear directly upon the problem of regulation as interpreted by the Gestaltists, save that they are far from adopting the familiar conclusions which the distinguished vitalist has drawn. In one of his experiments with the larvæ of a sea urchin, he destroyed one cell among four double cells. According to the "machine" theory of a rigid cell-net, one would expect that if the creature developed further a "cripple" would result, because of the lack of the corresponding part. Actually a complete organism appeared whose *total* size was one-fourth less than normal. These results have been confirmed by Roux in similar studies made in a later stage of development. The phenomenon evidently appears because of the division of another cell which assumes the function of the one removed. To Driesch, this is evidence that *the whole serves as the natural "entelechy,"* whereas Gestaltists prefer to think in terms of *Prägnanz,* a principle of lesser metaphysical shading because of its more recent promulgation.[4]

Weiss' Transplantation Work

In one of those unusual investigations which Americans have been led to consider typical of the Viennese school of biologists, Paul Weiss amputated complete mature limbs of salamanders and transplanted the extremity by placing it beside a normal one. In the many instances in which perfect healing ensued, the transplanted limb hung loosely at the side of the body during the first few weeks as a result of the severing of the nerve-fibers. After an interval of uselessness, the transplanted limb slowly recovered the power of motion and finally was functionally normal, its action in no way being distinguishable from that of an intact member. At this stage, the normal and the transplanted extremity invariably moved together like a pair of well-coördinated structures.

In all cases where the supernumerary limb received a part of its reinnervation from the limb level of the spinal cord it finally came to perform precisely as did the host limb. Weiss refers to this as the *homologous* function of the supernumerary and host. When an arm was inserted in the region of the host's leg, it performed homologously with the host limb, i.e., by bending at the elbows when the host bent its knee, bending the wrist with the host's ankle flexions, etc. This effect held irrespective of the point of attachment, the location, or the orientation of the grafted member. In one experiment, the upper arm was removed and the elbow inserted where the shoulder had been. The hand nevertheless continued to function (after recuperation) as a hand, never as an elbow, whose place relative to the

[4] Schaxel, the Jena biologist, and Bertalanffy (*Kritische Theorie der Formbildung,* Berlin, 1928) lean heavily in the Gestalt direction. Both have been influential in moulding Lewin's thought, according to his own admission. (It may be worth noting that a century ago, Von Baer compared the growth of an individual with a melody.)

body it now occupied. Certainly neither re-established direct connection nor "learning" in the usual sense account for these phenomena.

Obviously, some kind of connection with the central nervous system of the new animal must have been established. Weiss offers a theory of nervous resonance [5] to explain this extraordinary fact, according to which each muscle does not react to every efferent discharge, but only to excitation of a quite definite form characteristic for it (isochronisms). He believes that the muscles, end-plates, and possibly the motor fibers (provided the latter acquire specificity under the dominance of the particular muscle) must themselves possess properties of *selectivity* which enable them to respond to the appropriate action currents and not to others which reach them. His evidence indicates a dynamic coördinated interaction between (1) a central "broadcasting" system, (2) transmitting motor nerves, and (3) a motor receiving system, which we can understand only in terms of the properties of all three. Weiss agrees with Köhler's hypothesis to the extent that he rejects any point-to-point coördination between periphery and center and discards the notion of constant geometrical-anatomical connection in favor of a more dynamic distribution process.

Marinà's Eye-Muscle Surgery

A rare study which the Gestalt theorists delight to cite as confirmation of their viewpoint, but which seriously needs competent verification, is the novel experiment of A. Marina on the effects of interchanging the eye muscles of the ape. Marina published in 1905 and 1910 the results of his visual operations in which he interchanged first the medial rectus and lateral rectus, and later substituted the superior rectus for the lateral rectus. This meant in the first instance that the eye was moved outward by the previously inward-moving muscle, and *vice versa;* while in the second instance, the muscle moving the eye

[5] Best described in an article on "Erregungsresonanz und Erregungsspecifizität" in *Ergebnisse der Biologie,* 1928, *3,* 1–151. The neurological explanation of Gestalt phenomena must be sought along such lines as here indicated or in conjunction with Lapicque's conception of chronaxy. (A convenient English summary of Weiss' work may be found in "Changing Conceptions in Physiological Psychology" by H. R. De Silva and W. D. Ellis, *J. Gen. Psychol.,* 1934, *11,* 145–159.)

outward was eliminated and its place taken by a lifting muscle. Having accomplished this curious rearrangement of the natural alignment, the animal ought to have exhibited a most extraordinary type of nystagmus on the principle that a definite impulse is conducted from the brain center through a fixed pathway to each muscle. Instead, as soon as the wound had healed, the voluntary and automatic sideward movements of the eye were executed in normal fashion! Certainly, as the author himself suggests, such an outcome argues very strongly for the indifference or lack of pre-determination of function in the conduction pathways.

Coghill and Minkowski on the Origin of Reflexes

Coghill is another experimenter whose work is a powerful aid to the configurationist cause. In his embryological study of the common salamander, he found that the earliest movements are made by the most anterior part of the muscle system of the trunk. As the external gills, fore limbs, and hind limbs develop, their first movements are performed only as the trunk moves. According to Coghill, this method of "expanding" the behavior pattern is applicable to all vertebrates, and he has assembled some valuable testimony concerning the origin of reflexes in man. The Swiss neurologist, Minkowski, has similarly shown that with human fetuses only a few centimeters in length the reflexes never occur as discrete acts but are always allied with other movements. The pattern of movement of the toes as a group "individuates" out of the larger pattern of movement of the leg, foot, and toes; the characteristic Babinski sign is a relatively late development. There can be little question that such an entity as the "simple reflex" never occurs in the life of the individual, a point recognized by Sherrington, for in 1905 he had called the simple reflex a "pure abstract conception." This apparently had been forgotten by many of the less critical, so that now new material is required to show that complexity of behavior is not derived by the progressive integration of more and more originally discrete units.[6]

[6] "The Early Development of Behavior in *Amblystoma* and Man," *Archives of Neurology and Psychiatry*, 1929, 21, 989–1009. A less specialized but more complete account of the implications of these facts is found in Coghill's *Anatomy of Behavior*, Cambridge, 1929.

CHAPTER 4

THE PHILOSOPHICAL FOUNDATIONS

Wertheimer's Anti-Synthetic Position

In less systematic but in far more dramatic manner than Köhler, Wertheimer has laid down the broad outlines of Gestalt theory. In a semi-popular address,[1] he has characterized the basic doctrine of configurationism as follows: There exist natural circumstances [2] in which what happens in the total is not conditioned by the nature of the parts or their mode of combination, but on the contrary, what occurs in any part of this whole is determined by the inner structural laws of this entirety. As he told his audience, *all* of Gestalt theory is embraced in this formula—neither more, nor less.

If one asks how this differs from Ehrenfels' position, the answer is readily given. If a melody consisting of six tones is reproduced and recognized when six utterly different notes are played, what has happened? The six elements are surely present, but in addition thereto one must presuppose a seventh, the so-called *Gestaltqualität*. It is this seventh datum which makes possible the recognition of the melody. So runs Ehrenfels' argument. But contemporary configurationism takes a much more radical view. According to it, the flesh and blood of a single tone is dependent upon its rôle in the melody. When *b* is a predecessor to *c*, it is something altogether different from *b* as the tonic. This dynamic position is understood only when one appreciates the presence of total-tendencies in a broader field of energy.

The Gestalt conception is not just limited to the provincial domain of psychology, but involves a characteristic approach

[1] "Ueber Gestalttheorie," *Symposion*, I, 1927, 39–60.

[2] Note that this phrase does not claim *universal* applicability. However, the implication at least of most Gestalt language is that the principle possesses cosmic dimensions and is true without exception.

to all science and all knowledge. Suppose I look at the universe from the standpoint of a "collective" theory and ask, "How must a world appear within which there can be no science, no understanding, no penetration into and comprehension of inner relations?" The answer is very simple. Such a situation results whenever we have a multiplicity of purely disparate sections. Again, how must the world be constituted, or how must the manifold it presents be conceived in order that science of the piecemeal variety may be pursued? For this one needs nothing more than repeated meaningless connections, which is all one has to postulate in order to carry on traditional logic, mathematics and science. This is the view most people still hold of physics. But actual physical enterprise, rightly considered, shows the world in a different light. It is more like a Beethoven symphony, wherein we have the possibility of sensing the whole from one of its parts, which permits some premonition of the structural principle of the total, and in which the fundamental laws are not laws of the parts, but properties of the entire event.

There are two doctrines implicit in the older psychology to which the Gestalt position is flatly opposed. These are (1) the mosaic or "bundle" hypothesis and (2) the associationist thesis. The first holds that all complex mental states rest upon a collection of juxtaposed simpler contents in much the same way that a sand heap consists of a multitude of separate grains of sand. The second proposition fundamentally states that if a given mental content *a* has occurred together (in spatio-temporal contiguity) with another content *b*, a tendency for *a* to draw *b* after it is thereby established. Both views are essentially alike, the first thesis supplying the bricks and the second the mortar of the psychic structure. Should it be said that no serious psychologist since James Mill has held these ideas in their raw form, Wertheimer would retort that they are implicit in most attacks on concrete problems made by contemporary research, regardless of the occasional modifications (which do not basically alter the situation, for they, too, are handled "analytically") introduced by the use of "simultaneous attention," "imageless thoughts," "determining tendencies," or "meaning functions."

Now while it is true that behavior occasionally exhibits phenomena which approach this summative type of response, it is far from *typical* of mental events, being only a limiting case and occurring under rare and very special conditions. On the contrary, all reality (= the "given") is structured, formed, or patterned with highly concrete total attributes and invariably obeys the law that *total processes define what shall take place in subordinate areas.*[3] Consequently, fidelity to the facts demands that one speak of a stimulus "constellation" and never of *a* stimulus, of an "action-total" and not of *a* movement. The Gestalt concept restores meaning to our conduct by its recognition of the primacy of restricted "wholes" and the derivative and dependent nature of all part-processes.

Lewin on Scientific Method

Following the heavy philosophical penchant of German psychological literature, Lewin has elaborated in an impressively original paper[4] his belief that the study of behavior is passing from the Aristotelian stage into the Galilean phase, and that at present we are witnessing a reconstruction of fundamental views akin to that which accompanied the birth of modern physics in the seventeenth century. Aristotelianism in psychology means among other things, (1) the persistence of valuational attitudes so well represented in the outworn distinction between normal and pathological phenomena. We still speak of "childish" errors, of drill, and "improvement" in the same anthropomorphic sense with which early botany considered weeds and parasites. (2) The Aristotelian standpoint—which is usually but not necessarily exhibited in the actual writings of the Stagirite—tends to identify the *individual* with the *accidental.* Ordinary observers exhibit this bias to perfection when watching some unique bit of child behavior. Do *all* or at least *most* youngsters do that? If the answer is negative,

[3] Max Wertheimer, "Untersuchungen zur Lehre von der Gestalt: I. Prinzipielle Bemerkungen," *Psychol. Forschung,* 1922, *1,* 47–58. It is curious that in his Dozent days, Wertheimer actually won some repute as an authority on the diagnostic or detective use of the free-association method!

[4] "Der Uebergang von der aristotelischen zur galileischen Denkweise in Biologie und Psychologie," *Erkenntnis,* 1930, *1,* 421–466. Dr. Donald Adams has made a faithful translation of this paper for the *J. General Psychol.,* 1931, *5,* 141–177.

the silent assumption is that the action lacks scientific interest. (3) The historical Aristotle did restrict the reign of natural law to regularly recurrent or oft-recurring events, with the result that law and individual were considered opposites, since law was limited to those cases in which something common was repeated. The general or the abstract had to be discerned in the particular and the concrete. This emphasis upon the frequency feature has led to a one-sided use of mathematics in psychology with almost exclusive devotion to statistical methods and "unreal" averages, and a consequent neglect of procedures for apprehending the full reality of the single situation.[5] It has also nourished the belief that quality and quantity are irreconcilably opposed in psychology, a situation similar to that which the followers of Galileo had to meet when it was objected: How can one comprehend under one rule of motion such utterly different events as the movement of the stars, the drift of leaves with the wind, the descent of the rolling stone, and the flight of birds? One still encounters a subtle version of this attitude in the assertion that a law is simply an extreme instance of regularity and probability; whereas, a true Galileian must maintain the universal validity of psychological laws.[6]

The contrast between the two systems of thinking is most decisive in the different explanations of movement. In Aristotelian dynamics, the manner and direction of the physical vec-

[5] In another article, Lewin writes, "The statistical method is usually compelled to define its groups on the basis, not of purely psychical characteristics, but of more or less extrinsic ones (such as number of siblings), so that particular cases having quite different or even opposed psychological structures may be included in the same group. . . . But the very relation that is decisive for the investigation of *dynamics*—viz., that of the position of the actual individual child in the actual concrete total situation—is thereby 'abstracted.' An inference from the concepts of the average child and of the average situation are abstractions that have no utility whatever for the investigation of dynamics. The laws of falling bodies in physics cannot be discovered by taking the average of actual falling movements, say of leaves, stones, and other objects, but only by proceeding from so-called 'pure cases.' "—Essay on "Environmental Forces in Child Behavior and Development" in Murchison's *Handbook of Child Psychology*, 1931, p. 95. For a pleasant satire of statistical quantification, see Waller, "Scientific Method and Insight," *Amer. J. Sociol.*, 1934, *40*, 285–297. The entire essay is Lewinian in spirit.

[6] Gestaltists object to the usual view of causation as an inevitable chain-like sequence of cause and effect, and prefer to predict consequences in terms of general "conditions" which must be met. Even the notion of cause is made ancillary to their leading idea. Thus, Koffka says, "According to the only significant law, A B C form one series, A, B, C, another. Then law can no longer mean the mere statement of sequences, but must refer to real functional wholes akin to melodies. Scientific law must state, under the Gestalt category, the intrinsic properties of such spatial and temporal wholes." See his article on Gestalt in the *Encyclopaedia of the Social Sciences*. In Lewin's language, a natural law is then essentially an action-total. Only such facts can affect each other which have a place in the same field. The *cause* of the events is the *relationship between the parts of the situation as dynamical facts* and a complete characterization of these dynamical facts would be a complete analysis.

tor is completely determined in advance by the nature of the object in question; in modern physics, however, the occurrence of physical vectors always rests upon a conjunction of several physical factors, especially upon some relation of the object to its surroundings (cf. the "total situation" in psychology). If, then, as seems generally acknowledged, the dynamics of an event is not only dependent upon the object but also primarily conditioned by the situation, then it is indeed absurd to assume that general laws can be revealed by ruling out the influences of the different circumstances as much as possible.

The reader need hardly be told now that Lewin, in presenting the distinction between Aristotelian and Galileian approaches to scientific problems, is really interested in magnifying—via the principle of *Prägnanz!*—the fundamental opposition in methodology between traditional nineteenth-century psychology and the spirit of configurationism. The conflict is not based solely nor even primarily upon questions of fact or content, such as the rôle of kinæsthetic images in the thought process, but upon a basic cleavage in the general principles governing experimental technique and interpretation. A little table may assist in picturing the character of some of the more significant contrasts:

	Aristotle	Galileo
1. The Regular and Uniform The Frequent	are subject to law	subject to law
The Individual	is a matter of chance	
2. Criteria of Natural Law are	uniformity frequency	not required
3. That which is common to historically and geographically given instances is—	a manifestation of the essence of the occasion; an expression of the nature of the thing	an "accident," i.e., only historically conditioned

An American disciple of Lewin's, J. F. Brown,[7] has prepared a more extended parallel between the two modes of thinking under the general caption of "class" versus "field" theory. The

[7] "Freud and the Scientific Method," *Phil. of Sci.*, 1934, *I*, 323–337.

central idea of a "field" theory (of which post-Copernican astronomy and physics and contemporary Gestalt psychology are examples) is that the behavior of an object is determined by the field structure or spatio-temporal configuration of the energy within the field. The central idea of a "class" theory (pure illustrations are difficult to find but differential and abnormal psychology are saturated with this viewpoint) is that membership in a certain class determines the behavior of an object. A summary in terms of ten sharply opposed characteristics of the two approaches is reproduced below:

Criteria for Class Theory	Criteria for Field Theory
1. The behavior of objects is determined by the *class* to which they belong.	1. The behavior of objects is determined by the structure of the *field* of which they are a part.
2. The force directing behavior shows the properties of an *entelechy.*	2. The force directing behavior shows the properties of a *vector.*
3. There is *local* determination.	3. There is *no* local determination.
4. The concepts used in "class" theory are primarily *substantial.*	4. The concepts used in "field" theory are mainly *functional.*
5. The method of scientific analysis is largely *structural.*	5. The method of scientific analysis is primarily *relational.*
6. The analysis is in terms of historically and geographically conditioned *regularities.*	6. The analysis is in terms of ahistorical-typical *laws.*
7. The method is primarily *empirical.*	7. The method is hypothetical-*deductive.*
8. The analysis allows *dichotomies.*	8. The analysis allows *no* dichotomies.
9. Class theory tends to use *valuative* concepts.	9. Field theory insists on *non-valuative* concepts.
10. Class theory attempts to answer a *metaphysical* "why?"	10. Field theory attempts to answer a *scientific* "how?"

In another disquisition [8] on the problem of method, Lewin attacks the customary theory of induction, viz., that the universal necessity of law rests upon a leap "from many cases to all cases." There are two kinds of uniformity which must be distinguished: (1) those dependent upon *historico-geographical* connections and (2) those involving *conditional-genetic* factors. The former is illustrated by the sequence of omnibus

[8] "Gesetz und Experiment in der Psychologie," *Symposion*, 1927, *1*, 375–421.

lines passing a given corner: if one watches long enough, one may notice that a No. 12 car passing in one direction is followed within a short time by a No. 14 going in the opposite direction. This sequence, however, is not a true causal connection, but the result of a time-schedule and the plan of the city streets. The latter is represented by the step from "example" to "type," the type remaining invariant with reference to spatio-temporal indices, just as a plant grown at different altitudes. Gold as a "type" is *not* identical with the aggregate of all the gold in the world. Similarly, the relation between individual things or structures and thing-types is paralleled by the relation between individual "happenings" and occurrence-types.

Lewin holds that a natural law is none other than the description of a definite conditional-genetic occurrence-type. To say that an event obeys a certain law is to say nothing more than that it belongs to a specific type of occurrence. For instance, the meaning back of the various gas formulæ in physics is simply that events *a* and *b* are necessarily *dependent moments* of a unitary happening. In order to determine whether an event belongs in the historico-geographical or the conditional-genetic category, one must have recourse to experiment. That is why a *single* experiment is able to disprove a rule which one has tended to accept as a consequence of thousandfold repeated experience in daily life. The major difficulty lies in the selection of crucial examples, but once found, the penetrating analysis of a single experiment is better than the accumulation of statistical cases.[9] To use terms of a biological origin, the *genotypical* experiment leads to causal explanation in terms of laws, while *phenotypical* observation is limited to a here-and-now description of characteristics, many of which are irrelevant to the event. Explaining an event consists in adequately describing the underlying genotype and seeing if the phenotype (experience or data) may be precisely *ordered* to it. Laws are descriptions of genotypes.

[9] Lewin acknowledges that he obtained this epistemological idea from the writings of the distinguished Hamburg philosopher, Ernst Cassirer. Lewin's rule is that for an "explanation" or prediction of events, we must know (in psychology as in every science): (1) the general laws of the particular events; (2) the momentary constitution of the whole situation.

Wheeler's Organismic Laws

The one American writer who has offered the most systematic and encyclopædic exposition of Gestalt psychology has been Raymond Wheeler. In a series of four volumes[10] (in which he has always been the senior author) published in rapid succession between the years 1929 and 1932, he has tried to give a comprehensive picture of the development, and to demonstrate its teachableness by reducing the widely scattered interpretative literature to the confines of a compact textbook. Not only has he gone farther than his German predecessors in this highly valuable pedagogical contribution, but he has attempted to make the Gestalt edifice "hang together" through the consistent application to each of its divisions of eight organismic laws of his own formulation. Although not original with him, their extensive use as fundamental explanatory principles in psychological science was first made through his efforts. At bottom, the conceptions are Köhler's, but broadened and freely employed with an enthusiasm which shows how readily the disciple's ardor may exceed that of his prophet.

Like Köhler, he upholds the identity of physical and mental laws and rejects the ancient problem of materialism *versus* vitalism as the artificial dichotomy of dualistic ignorance. He traces it to the difficulty the Greeks encountered in applying the structural and functional points of views with apparently opposed conclusions. The one is a question of *composition* and the other a matter of *activity*. This grand problem of antiquity became one of the persistent traditions of European philosophy, a heritage which might have been avoided had the originators appreciated that "structure and function are merely aspects of each other; the same thing is envisaged first from a static and then from a dynamic point of view. Structure is the form of an activity, a something moving, or a something that changes; function is the activity of the form, the moving or changing of the thing. Structure and function have opposite but mutually dependent meanings" (*Laws of Human Nature,* p. 9). This is

[10] The books referred to are, in order: (1) *The Science of Psychology,* 1929; (2) *Readings in Psychology,* 1930; (3) *The Laws of Human Nature,* 1932 (Appleton, New York); (4) *Principles of Mental Development,* 1932—all but (3) published by Crowell, New York.

the larger whole into which both mind and matter fit. Physics and psychology instead of being diametrically apart are fundamentally akin in their efforts to understand natural phenomena.

This structure-function antinomy has exaggerated the common-sense disparity between the physical and the psychical. Wheeler offers a brief illustration to demonstrate the unreality of this logical distinction: "Hold up your little finger and wiggle it. You can cut your finger, for the finger is structure. Where is the movement? In the finger? Cut it open and see. No, the movement is not inside. The movement is not in the finger, nor is it outside of it; it is *of* the finger; it is something the finger does. Similarly, an idea is not in or outside of the brain. It is something the brain does. These ABC's of dialectics are useful, in spite of the fact that they sound rather foolish; for they show how there are just as many phenomena of the so-called physical world that cannot be cut and burned as there are of the mental. These phenomena are processes, events. *Science investigates events that have no claim to material versus mental substantiality*" (*op. cit.*, p. 23). Those who protest that mental events are after all unique are exaggerating the qualitative distinctions which admittedly exist, but forget that these variations do not require a different set of laws. Oil and water are decidedly unique fluids, but both obey hydrodynamic principles.

The mechanistic[11] bias of modern psychology was a one-sided and well-intentioned endeavor to avoid the tangles of an impossible dualism, but it suffered from the atomistic logic and elementarism which dominated Western thought in the nineteenth century. Its efforts to explain mental organization by means of creative synthesis out of a chaos of unrelated primordial parts proved abortive because the relations had to be "forced"

[11] Gestalt theorists are in part responsible for the misunderstanding of their anti-mechanistic position because of their neglect of the overtones of this phrase. Wheeler apparently is guilty of the same tactical error here. To the ordinary laboratory scientist, "mechanism" implies a belief in immanent law and order in the natural world. However, mechanism is only one variety of "naturalism" which configurationists, of course, adopt. It is mechanism of the atomistic variety against which the Gestalt writers protest and the postulates which they use in their arguments are just as "naturalistic" or "non-spiritual" as those held by their opponents. Intrinsically, the realism of Gestalt considers mind, or rather mental processes, not as something outside of nature, but as just such natural events as any others. They are links in the chains of reactions produced by an organism in an environment, and cannot legitimately be isolated from this context. The monism of Gestalt is implied in the assertion that one and the same reality are expressed in two different *conceptual* systems—the psychological and the physical. The gestalt is the *tertium comparationis* which permits one to equate bodily with mental events since the same configuration is found in both.

upon them from without. Actually, there are no disconnected pre-existing items: the elements are always related. The fundamental conception which promises to displace the "psychic atom" is the "potential," which implicitly has no existence outside of a field of stresses and strains. Unity is no longer to be derived from discord but is present from the very first. If this be granted, the soul or thought (entities which have previously been supposed to create this unity) become superfluous as separate explanatory concepts.

Since Gestalt has taught psychology to speak the language of twentieth-century physics, it is an asset to know the helpful features of that idiom. The basic term is the complex organic whole. *All measurable and observable phenomena in nature are differentiations of a pre-existing organic system, whether that be a gravitational field or a human being.* From this fact, Heisenberg, the brilliant young Leipzig theorist, has drawn his controversial but appealing "principle of uncertainty," which maintains that accuracy of prediction is proportional to the knowledge of the totality within which an event is occurring. The more isolated the part the less certain the prophecy of its behavior. For this reason, the orthodox assumption that psychological phenomena must ultimately be reduced to physiological terms and these in turn to physico-chemical properties is grossly misleading, for such "parts" can never explain the whole. All things and events are subject to the primary fact of relativity and interdependence. Actually, the universal laws of nature are no more peculiarly physical than they are psychological. Man and the cosmos are governed by the *same* rules and not just the same *kind* of rules. The laws of perception *are* the laws of learning and emotion. These are the laws of energy and dynamics, neutral concepts which all the sciences or any human enterprise may share. These general principles—termed by Wheeler his eight organismic laws—are as readily applicable to problems of conscious behavior as to conventional physical and biological affairs, and are defined as follows:

1. *The Law of Field Properties:* Any item of reality is in its own right an integrated whole that is more than the sum of

its parts. Note that this principle is not just a psychological curio, but is claimed to be a universal truth. The earth has a density-gradient from its surface to its center which no separate portion possesses. Water has properties which are not characteristic of either hydrogen or oxygen. A step on a stairway is merely a board in the lumber pile. Metabolic fields of force or physiological gradients are likewise attributes of the entire animal body and not of its cells and organs as such. *Meaning* is a field property of any perceptual experience; a "fractional" meaning is a fiction.

2. *The Law of Derived Properties:* Parts derive their properties from the whole. A stone, e.g., has weight and yet that weight has no independent existence. The weight is merely a relation between the body and the gravitational system which contains it. As Lashley and other students have shown, the function of a certain cerebral region hinges upon what is occurring throughout the entire neural system.

3. *The Law of Determined Action:* The whole conditions the activities of its parts. This principle states the Gestalt position on causation or determination, which, as a logical concept holds only between a whole and its parts, and never from part to part. Exact prediction of an event is possible only when the larger framework within which it occurs is known. This is why the behavior of electrons has recently been explained by subatomic researches in terms of statistical probabilities because the structure within which the members would conduct themselves "lawfully" has been destroyed. Early transplantation of tissue from the head end to the tail results in the growth of a tail and not a head because the developmental future of each cell is conditioned by the total organism. The phenomena of polarization and neurobiotaxis illustrate the same point.[12]

4. *The Law of Individuation:* Parts emerge from wholes through a process of differentiation or individuation, as every user of a tachistoscope knows. This is the configurationist key to the evolution of species and the development of the person.

[12] Perhaps this is the way in which the somewhat figurative expression, "the end determines the means" becomes neurologically understandable. The end is the position of equilibrium finally attained; the means are the events which will take place until equilibrium is attained.

Out of a physiological field or ground there arise segregated patterns or figures—an idea strangely reminiscent of Spencer's famous definition of evolution and Lloyd Morgan's emergent philosophy, and an interesting support to the notion of correspondence between organic and inorganic evolution.[13]

5. *The Law of Field Genesis:* Wholes evolve as wholes. This is largely a corollary to the preceding law. The teeth, heart, and brain do not change their size or texture in isolation, but the embracing organism undergoes an expansion or new structuration. Sheer physiological growth is "a function of the organism-as-a-whole; it is the progressive internal differentiation of a single protoplasmic individual."

6. *The Law of Least Action:* Energy interchange takes place through the shortest spatio-temporal interval. Air currents move from regions of high atmospheric pressure to those of low; electricity "flows" from high to low potential; nerve fibers grow maximally at those points where metabolic rates are highest; and art is dominated by symmetry and harmony. This law was first publicly enunciated by Maupertuis in the eighteenth century and later put into serviceable form by Euler.

7. *The Law of Maximum Work:* Where the balance of a system is disturbed, all the available energy is employed in restoring equilibrium. The all-or-none character of nerve fibre conduction and the "self-preservation" efforts of the organism are illustrations of this principle.

8. *The Law of Configuration:* One isolated, discrete event can never interact with another because things of this character are non-existent. The present determines the future in no more real sense than the future governs the past! *Temporal acts are unified in the same way that spatial patterns are*—a conclusion implicit in the phi-phenomenon.

These eight fundamental organismic laws Wheeler applies to all the chapter headings of the standard textbooks. They are assumed to be adequate to account for all psychological phe-

[13] In evolution, the accidental emergence of forms, in the Darwinian sense of selection, is supplanted by the creative dynamic pressure of an organic system. Köhler has expressed this idea in "Gestaltprobleme und Anfänge einer Gestalttheorie," *Jahresbericht ü. d. ges. Physiol. u. exp. Pharmakologie,* 1925, *3,* 512–539.

nomena and consequently other explanatory principles such as attention, association, experience, and memory-traces are rejected as tautologous. To explain learning in terms of exercise, or by the use or disuse of neural arcs, is gratuitous. "Drop a ball a million times and it will not fall more easily the last time than the first. . . . An electric current will travel just as well through a switch the first time as it will the thousandth. Repetition makes no difference to the switch nor to the current." No one benefits by experience unless he has enough insight into that experience to profit from it. A child or an imbecile could read, or better, gaze at, the text of Newton's "Principia" for a year at a time and not gain any more than a few simple percepts. The experience hypothesis is unable to explain how the *first* learning process in the life of the learner occurs when prior to it there has been no experience. If the initial act cannot be explained on this basis, neither can the tenth nor the thousandth. Instead, learning is a growth in insight derived from the properly-timed environmental stimulation of a maturing organism. If the inner maturation has not gone far enough to enable the learner to master the situation, learning, of course, fails to take place. That is why concentrated learning is so inferior to distributed learning—the "rest" or recess periods are as important as the practice sessions!

Wheeler's theory of recall is interesting because of its resemblance to Hollingworth's account of learning as a "reduction of cues," the fundamental difference lying in the former's appeal to "closure" or *Prägnanz* and the latter's associationist version of redintegration. The configurationist explanation is as follows: The same organization of potentials in the nervous system and the same stimulus pattern that were present in the original observation function in recall, "except that (1) maturation has taken place meanwhile, and (2) there is only a partial duplication of the original stimulus pattern. Suppose you climb a mountain on your vacation. When you return you are able to recall the scenery. You are doing nothing more than to see the scenery with part of the stimulus pattern missing, the scenery itself. When you were actually looking at the mountain you were responding to many more stimuli than the mountain itself. There were your companions, your camping equipment and your conversations with each other, even with yourself. You return home, bringing these stimuli with you, including language. Circumstances, then, construct a stimulus pattern partly duplicating the original; the response partly duplicates the original, and we designate it a recall. If the repeated stimulus-pattern were as complete as the original, the perception would have been equally as complete. You would then be re-observing the mountain, for, by assumption, it would be in front of you again. Errors in the recall are to be explained in terms of maturation on the one hand, and removal from stimulus-patterns on the other" (*Laws of Human Nature,* pp. 168-169).

One feature of Wheeler's personal version of the implications of configurationism, which should appeal to those who believe that the coming century belongs to the social sciences, is his insistence that an individual (or any "scientific object") cannot be defined adequately in terms of himself alone. The logical starting-point for all psychology should be social psychology, for it is out of the social matrix that individual behavior emerges. The most complex situation is in a certain sense also the most primitive. The human being must first be thought of as a "member-of-a-group," and only later under narrowly restricted conditions can he be studied as an isolated biological individual. The group has been shown by anthropologists to be the true evolutionary unit, and no theory of personality or the self (or of any other mental feature) can be correct which disregards the formative influence of powerful social forces. "A person could no more acquire a personality in the absence of the social group than a man could become a soldier without being in an army." Human nature itself is a pattern or group phenomenon, as most of the early sociologists insisted it was.

Concerning the problem of intelligent behavior, many non-Gestalt critics have found themselves questioning the dogma of the "constancy of the I. Q." Without denying the figures which seem to support this view, Wheeler maintains that this assertion violates a basic scientific principle; viz., that any event is a product of its conditions. The score which a person makes on a mental test is partly, but not exclusively, conditioned by his inheritance; social status, physical constitution, and emotional blocking are also significant factors. When the intelligence quotient appears to remain relatively stable, it is because the environment and these other influences have undergone no marked change. Capacities being potentials of some kind are as dependent upon the environment as upon the race. Within limits, then, the intelligence of the individual is under the control of the social group—certainly a more hopeful view to an enlightened educational system than the notion that it is exclusively a result of native endowment. The efforts of nature-nurture theorists to measure the percentage contributions from each source are absurd because there would be no achievement-product at all without the constant use and simultaneous coöperation of both.

CHAPTER 5

VARIETIES OF GESTALT THEORY

In the very nature of things, it is impossible for a universal concept such as the relation of the whole to its parts to receive the same systematic interpretation at the hands of different thinkers, despite their common acceptance of certain major postulates. The psychological circles of German-speaking countries to-day are virtually unanimous in affirming the merits of the "totality" mode of thinking, but they differ violently in the consequences to be drawn therefrom. The leading Gestalt school (by which we may mean nothing more than the "best-known") is the Wertheimer-Köhler-Koffka group, for brevity's sake often identified as the Berlin school from the name of the laboratory which has given rise to most of its positive contributions. It is curious, too, that this group has preserved the greatest degree of internal unity and presented a closed front to the "opposition," in spite of a rather large number of adherents. Since it is almost proverbial that there are as many psychologies as psychologists, some observers have commented on the distinction to be made between the Gestalt theory and the Gestalt movement—the former being an intellectual construction which most scientists can envision with dispassionate detachment, while the latter is a band of aggressive personalities engaged in propagating the faith. Although this book will be mainly devoted to the narrower version of configurationism, the demands of perspective make it necessary to examine a few alternative interpretations.

The picture is complicated by the presence of a number of contenders, each asserting the honor of priority in announcing the main outlines of the new theory. To state the matter vulgarly, many individuals appear to be dominated by the "I-said-it-myself-first" complex, which may lend animation to the ensuing polemics, but certainly adds confusion to both the befuddled reader and the distressed historian who must weigh the rival claims. Just as Binet complained with some justice that the famous Würzburg school of imageless thought could with equal fairness have been termed the Paris school (one might also add a New York school in the person of Woodworth), so configurationism might—but for the accidents of emphasis and opportunity—have been associated with the schools of Leipzig, Vienna,[1] Marburg,[2] Rostock,[3] and Hamburg,[4] to mention only a few of the more prominent varieties. Each offers an attractive and stimulating variation from the main theme, and it would be profitable to inspect all of them with some care, but to avoid complicating the story unduly, only the point of view of a single competing group will be presented.

Krueger and the Leipzig School

The major novelty in Felix Krueger's position[5] (since 1917 Wundt's successor at Leipzig) is the strategic rôle in mental life allotted to feeling; but as with every other system-builder, one must look to the entire framework of ideas before this division can be appreciated. The heavy philosophical and valuational undertone in Krueger's schema has repelled many of the "tough-minded," yet basically it involves little more than an insistence that experimental and non-experimental methods must operate conjointly to advance the realm of psychological discovery, a view championed by many authorities, particularly in the fields of applied and abnormal psychology. He holds that the associ-

---

[1] Bühler, Brunswik, and the child psychologists centering about them. The lack of rigorous experimental productions from the Vienna laboratory in the last decade is probably accountable for its failure to shine more prominently in the debate.

[2] Jaensch and his numerous disciples. His voluminous writings defy digestion, but the most representative of the "wholeness" approach is "Ueber den Aufbau der Wahrnehmungswelt und ihre Struktur in Jugendalter," *Zsch. f. Psychol.*, 1923, *93*. Spranger has acknowledged its influence over him. Pre-occupation with his extraordinary eidetic discoveries has probably led to a neglect of his configurationist views by others.

[3] Katz, of course. A provincial university, outside the main current of international traffic in scholars, explains this particular case of obscurity.

[4] William Stern, Werner, Muchow, and others. The influence of Stern's peculiar version of "personalism" has been limited to his own immediate circle. Werner's clever experimental program is an extremely promising development. A little late in arriving, his ideas have not been publicized by foreign lecture-tours to the extent that the Berlin groups have. The latter have been conspicuously successful in retailing their wares, and their success has led to much domestic criticism, the motivation of which is not always certain.

[5] "Ueber psychische Ganzheit," *Neue Psychologische Studien*, Vol. 1, Beck, München, 1926, 1–121.

ationist systems of Ziehen and G. E. Müller are in process of dissolution, despite the efforts to preserve the mechanistic play of ideas or "residues" by means of attention in its many guises, apperception, determining tendencies, etc. Instead, there has developed a growing recognition of the social and genetic conditioning of all mental events. Like Wertheimer, he deprecates the extreme analytic approach to scientific problems, but preserves a better balance and saves himself from misunderstanding by citing with approval one of Goethe's utterances, "Analysis and synthesis are both as necessary to the thinking spirit as inspiration and expiration to the organism."

To a certain extent, Krueger disclaims any marked originality for his view and points in a sober nationalistic vein to its kinship with the ideas shared by a long line of distinguished German teachers. The dynamics of Leibniz (his monads correspond to the "segregated wholes" of contemporary theory) and his conflict with the dogmatic rationalism of the Cartesians and the sensualism of the British empiricists began a tradition of broad inclusiveness which was steadily developed by Herder, Tetens, Kant (in his emphasis on the creative activity of the subject in perception) and Hegel (with his familiar triad and stress upon "becoming"). The fullest sweep of the totality problem is seen in the efforts of such metaphysicians to systematize into comprehensive unities all cosmic processes and existences, the most plausible means of effecting this integration being the evolutionary principle.

It must not be supposed that this standpoint is vague or irrelevant to psychological research, although these terms probably describe the average American psychologist's reaction to such a position. One must regret that to the strict experimentalist, philosophy has come to mean futile verbal disputation of uninteresting private opinions tinged with irresponsible emotions, when, as a matter of fact, his own attitude reflects but one among many possible intellectual adjustments. For the representative German scientist, however, the *Weltanschauung* prescribes his methodology and serves as a heuristic device in all investigations. To be sure, it has the same effect in the work of others, the only difference being that they usually seem to be unaware of it!

It appears that Krueger was led to his present theories on the basis of his older acoustic studies. These observations clearly indicated that consonance and dissonance of all types were *Komplexqualitäten;* i.e., they did not occur with single tones but were inevitably aspects of a chord. Every one can appreciate the simple truth of this contention, itself implicit in Ehrenfels' earlier illustrations.

Krueger acknowledges his indebtedness to his teacher, Hans Cornelius, for the suggestion that the feelings are Gestalt qualities in Ehrenfels' sense, although the latter rejected this particular identification. On the basis of the best introspection available, Krueger holds that the feelings are functionally to be reckoned among the complex-qualities as the specific total coloration of every experienced whole and as the mode in which the unitariness of psychic processes is directly and originally made conscious (Krueger, p. 26).

Physiological and biological evidence is freely appealed to. The effect of a local stimulus is not a local response; on the contrary, an irradiation throughout the total organism ensues. Neurologists appreciate the general influence of localized traumata and surgeons realize that their work not only affects the regional organ, but the whole personality. It is a commonplace among orthopedists that their patients are not only handicapped directly by their deformity or distortion of movement, but that a general internal deviation from the norm usually appears. Without going very far into either physiology or pathology, one can discern the operation of holistic principles in organic as well as psychic occasions. Structures and total performances appear in both regions of living activity, but *an experienced whole can occur only within the mental world;* it can be known more completely than all other whole forms because we understand it from within.

Although it is possible to study the peripheral data of psychology with little or no sociogenetic postulates, the atomism which this involves collapses utterly when brought to bear upon the cultural behaviour of man, especially as studied by the normative disciplines. Dilthey was one of the first to see this clearly and he made a fine pioneering endeavor to overcome this limitation by a liberal and flexible use of his favorite expression "structure" in connection with the more complex aspects of conduct. However, it remained for Driesch to be the first to erect a thorough-going system of philosophy upon the idea of the whole. His classic demonstration of organic regulation in the maintenance of form in the embryo is a beautiful experiment, but the assertion that every genuine totality in the world is "produced" by spiritual factors is a pure metaphysical hunch. Krueger pleads for a sharper distinction between real and ideal wholes to save us from such errors. Any part of a present experience approaches the character of a feeling the more of the perception it comprises and the less it is "membered" or distinguished from the rest. Feelings are qualities of total immediately-given wholes—each feeling being a diffused whole, preserved at every level of growth, and either entirely or largely without members. The course of both mental and cultural development moves steadily from a primitive totality to a less primitive, that is, more "structural" whole. Krueger finds the Berlin school of configurationism grossly neglectful of the importance of the feelings, a charge which had considerable justification before 1925, but which the researches of Lewin and his pupils since then amply refute. Köhler's brain-theory and his interpretation of structure-functions are anathema to Krueger who sees in them a revival of a meaningless physicalism. His anti-rationalist bias is clearly presented in his treatment of Spearman's account of spatial shapes, the main weakness of which he finds to be an overintellectualistic brand of "relationism." The "g" factor problem, however, upon which the two men labored in conjunction some years ago[6] is held to support his conception of a stable and enduring total structure underlying personality.

One sees, then, how insistent Krueger is that *the unitary character of all experience is earliest, most strongly and most*

[6] Krueger and Spearman, *Zsch. f. Psychol.*, 1906.

richly expressed in the domain of feeling. However, feelings, with which the emotions are grouped, are not usually configurations, although timbre and rhythm are such, and Krueger goes to great length in distinguishing between *Gestalt* (pattern) and *Ganzheit* (totality), the former being a species of the latter genus and marked by a preservation of the "membership traits" of the component parts. Gestalt phenomena are present only where experienced wholes occur; but this proposition cannot be reversed.[7]

The climax of Krueger's structuralism (the meaning of which is worlds removed from the connotation which Titchener gave to the term in America) is found in his interpretation of values. These most influential forms of psychic structuration rest upon instinctive bases and are the dominant forces in mental life. They constitute the core of personality and character and are the determinants of all typical and essential individual differences. Even the remote but fundamental field of epistemology profits from the suggestion that meaning or significance bears the traits of specific wholes, particularly the features of "belonging together."

In this system it is clear that the notion of feeling becomes much broader than the simple opposition of pleasantness-unpleasantness.[8] On the other hand, many familiar doctrines are retained even though submitted to a new interpretation; e.g., "an emotional complex loses in the intensity and plasticity of its emotional character to the degree that it becomes analyzed, so that its parts become relatively separated, or that the partial moments in it come out clearly as such" (Krueger, p. 62). This, of course, is simply a rephrasing of the elementary truth that an emotional state tends to be dissipated by attention to it as such. One sees, too, how some of the difficulties resulting from the James-Lange theory can be understood in a new light. The now

[7] "Der Strukturbegriff in der Psychologie," *Bericht über den VIII, Kong. f. exp. Psychologie*, Leipzig, 1923, 31–56. Jena, Fischer, 1924.

[8] This aspect of his doctrine has been most conveniently presented by Krueger in his contribution to the Wittenberg Symposium on the *Feelings and Emotions*, Clark University Press, 1928, 58–88.

A similar position had been outlined earlier by Claparède in an article published in the *Archives de Psychologie*, 1908, *7*, p. 195. The emotion is nothing other than the consciousness of a "form" of multiple organic impressions, i.e., the emotion is the consciousness of a global attitude of the organism. This confused, primitive, and general perception of the whole. Claparède called "syncretic perception."

generally admitted evidence indicates that the organic and visceral changes accompanying many distinct emotions are surprisingly alike if not identical (cf. for instance, the glandular accompaniments of fear and rage). Apparently the same internal elements have a different function depending upon the nature of the total mental state or even the total objective situation to which they refer or within which they operate.

Since there is a grave danger that even repetition with variation will not convey the precise outlines of Krueger's unfamiliar theory, it may be wise to let him state his position in his own language. "Never are the differentiable parts or sides of real experience as isolated from one another as the parts of physical substance, i.e., its molecules or its atoms. All things which we can differentiate there, by comparison, always grip into one another and around one another in the greatest elaboration. And every time it is, without exception, imbedded within a *total-whole,* by which it is penetrated and more or less completely enclosed. *Feelings are the qualities of experience of this total-whole. . . .* The total-whole of experience always has a specific, immediately observable quality which changes in a particular, continuous way. Such qualities of the total-whole are the different kinds of pleasantness and unpleasantness, excitement, tension, relaxation; and many other manifold tintings, shadings and forms of flight of total experience cannot be limited by number, and, until some future time, cannot be completely classified" (Krueger, pp. 67-69).

Some persons, repelled by the disorder which appears to result from the abandonment of the traditional categories, will wonder if this view does not eliminate the standard opposition between the emotional and the non-emotional. Krueger would willingly admit this, but believes a closer approximation to reality results therefrom. "It is certainly a fact," he says, "that feelings (e.g., of excitement without an object, of excitement resembling fury, of purely moody excitement), always pass over into qualities of more circumscribed and, primarily, of less organized *part*-complexes, e.g., into the consciousness of that about which I become excited, of that for which I hope, of that which I seek or of which I am afraid; and conversely, it is a fact that the one set of events is, moreover, qualitatively related to the other. The conception of the feeling-*like* is necessary to designate those phenomenological similarities and transformations. . . . Everywhere isolated sensations, perceptions, relations, also memories, clear ideas, decided volitions—in brief, all experience-organization—split off only after some time from the diffuse tendencies of emotion, and secondly, they always remain functionally dominated by them" (Krueger, pp. 70-72).

Sander

This genetic primacy of feeling over perception and thought is buttressed by numerous investigations from the Leipzig laboratory, especially those coming from the hands of Volkelt and Sander (now at Giessen). The former has shown that the

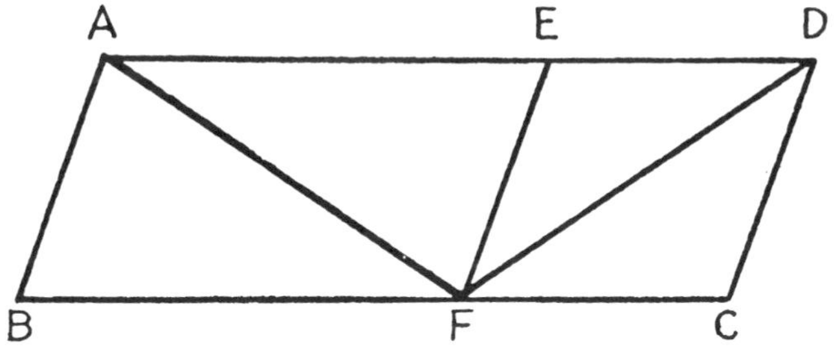

Figure 7. Sander's Parallelogram Illusion

Which of the two diagonals is the longer? Verify your impression by measurement.

younger the child the more overwhelming are the evidences of perception according to larger wholes, indicating that the analytical trend of adult observation is a derived tendency. Sander[9] has also constructed his new parallelogram illusion (see Figure 7) on this general principle and finds that the coefficient of illusory effect drops with increasing age.

Here two objectively equal lengths, *AF* and *FD,* are seen as unequal because they belong to two parallelograms of different size. The "apparent" size of an important member is domi-

[9] F. Sander, "Experimentelle Ergebnisse der Gestaltpsychologie," *X, Kong. f. exp. Psychol.,* Jena, 1928.

nated by the "actual" size of the whole and consequently shifts in that direction. If, however, the equilateral triangle *AFD* is "lifted" out of the complex, the two sides tend toward equivalence.[10]

Since the Leipzig school is decidedly more historically minded than the Berlin group, one need not be surprised to see them searching the records of older studies for support of their brand of configurationism. The have examined the handiwork of the naïve painters of the German Renaissance and find the law of *Prägnanz* operative in the unusual regularity of the sketched thunderbolt among one of these "primitives," thus . While the exaggeration here is extreme, we know that the customary representation of lightning shows nothing of the highly irregular gnarled branching which the photograph reveals. This same drift toward symmetry appears in innumerable cases. Incited by Goethe's interest in entoptic pictures (easily evoked by rubbing one's eyes in the dark), Purkinje sketched some of them and found them unusually regular; in fact, they approached snowflake patterns in appearance. One is tempted to apply Köhler's concept of physical configurations to the actual falling snow with its hexagonal flakes, but that would lead us too far afield from our own alluring quest.

Less spectacular but still impressive laboratory studies confirm this natural struggle for proportion. Kirschmann observed that when polygons were arranged to stimulate the peripheral areas of the retina, they were seen as circles, and it is well known that very brief tachistoscopic exposures of complicated plane figures result in the reproduction of the latter as circular objects. Figures apprehended in twilight or at a great distance exhibit a

[10] Note: The isolation is facilitated by mentally erecting a perpendicular at *F*.

In general, a change in one part or aspect of a configuration can be made only at the cost of or change in another. Thus two *objects of unlike size but equal weights are judged to differ* in weight, the smaller being the heavier (size-weight illusion). Here what the larger gains in size it loses in weight; what the smaller loses in size it gains in weight, phenomenally. Shortening the temporal interval between stimuli (visual, auditory or tactual) results in shortening the experienced spatial interval; brighter objects are judged to weigh less than darker (DeCamp); objects that leave the ground at a higher speed are judged to be lighter than those leaving at a slower rate. As Helson says, "In all these cases the experienced change (usually called the 'illusion') carries all the ear-marks of reality and can be explained only by the assumption of a unitary underlying process in which the various aspects exert real and mutual effects upon each other." See his useful summarization entitled, "The Fundamental Propositions of Gestalt Psychology," *Psy. Rev.*, 1933, *40*, 13–32.

kindred uniformity; e.g., in measuring visual acuity, one can take the letter K (which lacks all rounded features) and if held well beyond the point of distinct vision, it will be traced as a small ball or dot, provided, of course, the subject is kept in ignorance of the real nature of the stimulus.

The Hunger Studies of David Katz

In a few well-chosen studies on the appetite of barnyard fowl, Katz neatly demonstrated the dependence of an animal's "instinctive" and motor behavior upon systematic or configurational influences. He was able to show that the functioning of the hunger drive does not rest on a purely physiological basis, but that it is surprisingly independent of the physical state of the organism and depends to a high degree on outer circumstances.

If one places a hen before a pile of 100 grams of wheat, she will eat on the average 50 grams, and leave 50 grams. The hen in the same hunger condition eats from 33 to 54 grams more when confronted with a 200 gram pile. In general, the amount of food consumed increased with the amount of food presented, a fact applicable to all hens and all grains.

In another arrangement, a hen was allowed to remain before a food pile until fully satisfied. The remaining food was then removed with a brush and immediately replaced. When this was done the hen invariably began to eat again. When it ceased to eat the experiment was repeated once again with a similar result. There were hens with which the operation could be successfully repeated eight or more times. Many hens ate as much as 67% more. Katz triumphantly remarks that we have here a method in applied animal psychology which might profitably be used for fattening hens of other poultry!

The size of the single grains appear to exert an astonishing influence upon the quantity of food eaten. In a similar state of hunger, a hen ate two or three times as much in weight from a pile of whole rice as from one of cracked rice. The grains of the latter were only one-quarter as large as the former. Katz explains the difference in terms of the painful vibrations in the hen's beak caused by excessive pecking, a view supported by the fact that hens peck only about 40 grams of food from a hard wooden surface but twice as much from soft felt. When confronted with a choice, the animals always preferred the soft surface.

Some clever observations on the social behavior of hens are relevant to this discussion. A hen No. 1 is allowed to peck until motionless. Then a second hungry hen is brought in before the same heap. Instantly she begins to peck. Then the behavior of the first hen differs according to whether she has previously tyrannized over the other or has been subdued by her. In the former case, she tries to hinder the second hen from pecking the food, and if she fails immediately begins to peck again herself; in the latter case, she immediately resumes eating. Under the social influence of the second hen, hen No. 1 eats 60% or more food than when alone. This amount is still further increased if three hens instead of one are brought in, which shows that up to a certain limit the hunger behavior of the first hen is influenced by the number of hens brought in.

The reverse process was also followed. Three hens are put before a large hill of grain and satiated. If now a fourth hen is brought into this circle, she immediately begins to peck, and the other three remain almost motionless; they peck very little. They form, to a certain extent, a unity of behavior, no longer susceptible to the influence of the isolated fourth hen, who in turn is not noticeably affected by the "trinity."

The human analogues to this sort of behavior are numerous and convincing. Most people realize that they eat more when the table is loaded with an abundance of food, and every one recognizes the potency of social influence. The bachelor who goes to the hotel to dine because he wants to eat with other people gives evidence of the fact that in isolation his appetite is insufficient. Perhaps the added weight which most married couples exhibit is not solely attributable to maturity or the effect of wedded contentment—social facilitation may be the real cause. Katz suggests that the best way of improving a child's appetite is to let him eat with the other children. He claims that in earlier times lack of appetite was seldom heard of and that it has resulted largely from the reduction in the number of children in the family.[11]

Different Attempts to Solve the Part-Whole Problem

Both the strength and weakness of the Leipzig school have resided in its pronounced eclectic leanings which have kept it in close touch with other research centers without involving the abandonment of its characteristic viewpoint. One of its younger members, Burkhardt,[12] has examined the major German efforts to deal with the problem of totality, which for purposes of summary, may well be reproduced here. He finds that all represent attempts to solve the two following basic questions:

1. How does psychic "wholeness" arise?
2. In what does this totality exist?

Three different answers have been given to the first problem:

1. The production theory
2. The physical theory
3. The psychical theory

The first view is historically the oldest and was shared by such diverse individuals as the founders of the Graz school, Schumann and G. E. Müller. Meinong and most of his followers held that the intellect or "intelligence" was responsible for the integrations observed in experience; Schumann simply adopted the general view that the gap between summation and "wholeness" was bridged by some synthetic function, and Witasek and Müller boldly identified this with attention. However, Müller's admission[13] of the existence of "involuntary collective apprehension" is tantamount to a confession of the failure of this principle to operate satisfactorily as a universal explanation.

[11] The material for this section is largely derived from "The Vibratory Sense and other Lectures" in the University of Maine Studies, Second Series, No. 14, 1930, Orono.

Yoshioka later discovered that both wild grey rats and tame albino rats, when presented with an equal number of "large" and "small" sunflower seeds, tended in any given time to eat a greater number of large seeds than of small ones. See his "Size Preference of Wild and Albino Rats," *J. Genet. Psychol.*, 1930, *37*, 159–162, 427–430.

[12] *Zum Problem der Ganzheit,* "Ein Beitrag zur Theorie des Psychischen" (dissertation), Leipzig, 1925. The issue at stake may well vie in significance with the historic problem of the three bodies.

[13] *Komplextheorie und Gestalttheorie,* Göttingen, 1923, p. 101.

The second type of explanation is best represented by Wertheimer's pupils, Köhler, and the Berlin school in general. It is a form of psychophysical monism with its weakest point in the alleged physical parallelism. An appreciation of the qualitative difference between causally effective units like *extended* physico-chemical wholes and the *intensive* psychic totals makes difficult the acceptance of this view. Driesch,[14] the great vitalist, considers Köhler an opponent because of the latter's rejection of the autonomy of the living, i.e., the Berlin group is committed to pan-vitalism and not vitalism as a distinctly limited explanatory concept. Köhler's physical gestalten prove only the *unity* of his systems and not their *wholeness;* how frightened, e.g., we would be if a broken Leyden jar were suddenly to transform itself into two proportionately exact smaller jars! However, no one has ever denied that everything is dynamically joined to everything else in inanimate nature and that unities of effect thus obtain. A Mid-Victorian physicist had already maintained, "If I strike upon the table Sirius trembles." But it is not true as the Berliners allege that a change in a system composed of *n* parts changes its essence so that a total of *n—1* parts is utterly different from it; e.g. (ironically!), a dog still remains a dog even though I cut off some of his parts, such as his hairs.

The third view, represented by Driesch and Krueger, is truly dualistic and a psychology *with* a soul. There is a qualitative peculiarity about mental totalities which is not found elsewhere in nature—a fact which in itself makes of psychology an autonomous research discipline. This original uniqueness of psychic wholes constitutes the starting point for all investigations concerning them.

Turning to the second of the problems with which we began this section, we find that here, too, there have been three correspondingly different answers:

1. The theory of relations
2. The theory of structure-functions
3. The theory of qualities

---

[14] "Physische Gestalten und Organismen," *Annalen der Philos.*, 1925, 5, 1–11; and "Kritisches zur Ganzheitslehre," same journal and volume, pages 281–304.

Ehrenfels, Bühler, and Spearman are all inclined to adopt the first position which would make logical constructs of all complexes and gestalten. The inadequacy of this approach is most conspicuously revealed in feeling and will in which relations as ordinarily understood play almost no part. Köhler's account in terms of structure-function suffers from its objectivistic orientation and cannot satisfactorily explain in naturalistic terms why the same cliff side can be successively apprehended as a chaotic complex, as an animal figure, and as a bit of scenery. The third view is the right one in Burkhardt's opinion, and consists in the realization that wholes are qualitatively *irreducibles;* they are given existents with which we must work.

PART III—EMPIRICAL

CHAPTER 6

PHENOMENA OF VISUAL PERCEPTION

The limitations of the human mind make necessary the classificatory rubrics which segregate the divisions of every science. Despite the obvious logical service which they render, particularly to the novice in the field, there is always the grave and persistent danger of reification which accompanies their use. The topics of heat and light illustrate this plainly in physics, while it is but recently in psychology that we have begun to question the substantive character of memory, will, and other traditional chapter headings.[1] With the breakdown of the standard nineteenth-century forms of pigeon-holing data, it has become notorious that the same item can appear in the most unexpected of places, depending solely upon the whim of the writer. Many have assumed that this question of "labels" is a matter of indifference, but any one with a minimum of pedagogical insight knows this to be false.

This problem of the categories is especially pertinent to the present discussion because configurationism is a bold attempt to sweep away these lines of cleavage within the subject-matter and to substitute a more unified picture by means of such basic concepts as figure-ground, whole-part, pattern, insight, and tension, which are designed to offer a *comprehensive* interpretation of *all* the organism's activities. Conceivably one could center the experimental data around each of these themes, but since they are fundamentally interrelated, it would be difficult to do justice to any one of them without undue overlapping of the others—which, while psychologically inevitable, is logically in-

[1] Cf. on this point, the second chapter of Woodworth's revised *Psychology* (New York, 1934), in which he suggests the use of verbal forms—memorizing, willing, etc.—instead of nouns.

convenient. Although the same objection arises with any alternative treatment, it appears to be less pronounced with the revised functional groupings of recent texts. This method of presentation has been adopted here, not only because it minimizes the air of "queerness" which might otherwise result, but because it permits a readier appraisal of the genuine contributions of Gestalt to the orthodox concerns of experimental psychology.

Sensation and Perception: Fundamental Laws

For the Gestalt psychologist the subtle distinction between a "pure" sensory experience and a percept is dissolved by the recognition that they both involve perceptual processes which differ only in complexity, just as a chemical element and a compound are both "matter." A so-called sensation of brightness, e.g., is always attached to something: we do not see redness disembodied and independent but only a red object. The attempt of the Titchenerians to reduce all mental states to little psychic units, devoid of meaning and merely "existent," is said to involve the grossest sort of "stimulus error" because of its impossibility. For one who wishes to think clearly in this tangled field it is distressing to encounter at the start the vexed problem of meaning, so heavily tarred with the metaphysical brush. To wave the question aside may seem like a gesture of contempt for anything even faintly tinctured with philosophy, a procedure which is too often only a veiled retreat from an uncomfortable problem. Perhaps it is best for psychologists to err on the side of positivism, for while it may lead to wrong views at least it rarely encourages vague ones!

The classic account of configurationism's stand on the matter is undoubtedly Wertheimer's brilliant essay[2] in one of the early volumes of the *Forschung*. With magnificent directness he asks us to consider the following situation:

I look out of my window and see a house, some trees, the sky. On theoretical grounds I could say: There are 327 brightnesses and color-

[2] "Untersuchungen zur Lehre von der Gestalt," *Psychol. Forsch.*, 1923, *4*, 301–350. Some interesting new illustrations appear in his "Zu dem Problem der Unterscheidung von Einzelinhalt und Teil," *Zsch. f. Psychol.*, 1933, *129*, 353–357.

tones. Do I observe 327? No. Sky, house, trees, and the experiencing of the 327 items as such no one can realize. If in this odd reckoning we assume house as 120, trees 90, and sky 117, then I have *this* "togetherness," this "separateness," and not 127 and 100 and 100. Or suppose I hear a melody of 17 tones with an accompaniment of 32 tones. I hear the *melody* and *accompaniment,* not simply 49, or at least certainly not normally and *ad libitum* 20 plus 29. (p. 301.)

Although Wertheimer's cryptic and choppy style is not the kind of writing most in keeping with his exaltation of integrated patterns, it is clear that he is *denying* the reality of haphazard perceptual combinations which psychic atomism makes possible when pushed to its logical extreme. That there must be fixed laws governing the order found in our visual world is illustrated with numerous little drawings. He is trying to answer the following general question: Suppose stimuli *a b c d e* . . . . are conjointly effective; what are the principles responsible for the typical appearance of such a constellation as the grouping or division *a b c / d e* instead of *a b / c d e* (Wertheimer, p. 302)? In the example below (Figure 8) the diagonally-placed dots are *seen* as units, but not the other diagonal passing through *a b c.* Why?

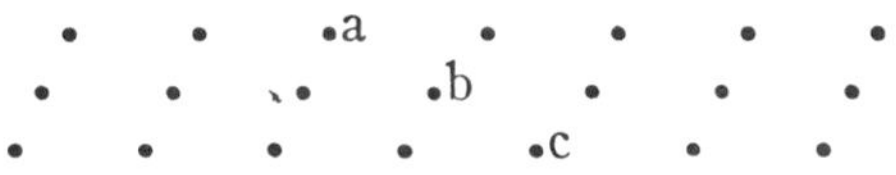

Figure 8. One of Wertheimer's dot patterns

With a little critical examination, even the untrained reader will hit upon likely and partial explanation. The formation of a dot-group with small distances is the one resulting naturally; the point-set involving larger spaces either does not occur at all, or when it does arise, is more difficult, artificial, uncertain, and labile. Tentatively one may say the unification takes place (*ceteris paribus*) according to the *principle of least distance* (= the factor of *nearness*).[3] This rule holds true for more than

[3] Schroff, working with Heidelberg school children, found that the great majority of them obeyed this factor of nearness in indicating what patterns "belonged together." The principle worked most powerfully with younger children, suggesting that with experience other factors beside nearness operate to produce "natural" groupings. See "*Ueber Gestaltauffassung bei Kindern im Alter von 6 bis 14 Jahren,*" *Psychol. Forsch.*, 1928, *11*, 235–266.

just optical and spatial data as may be seen if one taps out the following rhythm:

•	•	•	•	•	•
1	2	3	4	5	6

1-2 and 3-4 are organically united but 2-3 are not.

Consider now a somewhat more elaborate situation as represented below:

o	•	o	•	o	•	o
o	•	o	•	o	•	o
o	•	o	•	o	•	o
o	•	o	•	o	•	o
o	•	o	•	o	•	o

If one is asked to describe what is first discerned, the usual answer is that the verticals are readily seen but the horizontals are not! This leads to a second principle with this wording: If several stimuli be conjointly operative, there is a tendency for a pattern composed of like stimuli to appear (= factor of *likeness*). This maxim, too, is not restricted to the optical field as may be observed from any tonal sequence with similar emphases:

– – – ! ! ! – – – ! ! ! etc.

These two simple principles can be made the subject of further study when they function in the same or opposed directions. Which, for example, is the stronger when counteracting—nearness or similarity? But there are other supplementary factors operative in many special situations with a less static character. Suppose in the following series *c d e i k l* are simultaneously thrust upward above the original line of writing: this *common* movement evokes a new gestalt, for instead of seeing *a b c / d e f* . . . one observes *a b / c d e / f g h / i k l*.

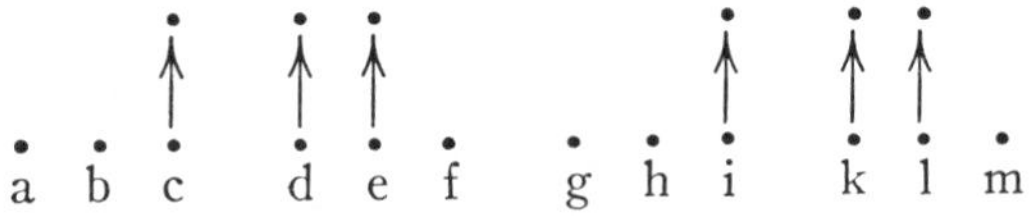

Wertheimer calls this third influence the law of "*common fate*," or "joint destiny," which can also function counter to the factor of nearness as in this case (Wertheimer, p. 316).

A fourth factor is that of *objective* set [4] (or *Einstellung*) which explains why a stimulus constellation or series C appears differently organized if series A and B have preceded it than if G, F, E came before. It is the familiar agency of anticipation or expectancy which helps determine the structure of our percepts.

Another interesting principle is exemplified in Figure 9. In the first drawing we spontaneously see "a vertical standing upon a horizontal line" or A C / B, despite the fact that geometrically all points in C are nearer to B than to A. In the second sketch one sees just a long straight line with diagonal "hooks." The third figure is seen as A C / B, and in the last

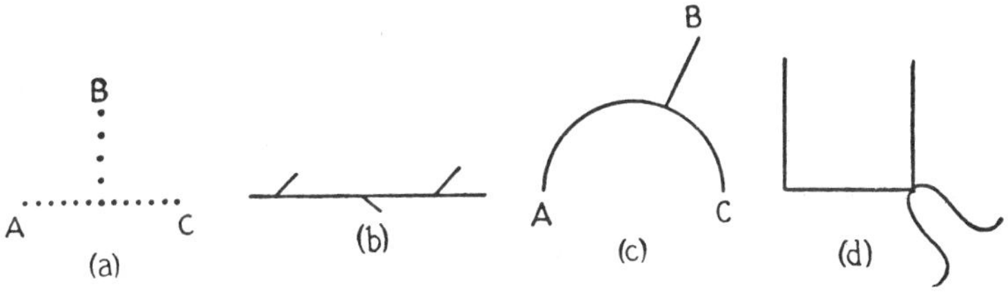

Figure 9. Illustrations of Wertheimer's Principles
Certain lines are more readily seen as prolongations of some parts than of others.

it is obvious what parts are to be considered as continuations of others. Continuous lines or dot-constellations are interchangeable and produce identical effects. Certain items which belong together are seen as a whole; those which do not, are differently segregated. Lines which go all the way through or groups in *one* direction are preferred to others. Wertheimer's idiomatic German is all but untranslatable at this point; he speaks of "immanent necessities" and "intrinsic togetherness" —or, more generally, the *principle of the "good gestalt"* [5] (Wertheimer, p. 324).

Still another factor is operative in this situation (Figure 10), which Wertheimer calls: "closure" (*Geschlossenheit*) or compactness. It may be formulated thus: Where A, B, C, D, are

[4] Later more commonly known as "gestalt-disposition." This factor is a weak point in the system as Petermann has indicated.

[5] This seems to be considered the most fundamental "law" of all by its adherents. As a theoretical maid-of-all-work, it is called upon as the explanatory factor in an extraordinary variety of circumstances.

present and A B / C D yield two enclosed or completed processes and A C / B D open and unclosed ones, then A B / C D is preferred in the perceptual response (Wertheimer, p. 325).

The factor of *position* is also effective, which one might expect on the general ground that field forces alter with it. Note carefully the left and right arrangement in Figure 11.

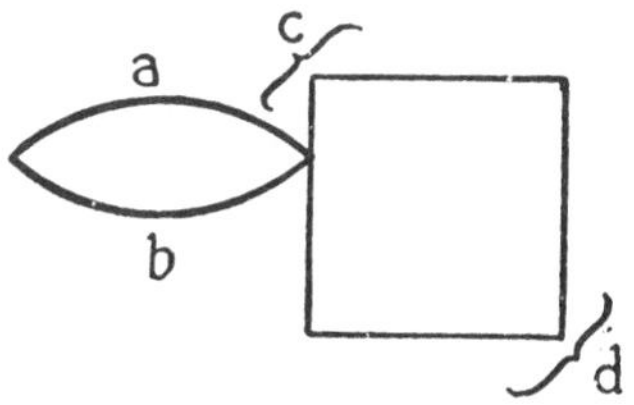

Figure 10. Diagram Exemplifying the Principle of "Closure"
Although contiguous, *ab* forms one clear-cut outline, *bd* another equally distinct.

In the one case, two hexagons with a minimum of common area are easily perceived; but in the other instance, one typically observes a single long hexagon with a little lozenge in the center, despite the fact that this little rectangle is formed by a slight overlapping of the bases of the two smaller constituent hexa-

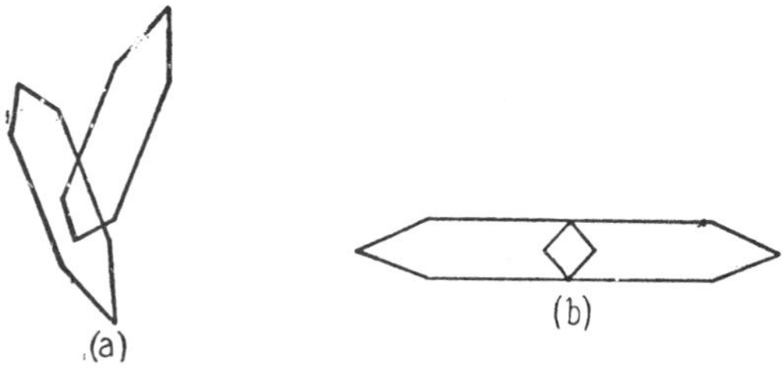

Figure 11. Sketch Indicating the Changes Effected by Different Positions of the Component Parts of Patterns

gons. The total field in the "set-up" on the right is more unitary and homogeneous than its partner. Position, then, seems to be capable of destroying as well as producing configurations.

The principle of *experience or habit,* which many behaviorists would insist is the factor underlying all the preceding laws, is acknowledged to be influential, but to play a strictly subordinate rôle. For instance, it is previous custom which prompts us to respond to 314 cm. as *a b c / d e* and not as 31/4 cm. or 314 c/m. An even happier illustration is found in this datum (Figure 12) which a Hellenist would see as a dual pattern (cursive sigma and gamma) while a Latinist would observe a unitary organization (an embellished V).

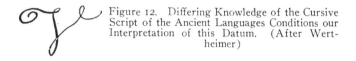

Figure 12. Differing Knowledge of the Cursive Script of the Ancient Languages Conditions our Interpretation of this Datum. (After Wertheimer)

While thus admitting the presence of earlier repetitions or custom as a partial explanation of certain common reactions or individual differences, Wertheimer explicitly denies that *all* of the above principles are matters of prior "experience." To account for the preference for right angles and circles in these situations, some would say that is simply due to the omnipresence of these forms in the visual world as in house, room, and furniture dimensions. However, even assuming that right angles occur more often in nature than others—which is very unlikely as a casual inspection of the twigs of any tree will show —*subjectively,* we see right angles only in a frontal-parallel

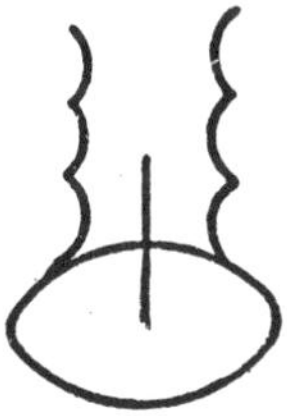

Figure 13. How Internal Organization Outweighs Effects Traceable to Past Experience

No one normally sees the familiar 3 or 4, or the E and S contained within the pattern.

position of the eyes. Similarly, the circles of our environment are overwhelmingly distorted ellipses when projected upon the retina. The untenability of the "empirical" theory is almost dramatically exhibited in the case of a novel figure (Figure 13) where field forces compel one to see something odd and not the familiar 3 + 4 + E + S, all of which are parts of the constellation.

Although the major part of this work was done between 1911 and 1914 and hence could not have been directly influenced by Rubin's significant monograph, nevertheless, it is plain that the figure-ground concept is basic in Wertheimer's analyses. There is not a single instance cited in the foregoing paragraphs which does not support the view that *the nature of the perceived figure is dependent upon the character of the surrounding field,* which may, and as a matter of fact usually does, comprise not only a simple "ground" but also other "figures." The direction of influence, however, does not only converge from the field upon the figure, but may diverge from that pattern and also affect the quality of the ground, thus establishing a condition of equilibrium characterized by reciprocity.

The burden of Wertheimer's study is that we do not react in uniform or constant ways to specific stimuli as though they were always insulated, but that the nature of the setting in which they are found determines the mode of organismic response. In psychology, the right formula is, *Constellation of stimuli* $\longrightarrow$ *Organization* $\longrightarrow$ *Reaction to results of organization,* rather than the usual S $\longrightarrow$ R type. The organism is not barren functionally, it is not a box containing conductors each with a separate function; it responds to a situation, first, by dynamical events peculiar to it as a system and, then, by behavior which depends upon the results of that dynamical organization and order. This is the cardinal principle of all Gestalt psychology: the *whole* is something other than the sum of its parts—it is genetically and functionally prior to them.[6] Such is the *Leitmotiv* which runs through the impressive mass of experimental literature reported in the *Psychologische Forschung* and liberally scattered through other periodicals. Since a general theory becomes convincing to the extent that it offers satisfactory interpretations and predictions in diverse fields, it will be desirable to follow its application in the various situations to be described below.

Methodology is often pushed into the foreground with the advent of new theoretical positions as psychologists have re-

[6] Most persons can retain a melody, fewer recognize a definite interval, and still fewer the individual tones, as shown by the rarity of absolute pitch.

cently seen in the debates concerning the adequacy of behavioristic technique or the psychoanalysts' "talking cures." Few writers have seriously questioned the legitimacy of the procedure used by the configurationist school, since in the main it conforms to the naturalistic and experimental tradition of modern and scientific positivism. However, since there is some reason for believing that the *way* in which facts are discovered is often as important as the facts themselves, researches which are primarily directed toward specifying the differential effects of various methods upon the data obtained have a significance all their own.

A study by Katona [7] falls into this category. He was concerned with an examination of the consequences of successive and simultaneous comparison of stimuli. In one division of his work, he exposed six nonsense drawings rapidly one after another like a pack of cards, or presented them all at once by withdrawing a screen placed before six adjacent figures. In the critical test series, three of the old pictures and three new were mingled, and the subject indicated which were familiar. To remove the objection that the manner in which the testing was done was influential, a *successive* learning exposure was measured later by the *simultaneous* procedure and *vice versa,* with results from three subjects as indicated in Table I.

TABLE I. INFLUENCE OF THE MANNER IN WHICH VISUAL LEARNING AND RECALL ARE MADE UPON THE FREQUENCY OF ERROR. (AFTER KATONA)

Manner of Impression	Test Method	Average Number of Errors
Successive	Simultaneous	5.33
Simultaneous	Successive	11.13

The inferiority of the simultaneous-successive sequence to its converse is explained in terms of the whole-part contrast, simultaneous comparison being favorable to the formation of

[7] "Experimentelle Untersuchungen über simultane und sukzessive Gesichtswahrnehmungen," *Psychol. Forsch.*, 1926, *7*, 226–256.

a total but unfavorable to isolated units, while the opposite situation holds for the successive impression. As far back as 1846, E. H. Weber had announced that two simultaneous touch sensations cannot be distinguished as well as two successive ones, because of the mutual disturbance they exercise upon each other. Stumpf [8] stated in connection with tonal experiences that "successive sensations constitute a mere sum, but simultaneous ones form a whole." Contiguity in time, the fundamental law of association, would seem to be the non-Gestalt phrase which best accounts for the peculiarities of simultaneous sensitivity. To configurationism, comparison is no longer a new act supervening upon the given sensation. The question how the two sensations are compared no longer exists, because the two sensations themselves do not exist. All that is found is an undivided, articulated whole.

Dependence of Form and Space Qualities upon the Configuration

Some of the more powerful supports of the correctness of the configurationist's thesis are found in the facts of animal, child, and primitive behavior. The reason is simple: if among relatively undeveloped mentalities one finds phenomena which are more in accord with the Gestalt hypothesis than with any alternative explanation, the arguments in its favor are strengthened. Whatever laws may govern human conduct presumably are best studied under less complex conditions than those affecting the "normal adult European white male." The restriction in variability which more primitive circumstances impose makes the investigator much more certain of the generality of his findings.

Consequently, especial interest attaches to a novel study of crows' responses to figural elements made by Mathilde Hertz.[9] She arranged a large number of inverted brown clay flower pots about five centimeters in diameter in various patterns; under

[8] *Tonpsychologie*, 1890, *II*, 64.

[9] Daughter of the distinguished physicist. Her researches appear in "Wahrnehmungspsychologische Untersuchungen an Eichelhäher," *Zsch. f. vergl. Physiol.*, 1928, *7*, 144–194 and 617–656.

one of the pots within sight of the confined bird, a piece of food was placed. Most of the items were, therefore, "negative" and only one "positive." When the bird was released, the combined memory and perceptual difficulties confronting him were similar to those which we experience in trying to keep track of a particular individual in a swarm of sea-gulls. In this ex-

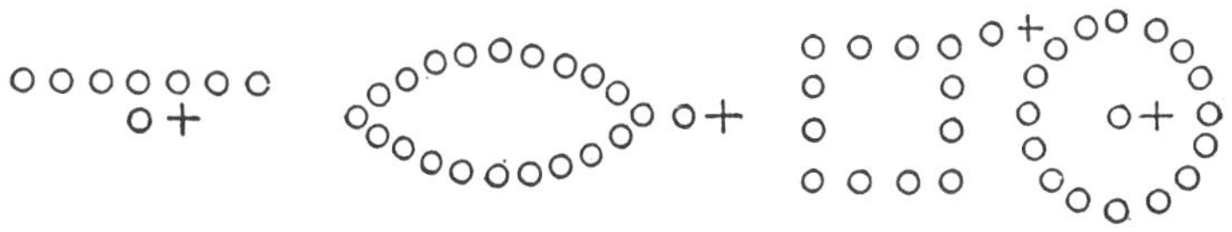

Figure 14. Each Circle Symbolizes a Clay Pot

The plus sign marks the one containing the objective.

periment the crows had no difficulty with pots distinguished as to *form, size,* or *color* from the rest of the complex situation, but made errors when *position* was the sole clue, unless that location happened to be *prägnant* or in some way set off from the confusion stimuli, as in the examples in Figure 14. Any type of cen-

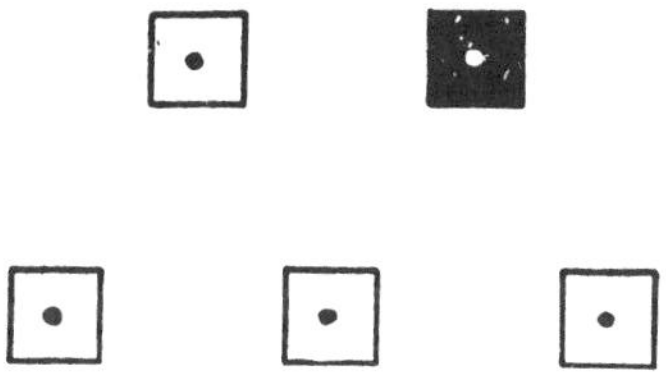

Figure 15. Materials Employed in the Training Series with Crows to Test their Ability to "Transfer" Habits of Brightness Discrimination. (After Hertz)

The birds responded correctly in critical situations when other figures than circles were substituted as "inner fields."

tral cluster with the goal placed peripherally to the main mass succeeds with a minimum of error.

This pronounced form-sense of the crow is even more spectacularly demonstrated in a supplementary account of figure-ground transfer. The birds were trained to react positively to all objects with a light figure on a dark ground, and to disregard the items having a dark figure on a light field as in Figure 15.

So well was the appropriate figure-ground relationship appreciated that the crows had no difficulty in responding successfully according to the comparative brightness difference when crosses, squares, stars, and other "figures" were used in place of the circles shown in the figure.

An impressive rejoinder to the common "empirical" explanation of Gestalt phenomena is provided by Kurt Gottschaldt[10] in an experimental procedure which is all but Euclidean in character. Normally, most psychologists shrug their shoulders when the nativistic-empiristic controversy is mentioned, because it appears so futile and impossible to set up the requisite conditions early enough in the life of the developing organism which would be adequate to test either hypothesis. However, Gottschaldt's highly original attack consisted in submitting to his subjects several hundred times a simple figure for overlearning and then presenting a novel context in which the original was "imbedded" to see if it could be spontaneously identified. For instance, the *a*-figures in Figure 16 were presented a varying number of times and then the corresponding *b*-figures were exposed, the observer being required to describe what he first saw. Only in rare instances did the *a*-figure "spring out" of its *b*-setting. To one who has pinned his faith in the explanation of visual organization by experience, it is startling to encounter Gottschaldt's evidence that when the *a*-figure forms a dependent part of a larger whole, the fact that it has been presented more than 500 times as an independent total does not noticeably increase the chances of its being seen as such in the new setting.

Since it is doubtful if the casual experience of ordinary life ever gives one as many repetitions of the stimuli commonly in-

---

[10] "Ueber den Einfluss der Erfahrung auf die Wahrnehmung von Figuren," *Psychol. Forsch.*, 1926, *8*, 261–317, and 1929, *12*, 1–87. Koffka had earlier called attention to the fact that the experience explanation was unable to account for the apparent "translation" of a red square into a yellow circle, which is a familiar stroboscopic effect. No observer has ever witnessed such an event and yet it can be obtained by presenting one object to the left eye and another to the right. Koffka holds that empiricism and nativism are both false, or better, that the opposition between them is resolved by this new way of viewing sensory impressions, i.e., as dynamic resultants of the complex immediately-given situation. See his article under a title similar to Gottschaldt's in *Die Naturwissenschaften*, 1919, 7, 597–605.

At Heidelberg, Strauss had made a similar study, emphasizing, however, the ability of the subject to isolate a constant pattern in a succession of varying forms. She found, of course, that a part can only be seen as a sub-whole in a larger constellation where Wertheimer's Gestalt factors are operative. Cf. "Untersuchungen über das Erlöschen und Herausspringen von Gestalten," *Psychol. Forsch.*, 1927, *10*, 57–83.

volved in laboratory studies as those deliberately secured here, and since even directions to search for the original figure did not noticeably aid the subject in discovering it, Gottschaldt concludes that the total configuration must have completely altered the functions of the parts. As soon as certain contours of the *a*-figure serve to outline some strange sub-wholes in the *b*-figure, they lose their original character and acquire wholly new functional properties.[11]

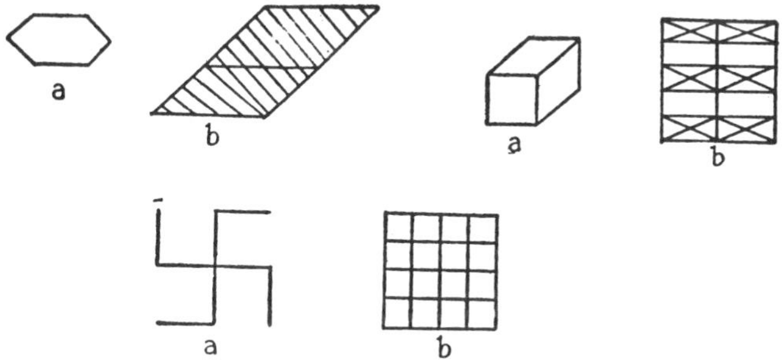

Figure 16. How Distinctive Figures Become "Lost" when Imbedded in a Different Perceptual Setting. (After Gottschaldt)

The "a" figures are all contained in their corresponding "b" patterns.

The problem of depth perception was cleverly attacked by Kopfermann[12] with the guidance which earlier configurationist experiments provided. She was concerned primarily with the question, "How do two-dimensional sketches succeed in giving an impression of spatiality?" The common theory holds that the way in which attention is divided on the basis of prior experience is the determining agent: certain parts of the figure are interpreted as "front" and others as "rear." However, careful observation shows that in the transition from a plane to a spatial apprehension the changes which occur are not restricted to depth values and "attensity"; there also occur characteristic structural transformations, re-groupings within the figure, clo-

[11] An American critic has objected that the connotation of "experience" as used in Gottschaldt's research has been unwarrantedly limited to *frequency* of repetition. Cf. M. G. Moore, "Gestalt vs. Experience," *Amer. J. Psychol.*, 1930, *42*, 453–455.

[12] "Psychologische Untersuchungen über die Wirkung zweidimensionaler Darstellung körperlicher Gebilde," *Psychol. Forsch.*, 1930, *13*, 289–364.

sure effects, etc. How is this process of reversal to be described phenomenally?

If one looks at Figure 17a, one will probably see first an "uneven rectangle with diagonals" followed suddenly by a "tetrahedron." Geometrically, the transition is accomplished by the following shift: At first, the "composition" present is (a, b, c, d); (e, f), (g, h), but after the conversion into the third-dimension, one sees $[a, d, (e + f)]$; $[a, b, (g + h)]$; $[d, c, (h + g)]$; $[b, c, (e + f)]$. It is psychologically impossible to maintain the former "togetherness" and realize a solid, and the converse is equally true. This perception of the parts in a definite rôle is the essence of understanding a figure. The individual parts need not be observed but their union must be, as, e.g., when we see a complicated crystal and react to it spatially.

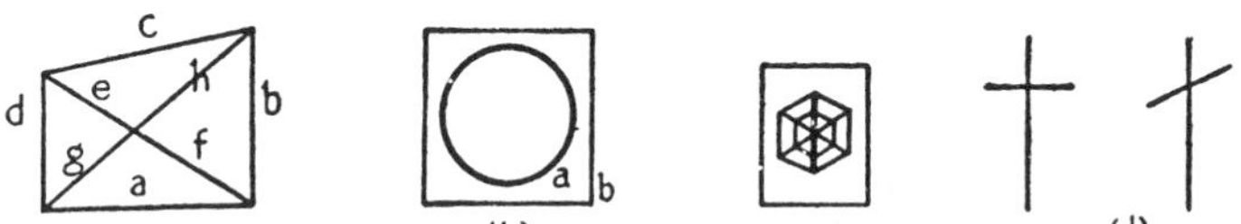

Figure 17. The Third Dimension as a Product of Gestalt Factors

Whether (a) is perceived as a plane or as a solid hinges upon the manner in which the parts are subjectively combined. The "depth" character in (b) is due to the double function of the contour *a* as opposed to the unitary function of contour *b*. Conversely, the "plane" quality of (c) results from viewing two transparent solids in perspective. In (d) the tilt of the transverse bar obviously determines the different spatial effects of the two crosses.

Kopfermann believes that the boundary-functions of various linear forms which fluctuate with the setting in which they are found play an important part in determining whether a two-dimensional or three-dimensional figure shall be seen. For example, a circle drawn on a white surface will normally be seen as a plane, but if a square be drawn around it, as in Figure 17b, so that it becomes a figure within an enclosing area, the double function of its contours stand out more sharply and the entire figure acquires a "depth" property. Contour *b* has only a limiting function toward within, but contour *a* limits the circle centripetally and the square centrifugally.

Spatiality would seem, then, to be a product of field forces. This view was experimentally tested by means of a light-proof "tunnel" box in which glass plates were arranged one behind the other, each containing a different section of some drawing. Figure 17c, for instance, was produced by two *separate* but identical sketches of a cube, held some distance apart. When placed in a straight-line vision, most observers saw this as a symbolic or formal "web" instead of a doubled cube, indicating that the objectively existing differences in depth were overcome by such figural factors as the nature of the "composition," the contour-functions, and the relation of the parts to the whole.[13] The influence of mere position within the field is also important as one may see from the non-spatial effect created by the symmetrical cross in Figure 17d and the definite spatial character of its asymmetrical neighbor.

The "wholeness" of our visual percepts is curiously illustrated by some quaint observations of Hornbostel on optic inversion, from which he concludes that convexity and concavity are "total" properties. He constructed some wire models of solids of the type sketched in Figure 18, and held them before a mirror in various positions. When such a figure is turned in different planes, it "tumbles" from one apparent shape to another like the familiar figure-ground reversals, save that with a tri-dimensional object more possibilities are opened; Figure 18, e.g., can be apprehended in at least four ways. *When the inversions occur, they come as a single complete unified movement:* one part does not "tip," then another, and so on. These quasi-solid inversions are neither illusory nor ideational "constructs," but things which under special conditions we *perceive.*

The phenomenal properties of a "convex" percept are typically distinct from a "concave" one. A convex affair is closed,

[13] Contrast this explanation with Washburn's motor account: "In the ambiguous cube, whether a cube resting on the ground or one suspended in air is perceived may depend upon whether one fixates one point or another; the point fixated seems to be nearer, i.e., suggests a shorter reaching movement, because in looking at an object we generally look at its nearest point, which, of course, carries with it that surface of the cube to which it belongs. Further, if a record is kept of the duration of the phases of the cube, we usually find that it is seen longer as a cube resting on the ground than as a hanging cube; this may be explained by the fact that we have a stronger tendency, due to habit, towards sitting down on cubes than towards looking up at them." "Gestalt Psychology and Motor Psychology," *Amer. J. Psychol.*, 1926, *37*, 516–520. Her entire criticism of configurationism is based upon a preference for an explanation in terms of our muscular activity in connection with objects previously experienced. Whether one is entitled to maintain this position after Gottschaldt's and Kopfermann's experiments is an open question.

excludes the observer, projects forward, cannot be penetrated visually because of its opacity or *manipulated* because of its impenetrability. Visual "objects" are convex. A concave item, on the other hand, is open, embraces the observer, permits visual and manual exploration, and possesses the characteristics of an empty background. "Spaces" are concave. The entire process of inversion involves making a convex item concave and *vice versa,* although for some reason it is normally harder to invert a convex object than a concave one.[14]

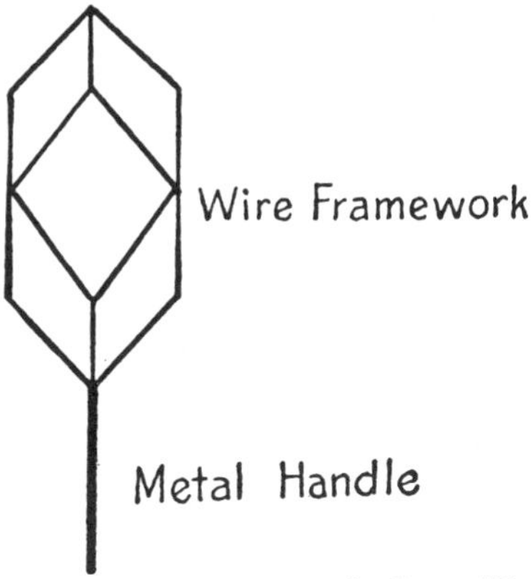

Figure 18. One of Hornbostel's Reversible Solids

When held before a mirror and properly rotated, the image alternately produces a convex or concave impression. For details, see the description in the text.

A considerable number of American psychologists have been interested in taking experimental hints from the continental Gestalt group and by repeating, refining, and checking their technical procedures have contributed to advance our understanding of configurationist theory and data. Wever,[15] e.g., took Rubin's "nonsense figures" and by a series of tachistoscopic exposures of varying lengths studied the characteristic changes in appearance which occurred as a result of the different presentation-times. The most primitive figure-ground experi-

[14] "Ueber optische Inversion," *Psychol. Forsch.,* 1922, *1,* 130–156. The familiar clinical reading disability of confusing "saw," "was," "b," "d," etc., may be more than just a case of poor directional habits!

[15] "Figure and Ground in the Visual Perception of Form," *Amer. J. Psychol.,* 1927, *38,* 194–226; "Attention and Clearness in the Perception of Figure and Ground," *ibid.,* 1928, *40,* 51–74.

ence apparently arises when the exposure lasts about ten milliseconds. The indispensable characteristic of such a perception appears to be a certain type of heterogeneity in the visual field: the field is so differentiated that two separate, intrinsically homogeneous regions are seen. As one would expect, with this feature of heterogeneity is always correlated a difference in brightness between the two fields. A primitive bounding mechanism is thus established. The limen for a continuous or completely enclosed contour is somewhat higher—around 13-14 milliseconds. Localization effects next emerge, and as Rubin observed, the figure seems to protrude, but the ground is recessive. In general, as the time of the presentation is increased the "goodness" of the figure-ground experience is enhanced. These time-relations easily make a dull recital, but they do show plainly what are the essential and the less significant qualities of the figural experience. One important finding of Wever's is his "discovery" that clearness is the *presence of something that can be reported upon;* since clearness is introspectively the heart of attention, its dependence upon the figure-ground opposition is of high theoretical importance as Rubin and the Gestalt school have maintained.

Contours acquire a special significance in Gestalt theory, because, whether sharp or weak, they serve to mark a figure off from its ground and thus establish the "natural" wholes with which configurationism prefers to deal. If the contour were not present to differentiate the two fields, no figure would be present, and no meaning or significance would attach to the presentation. The physico-chemical forces which operate *within* the contour are very distinct from those *outside,* and the perception of the resulting figures presumably rests upon an emergence or a central physiological delimitation of a specific area within a field. However, in our present state of knowledge these underlying dynamic agents cannot be identified except in terms of the grosser designations of nearness, similarity, etc., as indicated by Wertheimer. Nevertheless, some comparison of their relative strength can be made. Liebmann [16]

[16] "Ueber das Verhalten farbiger Formen bei Helligkeitsgleichheit von Figur und Grund," *Psychol. Forsch.,* 1927, *9,* 300–353.

reports marked phenomenal differences in the appearance of colored objects with and without brightness equivalence. Apparently, when variations in brightness are excluded, colored figures exhibit a lack of solidity, firm outlines, and "thing"—character. Based upon threshold determinations for both grey and colored fields, she found that brightness differences are far more influential than color distinctions in producing the fundamental perceptual situation of a figure upon a ground.

A curious incidental finding is worthy of record. If an observer is placed at a distance so that the accompanying figures *a* and *b* appear united without a gap, and then gradually allowed to approach the stimuli, he must come *nearer* in order to discern the little break in the plus sign than to distinguish as separate the two complete figures, despite the objective equality of the spatial interval. The reader will probably be reminded of the "closure" explanation [17] as pertinent here and in view of Gottschaldt's evidence on the untenability of the experience hypothesis it must be admitted as a plausible alternative.

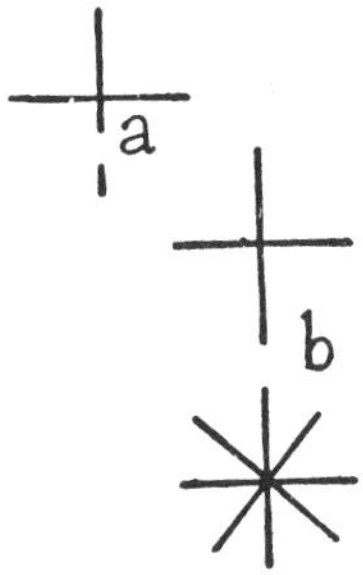

What has since come to be known as the "Liebmann effect" has been subjected to an exhaustive analysis by Koffka and Harrower.[18] As stated above, this name refers to the observation that mere color difference without the aid of a concomitant difference in brightness has surprisingly little organizing power. Colored figures on a neutral or colored ground lose their definition, become blurred and utterly diffuse if the brightness of figure and ground are made equal. Evidently pure color difference is not the main factor in segregating an area from its surrounding area.

Koffka and Harrower devised a photoprojector for varying the color and brightness of various figure-ground combinations. They were primarily interested in noting the effect of the presence or absence of thin black or white contours upon the prop-

[17] Note in this connection how the assumed "canals" of Mars may be as much a psychological reality as an astronomical. The Landolt ring in optometry is also affected by this interpretation.

[18] "Color and Organization," *Psychol. Forsch.*, 1931, *15*, 145–192 and 193–275.

erties of the contained color. They found the non-contour figure more highly saturated than the contour figure, the color of the contour figure being hard, glossy and condensed, that of the non-contour figure soft and spongy. *A contour, whether black or white, makes the color within the figure darker.* Since both black and white contours have the same effect of darkening the color of the enclosed figure, this cannot be produced either by contrast or by assimilation, but must be due to the higher degree of segregation which the contour figure possesses with regard to the non-contour ones. It appears as though the energy consumed in producing the better organization were supplied by a loss in brightness.

Regardless of the contour influence, red and yellow have relatively high articulatory power, i.e., they are "hard" colors, whereas green and yellow are low in articulatory power, i.e., they are "soft" colors. Throughout these observations the general Gestalt thesis appears to be upheld, viz., that the color in any part of the field depends upon the formal or figural characteristics of this region, and conversely the articulation of the field into different units depends upon the differences of brightness and color within its boundaries.

Perhaps one of the finest examples of the integrating possibilities of Gestalt theory is a study executed by Erna Schur [19] under Köhler's direction on the ancient problem of the moon illusion and its relation to the constancy of visual magnitude. This issue has baffled some of the world's keenest intellects, largely because the appropriate experimental insight was lacking. Aristotle supposed that atmospheric conditions near the horizon were responsible for the differences in the optical size of the heavenly bodies, but photography and exact physical measurements do not yield variations large enough to account for the extraordinary change in appearance at the zenith. The moon really casts a larger retinal picture at the zenith than at the horizon, since the observer is nearer by the distance of the earth's radius. With the discarding of explanations based upon refraction have appeared many built around the so-called errors

[19] "Mondtäuschung und Sehgrössenkonstanz," *Psychol. Forsch.*, 1926, *7*, 44–80.

of judgment; e. g., the moon near the horizon is said to look larger because of the greater contrast with "neighboring" earthly objects in the same line of sight. However, when one looks upward in a canyon where terrestrial objects are also visually "near" the zenith, the moon reveals no such equivalent increase in size, since the apparent ratio of the average lunar diameter in culmination and at the horizon is about 1 to 2.5.

Acting upon some earlier abortive investigations of Stroobant, Zoth,[20] and Guttmann, Schur prepared to reproduce the essence of the celestial phenomenon on a terrestrial scale. A simple apparatus was designed capable of throwing a circular disk of light upon a homogeneous dark background from a central floor position to the ceiling and directly forward upon one of the walls. The distances compared ranged all the way from a 3-meter room to a 32-meter height in a large theatre and Zeppelin hangar. Adjustments in the size of the comparison disc were made until it was judged subjectively equal to the standard. Typical data for one observer are given below:

TABLE II. SUBJECTIVE DIFFERENCES IN EQUATING LIGHT DISCS FOR SIZE WHEN ONE IS PROJECTED FORWARD AND THE OTHER ABOVE. (SCHUR)

Actual distance (in meters)	3	4.80	6	13.5	22
Overhead diameter (in cm.)	6.8	10.9	13.6	30	50
Mean diameter of the lower circle	5.8	9.1	10.1	17	27

From the corresponding curve one can compute that after a distance of 100 meters the magnitude of the illusory effect remains constant. A control test was instituted by reversing the direction of the head and eye movements, a requirement which was met by having the observer stand upon an elevated platform. In this case, when the diameter of the disc *below* was 18 cm. at a distance of 3.60 meters, the circle straight ahead had to be about 20.5 cm., or 14% larger, before a judgment of equality was reached.

[20] This writer interpreted the "illusion" as a result of over-compensated convergence tendencies of the eyeballs.

Gauss and Zoth had independently pointed out the probable influence of differences in the degree of convergence of the eye musculature upon the presence of the illusion, and it is more than accidental that the effect increases up to 100 meters, the customary limits of convergence, although the curves for the two are far from running parallel. That the direction of the visual axes is significant is clear from the fact that the negative after-image of the setting sun is much smaller at the zenith than at any point on the horizon. This change is all the more remarkable when one remembers that the size of the retinal region affected is unaltered. Moreover, that this is not a solar peculiarity is easily demonstrated by using an analogous white paper circle on a black background where the same results are obtained.

The dependence of the phenomenon upon the position of the observer was neatly elicited under circumstances which exaggerated the rôle of the extrinsic eye muscles. The subject lay flat upon his back and compared a "moon" upon the ceiling at a distance of 5.20 meters with one equidistant on the wall behind him! Since the essential conditions of the illusion were maintained, it was anticipated that the object on the wall would appear smaller because it corresponded to the normal zenith position of the moon to an erect observer. Actually, the expected diminution occurred but it was relatively small (5-13%), probably because of complicating influences exerted by the static organs and tonic tensions of the neck musculature. At any rate, the fertile character of the Gestalt hypothesis in leading to new experimental proposals is amply demonstrated by this study.

One of the most positive results of Gestalt experimentation has been the complete refutation of the conventional theories of the "blind spot." Since the blind spot contains no rods and cones it is easy to show that if an isolated object falls within that area of the retina it is not seen. Every undergraduate is familiar with the simple and impressive demonstration supporting this view. Nevertheless, it is well to remember that this blindness is relative, for while it is true that one does not see clearly the figure at that point, the background, no matter how homogeneous it may be, is preserved intact. Field-forces operating according to the principle of closure give the Gestalt version of the phenomenon. Moreover, Tschermak somewhere reports that if a colored patch, say blue, is projected upon the blind spot, the subject perceives a ring-like halo of yellow, indicating that contrast effects—which are fundamentally dual in character—are not suspended at this point and that light sensitivity of some kind must be preserved.

Stern[21] showed that the perception of motion is still possible when the path traversed by the "object" must pass through the

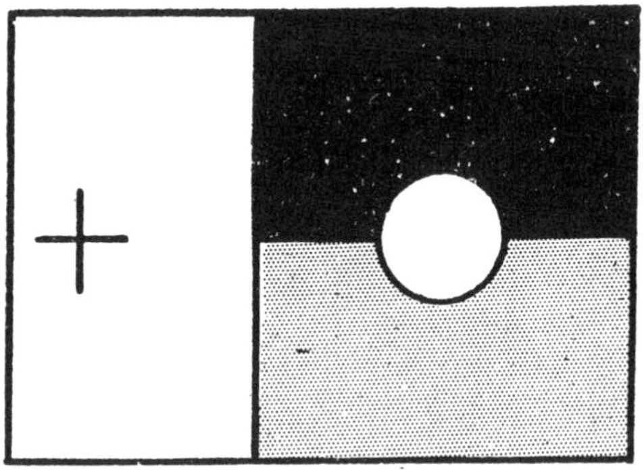

Figure 19. A Blind-Spot Card Modelled after Scripture's

Close the left eye and fixate the cross at a distance of about six inches. If the eye movements are carefully controlled, the white circle disappears entirely and a perfectly straight line border between the black and grey areas takes its place.

blind spot. Using a modification of Wertheimer's technique for exhibiting apparent movement, she found that the phi-phenomenon occurred if two light points were successively exposed on the upper and lower border of the blind spots; in fact, movement was actually perceived more readily and distinctly than upon the rest of the retina! Even more spectacular was her discovery that motion was present if one or both of the necessary light points was exposed within the "blind" area, despite inability to see each point when exposed singly. It is known that a straight line or circular circumference passing through

[21] "Die Wahrnehmung von Bewegungen in der Gegend des blinden Flecks," *Psychol. Forsch.*, 1926, *7*, 1–15.

the blind spot is not seen as "broken"—a fact for which the configurationist can easily account by the photo-electric gradients responsible for gestalt completion and the law of *Prägnanz*. The reader can easily determine this for himself by projecting the white circle in the Figure 19 upon his blind spot when the eye is fixated upon the cross. Although the white circle "disappears," the boundary line between the black and grey surfaces appears straight and the "ground" figures show no evidence of indentation. A small isolated form vanishes when cast upon the blind spot but a larger figure is preserved intact by a completional or totalizing process released by the rest of the field.

It should be emphasized that the completion observed is not at all "mental" (as Poppelreuter has maintained) but takes place wholly within the sensory sector. The difference can be made clear by the following trick: Stand a friend against a wall surface in such a way that his head falls within the blind spot. In spite of our experience that every person has a head, the head is not seen! Commonly, a rounded light impression is preserved, but the facial details vanish. Why? Presumably because a head is in itself a natural sub-total, whereas sections of a stick or simple circular figure obey the dynamics of closure under these circumstances.

Helson's extensive investigation[22] has also shown that the optic disk—he prefers this term to the misleading label of "blind-spot"—can be illuminated while the rest of the retinal field is dark, and that under these conditions after-images, contrast effects, adaptation, and many other color phenomena characteristic of normal vision will be found in the blind-spot, only in somewhat different degree.

Dependence of Brightness and Color Qualities upon the Configuration

One of Köhler's classic experiments[23] was designed to reveal the principle of relativity in animal conduct. The idea was

[22] "The Effects of Direct Stimulation of the Blind Spot," *Amer. J. Psychol.*, 1929, *41*, 345–397.

[23] "Optische Untersuchungen am Schimpansen und am Haushuhn," *Abhandlungen d. K. Preuss. Akad. d. Wissenschaften*, 1915, Phys.-math. Kl., Nr. 3.

very simple. A number of hens were trained to eat kernels of corn from the darker of two grey paper surfaces, A and B, and to avoid the lighter. As in all good objective studies, the grey grounds were alternately placed on the right or the left during the pecking process, so as to avoid the position habits which animals readily establish. The training was continued long enough (400 to 600 trials) to ensure a certain degree of over-learning as measured by a succession of errorless choices.

Suppose now the perceptual field is changed. If A in the above situation represents a *light* grey and B a *middle* grey, and a new *dark* grey ground C is paired off with B in place of A, from which surface will the hens now peck? According to the theory of restricted bonds, one would expect the chick to go to B, since that is the identical surface which was presented in the first series and consequently has the advantage of familiarity. However, in about 70% of the critical series the hens pecked from the *new* grey paper C.[24] Why? This utterly unforeseen result makes one question the validity of the original basis of prediction. But on Gestalt principles, the outcome is very simply explained. The animals had not responded to a *particular* brightness value[25] but to a *relation*—the "darker of the two!" When this interpretation is checked in a new training series by positive drill upon the *lighter* of a pair instead of the darker, similar behavior occurs and the configurational account is confirmed. Have we not here a species of transfer which satisfies neither Thorndike's theory of identical elements, nor Judd's theory of generalization, nor any other of the classical transfer hypotheses?

This has been a hard nut for opponents to crack. The statistical reliability of the differences between the choices has been questioned and some studies have reached opposite conclusions.[26]

[24] The same type of experiment had already been performed by H. C. Bingham in America. He trained chicks to select the larger of two circles and then presented them with circles reduced in size from the original, but with the size ratios maintained. Those animals who had been taught to pick a 6-cm. circle and to reject a 4-cm. one would select the latter when it was given in company with a 3-cm. circle. Evidently, relative rather than absolute magnitude had been discriminated. See "Size and Form Perception in *Gallus domesticus*," *J. Animal Behavior*, 1913, *3*, 65–113. This entire study has unfortunately been neglected and deserves to be much better known than it is.

[25] In his experiments, Pavlov found that a dog can be trained to a tone as a food signal with a coördination of the reaction to the *absolute* quality so striking and definite that no reaction occurred even with tones deviating only to a very small extent.

[26] See Howard Taylor, "A Study of Configuration Learning," *J. Comp. Psychol.*, 1932, *13*, 19–26. Taylor asks: If four hens in the critical series selected the neutral paper

Still the vast amount of controversy which has arisen around this special problem is one indication of its fundamental significance, not only for psychological research, but for the mechanics of social control, especially in education. Köhler's little supplementary experiment with a three-year-old child shows the "human" implications of his major study. A situation was arranged in which the brighter of two colored boxes always contained candy. Errorless responses were established after 45 trials, following which a new and brighter box was presented in the company of the original positive stimulus, replacing the darker negative box of the training series. Under these changed conditions—analogous to those confronting the hens—the child always selected the new bright container, rather than the one from which it had previously secured the candy. Presumably the native and primitive perceptual responses as they appear in both racial and individual development are more in harmony with a view which stresses *totals* and *wholes* than with one which maintains the primacy of elements.[27]

Koffka[28] has made many fine observations of out-of-the-way visual phenomena, but none which exceed in vividness his experiments pointing to a configurationist theory of marginal contrast. If one rotates a Masson disc with its familiar concentric grey rings, it is possible to isolate a single ring so that one can detect the contrast haze on both of its borders. If now a screen is held over the disc in such a way that it covers one of the marginal contrast bands of the ring attended to, the other forthwith disappears! The contrast apparently exists only be-

59 times and the original positive paper only 26 out of a total of 85 trials, is it not possible that the learning in the training series was inadequate to ensure perfect response later to a pattern stimulus? Moreover, can hens really distinguish slight brightness differences in greys? In his check, Taylor used black, white, and middle grey surfaces and shocked the animals electrically when they pecked the wrong kernels. In his critical test, 81.5% of the responses were made to the original "positive" grey, indicating—in flat opposition to Köhler—a reaction to specific sensory stimuli. This contradiction seriously needs to be resolved in the interests of both fact and theory. Perhaps there are gross individual differences among chicks, some behaving "analytically" and some "synthetically." Certainly children react in these two distinct ways.

[27] "Kleine Mitteilungen aus dem psychologischen Institut der Universität Giessen," *Psychol. Forsch.*, 1922, *2*, 145–153.

[28] "Ueber Feldbegrenzung und Felderfüllung," *Psychol. Forsch.*, 1922, *4*, 176–203. In 1878, Eugen Fick had reported some observations on "field forces" in perception. If a pin-hole is made in a cardboard and the latter laid over a bit of colored paper in bright illumination, it is impossible to identify the color at 6.5 meters. If now 15 added pin-holes (making a square of 16, four on a side) are inserted far enough apart to be differentiated, the color is quickly recognized. Cf. *Pflügers Archiv.*, *17*, 152–153.

cause of a brightness gradient, and as soon as one pole of the potential is destroyed the other simultaneously vanishes. This finding led Koffka to the generalization that marginal contrast can occur only in a field which is itself imbedded between a brighter and a darker. Elimination of this necessary gradient means the elimination of the effect.

A good way of appreciating some of the successes and positive contributions wrought by Gestalt theory is to follow the changes it has introduced into the very citadel of orthodox experimentalism—psychophysics. This division of the science, which has seemed hopelessly barren to every younger generation since James' fulminations, is, nevertheless, in its techniques of precision an imposing paradigm of methodology. Consequently, the uses which configurationism, the newest speculative position, makes of the psychophysical approach, perhaps the oldest quantitative procedure peculiar to psychology, cannot fail to be of interest.

The exact determination of absolute and differential thresholds in the separate sense modalities has been one of the major items of business assigned to the psychophysicist. Gelb and Granit[29] raised the original question whether the lower limen of color vision for the primary hues was influenced by the presence of the stimulus to be discriminated upon an area which could be seen either as figure or ground. Previous studies had considered only the effect of the brightness value of the field, but these investigators believed it made a difference if the field was a closed entity like a ring or a homogeneous field. Their subjects looked with one eye through a blackened tube at a grey Maltese cross (similar to Rubin's pattern; see Figure 4) outlined so as to yield a readily reversible combination. A subliminal spot of red light projected upon it was gradually increased in luminosity until distinguished as such. In all instances, the color threshold was *higher* when the light was cast upon the phenomenal figure than upon the ground; qualitatively, too, the color appeared suddenly within the figure, but emerged as from

[29] "Die Bedeutung von Figur und Grund für die Farbenschwelle," *Zsch. f. Psychol.*, 1923, *93*, 83–118. About the same time, L. Hartmann in his investigation of fusion, found that flicker for a white field disappears sooner if the field is perceived as ground rather than figure. Cf. "Neue Verschmelzungsprobleme," *Psychol. Forsch.*, 1923, *3*, 319–396.

a depth in the ground. As a control upon this observation, a red-white reversible cross was employed with a clear patch of red light upon the white region. In this case, the spot paled noticeably when the white cross was isolated as figure, but as soon as the red cross was thus apprehended its intensity was restored! Fluctuations in attention do not offer a plausible explanation, since in both figure and ground the projections of the light patch lay equidistant from the fixation point, the center of the cross. The interpretation which Gelb and Granit give is that the inner field or figure becomes functionally a "ground" when the light spot appears upon its surface. Its resistance to this fundamental change in its perceptual character is greater than that offered by the original ground; hence, a higher light intensity or threshold is required before it succumbs to the differentiation process.

The influence of *form,* even in the narrower sense of the word, is well illustrated in some fine observations of Benary,[30] who carried out the suggestions contained in one of Wertheimer's lecture-demonstrations: A plain black cross rests upon a white field. Of two objectively equal grey triangles, one (T_1) is placed upon the surface of the cross itself, the other (T_2) in a corner enclosed by two arms of the cross so that geometrically more black but less white adjoins it than in the case of T_1. According to summative theories of brightness contrast, the magnitude of the contrast effect is dependent upon the amount of black or white in the immediate neighborhood, on which basis T_2 should appear lighter than T_1. Actually T_1 appears brighter than T_2 (see Figure 20a).

It is characteristic of this presentation that even psychologically-trained observers fall into the error of maintaining that since T_1 lies *within* the black region it must have more black surrounding it until a little geometrical reflection shows that there is considerably more white in its environment than in T_2's. The extent of the black area contiguous with the triangle in the corner is substantially greater than the black area adjoining the other triangle. This phenomenon is not an artifact of a peculiar

[30] "Beobachtungen zu einem Experiment über Helligkeitskontrast," *Psychol. Forsch.,* 1924, *5,* 131–142.

example, since analogous effects are obtained with a large I and H. Moreover, reversal of the direction of contrast by means of white figures on black ground produced a corresponding result: T_1 now appeared *darker* than T_2.

In order to quantify his data, Benary inserted his critical grey fields of 180° black and 180° white in black figures on white ground in the cross-triangle comparison (Figure 20a matched with Figure 20b).

Seven subjects all saw T_1 as brighter than T_2; the brightness-difference, T_1-T_2, required on the average an additional 30°-40° black in T_1 to compensate or neutralize the figural stresses producing it.

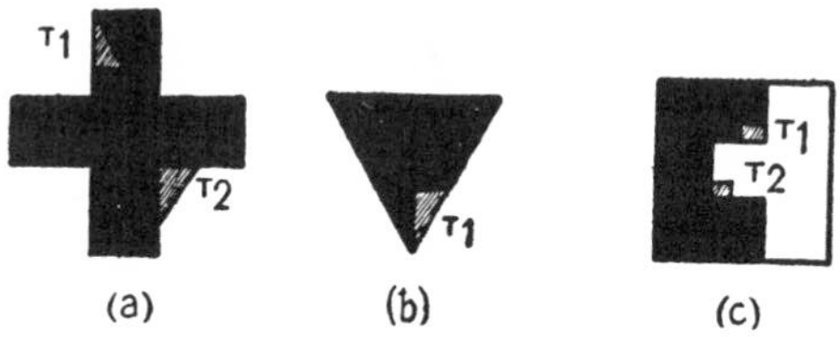

Figure 20. Benary's Figures Demonstrating the Influence of "Form" upon Brightness Properties

The T_1 homogeneous grey patches above are all seen as brighter than the corresponding T_2 sections, presumably because the first type clash with the "closure" tendencies of the figures upon which they are laid.

In the experiment above, T_1 always belonged to the figure, but T_2 did not. Is it just this relation to the figure as distinct from the ground which is responsible for the occurrence of the contrast phenomena described? In this neat configuration (Figure 20c), the grey wedge in the black, T_1, corresponds to the critical field in the preceding triangle, (Figure 20b), while the wedge upon the white, T_2, corresponds to the critical field in the cross. Normal observation makes T_1 seem brighter than T_2. It is possible for experienced observers to respond simultaneously to this configuration as two equivalent figures, one black and one white, with the included critical fields. But even under these conditions of apprehension, T_1 is brighter than T_2, suggesting that the brightness gradient is independent of the surface to which it "belongs," and that the division of the critical fields upon the figure and ground is not the condition *sine qua non* of the effect. Nevertheless, inclusion within a gestalt seems to be a more potent cause of brightness contrast than the kind, mass, and proximity of the inducing surface.[31]

Figure 21 prepared by Matthaei[32] is useful for many purposes, but especially good as a clear-cut instance of non-summative brightness contrast. The completely enclosed upper part of the "R" appears greyer than the white area above the letters which are exposed on three sides. Summatively, the upper field of the "R" should look brighter, but the central stripe is more strongly elevated, being a characteristically new structure. Even in those cases where the borders of the central stripe lie within the interior of a letter as in the "o" and more particularly in the second "n," the stripe as such is sharply set off.

Figure 21. The Central Stripe is the Brightest Single Region in the Figure. (After Matthaei)

A similar condition prevails in an interesting experiment of Helene Frank's [33] dealing with the effect of the pattern of the projection surface upon the behavior of after-images. If an after-image of a circle is cast upon a screen containing a drawing in perspective of a long corridor, the disc appears larger if projected upon the apparently remoter end and definitely smaller at the subjectively nearer end. A more dramatic effect is secured when the after-image of a plus (+) sign is projected orthogonally upon Rubin's cross pattern (cf. Figure 4, which appears alternately as an iron cross or a propeller); when the iron cross emerges as "figure," the after-image of the plus sign

[31] Mikesell and Bentley, in an elaborate repetition and more accurate extension of Benary's technique, confirmed his finding that the traditional laws of contrast need to be supplemented by other factors. They contend, however, that he confused configurations with geometrical or symbolic designs, and that the changed quality of the incorporated gray in mutilated patterns does not wholly support the Gestalt version. See "Configuration and Brightness Contrast," *J. Exper. Psychol.*, 1930, *13*, 1–23.

Jenkins has also shown that central and not peripheral factors are responsible for the changes of relative brightness of grey patches included in designs. "Inherence" must be added to *Prägnanz* as one of the fundamental laws of perceptual dynamics. Cf. "The Perception of Plane Designs," *ibid.*, pp. 24–46.

For a complete confirmation of Benary's work, see Atwater, "The Effect of Form on Color Contrast," *J. Gen. Psychol.*, 1933, *8*, 472–478.

[32] "Das Gestaltproblem," München, 1929, p. 60. Originally published in *Ergebnisse der Physiologie*, 1929, *29*, 1–82.

[33] "Ueber die Beeinflussung von Nachbildern durch die Gestalteigenschaften der Projektionsfläche," *Psychol. Forsch.*, 1923, *4*, 33–37. About the same time, Rotschild had found that slight irregularities in the contours of the original were eliminated in the after-image in accordance with the law of *Prägnanz*. This is of some importance for a theory of memory as will be seen later. Cf. "Ueber den Einfluss der Gestalt auf das negative Nachbild ruhender visueller Figuren," *Archiv. f. Ophthalmol.*, 1923, *112*, 1–28.

is clearly observed, but as soon as the propeller becomes focal it all but disappears; however, with the restoration of the "iron-cross attitude" the plus image becomes clear again.

A check upon this unique observation is found in the results obtained with the after-image of an eight-pointed star. When the iron cross is isolated only the plus (+) rays are clearly seen while the cross arms (×) appear dimly in the background.

Colored after-sensations follows the same rule, as was shown by using the hollow cross herein as background.

The after-image of this original was thrown upon it so that two alternating percepts were possible—one, a multiplication symbol and the other, two adjacent angles. When the "times" sign emerges as "figure" retinal color mixture apparently occurs, but in the double-angle response the definite bi-coloration is preserved. In general, these illustrations substantiate the claim that the visibility or clearness of the after-image is in part dependent upon its position within either figure or ground.[34]

In a series of experiments by Fuchs[35] some highly convincing evidence of the influence of formally-perceived combinations upon apparent color was accumulated. A typical illustration of this effect is afforded by the nine-spot figure (Figure 22), which permits one to see either a *yellow* plus sign (+) or a *blue-green* cross (×). The middle *yellow-green* circle can belong to either pattern. It is possible for experienced observers to see the mid-circle as belonging to the yellow plus-sign, in which case it becomes yellow, too, despite the simultaneous apprehension of the blue-green gestalt. Conversely, should it belong to the cross-

[34] Another favorite illustration in this: Place a 1-cm. thick gray ring about 8 cm. in diameter symmetrically upon a half-blue, half-yellow surface. One can see the ring as a whole or as two half-rings, but in the first case it seems homogeneously gray and in the second case, dark and blue upon the yellow ground, and bright and yellowish upon the blue; but it is impossible to see two equally grey half-rings. Here, too, the structure determines its own color. A thread separating diametrically the halves facilitates the effect.

An arrangement traceable to Benussi consists in placing twenty grey discs in a circular pattern upon an equally apportioned red and green field. With appropriate cognizance of the circle gestalt the contrast effect entirely disappears.

[35] "Experimentelle Untersuchungen über die Aenderung von Farben unter dem Einfluss von Gestalten," *Zsch. f. Psychol.*, 1923, 92, 249–325.

sign, the central disc becomes bluish-green like the other circles of that figure, although the yellow "square" is perceived at the same time. This double isolation of two figures, only one of which "contains" the middle circle is a neat procedure which disposes of the possibility that attention and not the configured percept is the cause of an adaptation in hue. Wundt had made a similar observation long before, but his interpretative bias led him to offer an explanation in terms of "associative effects" instead of a more vivid psychophysical dynamism.

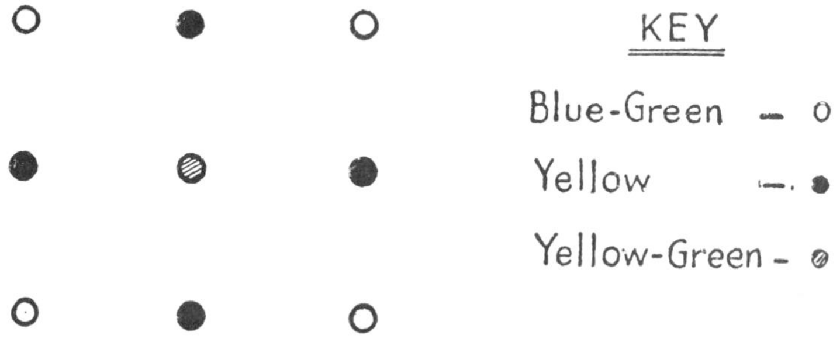

Figure 22. Schema Illustrating the Influence of "Form" upon Color Quality

The middle circle looks yellow if perceived as part of a plus-sign comprised mainly of the other yellow discs and more greenish if seen as part of an X primarily determined by the corner items.

Köhler himself has reported a simple observation which strengthens the view that such fundamental qualities of visual objects as brightness and color are properties of an extended field and depend upon more than local uniform stimulation. If we take a glass of water in which soap is dissolved, the aspect of such a liquid is defined by such adjectives as *dim* or *turbid*. Now if one looks at it through a little hole made in a piece of cardboard, one will see the hole filled with a certain grey hue (possibly a bit bluish or reddish), but the quality of "dimness" or "turbidness" will have disappeared. Why? Fundamentally, because the properties of parts are not the properties of wholes.

Movement as Conditioned by the Gestalt

Duncker's dissertation gives some of the best testimony in favor of the inevitability of a Gestalt explanation of perceptual experience, since it deals with phenomena with which every layman is familiar. There is a certain type of "induced" or apparent and illusory movement which occurs only as the result of simultaneously present and objectively "real" motion. It appears in its commonest form with two neighboring trains in a railroad station—one's own car seems to be moving when actually the adjoining one is in motion. Significantly enough, this illusion is all the more pronounced the less one sees of the stable or resting environment (= ground?) of the station. This explains the impressive effect of a reversal of direction when one's own coach is overtaken and passed by another train at night on an open stretch, since the normal "field" upon which motion is projected is absent.

There are other experiences which show that this phenomenon of relative or contrast movement demands at least two stimuli—one objectively at rest and the other in real motion.[36] If one stands upon a bridge and focuses upon a point in the stream, one seems ultimately to be moving with the bridge in a direction opposed to the flow of the water; again, an experience which is the more compulsive the less one sees of the firmly-anchored shores peripherally. The "wandering" moon when the clouds sweep by, the "floating" island in a rapidly moving stream, and the "falling" tower in a shifting fog are other perceptual effects conditioned by similar configurations. In all these cases, the common feature appears to be that phenomenal movement is essentially displacement in a natural system of relations.

One of Duncker's experiments revealed an important rule with respect to the production of induced movement, viz., the induction is solely a one-way affair from the larger to the smaller object and not reversible. A small light point was projected perpendicularly upon a cardboard surface attached to a moving band and fixated at a distance of one meter. When the carton moved, the objectively resting point also moved in an opposite direction and with an apparent velocity directly proportional to that of a real movement. This law was checked by

[36] "Ueber induzierte Bewegung," *Psychol. Forsch.*, 1929, *12*, 180–259.

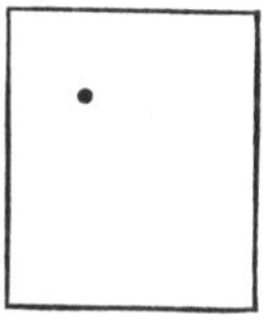

an arrangement in which a point in a rectangle could be either moved while the rectangle was fixed, or kept at rest while the rectangle moved. If the actually resting object was fixated in either instance, the *enclosed* object appeared to have the stronger movement, i.e., the figure is "livelier" than the ground. Oddly enough, an induced motion of the observer himself occurs if the distance from the fixation point is decreased to 30 cm.; seemingly the body of the observer becomes an annex to the induced motion of the point.

The appeal to "field forces" as the major determinants of organized wholes is cleverly illustrated in Koffka's persuasive ref-

Figure 23. Koffka's and Wittmann's Figures Modified from Linke's Originals

If the black ball is rapidly projected in different positions within the arcs, it appears to slide back and forth in contact with the circular rim.

utation[37] of Linke's empirical account of stroboscopic illusions. Linke prepared four identical semi-circles with the concave side turned *upward;* on the inner side of each and in contact with the rim a small black point was drawn—in the first semicircle toward the left, in the third toward the right, and in the other two below in the center. If one exposes the figures in the appropriate order, a definite impression of a ball rolling within the perisphere results. However, if the points are presented without the semi-circles (which apparently serve as a runway) the rolling movement disappears and the points simply hop from one position to another. Linke considered this evidence of the assimilating effect of past influences upon present experiences, since we have observed moving objects slide back and

[37] "Kleine Mitteilungen aus dem psychologischen Institut der Universität Giessen," *Psychol. Forsch.*, 1922, *2*, 144–155.

forth within vessels. Koffka nicely disposes of this explanation by simply inverting the figures so that the concave sides of the semi-circles are turned *downward.* Oddly enough, the point still clings to the periphery during its apparent movement under these conditions and describes a rolling motion along an arc rather than a jump across a chord! It slides up and down as though on the ceiling of a vault in a manner which defies all prior experience. Wittmann supports Koffka by his claim that a similar effect is indifferently obtained in other positions such as indicated by Figure 23. The most satisfactory explanation seems to be that the arcs by their "passive" presence exert some

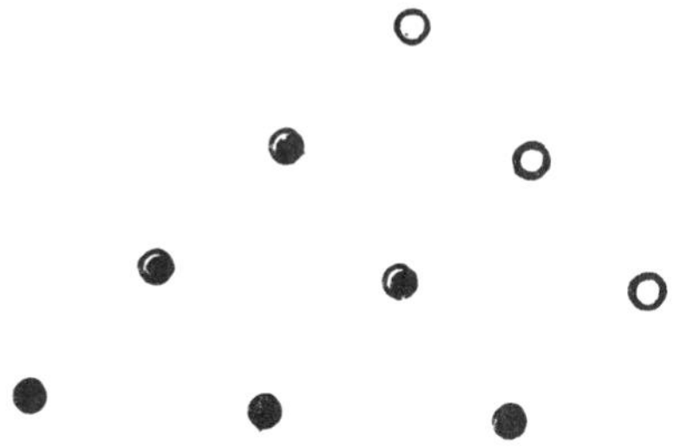

Figure 24. Ternus' Method of Demonstrating Phenomenal Identity Despite Objective Difference

Dots represent light points first exposed, circles those immediately following. Under these conditions the new points appear to be the old ones slightly displaced.

direct influence upon the adjacent curve of motion which is independent of individual experience.

A pupil of Wertheimer's, Ternus,[38] performed a number of simple but original experiments on the problem of phenomenal identity. This is a matter of some epistemological import since it is logically rather disturbing that two different points of light successively exposed should appear like the same point moving. By means of point patterns made by thrusting pin-holes into cardboard and a simple lever device which could be pushed in and out or up and down, thus exposing or screening certain points, Ternus was able to demonstrate that *phenomenal identity is preserved by the whole as such and not just by relations between the parts.* For example, in Figure 24 the dots indicate

[38] "Experimentelle Untersuchung über phänomenale Identität," *Psychol. Forsch.*, 1926, *7*, 81–136.

the first pattern briefly exposed and the circles the second one. If one moves the screening lever slightly, some of the original points (represented by dots) disappear and others (typified by the circles) appear. The subject, however, does not see some points go and others come; instead, he sees a general upward movement of the *entire* triangle. If old parts vanish and new ones assume their relative position, despite actual displacement, the integrity of the whole is preserved. A *dynamic* gestalt involving movement must be accounted for in terms of total field-forces just as much as a *static* gestalt (i.e., stable geometrical forms and figures).

A wealth of minor problems has been found in the experimental treatment of movement phenomena ever since Wertheimer scratched open a new vein. Lindemann[39] is responsible for a novel attack on the phenomenon which Kenkel in 1913 had termed the *gamma-movement.* This refers to a slight intrinsic apparent motion which appears in an object when tachistoscopically exposed. The evident expansion of an electric light bulb when the current is suddenly switched on is a special case of this effect; similarly, when the object disappears there is a definite contraction observable with the movement of the contours directed toward the center.

Working with very short exposures, Lindemann found that various geometrical figures presented in different ways behaved differently. In the case of a circle, the gamma movement was most pronounced along the horizontal direction, and the same held for an ellipse whether resting upon its long or short axis. A square resting upon one of its sides as a base also showed its maximum motion laterally, but when standing upon a point all four corners moved energetically in and out! To Lindemann, these observations suggest that the experiences of form and movement must be intimately related, a conclusion which is supported by the fact that an irregular aggregate of dots fails to show the phenomenon plainly until patterns of some kind emerge. *The gamma movement is an accompaniment of the*

[39] "Experimentelle Untersuchungen über das Entstehen und Vergehen von Gestalten," *Psychol. Forsch.*, 1922, *2*, 5–60. Cf. also the confirmation of Feinberg in "Experimentelle Untersuchungen über die Wahrnehmung im Gebiete des blinden Flecks," *ibid.*, pp. 16–43.

formation of a gestalt. The stationary resting figure is merely an end-state of a dynamic process, but it is all that concerns the organism practically. Biologically, this neglect of the preliminary function is of service because a creature's orientation in the visual world would be much disturbed by the unceasing dilation and contraction of the objects in his view!

Constancy Effects in Vision

Gestalt writers have had more than average interest in the phenomena of perceptual "constancy" because their theory seems to offer the most reasonable account of these unusual effects. Perceptual constancy refers to the fact the relative size, color, and brightness or other qualities of an object seem to be maintained under conditions where it must have different physical properties. Hering long ago was puzzled to know what mechanism was responsible for the fact that snow and coal in full sunlight and at dusk preserved their apparent blackness and whiteness, even though the absolute brightness of snow at twilight was less than that reflected by coal at high noon! One can place a grey surface beside a deep black one in such a way that one can see the grey as brighter (despite its presence in diffuse dim roomlight) than the black surface, which, when locally illuminated by a powerful lamp must necessarily be brighter, as can be shown by looking at a *small* section of both surfaces through a darkened tube. An explanation in terms of experience, such as suggested by the hypothesis of "memory-colors" clashes with our knowledge that the attributes of an inner field are functions of the qualities of the surroundings. The suspicion is not unwarranted that cases of "constancy" represent the determination of part-properties by a larger total constellation, i.e., they are conditioned by the coöperation of the environment with the object.

Frank[40] studied the problem of visual constancy of magnitude in young children, who are desirable subjects for this type of investigation, because the empirist holds that this phenomenon is a matter of acquisition. Köhler had shown in his Tenerife

[40] "Untersuchung über Sehgrössenkonstanz bei Kindern," *Psychol. Forsch.*, 1926, *7*, 137–145.

monographs that young chimpanzees behave in accordance with constancy principles, and Frank simply adapted his technique to her subjects. Thirty children, ranging from eleven months to seven years of age, were trained to go to the larger or smaller (depending upon the group) of two boxes: correct choices contained chocolate, fruit, or a toy hidden beneath. In the critical test-situations which followed, the boxes were so placed that the remote larger box cast a much smaller image upon the retina than the nearer small one. In some instances, the retinal image of the larger box had only 1% of the areal size of the smaller. Nevertheless, 23 out of 30 children made no errors on this basis at all and four made but one. Even the little youngsters, who were unable to walk, crawled a good distance to the objectively correct box. With six of the children, a transposition experiment modelled after Köhler's work on brightness discrimination in hens was undertaken. The subjects were trained to go to the larger of two boxes, and in the crucial test a still larger one was introduced. In all instances the results were positive, the choices taking place according to the principle of relative size.

Voigt[41] found that the accuracy of target-aiming is conditioned by a number of special configurational factors. He had his subjects shoot at a milk-glass plate target with a "light pistol," i.e., an instrument for projecting a circular beam of light upon a distant goal. The subjects aimed at the objective under the direct guidance of the motor system without optical control since no fine sighting was permitted. Contrary to ordinary expectations, the angle of error diminished with distance: thus, at 2 meters the mean angular error was 170′; at 4 meters, 158′; at 6 meters, 109′; and at 8 meters, 101′.

The same decrease in angular error occurred when retinal constancy of the target was achieved, i.e., a target 15 cm. in diameter at 3 meters gave a mean error of 104′ while its retinal equivalent of 150 cm. at 30 meters showed an error of only 49′. With the same objective target size at these distances, the errors were 105′ and 60′ respectively, values directly comparable in

[41] "Ueber die Richtungspräzision einer Fernhandlung," *Psychol. Forsch.*, 1931, *16*, 70–113.

magnitude. Evidently, this factor could not be the cause of the reduction.

Believing the crux of the situation to lie in some alteration in the optical structure of the field of action, Voigt set a box directly adjacent to the target on either the right or left edges. The resulting shots were displaced toward the side with which the box was in contact. The errors now clustered around a new center of gravity. Voigt explains his paradoxical reduction in relative error with increasing distance in terms of phenomenal accentuation of the distance element. In the case of the nearby target, the *internal diameter* of the target is emphasized in the subject's experience; with the far target, on the other hand, the *gap* between the marksman and the target is more prominent. The more sharply and strongly this gap is perceived, the greater the accuracy of shooting.

Another related problem was studied by Brown.[42] If I observe a specific objective speed at a distance of two and four meters respectively, then as far as the retinal projections of the moving contours are concerned, unequal retinal extents are traversed in equal times. The objective distance covered in one second is twice as great in the first case as in the second, so that the corresponding "retinal velocity" must also be in the ratio of two to one. Nevertheless, no such discrepancy is perceived (as we all know from watching automobile traffic) and it would seem as though there were a constancy of velocity analogous to the constancy of visual magnitude, of which it may, as a matter of fact, be but a special case.

In Brown's experiment on this topic, he had his subjects adjust the speed of a comparison motor driving an endless paper-band with a dot and other simple geometrical figures with that of a similar standard: the two moving fields were successively compared by being placed at right angles to each other. Despite the fact that the distance of the comparison field from the observer varied from three to ten meters, its adjusted velocity remained approximately constant, i.e., the ratio of the two speeds at different distances approached unity. More important

[42] "Ueber gesehene Geschwindigkeiten," *Psychol. Forsch.*, 1928, *10*, 84–106; also a series of three English papers on the same theme in the same journal, 1931, *14*, 183–268.

than this was Brown's discovery that if a moving field in a homogeneous surrounding field is transposed in its linear relations as 1 :2 the stimulus velocity must be transposed by a like amount in order that the phenomenal velocity in both cases be identical; e.g., if the "constant" figures are twice as large as the "comparison" ones and if the former are also twice as far away from the observer as the latter, the constant speed of the first divided by the mean of the adjusted speeds of the second approaches two (1.92 in the report). This indicates that phenomenal velocities (or movements) are determined in a dynamical *field,* the essential nature of which cannot be described as a sum of independent local events. They correspond to dependent events in the functional whole. "Therefore, the whole structure of the excited field, not the excitation present at any given point within the field, must be considered in order that one understand the physiology of the visual perception of velocity." We can now appreciate why there is little difference between saying, "It moves quickly" and "It takes a short time to get there." Whatever *structural* change alters phenomenal velocity affects phenomenal time by a corresponding amount. The relativity of Einstein and the configurationism of Wertheimer converge at this point.

The uniqueness of the Gestalt explanation of all types of "constancy" is clearly seen in its treatment of the brightness variety. Is it really an illusion if a white tablecloth remains phenomenally bright under yellow illumination? Does our judgment play a trick upon us in this and similar cases? Hardly; for it would be much more of an illusion if we saw the white tablecloth by lamplight as yellow, or the man at the other end of the room as a dwarf! *Prägnanz* affects shape, size, and surface attributes so that the most significant aspects of an object are preserved if the field conditions are not altered too severely; i.e., a "thing" is invariant or transposable just like a melody!

CHAPTER 7

STUDIES IN AUDITION AND THE SKIN SENSES

Experiments in the Perception of Sound

Exhaustive investigations in the field of sound had been continued long enough in Stumpf's day to establish a tradition of specialization for the Berlin laboratory, and it was only natural that when the Gestalt theorists captured this stronghold that they should turn some of their energies in this direction. One of the first fruits of this union of a new theory and excellent, if old, material equipment was a paper by Eberhardt [1] on the phenomenal pitch and intensity of partial tones. Using Lewin's mirror-membrane apparatus for measuring tonal intensities and resonators for "hearing out" partials, she sought to determine whether a partial picked out of a clang could be compared in intensity with a pure individual tone of the same character. When successive pairs were thus presented and judged under conditions of objectively equal strength, in no case did the intensity of the resonator partial exceed 90% of its intensity when isolated, and it often dropped as low as 1%! Apparently the sound context makes any single tone lose in intensity to an extraordinary degree. In addition, Eberhardt was able to make the important demonstration that a partial tone which was too feeble to be heard through the resonator was nevertheless able to influence the timbre of the clang. Any summative theory was bound to be weakened by the discovery of these incontestable facts.

Onoshima [2] performed a distinctive acoustic experiment concerning the influence of temporally adjoining tonal groups upon the judgment of intensity steps. Using an electrically-controlled

[1] "Ueber die phänomenale Höhe und Stärke von Teiltönen," *Psychol. Forsch.*, 1922, *2*, 346–367.

[2] "Ueber die Abhängigkeit akusticher Intensitätsschritte von einem unfassenden Tonverband," *Psychol. Forsch.*, 1928, *11*, 267–289.

hammer, he produced sounds of nine degrees of intensity and presented them to his subjects in symmetrical double pairs separated by a pause, thus *forẽ pair maiñ pair*. Two curious phenomena were observed. If the interval between the fore pair and the main pair was a step in the same direction (up or down) as that represented by the two tones in the fore pair or only weakly reversed, then an adaptation to this trend occurred within the two tones of the main pair, i.e., they also seemed to move up or down the intensity scale; but if the interval between the two pairs was sharply in the counter-direction to that indicated by the gradient between the two members of the first pair, then an opposed movement of the intensities of the main pair occurred. The first effect, however, was the more readily obtained with symmetrical pairs, irrespective of the times elapsing *within* or *between* the pairs; but the second effect was commoner with unsymmetrical time relations. This principle, like so many others of the Gestalt school, is a general sensory property and not peculiar to any modality, since Onoshima obtained analogous results with successive weight pairs in a supplementary study.

Köhler [3] has offered an interesting new version of the process of successive comparison and the time error which usually accompanies it.[4] The familiar phenomenon to which this refers was first noted in the early days of Wundt's laboratory in connection with sound intensities and pressures. According to these results, a slight difference in mass between two successively lifted weights is more readily discriminated if one first "lifts" the objectively lighter one and then the heavier (ascending step) than in the reversed case (descending order). Borak [5] found

[3] "Zur Theorie des Sukzessivvergleichs und der Zeitfehler," *Psychol. Forsch.*, 1923, *4*, 115–175. Lauenstein has extended this theory by showing that the same potential difference found between two immediately adjoining fields is not only the basis for the perception of contours but also necessary for the impression of relations. See his "Ansatz zu einer physiologischen Theorie des Vergleichs und der Zeitfehler," *ibid.*, 1933, *17*, 130–177.

[4] The time error normally occurs only in studies dealing with difference limens. It is perhaps significant that alcohol lowers the absolute and raises the differential threshold, a fact which suggests a functional distinction between the two structures—the one, a figure against a ground, and the other, a part against another part of a figure. See Specht, *Arch. f. d. Ges. Psychol.*, 1907, *9*, 180–295.

[5] "Ueber die Empfindlichkeit für Gewichtsunterschiede bei abnehmender Reizstärke," *Psychol. Forsch.*, 1922, 374–389. The main outlines of Köhler's theory are already implied among the possible explanations of the phenomena considered in Borak's paper. Any experience appears to the percipient as either a continuation of some previous one, on the same level, or as a rise or fall from a level, or as a change in figure within a given level. The reactions are not to "simple" stimuli, but rather to situations which represent "step-

that for any given pair the comparison in the ascending order always yielded more correct judgments (and consequently, a lower limen) than the other arrangement, and that even small descending steps were often interpreted not only as equal but as ascending! If this asymmetry has general neural significance and is not due to peripheral peculiarities, then Köhler argues the phenomenon should be found in *all successive perceptions of intensities.* He rejects a plausible interpretation which claims that all successive comparison is really a simultaneous comparison between a present second impression and a memory image of the first response. This explanation in terms of transitional experiences Köhler maintains is as inadequate as accounting for the essence of noon because it is then that the clock strikes twelve.

Neither is he willing to rest content with the task of description at the expense of explanatory efforts as certain pragmatic specialists would have us do. While some may protest against the spinning of intricate brain theories *ad libitum* because they are referred to a realm where facts elude us, nevertheless it is impossible to preserve all our hypotheses on a purely psychological level. The neural speculations which result from a search for the *raison d'être* of experimental findings are not really fantastic constructions, but if properly developed lead to definite consequences which can be tested by further investigation. Ordinarily, psychological theories have been so timid and indefinite that like the planks of a political platform one can read wellnigh everything into them!

Köhler's specific brain theory is built upon the biological fact that all sensory stimulation makes the excited area of the nervous system electronegative with respect to its environment. During this process positive hydrogen ions are liberated. Now it is probable that the stronger stimulus frees the ions in a greater concentration, producing an increase in the acid reaction and potential difference as contrasted with that of the environment.

---

wise" or differential aspects fundamentally related to figure and ground. Lauenstein (see footnote 3 above) found a *negative* time error when his paired stimuli were presented against a *dark* ground (in Hornbostel's sense) and a *positive* time error if *light* ground was used (relative to the brightness of the "figures"). This fact is in accordance with Lauenstein's theory that the "trace" of the first figural stimulus gradually accommodates itself to the nature of the ground, hence the interesting reversal of effect which can be demonstrated with both light and sound.

This simply means that the effects of the stimulus outlast its actual duration. If the phenomenon of the "time error" is caused by the dynamic transition from a slowly sinking "still picture" of the first excitation (reminiscent of Herbart's "residues" but devoid of their mechanical connotation) to a fresh second excitation, with the result that the gradient "upward" is stronger than the one "downward," then the time error must increase in proportion to the length of the time-interval as long as the "still picture" continues to sink. In other words, the relation of the judgments "higher" and "lower" is a function of the time-interval between the stimuli, a position which is confirmed by the following table with objectively *equal* auditory pairs (Köhler, page 152):

TABLE III. JUDGMENTS OF RELATIVE SOUND INTENSITIES OF PAIRED STIMULI WITH VARYING TIMES ELAPSING BETWEEN THE MEMBERS OF THE PAIRS. EIGHT SUBJECTS. (AFTER KÖHLER.)

[Italicized figures in parentheses represent data obtained from 12 subjects giving ten judgments each in response to repeated pipe-organ notes (from unpublished study by G. W. Hartmann).]

Reports	Intervals			
	1½ (*2*)	3 (*4*)	4½ (*6*)	6 (*8*) seconds
Rising (second-stronger) ..	1 (*43*)	7 (*62*)	13 (*71*)	15 (*88*)
Equal	8 (*62*)	5 (*32*)	5 (*24*)	7 (*16*)
Falling (second-weaker) ..	15 (*15*)	12 (*26*)	6 (*25*)	2 (*16*)
Total	24 (*120*)	24 (*120*)	24 (*120*)	24 (*120*)

Evidently the longer the gap between the two members to be compared, the more "intense" the second one appears to become, a fact known as the "negative" time error. Why? Presumably because the first stimulus changes in some way the electrochemical "level" of the nervous system so that the second stimulus is judged with reference to a wholly different "plane" of sensitivity—a plane which is constantly changing its altitude. Figuratively, the second stimulus leaps from a stool of varying height provided by the first stimulus, which when it appeared had to jump unaided from the floor.

Any perceptual hypothesis in which the time element becomes a central factor inevitably becomes a theory of memory as well.

Köhler saw this clearly in the paper under discussion but refrained from any immediate experimental extension of his position. Because of its peculiarly unifying character the point is important enough to be restated in Wheeler's [6] precise condensation:

> When an external stimulus impinges upon the nervous system, the existing state of the system changes until it is in equilibrium with the force that is acting upon the sense organ. Let another stimulus affect another part of the nervous system and the first approach to an equilibrium will be altered by the change going on toward equilibrium with the second stimulus, and *vice versa*. In this way, the responses to the two stimuli are interdependent and the final outcome depends upon the dynamic relation between the two levels of equilibrium. Second, it is supposed that the approach to equilibrium which commences upon stimulation so alters the concentration of reacting substances in the brain that a process of adjustment must continue after the stimulus is removed. This process of adjustment may determine for a considerable time the direction of changes elicited by subsequent stimuli. But this is after the "conscious" process associated with the first stimulus has disappeared; accordingly, the continuing brain process is called a "non-process condition," because it is not associated with conscious processes. The "non-process condition" is Köhler's substitute for the older concept of trace.

Theoretical attempts to appraise the respective merits of the Gestalt position and that of behaviorism of the conditioned response type have been numerous, but relatively few psychologists have put both to the sort of ingenious test which Humphrey [7] devised. His point of departure was the correct assumption that if Wertheimer's account be valid, then a musical note heard in isolation is a different thing from the same note heard in a musical melody. The technique consisted in drilling nine subjects to react with a withdrawal of the hand to a given note by means of an electric shock simultaneously applied. After "conditioning" had been established, the latency of the reaction was measured and found to be about 400 milliseconds, an interval about equal to the time required for a so-called "discriminative

---

[6] *The Science of Psychology,* New York, 1929, p. 276.

[7] "The Effect of Sequences of Indifferent Stimuli on a Reaction of the Conditioned Response Type," *J. Abn. & Soc. Psychol.*, 1927, *22,* 194–212.

In connection with Humphrey's point, it may be worth recalling that St. Catherine of Genoa at one time of her life vomited all food except that taken as part of the Eucharist!

response." Humphrey's significant discovery was that when presented in *isolation,* practically perfect responses were obtained with a given note; but when played in a *melody* it was in no case followed by a response. He states, "We may then fairly claim to have proved that the inclusion of a tone within a musical unity, such as a melody, scale, or arpeggio (*Home, Sweet Home*) may destroy the response habitually following the same note in isolation."

A defender of the conditioned response principle might reply, however, that Pavlov could easily explain this in terms of the inhibiting effect caused by companion stimuli. But Humphrey showed that these companion stimuli must have a very special kind of organization before they can exert any inhibiting influence, since a supplementary test demonstrated that a non-musical sequence failed to inhibit the response, while a musical one definitely did so.

An even more decisive objection to the usual neurological interpretation of the conditioning process has been made by Gibson and his associates.[8] They wished to see if a conditioned response was really limited to a connection between a fixed and definite type of stimulation and a specific muscle movement or whether there is any transfer or spread of effect to other regions. Using the familiar shock-and-buzzer combination for conditioning adult humans, they found that in 62% of the cases the establishment of a conditioned response of the right middle finger was accompanied by the formation of a similar conditioned response of the corresponding finger of the other hand. With several subjects the conditioned response readily transferred to the index finger of the same hand. Apparently a more inclusive process than that ordinarily alleged to occur takes place when a narrow S-R "bond" is established. The hypothesis seems justified that the conditioned withdrawal to shock involves, or perhaps is in itself, a *generalized* habit of avoiding or withdrawing when the buzzer is heard, which may be evoked from another part of the body than that in which the response was learned.

---

[8] "Bilateral Transfer of the Conditioned Response in the Human Subject," *J. Exp. Psychol.*, 1932, *15*, 416–421.

The Skin Senses

Passing from the auditory field to the cutaneous, we see again how Gestalt principles have revivified this standard type of investigation. Rosenbloom [9] stimulated ten subjects on the same region of the palm five times with the following seven figures—circle, square, triangle, open circle, open square, right angle, open triangle. The instrument applied followed the principle of the cookie-cutter, with pressure effects equalized by a one-pound weight placed on the top of each figure. An identification of the character of the tactual stimulus was demanded. Table IV shows that the number of correct reports was greatest with the triangle and circle and least with the open square. It is interesting to observe that those "figures" which are psychologically (not geometrically!) the simplest are also the ones least subject to confusion with others. The closed patterns are more easily perceived than the open ones; the square seems to be the weakest of the closed figures. A closure effect is noticeable, since the "open" figures are more often perceived as "closed" than the converse, with the open triangle showing the strongest tendency.

TABLE IV. NUMBER OF TIMES CERTAIN FIGURES WERE REPORTED IN RESPONSE TO A GIVEN PATTERN STIMULUS (ROSENBLOOM).

Stimuli	Responses						
	Circle	Square	Triangle	Open Circle	Open Square	Right Triangle	Open Triangle
Circle	40	0	0	4	0	0	0
Square	0	25	3	0	3	0	0
Triangle	0	0	40	0	0	0	1
Open Circle	9	1	0	27	1	0	0
Open Square	0	8	4	4	20	1	1
Right Triangle	0	0	6	2	0	37	0
Open Triangle	0	0	32	1	0	0	3

For decades psychologists have been reared in the belief that the reduction of cutaneous sensitivity from a generalized sense of "touch" to the four discrete properties of pain, cold, warmth,

[9] "Configurational Perception of Tactual Stimuli," *Amer. J. Psychol.*, 1929, *41*, 87–90.

and contact constituted one of the most conspicuous triumphs of the analytical method. The existence of a mosaic of tiny sensory areas in the skin has been unquestioned since the early work of Blix, Goldscheider, and von Frey. Nevertheless, careful researches made during the last decade have thrown doubt upon this convenient and plausible dogma of the punctate distribution of separate receptor systems. No one denies the anatomical existence of special nerve fibers but their functional discreteness has recently been made a matter of debate.

Waterston,[10] a British clinician, seems to have been the first to strengthen a latent suspicion that the assignment of limited functions to certain cell-bodies and corpuscles was purely hypothetical. He believes that the epithelium as a whole is the receptor organ for touch, for when a film of it is preserved in an experimental area the exposed surface is dry and a touch experience can be elicited from it, but when more of the epithelium is removed and the surface is raw and moist, no tactile sensation can be elicited, and only pain is excited by the stimulus. Especially significant is his discovery that the functions of given spots fluctuate considerably.[11] To quote:

> If the point of a fine metal probe cooled to the requisite degree is brought into contact with a cold spot, and the touch repeated again and again at intervals of about a second, at first the contact produces a clear and distinct sensation of cold. After a few contacts, however, the sensation of cold is no longer excited by the stimulus, but that of touch only. The cold sensation may disappear after two or three contacts, or only after some eleven or twelve, and it may disappear and then reappear once or twice and finally disappear. If now the stimulus point be moved slightly to one or other side, the sensation of cold is at once set up from a spot from which before no such sensation was elicited.

It is too early to reach any conclusion as to the degree to which these facts support the Gestalt contention, but the possibility of field conditions regulating the response of a given region has been much increased thereby. In fact, a novel experiment by Madlung[12] ends all doubt as to the reality of such

[10] Reports of the St. Andrews Institute for Clinical Research, Vol. 2, Oxford, 1924, 123–132.

[11] Dallenbach's painstaking and exhaustive experiments on the temperature spots and end-organs shows that the localization varies with the method of "mapping" employed. See *Amer. J. Psychol.*, 1927, *39*, 402–427.

[12] "Ueber anschauliche und funktionelle Nachbarschaft von Tasteindrücken," *Psychol. Forsch.*, 1934, *19*, 193–236.

"field" effects. Von Frey had found that two adjacent contact spots are experienced as closer together when stimulated simultaneously than when touched separately. More particularly, he had observed that an intense second stimulus tended to "suck up" a weaker predecessor, i.e., it exerted something like a gravitational pull toward itself. In this schema, $\underset{1}{\bullet}\ \underset{2}{\bullet}\ \underset{3}{\bullet}$, distance 2-3 may be experienced as smaller than distance 1-2.

Von Frey carried on his investigations with but one arm surface. Madlung used both arms laid parallel so that the fingers of one were near the elbow of the other; this gives two possible positions, dependent upon the relative location of the right or left arm to each other. His contact apparatus made it possible to strike two points or one arm surface and a third on the other. Surprisingly enough, Von Frey's attraction effect was demonstrated to take place from one member to another "through the air." The interspace between the two members is just as "real" a part of the gravitational field as the surfaces of the members themselves. Madlung showed that the attraction diminishes with the physical and phenomenal distance of the stimuli; where the physical or (anatomical) and phenomenal fields diverge, the latter is decisive in determining the character of the experience.

CHAPTER 8

THE UNITY OF THE SENSES

It must be clear now that one of the most interesting consequences of the Gestalt position has been the renewal of experimental activity in the ancient and honorable fields of sensation and perception. Probably most laboratory specialists who believe that a "brass instrument" psychology is the only kind worth developing appreciate the revivifying influence of configurationism which has swept through this division like a gust of fresh wind. Recently, the Gestalt theorists have been surprised to discover that the logic of their own thinking demanded an extension of the viewpoint to the problem of intersensory influences. If local action within any receptor area is undoubtedly affected by processes taking place in the total field, then it would appear plausible that the course of a sensory event in any modality would be conditioned by the character of the transformations simultaneously occurring in *all* the remaining receptors. Although the number of investigations motivated by this theme are still meagre, the prediction is not unwarranted that experiments of the intersensory type may grow with the same extraordinary rapidity that characterized the researches in mental tests during the last two decades. Certainly the present tendency of configurational experimentation seems to be toward extending configurational principles to the various sense modalities, unifying as many different fields as possible, and reducing apparently diverse phenomena, like movement and fusion, spatial extent and movement, form and quality, to more simple underlying configurational processes.

Hornbostel

Hornbostel is the German writer who has most clearly discerned the fundamental import of this question. In a delightful article on "the unity of the senses," he has expounded this doctrine in the charming literary manner of an intuitive philosopher of the romantic era.[1] The tenor of his paper is apt to repel the "he-men" among contemporary psychologists, the very people who owe their own hard-headed techniques to another rhapsodic mystic, Fechner. One beautiful thing about the proponents of Gestalt theories is that their own thought processes exemplify perfectly the principle which they proclaim, viz., that all mental development proceeds from an original vague undifferentiated total (=mysticism?) to well-defined and sharply-bounded patterns (the "clear and simple ideas" of Locke). With this in mind we may listen more sympathetically to Hornbostel's argument.

His first appeal is to philology which suggests that sensory functions have not been fully differentiated (at least conceptually) among primitive groups. Although we all know the sad fate which befell Grant Allen's hypothesis that the Homeric Greeks were color-blind because of the deficient color terminology of the early epics, still it is interesting to note that there is a Negro tribe which has a special word for "seeing," but only a common term to designate "hearing, tasting, smelling, touching." In French, *sentir* means to smell, touch, or feel in general. In modern German and English, "brightness" is a recognized attribute of both lights and sounds. When this relationship is mentioned, many persons maintain that sheer analogy has led to a transfer of meaning from the visual to the auditory realm, but as a matter of fact in Middle High German the sound connotation represented by *hell* (bright) was the exclusive one!

Hornbostel's personal contribution to this problem consists in the development of intersensory equations upon which his claim for the existence of a common supra-sensory factor of "brightness" is based.[2] This is the characteristic shared by most high-pitched tones, "loud" colors, penetrating but pleasant odors, sharp "pointed" tactile stimuli as opposed to dull, blunt surfaces, etc. The strongest evidence in favor of its existence

[1] "Die Einheit der Sinne," *Melos*, 1925, *4*, 290–297. A fuller experimental paper appears in his article, "Ueber Geruchshelligkeit," *Pflügers Archiv.*, 1931, *227*, 517–538.

[2] Köhler suggests that the corresponding psychophysical processes in the visual and auditory cortical areas may be similar in form. See his minor article on Tonpsychologie in Alexander and Marburg's *Handbuch der Neurologie des Ohres*, Vienna, 1923, 419–464. Is there any significance in the fact that most people pronounce "up" with a rising inflection and "down" with a falling (apart from the different vowel qualities of the words)?

is the curious triangular equation easily obtained from large groups of subjects. If one produces upon the color wheel greys resulting from five different proportions of black and white and presents with each a definite tone, there is considerable agreement—with the interesting exception of color-blind observers—that one and only one of the greys has a "brightness value" most like the sound.[3] Unanimity, of course, does not occur but even the most confirmed skeptic is surprised to find the "voting" far more uniform than chance could ever allow. The really startling demonstration, however, appears when one finds that a given odor can similarly be equated with a specific grey, and that this can be indirectly checked by equating the odor with the tone originally used! Things equal to the same thing (in some respect) must be equal to each other (in the same respect). The situation may be clarified by this table and equation, in which the subscript designates the brightness feature:

SENSE	BRIGHT	DARK
Vibratory	smooth	rough
Pressure	hard	soft
Contact	pointed	blunt
Kinesthetic	light	heavy
Temperature	cold	warm
Pain	"sharp"	"dull"
Organic	hunger	satiation
Gustatory	sweet?	bitter
Olfactory	flowery?	burnt?
Visual	"whitish"	"blackish"
Auditory	"high"	"low"

Grey X_b
(41° White + 319° Black)
// \\
Odor Y_b = Tone Z_b
(Benzol) (220 d.v.)

Consequently, there must be something sensory in nature which is not restricted to a single receptor. What has been popularly dubbed the "hearing" of the skin points in the same direction: with the fingertips one can detect which of two vibra-

[3] Among the Berlin *cognoscenti* the story goes that when Hornbostel first had the idea in embryo, he telephoned his friend, the late *Musikwissenschaftler*, Otto Abraham, and inquired what note on the piano corresponded to the odor of violet. When this extraordinary question was answered in the way that Hornbostel expected if the theory were sound, he was almost beside himself with joy.

tion frequencies is the "brighter," even if separated by a full "tone"; similarly, an octave dichord is sensed as consonant by the skin in contrast to a seventh. To Hornbostel, this means that brightness is the most primitive general sensory quality, all other specific attributes being later differentiations. The uniqueness of the eye is color, of the ear, musical quality—hence, being relatively new biological acquisitions they are most readily lost, as all clinical experience testifies.

It is with this special meaning in mind that one may legitimately speak of a transcendental sense-perception. There is no easy way to illustrate this phenomenon in the absence of the appropriate technical terms, but Hornbostel claims that he has distinct conscious states, akin to moods, but more tangible, which are equally well represented by a day in the Black Forest, a picture by Schwind, the works of Möricke, or the seventy-third movement of Wolf's "Foot Journey." The unity of the senses thereby becomes the fundamental reason for the unity of the arts. Perhaps Wagner dimly discerned this truth. At any rate, no one can allege that James stands alone in his endeavor to rehabilitate the "vague" and restore it to its proper psychological rights! Historically, it seems that the Viennese otologist, Urbantschitsch, made the first relevant observations in this field. James (*Principles,* II, p. 29), speaking of his work, says:

> All our sense-organs influence each other's sensations. The hue of patches of color so distant as not to be recognized was immediately perceived by Urbantschitsch's patients when a tuning-fork was sounded close to the ear. . . . The acuity of vision was increased, so that letters too far off to be read could be read when the tuning-fork was heard . . . sounds which were on the limits of audibility became audible when lights of various colors were exhibited to the eye. Smell, taste, touch, sense of temperature, etc., were all found to fluctuate when lights were seen and sounds were heard.

Possibly Weber's observation that a thaler laid on the skin of the forehead feels heavier when cold than warm represents an even earlier recognition of the existence of "convergent" stimulation. Indeed, the existence of this entire problem is a good example of the need for re-discovering old facts because at the time of the original researches the appropriate theoretical background for interpreting and assimilating them was missing.

If what we "see" is literally influenced by what we are hearing, touching, smelling, etc., it must be equally obvious that what we "hear" is similarly conditioned by what we see. A number of observations support this view. In 1669, the distinguished Copenhagen anatomist, Thomasius Bartholinus, announced that partially deaf individuals could hear better in the light than in the dark; improved hearing occurred even by the dim light of a candle. Otologists have long noted that the auditory perception of hard-of-hearing patients fluctuates with the weather—it tends to be better on bright warm days and poorer on raw and cloudy days. More recently, the Moscow biophysicist, Lazareff, has popularized the following simple demonstration: Strike a piano key with the pedal depressed and while the tone lasts, silently switch an electric light bulb on and off; one hears in the same rhythm the swelling and fading of the tonal intensity! If the eyes are closed or covered, the effect fails to occur. The discrimination of both pitch and intensity differences also undergoes a slight but consistent improvement under conditions of brilliant total illumination.

On the basis of these and other similar studies, the following tentative generalization has emerged: A simultaneous auxiliary heteromodal stimulus *augments* the main stimulus when the former is in the *background,* but it acts in an *inhibiting* way when it is *focal.* As *figure,* the auxiliary stimulus *diminishes* sensitivity in accordance with conventional expectations of the results of distraction, but it *increases* it as *ground* (when the main stimulus assumes the rôle of "figure"). The generalization readily harmonizes with Heymans' law (known since 1899), if we revise the latter to read: A more intense sensation (=figure) exerts an inhibitory action on a less intense one (=ground), the effect being proportional to the strength of the inhibitor.

Further Evidence of Intersensory Relations

The experimental possibilities of this far-reaching doctrine have only slowly begun to be appreciated by the rank-and-file of psychologists. Goldstein and Rosenthal-Veit,[4] who appear to have been among the first to follow out its implications in auditory localization under multi-sensory stimulation, found that a sound can be displaced toward the right from a subjective center by an eye movement toward the left, even though the head be kept stationary. More recently, the Russian scientist Kravkov [5] has unearthed new evidence of inter-sensory relationships which were formerly thought to be restricted to the oral cavity with its union of olfactory and gustatory elements. Using a telephone tied up with a low frequency cathode tube generator, Kravkov found that a tone of 2,100 vibrations per second increased the visual acuity of nine out of ten subjects tested with black figures on a white ground. This phenomenon was confirmed by the present writer for both high and low auxiliary sound stimuli, but even more astounding was the fact that simultaneous olfactory, tactual, and pain stimuli appeared to have equivalent effects in temporarily improving visual acuity.[6]

Zietz,[7] in a paper on the reciprocal influences of tonal and color experiences reports that an auxiliary sound exerted a powerful influence upon the course of an after-image, causing it to flicker when the tone "vibrated" intermittently, and extinguishing the image when it ceased. When the auxiliary tone had a vibration number of 200, the color became darker, warmer, softer, duller; the contours also tended to vanish.[8] With a tone of 550, the same color became brighter, colder, clearer, harder; and the contours were sharper. Occasionally, under the influence of a high tone (1,100 vibrations) a rounded after-image took on a squarish form! As far as the reversal of effect was concerned, it appeared that a tone sounded in a lighted room was judged higher than one acting in the dark.

---

[4] "Ueber akustische Lokalisation und deren Beeinflussbarkeit durch andere Sinnesreize," *Psychol. Forsch.*, 1926, *8*, 318–335.

[5] "Ueber die Abhängigkeit der Sehschärfe vom Schallreiz," *Arch. f. Ophthalmologie*, 1930, *124*, 334–338.

[6] G. W. Hartmann, "Changes in Visual Acuity through Simultaneous Stimulation of Other Sense Organs," *J. Exp. Psychol.*, 1933, *16*, 393–407; also "The Facilitating Effect of Strong General Illumination upon the Discrimination of Pitch and Intensity Differences," *ibid.*, 1934, *17*, 813–822.

[7] "Gegenseitige Beeinflussung von Farb-und Tonerlebnissen," *Zeitsch. f. Psychol.*, 1931, *121*, 257–356.

[8] Several years earlier, Noll had called attention to the exquisite obedience which after-images yield to Gestalt laws; e.g., the blurred contour of an after-image as it fades away is very easily drawn magnet-like within the sharply outlined boundaries of a simple gestalt should the image be projected somewhat eccentrically thereto. Cf. the rest of his interesting article on "Versuche über Nachbilder," *Psychol. Forsch.*, 1926, *8*, 3–27.

Von Schiller,[9] working in a similar situation involving "heteromodal" stimulation, found that "pulsation" or "coarseness" may be considered along with Hornbostel's "brightness" as another universal intersensory moment. Using the threshold of fusion with black-white discs as his "base," he found that beats from an auditory source strengthen and emphasize the flicker effect, while dichords in firsts and fifths (as well as the simultaneous finger "feeling" or exploration of smooth cardboard) minimize it. The prominence of the flicker increased as the beats rose from 4 to 12 per second, but at 20 a better fusion occurred. Although von Schiller finds ample evidence for mutual influences, the conditions most favorable for "intersensory induction," as we may term the general phenomenon, are provided when the "induced" experience is a sense-perception with an objective reference and the "inducing" event something affecting the entire subjective state of the organism;—the former, moreover, will have a figure-character and the latter a ground-character where optimal results are obtained.

A study of Usnadze[10] on the psychological basis for conferring certain names upon certain objects fits in very nicely with Hornbostel's view of a common sensory element in both auditory and visual experience. This author exposed six meaningless drawings to his subjects for about five seconds each with instructions to avoid any associations with familiar objects, and then had them select the most appropriate nonsense sound for each picture from a suggested list of 42 syllables. Each sound had an equal chance of being chosen, but as a matter of fact only 29 or 68% were selected, the remaining 32% simply not being considered. The degree of agreement among the subjects with respect to the matching of sound and picture was far greater than sheer probability would ever permit. According to Usnadze, this implies that there must be some equivalence of impression among the two members to be thus united. The modified onomatopoetic theory of language formation of which

[9] "Das optische Verschmelzen in seiner Abhängigkeit von heteromodaler Reizung," *Zeitsch. f. Psychol.*, 1932, *125*, 249–288. Schiller also found that motor performances were affected by sensory field conditions. In pouring water from one receptacle to another, 16% less spilling occurred when high tones were given than when lower ones accompanied the task. See his "Wirkung des Umfeldes auf motorische Leistungen," *Zsch. f. Psychol.*, 1934, *132*, 83–103.

[10] "Ein experimenteller Beitrag zum Problem der psychologischen Grundlagen der Namengebung," *Psychol. Forsch.*, 1924, *5*, 24–43.

this gives a hint is of more than passing interest: all vocal and verbal complexes possess a specific *Gestaltqualität* which fits them to become the designation of those objective visual forms which they most closely resemble in organization and emotional congruency. Conversely, if a given sound is to be pictorially represented, certain forms are recognized as fitting and others are not.

Certain hitherto incomprehensible facts now find an understandable niche in this portion of the Gestalt structure. Travis [11] noted that auditory acuity seemed to be lowered during the performance of certain mental tasks, such as solving problems, reading and memorizing—a result which was bound to puzzle those who had to work with the prevailing theories of attention and distraction. Laird [12] and his pupils reported that subjects estimate the quality of four identical commercial products higher if a faint agreeable odor—of which the observers remain ignorant—is fused with the other sensory impressions necessary for inspection.

Benussi [13] had noted that if three light points in a dark room were arranged in a straight line and the points successively illuminated, the apparent magnitudes of the two distances involved become functions of the corresponding time-intervals, i.e., the shorter the interval between the two exposures, the shorter the phenomenal distance. Working with telephonic stimuli, Kester [14] was able to secure a similar kind of "sound movement," analogous to Wertheimer's phi-phenomenon in that two sounds successively emitted from different places produced the effect of the same sound jumping from one place to another. Here, too, the shorter the time elapsing between the sounds, the shorter the apparent distance through which they "moved." This relativity and interdependence [15] of our percepts can be made plain

[11] "Changes in Auditory Acuity during the Performance of Certain Mental Tasks," *Amer. J. Psychol.*, 1926, *37*, 139–142.

[12] "How the Consumer Estimates Quality by Subconscious Sensory Impressions," *J. Applied Psychol.*, 1932, *16*, 241–246.

[13] *Psychologie der Zeitauffassung*, 1913.

[14] "Ueber Lokalisation und Bewegungserscheinungen bei Geräuschpaaren," *Psychol. Forsch.*, 1926, *8*, 75–113.

[15] "We of this generation are involved in Mid-Victorian physical thought, which separates time from space and thus tends to think of a situation as primarily a spatial complex; whereas modern physics makes no fundamental difference between the space and the time coördinates." George Humphrey, "Learning and the Living System," *Psychol. Rev.*, 1930, *37*, 497–510.

to any one by the following simple demonstration: Have a friend mark off three equidistant points on your bare forearm. Then, while you keep your gaze averted, have him tap each point in succession with the tip of his index finger, alternating a rapid and a slow movement, while you try to estimate which distance in each pair was greater. The Benussi phenomenon is thus easily observed on the cutaneous level, for the slow motion yields an impression of greater distances, whereas the same gap quickly traversed seems shorter. With naïve subjects, the variations in estimates are more pronounced. Much of this is common observation, but the advantage of a new theory is that isolated facts may now be intelligibly interconnected.

The numerous experimental possibilities of this single idea which inevitably suggest themselves to the most amateurish beginner are a tribute to the fruitfulness of the underlying theory.

Mogensen and English[16] performed an odd little experiment on the apparent warmth of colors which seems to fall within the Hornbostel schema. They made what some unsympathetic observers might consider an almost laughable attempt to see whether conventionally "warm" colors like red and yellow would lower the threshold for heat sensitivity; conversely, "cool" colors like blue and green were expected to raise it. Using a slightly modified method of paired comparison, they presented six saturated colors wrapped smoothly about two slide rheostats which were kept at a constant temperature of 42° C. The subjects simultaneously grasped both cylinders for one second while looking at them and making judgments of relative warmth. Strangely enough, the highest "warmth values" were ascribed to green and blue, while red had a surprisingly low position. The authors reached the conclusion that the apparent warmth of colors is insufficiently intrinsic to enter into the total configuration in such a way as to modify the judgments of tactual warmth.

To this attractive paper with its curious conclusion, Metzger,[17] a former assistant of Köhler, took violent exception. He

[16] See *Amer. J. Psychol.*, 1926, *37*, 427–428.

[17] "Certain Implications in the Concept of Gestalt," *Amer. J. Psychol.*, 1928, *40*, 162–166.

claimed that the experimenters made a technical and terminological error in supposing that the attributes of a whole could be found by adding the attributes of its parts. The visual and tactual warmth of the papers would have been in *configuration* in any case (in such a relative situation and proportion of extent in space or time as can be stated in geometrical terms, such as being close together, one surrounded by the other, and the like). But visual and tactual warmth are in a *gestalt* [18] only if a greater or lesser mutual modification is possible. To make a successful study out of the idea under discussion, it would be necessary to take the entire field into consideration by placing the observer within the center of a room and then seeing if a shift in color will balance a temperature increment or decrement. To date, no one has followed up this interesting suggestion.

Werner's Sensation-Stages

Werner,[19] a pupil and colleague of Stern at Hamburg, and consequently committed to a personalistic version of the Gestalt problem, is just as strongly convinced of the scientific and metaphysical significance [20] of the "unity of the senses" as Hornbostel is. In a less rhapsodic but equally persuasive vein, he has directed a series of experiments during the last decade which point definitely to synaesthesia of all forms as the original type of sensory functioning and support the view that the restriction of stimulation to a single modality is simply a limiting case. For instance, if one projects motion picture film so slowly that no motion can be seen, movement appears at once if one simultaneously presents corresponding acoustic rhythms; apparently, the dynamics of the bodily sensation-sphere, which was too weak to be propagated by purely optical stimulation, was supported by the dynamic consequences of acoustic excitation.

---

[18] It is doubtful if most English-speaking psychologists make this distinction or even consider it a desirable one to introduce. The words are used interchangeably in this volume. Both configuration and gestalt have come to include not only the *spatial configuration*, but also any and all factors which may change the experience, such as the time between the stimuli, the spatial distance, the intensity, and whatever else affects the phenomenal result: in other words, if the terms are not to be identified with the total situation, at least they mean very much the same as the total *effective* situation.

[19] "Das Problem der Empfindens und die Methoden seiner experimentellen Prüfung," *Zsch. f. Psychol.*, 1930, *114*, 152–166.

[20] Herder, the great German writer of the eighteenth century, evidently held the same view on semi-mystical grounds.

Apparent visual movement of the phi-phenomenon type either ceases or is completely deranged when presented in conjunction with irregular, unrhythmical beats from a sound source. Just as the constancy-hypothesis fails *within* any sensory area, so it fails to apply even to the isolated modality as a whole. It is the entire organism which responds and not just one of its structures.

Werner claims that all forms of sensation pass through four stages. In the first stage, when a tone is struck upon the piano, the sound is localized externally and has a purely objective character; in the case of a color, this stage is represented by the surface hue of a familiar article. In the second stage, the tone seems to lose its moorings and becomes a property of the total surrounding space; the visual analogies are the atmospheric colors of Katz. During the third stage, a significant transformation occurs and the object and the self are no longer distinguishable—both tone and color have entered *into* the percipient. He is the sounding vessel and the observer himself is filled with color. In the fourth stage, the ego itself recedes and there remains only the experience of a condition of bodily sensibility.

The report is also made that with certain observers the reverse sequence can be demonstrated, thus confirming the discreteness of these stages. A person experiencing blue, e.g., in all its totality finds himself in a general physical condition which is noticeably different from that involved in reacting to any other color. If one presents tachistoscopically certain words, such as "warm," the bodily sensation of something warm is occasionally experienced before the word is optically read or articulated, indicating that total organismic responses are possible even on the symbolic level. Premonitory stages before final clear perception occurs usually class the stimulus-word in its proper "species" or grammatical category; e.g., even though the subjects have an unclear view of the word, they "feel" it to be an adjective, verb, etc.

CHAPTER 9

MEMORY PROCESSES

Wulf's Experiment and Its American Extensions

The most characteristic memory experiment of the Gestalt school comes from the hands of Wulf.[1] His point of departure was G. E. Müller's "principle of convergence," which simply stated that with decreasing clearness memory images tend to lose their sharp outlines. The experimental procedure consisted in presenting samples of relatively simple line drawings to the subjects and requesting re-drawn reproductions after various intervals. These reproductions were then compared with the original specimens to see if the special figural peculiarities were *preserved, weakened,* or *strengthened;* the corresponding processes producing these effects may be called in order *conservation, levelling,* and *precision* (occasionally also termed *normalization* or *accentuation*), these last three all being manifestations of the general principle of *Prägnanz,* or "essentiality."

Contrary to Müller, Wulf finds that changes in the direction of indefiniteness are not the only shifts undergone by the visual image. For example, the original saw-tooth pattern in Figure 25 is changed during the interval so that sharper points in the angles result; similarly, the two arcs are made more regular and uniform by being construed as equivalent parts of concentric circles. The "normalizing" process seems to act in such a way that a familiar pattern ultimately forces its own shape upon the original so that a different reproduction is given.[2] The common feature in all cases is a change in the direction of a "better

[1] "Ueber die Veränderung von Vorstellungen," *Psychol. Forsch.*, 1922, *1*, 333–373.

[2] Meyer had earlier noted that a figure often approached in appearance the auxiliary memory aid more than the actually seen original; see *Zeitschr. f. Psychol.*, 1913. The after-image studies of Frank and Rotschild are also of pertinence here (see the chapter on visual phenomena).

gestalt." In perception, that which is phenomenally observed is subject to the general law of *Prägnanz,* which holds that every gestalt tends to become as good as possible, i.e., definite, pronounced forms are preferred in both nature and experience. In memory, the "engram" is still under the influence of this principle and any transformations it suffers must be accounted for in such terms.

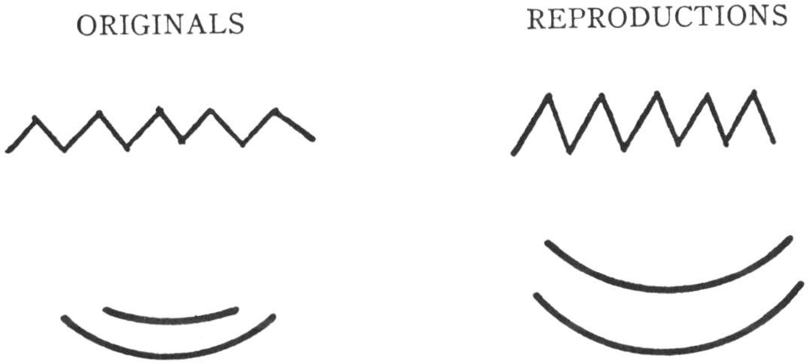

Figure 25. Wulf's Memory Figures

The items at the left represent the initial impressions, those at the right the delayed reproductions. Note the more marked "angularity" and "curvilinearity" in the latter drawing.

From this study emerges the generalization that *all* configurations change through accentuation or leveling of parts. Thus, in the field of sensation, visual contrast is a configurative change through membering of parts, while adaptation is a change involving leveling of parts.

Wulf's work has been provocative enough to call forth four different efforts to confirm his major thesis, viz., those of Gibson, Allport, Perkins, and Carmichael and his pupils. All of these experimenters appear to have been impressed by Wulf's remark that in some instances his subjects spontaneously identified the presented forms with different phenomenal objects. This identification involves the *linguistic* naming of the objects, and this naming appears to have been important in the production of the reproduced forms. Hence, it is little surprise that

Gibson[3] finds language association adequate to explain Wulf's results and his own, i.e., the nature of a change found in the reproduction depends upon the manner in which the figure was apprehended, e.g., as "irregular" or "Gothic" in appearance. This verbal label would suffice to produce changes in the engram without an appeal to the uncertain principle of *Prägnanz.*

Allport[4] made an elaborate investigation of the reproductions of two drawings (a simple Greek key pattern and a truncated pyramid) secured immediately, after two weeks, and after four months, from 350 pre-pubertal school children. He found definite evidence of the "self-distributing" nature of the deterioration since the change tends to persist in the same direction in which it starts. A reduction in size with time also occurs, but the shrinkage is confined to a certain range in the absolute size of the stimulus. Above all, "there can be no escape from the conclusion that one of the properties of the trace is for it to retain or to acquire symmetry." While Allport is just as dissatisfied as Gibson with the vagueness of the so-called law of *Prägnanz,* he does incline to accept the principle of the dynamical properties of the engram or trace as the most fruitful hypothesis for dealing with the decay of the memory image.

On the grounds of parsimony (or at least tradition) it should perhaps, wherever possible, be conceded that perceptual set, associative context, various influences of habit, etc., modify and change the nature of the image and the reproductions. But in the present investigation there seem to be several findings that offer grave difficulty to any associational explanation: the persistence of change in the direction in which it starts, the spontaneous commencement of a change after a lapse of time, the equalizing of strips and the changing of the rectangle to a square, the preservation of the old, or the achievement of a new, symmetry in the position of the loops, the retention of an impression of two, the frequency of displacements, the continuous shrinkage of the image, the rigidity of the rectilinear form, the continuity or cohesion in each of the figures, the relative lack of elaboration, and the tendency toward simplification. Still another feature, too subjective to sustain much weight, and yet important, is the fact that the recognizability of a design often remained even though every portion of it was incorrectly reproduced. (*Op. cit.,* p. 147.)

---

[3] "The Reproduction of Visually Perceived Forms," *J. Exp. Psychol.,* 1929, *12,* 1–39.

[4] "Change and Decay in the Visual Memory Image," *Brit. J. Psychol.,* 1930, *21:* 133–148.

An attractive variation of this theme is involved in a neat experiment performed by Carmichael[5] and his colleagues. They presented the same visual figure tachistoscopically to all their subjects, but before the exposure one list of names was read to one group and another list to a second group. A small control group was used to whom the forms were presented without the assignment of any name. In about three-fourths of those reproductions which deviated most from the original presentation, the figure appeared more like the object represented by the concomitantly given word, irrespective of the group concerned. While the authors prefer a description of the outcome in terms of a "dynamically considered process of association" it is clear that the following passage is not far removed from a configurational account and could readily be assimilated to it:

It seems that if a subject has just heard, e. g., the word "eyeglass," certain processes in his organism have been started that initiate other processes which are possible because of the past experience of that individual with *eye glasses* as words and as objects. If, while these processes are in progress, a figure of two visual circles connected by a line is presented to the subject, this figure may later be reproduced in a different manner than if the processes present in the individual at the time of the same visual presentation had been evoked by the word "dumbbell." In other words, without recourse to any elaborate theory, one who wishes to make an empirical statement of fact may say: If a verbal stimulus form and a visual stimulus form are presented to a subject in certain temporal relationships, the processes in question may be modified, or rather a new total process may result, which is in certain respects unlike either of the previous sets of processes. On subsequent arousal by any "part" stimulus the "reproduction" is thus a complexly determined total, and not either of its component processes. (*Op cit.*, p. 86.)

Perkins' experiment[6] is an enthusiastic acceptance of Wulf's main thesis. He presented to 150 subjects five simple nonsymmetrical geometrical figures, such as a disjointed "B" or "8." A change toward bilateral symmetry or proportionate relations between parts was the most conspicuous transformation found in periods of recall extending over fifty days. The greatest change toward standardization and simplification occurred

[5] "An Experimental Study of the Effect of Language on the Reproduction of Visually Perceived Form," *J. Exp. Psychol.*, 1932, *15*, 73–86.
[6] "Symmetry in Visual Recall," *Amer. J. Psychol.*, 1932, *44*, 473–490.

within the first ten days following the impression, but the drift toward maximum "balance" was still noticeable even after seven weeks.

Inadequacy of Associationism

At the bottom of all standard experiments and interpretations dealing with memory lies the concept of association. This doctrine, to be sure, has been protean in its manifestations, but even the most radical version has clung to contiguity in experience as an explanatory guide. In a long and unusually detailed monograph, Lewin [7] has assembled the evidence which constitutes the Gestalt refutation of this principle. He repeated Ach's famous experiment on the "associative equivalent of the will," in which the latter had his subjects overlearn certain paired associates such as *miv-jek,* and then later presented them with the first member (*miv*), with instructions to find a rhyming syllable such as *tiv.* This task was relatively easy when only a few repetitions were involved, but practically impossible with a hundred repetitions when failures to obey directions and relapses toward the old associates (i.e., the second members) invariably occurred. The will to rhyme, then, had a strength equal to 75 repetitions if below that there were no failures and beyond it no successes. These various intentions to perform certain tasks, such as rhyming, reversing, etc., Ach called "determining tendencies."

Lewin challenged this conception. Historically, the determining tendency was an outgrowth of Külpe's interest in imageless thought, the admission of which, as G. E. Müller pointed out, did not involve a rejection of associationism, because this mechanism applies only to behavior under given conditions. Lewin, however, considers the difference between imaginal and imageless thought an unimportant one, since there are many fluid transitional states between them, and views the "determining tendency" as a superfluous effort to patch a crumbling edifice like the Ptolemaic epicyclical theories.

In one of his sub-experiments on this topic, Lewin secured 270 repetitions of a nonsense syllable list so that it was learned

---

[7] "Das Problem der Willensmessung und das Grundgesetz der Assoziation," *Psychol. Forsch.,* 1922, *1,* 191–302; and 1922, *2,* 65–140.

to the saturation point within a period of fifteen days. In the later test series, a heterogeneous activity was introduced, consisting in *reversing* the syllable (*mut-tum*) and pronouncing it. In order to compare the resulting inhibiting effect,[8] a *neutral* series was also presented: these neutral syllables were not brand new, because unfamiliarity would probably have had a slowing-up effect, but they had been learned previously, except that on this occasion they appeared in a different sequence. Table V gives the comparison in terms of average reaction-times in milliseconds of each subject.

TABLE V. MEAN REACTION-TIMES OF SUBJECTS IN PERFORMING TASKS INVOLVING PAIRED ASSOCIATES (LEWIN).

	Neutral Syllables	Reversed Syllables	Difference
Median	581	602	21
A.M.	602	632	30
M.V.	49	71	
n	16	15	

Clearly, the preceding 270 associations failed completely to inhibit the "intent to reverse," as measured by the speed or accuracy of the responses. The inadequacy of the associationist explanation of reproduction was even more dramatically revealed by a comparison of the reaction times for three series, the first of which involved rhyming repeated with an X frequency, the second the same task, but with one-half $\left(\frac{X}{2}\right)$ that amount of practice, and the third an alternation on the odd and even items of different acts. In all instances, the obtained differences were of vanishing magnitude, indicating that the activities were on the same footing so far as ease of reproduction or execution was concerned.

[8] The neurology of inhibition remains a profound puzzle. Configurationists seemingly dislike the concept, for Dahl, who found that recognition of nonsense syllables was consistently 10% better if a sleeping rather than a waking interval intervened, rejects an explanation in terms of retroactive inhibition, claiming that this has never been demonstrated with recognition, whatever the facts in the case of reproductive recall may be. See his paper, "Ueber den Einfluss des Schlafens auf das Wiedererkennen," *Psychol. Forsch.*, 1928, *11*, 290–301.

Apparently the syllables simply serve as activating stimuli for a specific "readiness for performance." *No reproduction occurs without the attitudinal direction being one of reproducing.* The task itself is the important thing and the fact that certain items have been connected with one task in the past has little or no effect upon what will take place when they are joined with another task later on. The "task" may be considered as the larger "action-total" to which all part-performances are subsidiary, and there is reason for believing that genetically the whole performance is not the product of a chain-like union of minor acts, but that the mastery of the total appears earlier than the control of separate divisions. That this general adjustment of the organism must be more influential than the effects of serial activity is clear from Kühn's finding [9] that *attentively* reading the same syllable list without the intention of learning yielded no mastery of the material, and Hornbostel's confession that he had reached for cigarettes in a definite vest pocket 150,000 times, but when he wore another vest in which the tobacco pocket was in a different place, he made perhaps one failure at the start—but no more! Some larger organization must determine what shall happen to individual combinations previously established. As soon as this is appreciated, one's faith in associationism is dead.

The major defect of associationism was its implicit assumption that two things or processes can interact quite independently of their properties, an assumption which is contradicted by the data of every other natural science. In chemistry the intensity of the reaction or the failure of it to occur is determined by the relation of the properties of the atoms in any given case. In electricity the occurrence of attraction or repulsion depends upon the nature of the electric charges. And, of course, in astronomy, acceleration is conditioned by the masses of two or more bodies moving interdependently.

[9] "Ueber Einprägen durch Lesen und Rezitieren," *Zeitschrift f. Psychol.*, 1914, *68*, 396 ff. There are plenty of non-experimental observations which support this view. For example, familiar objects are certainly thoroughly associated with their names, yet when we walk along a street and attend successively to many well-known things, we are far from reproducing their names.

CHAPTER 10

LEARNING: DATA AND INTERPRETATIONS

Despite the extraordinary fruitfulness of Gestalt theories in many areas of psychological interest, they do not constitute at present a well-rounded and finished system of ideas. Common characteristics are found, to be sure, in the numerous explanations of varied mental phenomena, but the interpretative principles can hardly be considered fixed. This is probably inevitable in a young and growing movement and perhaps even desirable from the standpoint of rapid scientific advance, but it is a circumstance which helps account for the many *ad hoc* and purely suggestive views of configurationism. All fields of psychology to which the new school has directed its efforts exhibit this situation, but none to a less satisfactory extent—at least from the standpoint of the impartial critic—than the domain of learning. Nevertheless, the learning experiments with both animal and human subjects which the Gestalt position has inspired are usually unique and interesting on the theoretical side even to the most unconvinced skeptic, and a consideration of the more prominent and representative of these studies must now be undertaken.

The Anthropoid Studies

While marooned in Tenerife as a result of the World War, Köhler was able to make some very important observations of chimpanzee behavior at the Anthropoid Station established there by the Prussian Academy of Sciences. Disbelieving the low estimates of animal intelligence which the work of Thorndike and the American school in general had encouraged, he prepared different types of problems for solution which have now come to be known as *Umweg* or detour situations. These experiments were first reported in a monograph of the Berlin

Academy[1] for the year 1917, and are all characterized by a situation set up by the experimenter in which the direct path to the objective is blocked but a roundabout way left open, so that the animal must often go further away from his goal in order ultimately to attain it.[2] Sometimes this involved merely a detour around an obstacle,[3] or the use of implements such as sticks, ropes, etc., but in every instance all the general conditions needed for the solution were completely visible. All the experiments were qualitative in form, but executed with such high ingenuity that important evidence against the standard trial-and-error formula was established. Perhaps the best-known and most illuminating of all these observations is described in the following excerpt:

> Are two sticks ever combined so as to become technically useful? . . . Sultan's sticks are two hollow, but firm, bamboo rods, such as the animals often use for pulling along fruit. The one is so much smaller than the other that it can be pushed in at either end quite easily. Beyond the bars lies the objective (a banana), just so far away that the animal cannot reach it with either rod. They are about the same length. Nevertheless, he takes great pains to try to reach it with one stick or the other, even pushing his right shoulder through the bars (of the cage). When everything proves futile, Sultan commits a "bad error." . . . He pulls a box from the back of the room towards the bars; true, he pushes it away again at once as it is useless. . . . Immediately afterwards, he does something which, although practically useless, must be counted among the "good errors": he pushes one of the sticks out as far as it will go, then takes the second, and with it pokes the first one cautiously towards the objective, pushing it carefully from the nearer end and thus slowly urging it towards the fruit. This does not always succeed, but if he has got pretty close in this way, he takes even greater precaution; he pushes very gently, watches the movements of the stick that is lying on the ground, and actually touches the objective with its tip. Thus, all of a sudden, for the first time, the contact "animal-

---

[1] "Intelligenzprüfung an Anthropoiden," *Abhandlungen d. k. preuss. Akad. d. Wissenschaften*, 1917, I. Also in modified book form as *Intelligenzprüfungen an Menschenaffen, Berlin*, 1921. The English translation entitled *The Mentality of Apes* appeared in 1925, from which my own citations are taken.

[2] The difficulties some children encounter in learning to sit down is a case in point. In order to do this the child must abandon his customary straightforward orientation and turn his back upon the objective before he can attain it! (Lewin)

[3] Adams has made this fact the crux of his interesting "restatement of the problem of learning." If there is no *obstruction* in the field learning cannot occur because the creature's need is satisfied with maximal potential parsimony at once. By "parsimony" is meant the belief that animals approach a needed object or state of affairs by the shortest route or most economical means functionally possible. This is presumably a feature of all living behavior, for Adams suggests that some interesting *Umweg* experiments might be made with potato sprouts in cellars.—See *Brit. J. Psychol.*, 1931, *22*, 150–178.

objective" has been established, and Sultan visibly feels (we humans can sympathize) a certain satisfaction in having even so much power over the fruit that he can touch and slightly move it by pushing the stick. The proceeding is repeated; when the animal has pushed the stick on the ground so far out that he cannot possibly get it back by himself, it is given back to him. But although, in trying to steer it cautiously, he puts the stick in his hand exactly to the cut (i. e., the opening) of the stick on the ground, and although one might think that doing so would suggest the possibility of pushing one stick into the other, there is no indication whatever of such a practically valuable solution. Finally, the observer gives the animal some help by putting one finger into the opening of one stick under the animal's nose (without pointing to the other stick at all). This has no effect; Sultan, as before, pushes one stick with the other towards the objective, and as this pseudo-solution does not satisfy him any longer, he abandons his efforts altogether, and does not even pick up the sticks when they are both again thrown through the bars to him. The experiment has lasted over an hour, and is stopped for the present, as it seems hopeless, carried out like this. As we intend to take it up again after a while, Sultan is left in possession of his sticks; the keeper is left there to watch him.

Keeper's report: Sultan first of all squats indifferently on the box, which has been left standing a little back from the railings; then he gets up, picks up the two sticks, sits down again on the box and plays carelessly with them. While doing this, it happens that he finds himself holding one rod in either hand in such a way that they lie in a straight line; he pushes the thinner one a little way into the opening of the thicker, jumps up and is already on the run towards the railings, to which he has up to now half turned his back, and begins to draw a banana towards him with the double stick. I call the master: meanwhile, one of the animal's rods has fallen out of the other, as he has pushed one of them only a little way into the other; whereupon he connects them again.

Sticks were necessary implements to the apes in these experiments, since they were universally employed to pull in fruit. If sticks were unavailable, substitute "tools" were readily used. Thus, one ape pushed a blanket between the bars of the cage, flapped at the fruit a few feet away, and succeeded in beating it toward her. If the banana rolled on to the tip of the blanket, the procedure was instantly altered, and the blanket with the banana was drawn very gently toward the bars. Is this to be explained as learning through trial-and-error? Hardly, since the delicate adaptation occurred the first time it was needed. When the chimpanzee learned to use a stick in bringing in food, he came also to appreciate its functional or instrumental value in relation to his goals. Under certain conditions, a piece of wire, a blanket, an old straw hat, etc., may possess the same properties as tools and be used as substitutes. Climbing upon the shoulders of a human when a box was absent in order to reach an object out of convenient distance is another illustration of the chimpanzee's direct perception of significant spatial relations. A definite "transfer of training" appears to take place, since the essential relational features perceived in the first instance are present in later cases, even though the parts are all new.

On the basis of this and numerous other brilliant concrete observations, Köhler maintains that the processes of thinking and learning have been very much misinterpreted. According to the prevailing trial-and-error hypothesis, the succession of movements which leads to a solution is "as accidental as the winning numbers in a roulette." The parts of the finished act are put together in a purely external way without any "necessary" connection between them. To this Köhler opposes his version of learning by *insight*. "We can, from our own experience, distinguish sharply between the kind of conduct which from the very beginning arises out of a consideration of the characteristics of a situation, and one that does not. Only in the former cases do we speak of insight, and only that behavior of animals definitely appears to us intelligent which takes account from the beginning of the lie of the land, and proceeds to deal with it in a smooth, continuous course. Hence follows this characteristic: *to set up as the criterion of insight the appearance of a complete solution with reference to the whole lay-out of the field*" (Köhler, p. 198).

All the actions of animals in solving problems appear as unitary wholes and result directly from a visual survey of the situation. This conclusion is flatly opposed to the "chance" theory which maintains that the first smooth and correct execution of a relatively complex act is always the result of frequent repetition of the "component parts" which are put together through sheer "accident." According to this view, the apes' ability to use packing boxes as footstools required more or less extensive preliminary "practice." To this Köhler retorts that the ape would not even have made the first move toward the box unless it appreciated (i.e., had "insight") its possible function in helping reach a banana suspended overhead. Even the simple "imitation" of the child requires some understanding of the necessary inner relations of the action imitated before it can be done, and is far from being a purely fortuitous and mechanical affair.

Along with this novel interpretation of animal behavior, the configurationists introduced a different conception of the kind of experiment appropriate to infrahuman creatures. According to Köhler's remarks, "One must know and, if necessary, establish by preliminary observation, within which limits of difficulty and in which functions the chimpanzee *can possibly* show insight; negative or confused results from complicated and accidentally-chosen test-material, have obviously no bearing upon the fundamental question, and, in general, the experimenter should recognize that every intelligence test is a test, not only of the creature examined, but also of the experimenter himself" (*op. cit.*, p. 275). The implication is that if one's theoretical positions lead to the construction of problem-situations which can only be solved by "chance" movements, then of course one draws out of the experiment just exactly what was put into it.

The daring originality of the Gestalt position is often best seen in many incidental suggestions concerning fruitful possibilities of investigation in fields which the "hard-boiled" and "tough-minded" American psychologist of the behaviorist strain usually considers unworthy of a rigorous laboratory science. The following observation illustrates some of these curious and occasional "chips from a German workshop": One day Köhler approached the stockade within which the apes were confined and suddenly pulled over his head and face a cardboard copy of the mask of a primitive Cingalese plague demon; instantly every chimpanzee fled in horror from this appalling object.[4] Why? Surely not just because everything new and unknown appears

[4] The use of a military gas mask is said to have a similar effect upon domestic animals.

terrible to these creatures, since the changes in the clothing of the attendants never produced such fear. Köhler does not hesitate to draw upon all the imaginative possibilities which the Gestalt hypothesis makes available, and inquires, "Is it not an admissible hypothesis that certain shapes and outlines of things have in themselves the quality of weirdness and frightfulness (not because any special mechanism in us enables them to produce it), but because, granted our general nature and psyche, some shapes inevitably have the character of the terrible, others grace, or clumsiness, or energy, or decidedness" (*op. cit.*, p. 335)? That is, they do not acquire this fearful aspect through experience or association with another originally terrible object, but they possess it by virtue of their intrinsic constitution.[5] Not easy to demonstrate, indeed, but perfectly plausible in the light of configurationism.

The Nature of Mental Development

A more extensive application of the insight version of learning has been made by Koffka in his *Growth of the Mind.*[6] He is especially concerned here with the manner in which modifications in a child's behavior occur during the course of its development. The perennial problem of heredity and environment has been unjustly preëmpted by the rival positions of nativism and empiricism, according to which the major phenomena of mental life are either inborn functions or products of experience. Koffka, instead, is inclined to adopt as a more satisfactory description of the problem Stern's convergence theory, according to which every capacity is the result of the constant coöperation of both inner and outer conditions of development.

This position is nicely developed in an analysis of the eye reflexes of the infant by means of an illustration which has now become widespread. "Assume that the gaze of a child is first

---

[5] An obscure passage in one of Wertheimer's lesser known papers points in the same direction. "In the dance lie grace and joy. [If we think in terms of the usual body-soul hypothesis] does that mean that we really have on the one side a sum of physical muscle and limb movements, and on the other something psychically conscious? No. . . . There are many such processes in which if one only disregards the material character of the individual segments, a formal identity (*gestaltlich Identisches*) will be discerned." Cf. "Ueber Gestalttheorie," *Symposion, I*, 1927, 39–60. Objective beauty and spiritual loveliness are cast in the same *mould* or pattern even though their substances are distinct!

[6] New York, 1925. Reprinted with corrections in 1931.

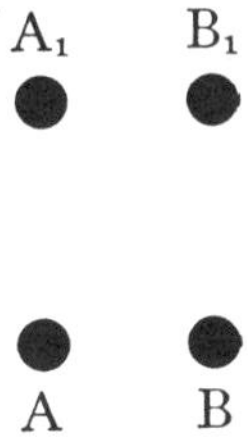

of all directed straight ahead upon a point A. There appears now in the same plane a point of light at B on the right. The eyes will then move so that this point falls upon the fovea. If now another point of light B_1, is introduced vertically above B, the eyes will move upward and fixate it. Let us assume that the eyes are again directed upon A, after which a point A_1 is flashed vertically above it. In passing from A to A_1 the same retinal position will be effected which received B_1 when the gaze was first directed upon B. Again, there is an upward movement of the eyes to effect the fixation of A_1; but although in this case A_1 stimulates the same retinal point which in the case of the first retinal movement from B to B_1 was stimulated by the point B_1, yet the two movements are not at all the same, because the movement from A to A_1 and that from B to B_1 require different innervations of the eye muscles. What is shown in this special case may be stated in general terms as follows: the innervations which the eye muscles undergo in movements of fixation are determined, not only by the position of the retinal points which arouse the movement, but also by the pre-existing position of the eyes. It, therefore, follows that every sensory fibre must possess not merely one connection with the motor nerves, but as many as may be required for all possible positions of the eyes" (Koffka, p. 77).

It is at this point that Koffka develops his "teleological" theory of the reflexes as opposed to the older and possibly simpler connectionist view. The empiristic standpoint accounts for the learning of optical fixation and coördination in terms of the establishment of *specific* connections between neurons, but in the illustration above we have a case of the same end (a peripheral point made foveal) accomplished by two different means (movements $A - A_1$ and $B - B_1$). The empirical position would thus needlessly demand an infinite number of neural connections before ordinary seeing could take place properly and it is clear that an infinite number of such separate acts are neither learned nor practiced. Without espousing a nativistic approach—which would explain everything in advance by maintaining that the entire complex mechanism comes ready-made—Koffka does insist that this event, like all other natural occurrences is fully defined by all the conditions determining it, and heredity is but one of these influences. The following radical pronouncement gives his explanation of the phenomenon:

> We can no longer assume that the sensory function serves merely to release the motor function without involving any *inner* or *material* connection between the two. Instead, the hypothesis is advanced that the specific pattern of the seen-object itself regulates the movements of the eye. From this it follows at once that the optical sensorium and motorium cannot be regarded as two independent pieces of apparatus,[7] since for many types of performance they constitute a *unitary organ*—a physical system—within which separate organic parts may react upon other parts. Accordingly, what happens at one point in the organism is never independent of, or without its influence upon, what is taking place at any other point in the organism (p. 80).

Clearly, if the concept of the reflex is thus seriously modified, a similar alteration is bound to affect the field of instinct. Gestalt theory inevitably takes exception to the "chain-reflex" explanation because it fails to account adequately for the significant characteristic of instinctive acts—"persistency with varied effort." If the instinct-apparatus is conceived as a system of predetermined pathways, then the fine adaptation of movements to a definite end or goal—such as one observes even in the sucking of the infant—becomes incomprehensible. Moreover, "when we consider a typical instinctive action as it appears in the natural course of an animal's life, the impression is not at all that of a summation of part-activities which have in themselves nothing to do with one another. On the contrary, an instinctive activity takes a *uniform course;* it is a *continuous* movement; it does not appear as a multiplicity of separate movements, but as one articulate whole embracing an end as well as a beginning. Every member of this activity seems to be determined, not only by its position with reference to what has gone before, but also with reference to all the members of the completed act,—especially to the last phase which leads to the result" (Koffka, pp. 98-99). To speak figuratively, the instinctive

[7] Cf. this utterance with Dewey's position in 1896 (*vide supra*, p. 20).

activity is a melody and not just a succession of tones; it is a reaction adjusted to its stimulus and not just released by it.[8] So long as the instinctive activity is incomplete, every new situation created by the animal is to it a transitional situation. Every member of the instinctive activity is determined not only by its position with reference to what has gone before, but with reference to all the members of the complete act and particularly, the last. "Native" behavior of this sort is much more like volition than like a concatenation of pure reflexes since it reveals the same forward direction that is characteristic of voluntary action.[9]

If it be objected that instinctive activity is not characterized by cognitive awareness of the end, Koffka would reply that this

Figure 26. A Simple Illustration of the Meaning of Closure. (After Koffka)

The nature of the situation practically "compels" one to see a completed triangle at the apex.

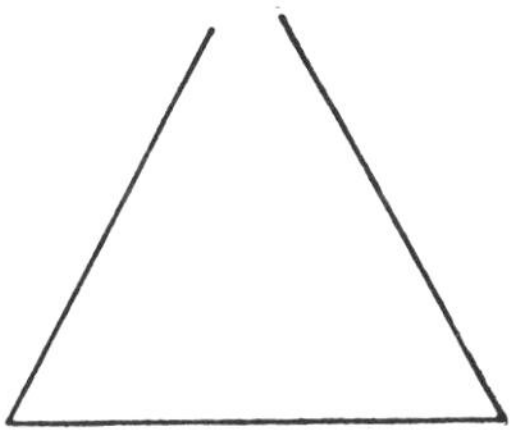

is only approximately true. As the goal draws near, appreciation of the end-situation is enhanced—a fact which exhibits the phenomenon of closure as represented by the open triangle below. This figure displays "non-closure" (like the transitional stages of an instinctive series) and yet indicates with a relatively high degree of certainty the direction in which closure is to be effected.

At this point, an interesting conclusion is reached. It is well-known that reflexes and instincts differ largely in degree of complexity, and even classifications made on this score tend to be

[8] The necessity for unitary organization in instinctive action was nicely shown by Grünbaum. If a dead fly is brought into contact with a spider's body the spinning reaction does not occur, but it does appear if the fly is fastened to a vibrating wire. A tuning fork causes the spider to wrap itself wildly around the tine as long as it vibrates. If the web is vibrated and no object found, no spinning takes place. Apparently the vibratory and tactile stimuli *separately* are ineffective but when *joined* or fused into one object the response ensues. Cf. "Ueber das Verhalten der Spinne (epeira diademata) etc.," *Psychol. Forsch.*, 1929, *9*, 275–299.

It is significant, too, that if a spider's web is slightly injured, it is invariably repaired, but if the destruction is extensive, the web is abandoned.

[9] Wundt, for different reasons, however, held a similar view.

uncertain. Instead, however, of looking upon the reflexive mechanism as the simplest and fundamental fact of behavior, upon which other more elaborate psychic structures are built, the configurationist reverses the process. Rather than trying to explain instincts in terms of reflexes, as Spencer and many latter-day behaviorists have done, he would explain reflexes as derived instincts. The whole is prior to the part. Genetically, the pure reflex is merely a product of instinctive fixation having become differentiated and segregated from a larger and more *massive* pattern of movement.[10]

Mental growth cannot be based, then, upon an assumption of inherited neural bonds, which permits only the possibility of a re-combination of old elements. On the other hand, if we allow for the initial existence of primitive figure-ground configurations, the possibilities for novel expansion and elaboration are infinite. The perceptual world of the new-born child is not the "blooming, buzzing confusion" of which James spoke, but plainly organized with qualities upon a ground. *The most primitive conscious phenomena are figural* as illustrated by a luminous point set off from a uniform field. The child recognizes its mother's face as early as the second month, and at six months it responds differently to a "friendly" face (i.e., a total aspect) than it does to an "angry" face—a difference which obliges us to conclude that "friendly" and "angry" faces are phenomenal facts[11] to the infant, and not mere distributions of light and shade. There is nothing in the reactions of the infant to indicate that it builds up its acquaintance with "objects" by uniting an original chaos of sensations. The fact that most of his definitions are in terms of use shows how hard it is for a

[10] Some excellent evidence of the correctness of this view has been obtained by Irwin in his continuous observation of four neonates during the first ten days. What he calls mass activity appears before local movements and seems to be more primitive than the individual reflexes. The infant cries at first only as the whole body moves, etc. See the detailed observations in "The Amount and Nature of Activities of New-Born Infants," *Genet. Psychol. Monog.*, 1930, *8*, 1–92.

These facts may help to interpret the *polymorphous perverse* sexuality which Freud attributes to the child. On Gestalt grounds the original sex urge would be diffuse, and the successive stages of narcissism, homosexuality, and heterosexuality merely representative of new differentiations or transformations of an evolving pattern.

[11] It may be of some incidental interest to report a much-needed observation by Stratton. Contrary to common view, he found that there is no correlation between the presence of a red flag and anger in cattle. The anger reaction is aroused only when the total situation is established—when the flag is waved in an annoying manner, when the waver jumps about, making peculiar vocal sounds and stirring into motion the dust about him. See his article on "The Color Red and the Anger of Cattle," *Psychol. Rev.*, 1924, *30*, p. 321.

child to form a concept of a thing outside of its "setting." His number ideas, too, originally refer to groups and not to arithmetic units. Mental life, even at the start, is always more or less well-organized.

All these interpretations are necessary preliminaries to the doctrine of insight, which is a natural outgrowth of them. The characteristic Gestalt ideology respecting the learning process is of especial significance in the light of its tremendous educational possibilities. Its point of departure is the question: *How does the first performance of any new act come about?* If the structure of an initial achievement can be understood, the problem will have been attacked at its most central point.

The trial-and-error hypothesis simply assumes that a large number of random movements are made from those already present in the learner's repertoire: the selection of the correct responses occurs by the gradual elimination of the useless movements, whereupon the useful ones fall into their proper serial order. The pleasure or pain accompanying these reactions serves to "stamp in" the "right" behavior or "stamp out" the wrong. Despite the admitted simplicity of this account, it fails utterly when the hypothesis is stated in terms which admit of an experimental test. Mere casual reflection upon the alleged rôle of frequency and repetition shows that the learner never duplicates exactly the same movement, but only the same general kind of behavior. A number of authors have observed that a cat which has once freed itself from a puzzle box by pulling a string with its foot, may upon another occasion pull the same string with its teeth, although the latter activity has never been exercised. The supplementary law of effect in turn suffers from the defect that the reward or punishment often occurs after a whole series of movements, some appropriate and some inappropriate, have been executed, so that it is difficult to see how any retroactive influence would help the learner to know which unit should be retained and which discarded.

¶In place of all this, configurationism would substitute the admitted fact that *improvement in efficiency goes hand in hand with an increased insight into the nature of the task.* If this insightful moment can be understood, then the problem of accounting for the first correct performance of any act is solved. Köhler's animal experiments are invariably brought in to illuminate this point. If insight be the name given to the perceptual reorganization of the visual field confronting the learner, then an alteration in the character or "meaning" of certain objects is the necessary condition of mastery. What initially was just an indifferent stick or plaything for the chimpanzee becomes, under the pressure of goal-seeking forces, an instrument for fetching fruit out of arm's reach. One of the principles affecting the formation of such optical units is spatial separation (Wertheimer, *vide supra*), and it is easy to comprehend why this factor might render this process difficult or at least delay it, because an isolated thing can spring into a complex (or be assimilated within a larger gestalt) more readily when it can

Figure 27. A Sample of "Wholeness" in Perceptual Experience

The most natural and primitive designation of this figure is "angle"; only upon later analysis do its constituents—a horizontal and a vertical line—spring forth.

be viewed simultaneously with the complex than when it is spatially remote from it. In Köhler's words, "the chance of a stick becoming a tool is a function of a geometrical constellation." What the learner eventually suceeds in doing is to make an irrelevant subject relevant to the situation, which is something quite different from an external connection between a certain stick in the field of perception, and a certain sequence of movements. On the contrary, an inadequate configuration must be broken up into a more adequate one. Chance, in the mathematical sense, may produce conditions favorable to such a transformation, but does not in itself explain the solution.

The reason that insight is possible is because things "hang together" in nature anyhow. This bearing of one datum, event, or experience upon another is a fundamental property of the phenomenal world and psychology is not the only science which must deal with this fact. When two colored surfaces are placed side by side, it is incorrect to maintain that nothing is given in this pair except one color here and another there, just as it would be incorrect to describe the figure above as one vertical and one horizontal line. What we actually see here is an angle. Similarly in the pair of colors what we notice is a combination, a configuration, for which we require no other transitional, secondary, derived, or superimposed experience.

Insight, then, takes the place of practice or repetition as the key word in a configurationist picture of learning. This does not deny that the frequency with which acts are performed may affect the course of progress in any performance. Instead, however, of serving to strengthen bonds, the chief function of repetition according to Koffka is to prepare the ground for the construction of an appropriate figure. In motor acts, e.g., a "movement-melody" must be composed, but it may be "played" well or poorly. After the configuration has once been constructed, repetition serves to make the behavior appreciably firmer and easier—but not before.

> This assumption seems to agree better than any other with the known facts. We know, for instance, that in a purely habitual achievement like that of mechanically learning a series of nonsense-syllables,[12] a "collective apprehension" is requisite, in which the several members are bound together in a uniform whole. Usually this construction of a unity occurs in the form of rhythmical groups, but in general what we mean to say is that in order to be learned the material must first receive some kind of figure, every facilitation in the construction of which is a facilitation of learning. . . . *All learning requires the arousal of configural patterns.* . . . It follows that repetitions without the achievement of a configuration remain ineffective whenever they are not positively harmful. In the broadest sense, practice means the formation of a figure, rather than the strengthening of bonds of connection (*op. cit.*, pp. 233-234).

The problem of learning is ineluctably joined to the question of the memory functions. In the associationist interpretation, memory is usually accounted for in terms of the re-activation of previously used paths or of "traces" left behind by earlier

[12] The "autochthonous organization" of ordinary visual perception is absent here. Most experiences are better self-organized when the subject encounters them, but in the case of the usual syllable lists, the members are so artificially homogeneous that the individual must create his own group structures. Symbolically, the resulting unity is better represented by (ABC) than by the conventional sequence A-B-C.

impressions. This hypothesis was neatly disposed of a generation ago by von Kries and Becher. Their argument ran as follows: Having once seen a figure we are still able to recognize it after its position, magnitude, and color have been so greatly altered that different neural pathways must now be involved. The whole process must take place in quite a different manner than it did before; indeed, no object is ever twice reflected in the eye in exactly the same way. If the same fixed paths and identical local "traces" are necessary to recognition, it is impossible to see how we ever recognize anything at all, since only in exceptional cases would the same avenues be traversed. The theory is killed by its own specificity. Nevertheless, it needs but a slight modification in order to be made acceptable to Gestalt. If the phenomena A, B, and C have been present once or oftener as members of a configuration, and if one of these reappears with its "membership-character," it will have a tendency to supplement itself more or less definitely and completely with the remainder of the total pattern.[13] The only ambiguity lies in the phrase "membership-character," which, however, may be taken to mean the simultaneous presence of the relevant *Aufgabe,* determining tendency, or mental set, so that the whole to which the part refers is at least roughly indicated.

One of the doctrines of associationism which plagued the more rigid mechanists of an older era was the principle of reproduction by *similarity.* According to it an idea X can reproduce another idea Y without any previous existential connection established by *contact,* provided that X and Y are sufficiently similar. The thought of thunder not only occurs *with* lightning, but also whenever we hear any other dull noise—or when a mountain, cross, or forest is recalled. To a poet, the drooping and snow-laden branches of certain evergreens may suggest the curious roof of a pagoda. Now this fact, if admitted—and there is ample experimental evidence in its favor—really lies outside the bounds of strict associationism, because a purely external tie is replaced by an "internal" connection. The name

[13] Note that "membership-character" is the key to the explanation. Shepard and Fogelsonger had earlier demonstrated in a memory experiment that the association will not work effectively when one attends to the syllables in a different combination from that in which they were learned. See their valuable "Studies in Association and Inhibition," *Psychol. Rev.,* 1913, *20,* 290-311.

"association by similarity" has served to obscure the fact that an entirely new principle of explanation had been introduced into mental life, although psychologists since the days of Hartley and Mill have felt uncomfortable in its presence, as indicated by their efforts to reduce this type to sheer *contiguity*. Koffka holds that this principle of reproduction by similarity and the fact of recognition are related, and thus avoids the difficulties of the fixed pathway hypothesis by considering both as special cases under a more general law.

Ogden's New Laws of Learning

An American psychologist, Dean Ogden of Cornell, who prepared the English translation of Koffka's *Growth of the Mind,* has offered in his own volume on *Psychology and Education,*[14] an interesting development of the same trend of thought. Like the originators of the Gestalt doctrine, upon whom he leans heavily for interpretative support, he holds the view that the whole organism, by virtue of its very organization, is so built that it must behave "pattern-wise." This conception leads to an annihilation of the old cleavage between a stimulus on one hand impinging upon a receptor and a response produced by an effector; in its place appears the methodological notion that behavior is not a response to a situation, but a *situation-response,* i.e., a total action-unit. An organism and its environment are one.[15] The basic facts for psychology (or any other science for that matter) are "not isolated, self-sufficient entities, but . . . dynamic patterns, the very existence of which involves form." Facts of any kind simply are not independent items, each existing in its own right quite apart from everything else.

In the field of native conduct, this approach is illustrated by the primacy of instinct, the larger whole, over reflex, the part. This sounds incomprehensible to many but is a conclusion buttressed by the neurological researches of Child, Herrick, Coghill, and others. Child[16] writes, "Summing up, the reflex, strictly speaking, is a specialized behavior-pattern depending on the presence of certain morphological mechanisms; but it is

[14] New York, 1926. A revision in conjunction with Freeman appeared in 1932.
[15] Cf. J. S. Haldane, *Organism and Environment,* 1917, 93-99.
[16] *Physiological Foundations of Behavior,* New York, 1924, p. 235.

physiologically a development from the primary organismic behavior-mechanism, the excitation-gradient." And a gradient, of course, always involves a reciprocal dynamic relation between at least two areas of high or low potential (or metabolic activity), respectively. Since the reflex itself is genetically a derived mode of reaction, the futility of attempting to derive intelligence and the higher mental faculties in general from reflexes, habits, or any other form of fixed or determinate behavior must be obvious to all, as Herrick has correctly observed.[17]

Just as the special reflexes differentiate from a broader matrix of behavior, so those fixated responses which we call "habits" emerge from total-responses, whose intrinsic wholeness has a voluntary character. The volitional process is a comprehensive adjustment of the entire organism to all phases of the situation confronting it, and consequently is more variable and less stereotyped than a segmental habit which is merely an isolated behavior-fragment.

This principle of differentiation is of considerable suggestive value to social psychology with its customary hostility to the group or "institutional fallacy," as the following excerpt shows:

> There are two conceptions of society. According to one of them a society consists of members which are "integrals" of the group. According to the other conception society consists of separate "integers," each a self-sufficient individual. In the first conception the group-whole is more significant than the individuals that compose it; whereas in the second the group, being constituted of individuals, is less significant than its members. In choosing the first of these two conceptions we maintain that a social group determines its members, each of whom will possess whatever degree of individuality the particular group makes possible. We, therefore, deny the opposite view that

[17] *Neurological Foundations of Animal Behavior,* New York, 1924, p. 234. Coghill, a careful student of the problem, has more recently expressed himself as follows: "In so far as the development of behavior is known in vertebrates, all reflexes emerge as partial or local patterns within an expanding or growing total pattern that normally is from the beginning perfectly integrated. They become partial or local only overtly. They are inherently components of the total pattern or they are under its dominance. An instinctive reaction, on the other hand, is the total pattern overtly in action. . . . The process of individuation of the partial pattern out of the total pattern consists in progressive restriction of the zone of stimulation adequate for the response, and in progressive reduction of the extent of muscular reaction. . . . Since the reflex and the instinct develop according to the same law and serve the same purpose, they cannot be regarded as two distinct categories of behavior. Their apparent difference with reference to the magnitude of the pattern is simply a function of growth." "The Genetic Interrelation of Instinctive Behavior and Reflexes," *Psychol. Rev.,* 1930, *37,* 264-266.

society accrues to individuals in congregation, and is, in effect, simply the sum of several distinct entities. Social integration is not a summation of "integers," instead, the members of a social group are the "integrals" of a whole. In other words, priority attaches to the group, not to its members.[18] (*op. cit.*, p. 90.)

By implication, of course, personality and biological uniqueness are derivatives of social life, since, like the formation of a figure upon a ground, individuality accrues to any body or any thing possessed of a degree of articulateness sufficient to define it and set it off from its surroundings. Contrary to the usual view, sociology and anthropology may rightly consider themselves more fundamental disciplines than psychology.

The remembering activities of the organism may similarly be assumed to represent differentiations from the original unitary "eidetic" phenomena of childhood. It is well-known that Jaensch and the Marburg school have assembled interesting evidence pointing to the eidetic image as either the bridge between impressions and ideas (in Hume's sense) or the matrix from which both emerged. What we call the perception of external or objective reality is a relatively late development in individual life like the awareness of self, both being produced by the establishment of stable configurations in experience.

With these premises, Ogden proceeds to the assertion that the conditions under which a phenomenal revival of memory occurs can be stated in three laws: (1) Perseveration, (2) Association, and (3) Practice. The law of perseveration simply holds that "any perceived configuration, the articulateness of which is marked, will persist for a brief period of time in a state of sub-arousal after the perception is over" (*op. cit.*, p. 182). Few persons will find difficulty with this statement, since it is a pure description of a familiar fact.

The second law of association is obviously not the historical version, reading as follows: "Whenever a number of more or less discrete perceptions (or ideas) enter into a configuration,

[18] The hyper-reality of the group finds expression in ancestor-worship and numerous primitive practices. The dead, though absent, are treated as integral parts of the social organization. Cf. the observations of D. Westermann, "Tod und Leben bei der Kpelle in Liberia," *Psychol. Forsch.*, 1922, *1*, 59-65.

The psychology of leadership, too, is illuminated by the fact that parts having a poor position within a whole may be made more impressive by change of position or function within the whole.

they become joined by virtue of their membership in a whole; the members are thereafter held together, not by the external agency of an associative 'glue,' but by the transformation which they have undergone in losing something of their individuality and becoming the members of a single pattern." *The pattern and not the individual contents constitutes the memorial residuum.* Ogden submits the following homely illustration as a sample of the operation of this principle:

> When I meet Jones and his wife, I am not just encountering two individuals, but I am meeting a "married couple." Later when I meet Jones alone, I recall his wife because I perceive him as one of a pair. The pattern is supplemented or "filled in" and practically becomes what it was upon the first encounter by virtue of the recollection of the missing member. If, however, the "context" in which I meet Jones later is such that I react to him as an "individual" only, or as a member of some other configuration, such as a team, society, etc., to which he also belongs, then I do not recall his wife.

Thus restated and limited, the law of association is derived from the more general law of configuration that controls all phenomena and all behavior. "Instead of likening association to a string of beads, each bead recalling the next in sequence, we remember first the string, and then supply the beads as best we can." First comes the purview, then the details; or, if one wishes, the entire figure must first arise, after which the parts or members fall into place.

Ogden's third law of practice defines the service of practice as "that of furnishing conditions favorable to a closer articulation and consequent fixation of whatever would otherwise be loose and inarticulate in form" (Ogden, p. 193). Frequency of repetition under certain favorable conditions facilitates this process, since it is all but impossible to repeat any sensori-motor coordination without promoting its articulation. To that extent even the dullest of drill may be helpful. To the familiar correction that "practice makes perfect" only when the *right* activity is rehearsed, Gestalt would add, "only when it favors articulation into a whole."

A recognition of the correctness of this picture of the memory process was for a long time delayed by the prestige accruing to the standard nonsense-syllable technique which apparently had demonstrated that meaningless material could be "linked together" purely through bonds formed by contiguity. Nevertheless, these artificial units can and do enter into a variety of configurations of order, rhythm, appearance, and sound. Indeed, Ogden alleges that "it is only when the series becomes a unified whole, with a certain articulatory progression, or with beat, measure, and melody, that the series can be memorized at all" (Ogden, p. 210). A pattern must be formed which suggests its own completion, a position which is strengthened by the acknowledged existence of remote forward and retrograde associations.

The bitter controversy begun by the Würzburgers concerning the function of imagery in mental life is nicely illuminated by an observation which apparently places the Gestalt theorist in the ranks of the "imageless thoughters." It is known that different minds attain the same ends in reasoning by methods, which, when analyzed as to their sensory qualities, vary markedly. "The *important thing is always the figure;* how this shall be clothed, sensorially and imaginally, is more or less a matter of taste in the selection of draperies which happen to be available," i.e., since the *dynamic* gestalt is transposable, the *material* vehicle by which it is borne is irrelevant.

Few adherents of configurationism have tried to give a more systematic portrayal of learning from that standpoint than has Ogden. Its chief characteristic is the close link established between it and the ancient category of perception, whereas previously the motor aspect of learning had received almost exclusive attention. According to the new version, learning begins with "the particularization of an objective," or, in more familiar language, the establishment of a goal. These objectives arise out of a general ground of experience in accordance with the same laws which govern the formation of any pattern of response. The end, it seems, corresponds to an area of low resistance upon which all the energies of the organism readily converge. That is why a motor act is best discharged by concentrating upon the desired objective, and why the same act suffers in smoothness of execution when attention is directed toward the parts. All learning depends upon this fundamental process of particularization whereby a limited coherence of forces is established, but since there are various conditions of perception, so also there are different ways of learning. There are four of them: differentiation, assimilation, gradation, and re-definition, each of which will demand some elaboration.

Learning by *differentiation* and *assimilation* corresponds to the analytic and synthetic methods respectively. In analysis of this type, an old whole or pattern disintegrates during perception and a new one takes its place or becomes subordinated to the original; similarly, the synthesis referred to here is not a compounding of behavior elements but the integration of a larger whole. *Gradation* is a form of learning involving the perception of a direction of change as in the responses of Köhler's hens to his paired greys. This ability to respond to a *gradient* or scale (such as brightness-darkness, big-little, left-right) is the true basis of all genuine transfer of training, and it is probably more than accidental that intellectual discrimination is also based less upon the absolute data of sense than upon the pattern of arrangement. *Re-definition,* finally, is illustrated by the varying reactions made to ambiguous figures: nothing is added or subtracted in making these transformations, but the same lines and angles enter into different patterns through the re-orientation of the figure. Presumably shifts in viewpoint on controversial topics as a result of prolonged reflection may be accounted for by this mechanism.

CHAPTER 11

THINKING AND REASONING

Primitive Thought

Anthropological and ethnological data concerning the thought processes of primitive men have attracted Gestalt authors because of the opportunity thus afforded to trace the emergence of differentiated patterns from cruder forms. They claim that the customary biases with which European investigators attack the problems of tribal life are serious obstacles to a proper understanding of the phenomena.[1] Our modern categories—number, causes, abstract concepts—have evolved as a result of the biological and social relations of a restricted historical development, and to apply these "prejudices" to simpler societies is often a barrier to the discovery of the true situation.

To us, number is a property of groups of objects which is unrelated to their material aspects, but its integration with reality is much closer among primitives. For instance, 1 horse + 1 horse = 2 horses; 1 man + 1 man = 2 men; but 1 man + 1 horse = a rider! This unification is a consequence of the existence of original natural groups from which separate subgroups eventually split off.[2] Six is really something other than 3 + 3. The "counting" of animals must have this rudimentary quality of form-perception, for if one kitten in a litter of four is removed, the mother behaves as though she knew one were missing. The gestalt resulting from four small creatures is obvi-

---

[1] A recent paper by Ruth Benedict indicates that anthropology has begun to be affected by Gestalt views. The strict diffusionists of the last decades operated solely with detached objects (pottery in particular!), never with their setting or function in the culture from which they came. The newer school is trying to obtain full-length portraits of primitive peoples on the principle that different tribes have different patterns of living (= cultures). Cf. "Configuration of Culture in North America," *Amer. Anthropologist*, 1932, *34*, 1–27.

[2] The ludicrous practice observed in many primitive families of the husband going to bed when a child is born is also based upon the primacy of the biological group. When any one is ill the medicine-man must treat the entire family! Reasoning itself appears to be the cerebral counterpart of the general biological differentiation of part patterns within larger wholes.

ously different from that produced by three. This dependence of thought upon natural units is still observed in the modern adult, for we do not consider as biologically meaningful many divisions which are mathematically irreproachable, such as a half-pot, 1/26 of a penny, 1/5 of a goose, 1/4 of an Armenian.

Time estimates similarly indicate that the temporal aspect was and is a dependent property of some other comprehensive unit. *Yesterday—to-day—tomorrow* constitute a single time interval for the child, and even now there are Bavarians who estimate distance in terms of the number of pipes of tobacco which can be smoked on the way! Our own ability to tell time correctly from a modernistic clock whose dial lacks the conventional Roman or Arabic figures is a more refined case of the primitive imbedding of the time factor in a spatial pattern.

The language of many tribes reveals this same imperfect isolation of the abstract "elements." [3] That Indian, who in the process of interpreting a speech lesson was asked to translate "The white man killed six bears to-day" and refused on the ground that it was impossible for a white man to kill that many bears in so short a time, illustrates how symbolism is significant to the primitive mind only when an agreement with his total experience is involved.[4] For much the same reason the fallacy of *post hoc ergo propter hoc* is so deeply rooted in the mind, not only of primitive man, but of the man-in-the-street to-day.

Formal Logic

Wertheimer has made an interesting contribution to the theory of the thought processes involved in deductive reasoning by showing that it obeys Gestalt principles. Logicians have long quarreled over the standard syllogism, especially over the mode Barbara—all men are mortal; Caius is a man; therefore, Caius is mortal—some arguing that this dull reasoning is a *petitio,* a mere recapitulation of something already known.

[3] The double meaning of *digit* in words of Latin origin, and the Teutonic ten = toes (cf. German *zehn, Zehen*), reveals the concrete origin of all mathematics. The persistence of rich declensions and conjugations in modern tongues shows that the sentence or phrase arose earlier than the word.

[4] These illustrations are taken from Wertheimer's essay "Ueber das Denken der Naturvölker" in his *Drei Abhandlungen zur Gestalt-theorie,* Erlangen, 1924. The paragraphs which follow are taken from another essay in the same volume entitled, "Ueber Schlussprozesse im produktiven Denken."

Wertheimer, however, holds with the scholastics that one can often penetrate ahead and increase one's knowledge through the use of this device. For example, a citizen who does not know in what fiscal district he lives comes to the city hall for information. The official says:

> You live in X street
> X street belongs to tax precinct 426 (reading from his record)
> Therefore, . . .

A genuine transformation has occurred here, because the notion one has of a thing is not only enriched, but altered, improved, and deepened. Or suppose I am looking for a slip of paper belonging to assignment A and am unable to locate it. I know that I have burnt all manuscript material pertaining to assignment B. Suddenly I realize that the A sheet which I am searching for also belongs to project B; therefore, . . . i.e., the desired slip appears in two configurations, once as part of A and again as part of B. The heart of the performance lies in changing the A slip into a B slip. This is exactly what happens when an ape breaks off a branch of a tree and converts it into a stick for reaching an objective. Again, is 1,000,008 divisible by 9, or not? Obscurity and confusion dominate until one sees that the major quantity is 999,999 plus 9, whereupon the matter is plain. In fact, the entire domain of reasoning bears testimony to the rule that the phenomenal pattern determines the reaction pattern; e.g., in his ape experiments, Köhler found that a rope wound around a beam presented insuperable obstacles to the animals; what appears to us as a clear, articulate structure evidently appears to these animals as a tangled, intricate structure.

A demonstration of Wertheimer's is another excellent example of the concrete projection of the operations of thought into the perceptual field. In the following problem the area of the square tangent to the circle is to be found; all that is given is the length of the radius R. The "gap" is: What help can the radius be in finding the area of the square? The solution is delayed until the radius "displaces" itself to a position parallel to the base line, where one no longer perceives it as *part of the circle* but *as part of the square;* i.e., as a half-side of the square. The answer is then read off directly: $A = (2R)^2$.

The same attack is illustrated in this problem: Given a square of nine dots (Figure 28b) draw four lines so that each dot will be passed through at least once. The pencil is not to be taken from the paper and no lines are to be retraced. This task is difficult because a person continues his attempts *within* the area of the square. As soon as it is suggested that one could go *outside* the area of the square, the solution is easily found.

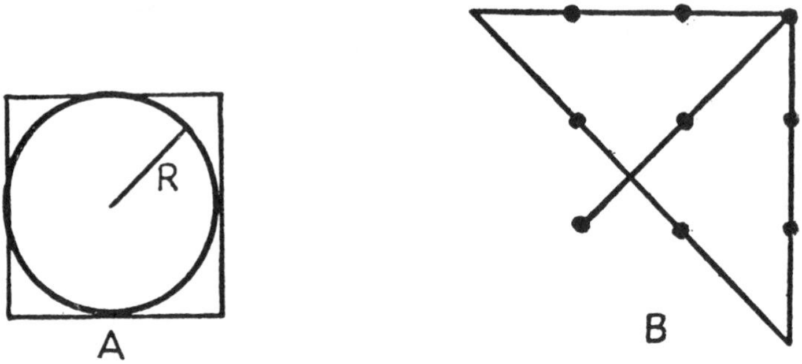

Figure 28. Problems. (From Scheerer)

(A) Find the area of the square when nothing is given but the radius of its inscribed circle. Hint: visualize R in a position parallel to either the horizontal or vertical sides of the square. (B) Without lifting the pencil from the paper or retracing any lines, draw four straight lines so that each dot will be passed through at least once. Hint: the lines may extend beyond the outlines of the square.

Again, from six matches construct four equilateral triangles having a side equal in length to a match. This is also difficult because one tries to place them in one plane. If one asks, "Why limit yourself to two dimensions?" a new way of looking at the problem (= direction) is seen and the solution is likely to follow.

Most logicians, unfortunately, have acted on the assumption that all cognitive operations must be executed with a knife (subtractive abstraction) or with a sack (the "class" concept); instead, even in the barest of syllogisms, certain definite moments may be pushed into the foreground or new *combinations* (not aggregations) may emerge. It would seem that thought can tease something new out of existing propositions by identifying the members of two different configurations (the premises) as belonging to a common *new* configuration (the conclusion.)

As one might expect, any revision of the logical processes leads to a new view of the nature of truth. The familiar "correspondence" theory of truth holds that any proposition is "true" if it can be matched with a fact or item of experience with which it agrees. Wertheimer [5] considers this literally a "partial" and one-sided approach. It is atomistic logic operating again at the very foundations of thought.

For example, a thing may be true in the piecemeal sense, and false, indeed a lie, as a part in its whole. We must distinguish the object as piece $|a|$, the object as part of its whole $\left|\begin{matrix}a\\abc\end{matrix}\right|$, the object as part of another $\left|\begin{matrix}a\\amn\end{matrix}\right|$. To illustrate his doctrine of the "two-fold truth," Wertheimer calls attention to the case of a man who persuaded another person to steal something, and yet who could honestly deny that *he* stole it, even though his responsibility is plain to any one fully acquainted with the situation. The number of false conclusions which can be encouraged by varying the inflection is another instance of this point.

These two kinds of truth may deal with the same data, but one (the "whole" truth?) goes to the heart of the matter, while the other may remain external—viz., when the set of facts is not merely a sum. That is why statistics lie when they fail to portray the entire picture. Similarly, an engineer discovers in his measurements that he has a straight line. Measurements taken in other subsections show that he is dealing not with a straight line, but with the asymptote of an hyperbola—and his equation alters accordingly. Again, on the moral level, it is plain that it is in the total conduct of men rather than in their statements that truth or falsehood lives.

Wertheimer does not state this explicitly, but it seems plain the Gestalt position strikes directly at the most fundamental rule of logic, viz., the law of identity. This solidly-established convention maintains that what is true of a group is also true of each individual component of the group. This law as it stands

[5] Presented in his first publication in English, *Social Research*, 1934, *I*, 135–146.

appears to forbid thought to contradict itself. Nevertheless, if group or "systemic" realities are different modes of existence from "elemental" ones, this ancient dogma will have to undergo appropriate modification if it is to be preserved as a guide to knowledge.

Closure

The closure concept is obviously a godsend to any theory of the reasoning process since it justifies one in saying that a felt "difficulty"—with which, according to Dewey, all thinking begins—is a partial pattern indicating more or less adequately the way it is to be completed. The function of reasoning or insight is simply to bridge the exposed gap.[6] Thorndike claims that the original thinker is one who is *dissatisfied* with old solutions, with the result that he makes an effort to reach interpretations which are more agreeable, but the configurationist would hold that the imperfectly formed neural patterns create tensions or gradients leading inevitably to their own completion. A problem presents itself as an open gestalt which "yearns" for solution, and it is the business of thought to find the solution by transforming the open gestalt into a closed one.[7] From this point of view, an intelligent person is one who is able to transpose one situation into another and to reconstruct his perceptual field.

The uniqueness of the Gestalt version of thought is, like its other contributions, best understood in the light of the associationist accounts which it hopes to supplant. According to the constellation-theory of Selz, which is the climax of associationist speculation, a cross-section of consciousness at any moment reveals a chaotic mass of competing reproductive tendencies. To explain the cosmos of our orderly thinking we need to know how the presentational series reaches the goals which it establishes for itself. Consequently, associationism

[6] Gestalt theory maintains that understanding and invention or discovery occur in accordance with the same principles, save that the first is easier. Consequently, the school child is never really passive, for every act of comprehension is something creative. The "born teacher" is simply one who presents and adjusts incomplete patterns in such a way that the proper closures are most readily made.

[7] Some excellent illustrations of this method may be found in O. L. Reiser, "The Logic of Gestalt Psychology," *Psychol. Rev.*, 1931, *38*, 359-368.

In general, configurationists claim that every item or event points to something beyond itself, closure effects simply being the most drastic instances of this universal process. This idea gives added richness to Nietzsche's well-known saying (Thus Spake Zarathustra): "What is great in man is that he is a bridge and no goal; what can be loved in man is that he is a going-over and a going-under."

postulates the presence of a relatively stable mental content from which other ideas or definite reproductive tendencies proceed and from which a selection is made. Koffka,[8] however, holds that the introduction of this conception of goal or direction is really an anti-associationist admission. To an idea I wish to find its opposite. The goal-presentation must be an idea that the concept sought is the "opposite." But what kind of an idea is this and how is this joined with the idea ultimately sought? By virtue of what associations is it able to inhibit or facilitate the numerous reproductive-tendencies at hand? This steady move toward a defined objective constitutes a difficulty which the associationist theory is unable to solve, because it makes thought essentially a memory-function.

The Gestalt solution is quite different. "Opposite-pair" is a gestalt and like all other gestalten it evokes a "gestalt-disposition" with an important property.[9] If a child has comprehended that "big" is the opposite of "little," then a gestalt disposition does not only exist for this and similar conceptual pairs but the configuration "opposite" in general has been acquired—just as the child which has learned to distinguish yellow and green finds it much easier to master the distinction between red and blue. What makes a task a task, a question a question? Nothing other than incomplete thought-structures, thought gestalten with gaps, and from the configuration as a whole proceed strong tendencies to close these gaps.

The difference between the two accounts has been so well expressed by Helson [10] that one can do no better than quote his pertinent paragraph in its entirety here:

> The logical analysis of the associationist is responsible for the plight he gets into; for, having begun with elements having no relation to one another, he must by some means connect them. The configurationists answer the question of thinking by asking how thought progresses from the beginning to the end of a problem. The historic antitheses of sense

[8] Cf. his section on "Psychologie" in *Lehrbuch der Philosophie,* ed. Dessoir, Berlin, 1925, 493-603.

[9] The gestalt-disposition is roughly equivalent to mental set or *Einstellung* in its reference to organismic conditions which determine the effects stimuli will have when they are operative. The following riddle is illustrative: A: "What is the lightest city?" B: "?" A: "Agram. And why?" B: "?" A: "Because it weighs just a gram. Now what is the largest city?" B: "?" A: "London. Because it has the most inhabitants."
The second question would have been correctly answered but for its predecessor, which established a latent *Einstellung.*

[10] "The Psychology of Gestalt," *Amer, J. Psychol.,* 1926, *37,* p. 54.

and intellect, sensation and thought, do not exist in configurational psychology; hence there is no need to build one on the other or to derive one from the other. . . . . For thought to progress along logical lines it must proceed within a structure, and this structure is very often furnished in perception. The relation of objects to one another are given in phenomenal configurations won in perception. A change in the object of perception may mean a change in the whole course of thinking, since rational insight demands the perception of the structure of the whole. Fruitful thinking, consists therefore, in approximating, either in perception or in thought, to the *sachlicher Zusammenhang* (= functional relation) of configurational structures. Configurational connections are not the results of frequent associations or blind juxtapositions, but are inner bonds imposed by the demands of the total structure. Once this structure is seen, the parts must follow one another in a certain way.

Relation versus Gestalt

To many persons the notion of gestalt is wrongly identified with that of "relation." Koffka tries to remove this difficulty by showing that *relation is the species of which gestalt is the genus.*[11] The relation-seeing attitude cannot be identified with the "structure-seeing" attitude because these are two entirely different perceptions and involve wholly different phenomenal patterns; the perception of a structure is prior to and independent of relational judgments. For instance, the impression of a rectangle or of any gestalt is not sufficient in itself for the apprehension of relation. If I see a rectangle, I see a regularly closed figure, but I do not see the equivalence of the two vertical or horizontal boundary lines. The presence of such a gestalt is not yet the basis of the judgment: $a = b$. However, that does not mean that a perceptual foundation for this judgment is absent. If I try to describe the phenomenal condition underlying the verdict, "Distances a and b are equally long," I find that the rectangular character is there but somewhat altered, so that the sides a and b are now the *main* part of the total and in tension with respect to each other, while the two other sides merely serve as the transition between them, the character of the transition—divergent or convergent—determining the relation.

[11] Of course, the genus-species "relation" is itself a gestalt! The common-sense difficulty with explaining a gestalt in terms of relations lies in determining which, among an innumerable variety of relations, are really decisive in making it what it is. Cf. the historical concept of "essence."

CHAPTER 12

RESEARCHES ON INSIGHT

To an outsider the greatest strength and weakness of the Gestalt position appears in the application of its central notion of insight or organized response to the problems of thought and learning. According to it, all learning occurs *via* insight; where there is no insight, there is no learning. We have already seen evidence of the positive power of this concept to illuminate older observations and to advance new types of research. Nevertheless, it remains the one feature of the configurationist program which has been least acceptable to the orthodox. Investigators who have reluctantly acknowledged the reality of field-forces in perception and who appreciate the derived character of the simple reflex bitterly attack the insight explanation as unscientific in the extreme, even where it means little more than transposability of the general properties of response from one problem to another. Why?

Terminology

Part of the difficulty has undoubtedly been a matter of terminology. In English "insight" is an acceptable popular and loose equivalent of understanding, comprehension, or occasionally, intuition. The colloquial "hunch" is probably a low-level form of insight in its stricter use. On the other hand, insight has also been employed in abnormal and social psychology to designate the personality trait involving awareness of one's condition or status. Supplementary to these uses (and perhaps embracing them all) is the more technical version, which strangely enough was not introduced by the Gestaltists as many suppose, but by Woodworth and Ruger [1] between 1908 and 1911. True they did not identify it with configurational learning, but emphasized

[1] *The Psychology of Efficiency,* New York, 1910.

the presence of sudden solutions in problem-solving, an exceptional fact which Thorndike had noted in his early animal experiments and which he had suggested might be explained by the presence of "a totally different mental function, namely, free ideas." [2]

Another limitation has been the failure to reach an acceptable set of criteria [3] by which the phenomenon of insight could be identified.[4] This has obviously been needed in animal studies and is equally desirable in describing the conduct of human subjects. The best single effort to meet this requirement has been made by Yerkes [5] in the following list:

> In acts which by us are performed with insight or understanding of relations of means to ends, we are familiar with certain characteristics which are important, if not also differential. These features are: (1) Survey, inspection, or persistent examination of problematic situations. (2) Hesitation, pause, attitude of concentrated attention. (3) Trial of more or less adequate mode of response. (4) In case initial mode of response proves inadequate, trial of some other mode of response, the transition from one method to the other being sharp and often sudden. (5) Persistent or frequently recurrent attention to the object or goal and motivation thereby. (6) Appearance of critical point at which the organism suddenly, directly, and definitely performs required adaptive act. (7) Ready repetition of adaptive response after once performed. (8) Notable ability to discover and attend to the essential aspect or relation in the problematic situation and to neglect, relatively, variations in non-essentials.

The definition of insight which would be most in accord with the Berlin school of Gestalt states it to be *the phenomenal correlate of the "closing" of a configuration.* This is merely another way of saying that when an experience is patterned so

[2] "Mental Life of Monkeys," *Psychol. Rev. Monog.*, 1901, *3*, No. 5, p. 16. How much the theoretical leanings of the observer affect his interpretation is seen in contrasting Thorndike's early work with the elaborate repetition of the "cat in the puzzle-box" problem made by Donald Adams, who found more evidence of intelligent adaptation of means to ends. See "Experimental Studies of Adaptive Behavior in Cats," *Comp. Psy. Monographs*, 1929, *6*, 1–162.

[3] For a more extensive discussion of this point the reader is referred to the writer's article on "The Concept and Criteria of Insight" in *Psychol. Rev.*, 1931, *38*, 242–253. Ogden holds that any criticism of the insight doctrine must be made within the framework of the configurationist hypothesis, and if made from any other standpoint is thereby irrelevant. See his note in *Amer. J. Psychol.*, 1932, *44*, 350–356, and the writer's dissenting reply entitled "Insight and the Context of Gestalt," *Amer. J. Psychol.*, 1932, *44*, 576–578.

[4] As logicians well know, things are often better characterized in terms of what they are *not* than in terms of what they are. Thus Koffka suggests a reciprocal criterion of "stupidity" when he says, "We call any behavior or action stupid which is not able to execute a performance for which *all conditions* for solving are given."—*Psychologie*, p. 578, in Dessoir's *Lehrbuch der Philosophie*, 1925.

[5] *The Great Apes*, New Haven, 1929, p. 156.

that certain aspects of the pattern are felt directly to depend upon other aspects, then the term insight may correctly be applied. Insight is the *how* and *why* of a situation, an understanding of the innermost nature of the field, the stresses not merely apprehended but comprehended. A highly important question dealing with the adequacy of the resulting configuration arises from this claim. Alpert [6] applied a variation of Köhler's stick and box-building devices to children aged 19-49 months with confirmatory results, but added the important modification of partial and gradual insight. One is tempted to believe that where insight is not immediate, or at least sudden, it has lost its essential character, and one may also suspect that where partial and gradual insights are admitted they represent either what would ordinarily be termed sheer trial-and-success or at best transition stages between that and insight *per se*. The main difficulty of the trial-and-error-hypothesis—how the correct solution could ever be hit upon by chance—is only partly removed by the insight view which means little more than "appropriateness" without explaining wherein the appropriateness consists, other than the pragmatic test provided by the solution.

In the same connection the work of Kreezer and Dallenbach [7] is of interest in showing that the relation of opposites is learned by varying percentages of children between five and seven and one-half years after but one or two illustrative examples. A sort of all-or-none law seemed to function on this level as the presence of insight was a *sine qua non* for mastering the task. Those who learned, learned by insight, and those to whom the insight did not come, did not learn at all. The only danger in such a bald statement of the fact is that it suggests that *the solution itself becomes the criterion of insight*—a conclusion which several critics have not hesitated to draw.

Zeininger [8] has noticed a type of thinking in young children which he characterizes as "If-then-thinking." It consists in a

[6] *The Solving of Problem-Situations by Pre-School Children,* New York, 1928.

[7] "Learning the Relation of Opposition," *Amer. J. Psychol.,* 1929, *41,* 432–441. Dallenbach had earlier made some rough investigations of this problem with his own and Ogden's children. See "A Note on the Immediacy of Understanding a Relation," *Psychol. Forsch.,* 1926, *I,* 268–269.

[8] "Magische Geisteshaltung im Kindesalter und ihre Bedeutung für die religiöse Entwicklung," *Zsch. f. angew. Psychol.,* 1929, Beiheft 47. Huang adopts this view with surprisingly few reservations in his "Children's Explanations of Strange Phenomena," *Psychol. Forsch.,* 1931, *14,* 63–182.

mere statement of what one has to do in order to realize certain ends, without insight into the situation. Many adults, too, know that if they wish to attain a desired result they must press a given button, but they are wholly ignorant concerning the "why" of the machine's behavior. One may also be compelled to distinguish two "levels" or kinds of insights—one involved in the internal solution of the problem itself and the other present as a sort of perception of the most promising way of approaching the task.

Varieties of Insight

Ideally, a demonstration of the presence of insight requires the solution of problems in such a way that errors abound up to the point at which the "principle" is discerned after which no further mistakes appear, i.e., 100% failure precedes the critical moment followed by 100% success. In an experiment conducted by the writer [9] ten types of problems of this sort were constructed. All of them were ludicrously easy as soon as the major common relations had been established by the subject. One series consisted of a reversed analogies test as follows:

1. steel : hard   burden : light
2. stomach : middle   head : bottom
3. sky : blue   snow : ______
4. Socrates : wise   Hercules : ______

The subject was shown the first line, told that *light* was the correct word because of a certain principle which the experimenter was consistently using, and then asked to insert the right term in the second line. If, as usually happened, he failed to respond properly after an arbitrary time limit had elapsed, the answer was given to him and he was directed to proceed further. Some subjects, of course, needed more illustrations than others before they saw the point of the arrangement, but all sooner or later realized that a word opposite to what one would normally give was correct; thus, *black* and *weak* are right answers in lines

[9] The full report may be found under the title, "Insight versus Trial-and-Error in the Solution of Problems," *Amer. J. Psychol.*, 1933, 45, 663–677. If insight be taken to mean that no problem-solving activity is ever planless but always involves a search for some pattern which can be applied, little reason for quarreling remains.

three and four respectively. In all cases introspective records [10] were used to throw light upon the mode of solution.

The main feature observed in every situation and confirmed by the subjects' reports was the frequency with which varying hypotheses were developed and rejected before the desired insight made its appearance.[11] A more or less extensive period of experimentation was evidently necessary before any of the problems were solved. During this preliminary struggle something very much like trial-and-error [12] learning unquestionably occurred, otherwise why should so many distinct possibilities of action have arisen only to be discarded?—and the time relations involved confirmed a classification of the varieties of insight made earlier by Alpert:

1. Solution with *immediate* insight (i.e., first "idea" correct)
2. Solution with *gradual* insight (= built up by accretion)
   a. *Partial* insight (= "good" errors)
   b. *Complete* insight
3. Solution with *sudden* insight (sharp transition occurring after perception of crucial factor)

Another study by the writer [13] on this theme may be referred to here to indicate that Gestalt theorists do not restrict the use of insight to the "rational" aspects of man's conduct. It is as

[10] Most phenomenological descriptions of the moment of insight tend to be disappointingly meager and barren. The *process* seems never to be as amenable to observation as the *product.* Benussi mentions his ability to produce the insightful experience in hypnotized subjects without requiring any conscious efforts at problem-solving. This notion of an autonomous or transcendental insight in which the function is divorced from both the normal content and situation is puzzling in the extreme, but it may account for the divine illumination reported by many mystics, both medieval and modern. See his little-known study, "Zur experimentellen Grundlegung hypno-suggestiver Methoden psychischer Analyse," *Pschol. Forsch.*, 1927, *9*, 197–274.

[11] This same point was independently made by Patton, whose subjects in a more limited perceptual task always worked on the basis of some theory or principle. The present writer holds that this systematic sampling by hypotheses and "guesses" (rather than disjointed movements) is all that the trial-and-error position maintains. Why should the last trial which happens to be correct be dignified with the special label of "insight"? To demonstrate that no behavior occurs without a goal is not proof of the presence of either insight or trial-and-error since the same objective can often be obtained by both means. See "*An Experimental Study of the Emergence of Insightful Behavior,*" *Psychol. Mono.*, 1933, *44*, 98–124. From the Gestalt standpoint, what seems to be trial-and-error learning is simply behavior whose "maturation" is incomplete, and hence the responses are gross and inadequate. Unfortunately, there is a lot of ambiguity and mystery about the maturation process.

[12] This would seem to dispose of Wheeler and Perkins' claim that to deny insight to animal conduct is to commit the "fallacy of the double standard" (*Principles of Mental Development*, p. 85). While there may be some legitimate doubt as to the relevancy of the human standard when imposed upon animals through the experimentally-controlled situation, there is simply no other standard which can be followed in observing adult behavior, especially if one combines objective records and introspective testimony.

[13] Cf. the original, "Configurational Factors in the Understanding of Actions," *J. General Psychol.*, 1932, *7*, 438–452.

immanent a factor in our crudest social perceptions as in the more severe forms of thought and learning, characterizing static visual figures as well as dynamic action-totals. Our comprehension of another's behavior is alleged to be dependent upon this condition, e.g., an identical act such as wiping a tear from the eye has one meaning when it occurs in the spectator of a stage tragedy and another on a windy road. No isolated act can be comprehended by itself.[14] To understand is equivalent to taking into consideration the *total situations*.

Köhler's remark that one must never cease to wonder at the obvious and commonplace details of experience is a useful introduction to the experiment under discussion. In outline it was absurdly simple, consisting only of a number of acts partially completed by the performer in the presence of an observer who was then asked to tell what the experimenter intended doing. The identical words and actions were carried out in two slightly different settings in which the physical articles of the room were the only items displaced, added, or removed.

Example: Upon the work-table were the following objects: Left (of the performer), a small torn colored map of Europe; right, a fair-sized piece of stiff yellow paper, upon which small paper strips had been pasted to form geometrical figures—one a complete triangle, the other a hexagon with two sides missing. In the middle of the table were scissors, ruler, a tube of paste, and white paper of the same kind as the paper strips described.

The subject, who was seated opposite the experimenter, observed the following action which he was prepared to interpret: The experimenter soliloquized, "The length is about 14 cm" and slowly cut out two equal paper strips, whose dimensions corresponded to the strips forming the figures (but also to the length of the rent in the map). After the experimenter had smeared the surface of one strip with some paste, he broke off the action.

Under the conditions just described the subjects in every single case declared that the intention was to complete the hexagon, whereas in a parallel experiment, in which this unfinished design was removed, every observer maintained that the purpose

---

[14] Hermann-Cziner showed this with word-material in "Experimentelle Untersuchungen zum Problem des Verstehens," *Zsch. f. Psychol.*, 1923, *92*, 88–109.

was plainly to repair the map. The vectors or field-forces in one case pointed clearly to a certain inevitable outcome while the goal in the second seemed equally obvious. Two distinct perceptual organizations resulted from two slightly altered objective configurations in which the rôle of every remaining part had been changed by the removal of one. There is some reason for believing that the situations here portrayed may represent the most primitive and general stage of the phenomenon of insight.[15]

Patterns and Learning

Guilford's study on the rôle of form in learning [16] is an excellent demonstration of the familiar fact that the perception of the system and organization of the material to be mastered is a facilitating factor of the first order. Nonsense syllables are notoriously more difficult to learn than a random list of numbers or meaningful disconnected words and these in turn are far more difficult than items with a plan or pattern uniting them. The way in which the "form" emerges is of interest for the light it throws upon the development of insight. To illustrate, let the reader endeavor to memorize the two lists here given:

force	thick
Korans	wall
heaven	it
ye	tea
sago	of
are	myrrh
feathers	seize
brat	knot
four	strain
than	debt
this	drop
count	path
anent	Asa
anew	gent
neigh	tell
shun	reign

[15] According to Erismann, the presence of insight is the major trait of the psychical as opposed to the physical. His claim, however, that insightful knowledge can never be false is rejected by configurationists as a confusion of the epistemological and psychological standpoints. See *Die Eigenart des Geistigen*, Leipzig, 1924.

[16] *J. Exp. Psychol.*, 1927, *10*, 415–423. For a more extended demonstration of the thesis that grouping is a necessary phenomenon in learning, see F. H. Lumley, "An Investigation of the Responses Made in Learning a Multiple Choice Maze," *Psychol. Mono.*, 1931, *42*, No. 189.

The first oral reading or so rarely suggests the scheme involved in the series, but there is a definite evolution through quick stages until the order comes with a flash. As soon as the Gettysburg speech and Portia's plea are seen to apply, the learner's difficulties are over. James, of course, had earlier referred to the same phenomenon in his clever illustration, *pas de lieu Rhône que nous.*

There is an extraordinary incident in the childhood life of Helen Keller,[17] who was born without the power to use her major sense organs, which is pertinent to any discussion of insight, for it shows how this distinguished woman became aware of the existence of language and discovered that everything has a name. She had been taught certain ideas and symbols by means of tactile stimulation but even at the age of seven her vocabulary was very meagre, the words employed designating only total situations and not specific individual objects. On one occasion, the teacher took the girl to the pump and while Helen was pumping water into a container, she spelled into the child's hand the word *w-a-t-e-r.* As the cold water touched her skin, Helen suddenly recognized that the manually spelled letters had the definite meaning of water. She had never before understood that a word had reference to a distinct and limited item of experience. Excitedly she pointed to the ground while its name was similarly impressed upon her hand, a process which continued with other familiar objects, so that within a few hours she had enormously increased her vocabulary and understanding of common concrete things.

An experiment by Lewis [18] on the configural response in the chick is an excellent case of learning of the non-specific type. He trained his animals to select the correct light of three *absolutely* different intensities (bright, moderate, or dim) in varying positions with reference to each other, and then "stepped" the illumination up or down so that all the original intensities were altered. Almost perfect transfer was found to prevail when the total situations were changed, indicating clearly that the

---

[17] See her appealing *Story of My Life,* New York, 1920, pp. 315–316. The entire autobiography is a mine of excellent psychological illustrations.

[18] *Journal of Experimental Psychol.,* 1930, *13,* 61–75.

chicks saw the lights in their mutual brightness relations; e.g., the chicks who were trained to select the medium light must have been able to do so only because they perceived it in connection with a brighter and a dimmer.[19] Most of the learning was sudden and the obvious initial delays before choice argue against any simple mechanical view of learning. In many trials, the chick, although hungry, would remain motionless upon being placed in the apparatus and would run to a compartment only after surveying the situation. The following observation is of interest because of the theoretical reconstruction it demands: "The box furnished us with a convincing bit of evidence against the theory of identical elements. A light of moderate intensity was placed in the box and on succeeding trials only the lights in the semi-circle were changed. Thus the box-light, remaining constant, would assume all possible relationships to the total pattern, now the brightest, now medium, and now dimmest; but as it was of the same absolute nature both in position and in intensity, it was an identical element of all identical elements. When the light was correct or incorrect the chicks chose or deserted it, as the case might be, without the slightest compunction; the light changed its identity with the changing conditions related to it." (*Op. cit.*, p. 70.)

A Canadian psychologist, George Humphrey,[20] without committing himself to a thorough-going Gestalt schema, has nevertheless lent credence to the insight doctrine by showing that all learning or modifications of the organism *must* obey systemic laws involving more than purely local effects. Going to biophysics for his inspiration, he has reasoned that there are certain properties of systems in general which, if the phrase "biological system" is anything more than a pious metaphor, should be found to belong not less to living than to non-living complexes. Le Chatelier's rule, originating in physical chemistry, would also appear applicable to the problem of habituation in animals: "If

---

[19] DeCamp, in an unpublished experiment performed at the Pennsylvania State College, finds that rats can learn to go to the first of two entrances successively illuminated or even to the middle of three, lighted one after another, provided the correct entrance is illuminated a little longer than the incorrect. When one considers how many combinations of order the three entrances permit, the *generality* of the number pattern response is striking.

[20] "Le Chatelier's Rule, and the Problem of Habit and Dehabituation in *Helix albolabris*," *Psychol. Forsch.*, 1930, *13*, 113–127; also "A Note on the Applicability of Le Chatelier's Rule to Biological Systems," *ibid.*, pp. 365–367.

a change occurs in one of the factors determining a condition of equilibrium, the equilibrium shifts in such a way as to tend to annul the effect of the change." While it is true that there is a difference between chemical and physiological equilibrium in that the latter must call upon outside energy to maintain itself, intra-organic changes of a compensatory character take place after every stimulation with the result that a fresh equilibrium—or new stationary condition consistent with the new external or internal environment—is brought about. Although Humphrey does not say this directly, it is clear that if no learning can occur without a rearrangement of neural patterns [21] we have precisely that sort of reconstruction of conduct which the insight hypothesis demands.

Thorndike and Belongingness

The one author who has had to bear the brunt of the Gestaltists' attacks because he seems to them the stoutest champion of the trial-and-error version of learning is Thorndike. Much of their criticism has an element of unfairness born from limited acquaintance with only a fraction of his writings, for he has always stressed the importance of the *situation* as contrasted with the individual stimulus. However, it is true that Thorndike has exhibited to perfection the analytical trend—which is anathema to the configurationists—in his emphasis upon the reality of bonds and connections, but this position is far from being as naïve neurologically as many opponents seem to believe.

One fact which is not yet sufficiently appreciated is that Thorndike himself [22] is responsible for some of the strongest evidence against the crude repetition or frequency theory of learning as advanced by Watson. As every critic realizes, the law of use never intended to explain more than the *strengthening* of an association without accounting in the least for the original

[21] The "tumble" and "flop" of colloquial speech and slang express the same process more picturesquely, and at the same time suggest the interesting kinship with reversible figures.

It is significant that the transition from waking life to sleep and *vice versa* takes place suddenly. If the physiological processes of the cortex overstep the threshold with respect to quantity, intensity, or complexity, by ever so little, consciousness is present.

[22] *Human Learning*, New York, 1931. See also Brown and Feder, "Thorndike's Theory of Learning as Gestalt Psychology," *Psy. Bull.*, 1934, *31*, 426–437.

formation. From the beginning he has maintained the greater significance of the Law of Effect and in recent years has made a certain concession to the Gestalt claim by admitting a new principle of "belongingness." [23] This is simply illustrated by reading repeatedly to an audience such sentences as

> Norman Foster and his mother bought much.
> Alice Hanson and her teacher came yesterday.

If one then asks, "What word came after 'Norman Foster and his mother'?" the correct answer comes much more often than if one asks for the word following "much." In Thorndike's opinion, the temporal contiguity of one item with the word following it, the mere sequence without belonging, does little or nothing to the connection. In our example, the last word of the first sentence did not arouse the first word of the next because it belonged to a different thought unit. Repetition of a "connection" in the sense of the mere sequence of the two things in time has very little power as a cause of learning. Belonging is necessary. To quote a striking instance:

> If a man simply experiences A and B in succession repeatedly without any sense that B after A is right and proper, or even that B belongs with A, and without himself producing B when he suffers A, the influence upon the man is very, very slight. You practically always raise the body and bend it back after tying your shoes, and so have the sensations of bending the body back as a sequent to those of tying your shoes. You have done this from say 10,000 to 40,000 times (according to your respective ages and predilections about changing your shoes often) but the experience of tying your shoes has probably never called to mind any sensation, image, or idea of the backward body-bend in one person in 1,000. Mere sequence with no fitness or belonging has done little or nothing. (p. 19.)

On the other hand, Thorndike holds all the more insistently to his basic Law of Effect, claiming that any action which fosters the life processes of the neurons is thereby "stamped in" or learned and anything which has disagreeable consequences is eliminated. In an analysis of this concept, Cason [24] endeavors to show its untenability by pointing to the fact that numerous

[23] His less clearly-defined principle of identifiability which is now first specified is very similar to his opponents' notion of degree of structuration or "goodness" of gestalt, *op. cit.*, pp. 87–90.

[24] "Criticism of the Laws of Exercise and Effect," *Psychol. Review*, 1924, *31*, 397–417.

associations, as in reading, are formed without the accompaniment of any feelings, either pleasant or unpleasant. In considering the question of the elimination of useless movements, it is pointed out that the rat in the maze cannot distinguish between the "successful" and the "unsuccessful" turns at the time he makes them, and, of course, a human subject in similar situations has the same difficulty. "One turn looks like the other to the rat at the time he makes it, and it is difficult to understand how the *successful* turn could have been 'stamped in' and the *unsuccessful* turn 'stamped out' at the time they were made." Moreover, it is highly improbable that readiness or unreadiness of certain specific reaction-arcs to conduct can influence the satisfaction of the whole organism, for whatever entities pleasure and pain may ultimately be proved to be, they indubitably affect the total personality and not just a limited function of it.

Humor

The Gestalt position readily provides an additional hypothesis to the long list of theories of humor by calling into action its handy concept of insight. The sudden laughter which accompanies "seeing the point" is an obvious feature of kinship between the two. According to Maier,[25] who has developed this relation most explicitly, humor is essentially like insight and differs from reasoning or understanding only in so far as it contains the elements of the ridiculous. A pun is the clearest example of humor created by displacing an item from one setting to another. Kant's intellectualistic version of laughter is the nearest of the classical interpretations to the configurationist's schema, and Maier's account may be considered as a modernization of the Kantian theory of incongruity. He says:

> The thought-configuration which makes for a humorous experience must (1) be unprepared for; (2) appear suddenly and bring with it a change in the meaning of its elements; (3) be made up of elements which are experienced entirely objectively (no emotional factors can

[25] A "Gestalt Theory of Humor," *Brit. J. Psychol.*, 1932, *23*, 69–74. Conceptually the main difficulty of this highly plausible theory is that while the ridiculous is always the incongruous, the converse cannot be held. Hence, the numerous provisos attached.

Perhaps Emerson caught a glimpse of this notion in his "Essay on the Comic," for he writes, "Separate any particular object from the *connection* of things, and contemplate it alone, standing there in absolute nature, it becomes at once comic."

be part of the configuration); (4) contain as its elements the facts appearing in the story, and these facts must be harmonized, explained, and unified; and (5) have the characteristics of the ridiculous in that its harmony and logic apply only to its own elements.

In Harrower's study,[26] the Gestalt view of this problem is supported by an appeal to experimental data. She assumes that one can find structured wholes in non-perceptual content, and that such wholes possess the same or similar functional properties as the corresponding perceptual structures. In her judgment a *joke* is just such a non-perceptual unit. A joke, told among other casual items, stands out as a unity with its own particular flavor: it has unmistakable boundary lines as to its beginning and end. Further, no one who has been told two jokes, and is then asked to make a natural division in his flow of consciousness over that period, would take half of one joke as a unit, over and against one and a half jokes as the other.

Harrower's method was a derivative of the one earlier employed by Flach,[27] Arnheim (footnote 5, page 254) and Usnadze (footnote 10, page 147). One of Flach's subjects, on being asked to express Bach's music, Gothic architecture and a "compromise" by means of drawings, had sketched the accompanying diagrams in the order given:

Harrower's technique was to read a joke to her subjects and show how it might be diagrammed; the diagram was not meant as a pictorial representation of any detail or part of the joke, but was an expression of the distribution of the meaning as a whole. Then a number of jokes were read and a page of miscellaneous symbolic drawings placed before the subject with instructions to select that drawing which seemed to approximate a given joke. It is to be understood, of course, that it is not the geometrical figure, drawn in pencil on paper, that can bear any

[26] "Organization in Higher Mental Processes," *Psychol. Forsch.*, 1933, *17*, 56–120.
[27] "Ueber symbolische Schemata im produktiven Denkprozess," *Arch. f.d. ges. Psychol.*, 1925, *52*, 438 ff.

resemblance to the joke, but it is the subject's "experience," *arising from the diagram,* which may have similar properties to the experience resulting from listening to the joke.

This illustration is typical of the preliminary procedure used: The old pawnbroker was on his death bed, his entire family had gathered there in the little back bedroom of the pawn-shop. At last the old man spoke:

Is Momma here?
Yes, Poppa.
Is Rifka here?
Yes, Poppa.
Is Max here?
Yes, Poppa.
Is de whole family here?
Yes, Poppa.
Den who in heaven's name is out front minding de shop?

The regular increasing steps and the final outburst will be seen as the properties intended to be conveyed by the diagram. When the companion diagram was interspersed among a number of confusion stimuli, a correct choice was made in roughly 73% of the cases, a value obviously well beyond chance.

To study the closure effect, Harrower read aloud fifteen unfinished jokes to twenty-two subjects who were told to put down on paper any completion that occurred to them. When these spontaneous completions were analyzed, the most outstanding characteristic was the fact that there may be two answers of an exactly *opposite meaning* which are given as the closure of the structure. Here is a concrete example:

The Prisoner in Court: But your worship, I wasn't going 50 miles an hour, nor 40, nor even 30 . . .
The Judge: ....

For the judge's answer two very different statements were obtained—the one continues the descrescendo already indicated in the unfinished situation, viz.:

"Well, you'll be going backwards soon."

The other type of answer appears in:

"No, I suppose you were going 70 miles an hour."

Diagrammatically, the first alternative is the simpler since it merely continues the "direction" of thought already established by the interrupted statement; but the second alternative is not arbitrary because the simple reversal of "movement" is also implicit in the situation. The two possibilities are organized with respect to some common center.

Harrower obviously is committed to the view that meaning and organization are closely related. The following examples are offered to show the *possibility* of changing from sense to nonsense by a re-distribution of emphasis:

> That that is is that that is not is not is not that so that's so.
> It was and I said not so.
> Time flies you cannot they alight at such irregular intervals.

The first of these sentences is generally read by the naïve observer as:

> That that, is is, that that, is not, is not, is not, that so, that's so.

and he pronounces it utter nonsense (or a passage from Gertrude Stein!). The correct and meaningful structure reads:

> That that is, is; that that is not, is not. Is not that so? That's so.

The second is almost invariably read as:

> It was, and I said, "not so."

which, though not sheer nonsense, is at least not a completely meaningful sentence. The correct structuring yields the meaning:

> "It was 'and,' I said, not 'so'."

In the third sentence we get:

> *Time* (emphasized) flies, *you* (emphasized) cannot, they alight at such irregular intervals.

whereas meaning demands:

> Time (verb) *flies* (noun), you cannot, *they* alight at such irregular intervals.

Clearly, the organizing power of punctuation and intonation is the decisive factor in these cases.

CHAPTER 13

ACTION, EMOTION, AND WILL

Any system of psychology which pretends to be valid for all manifestations of mental life must demonstrate its claims with approximately equal effectiveness in every field whose problems can be investigated by way of the experimental method. It is a commonplace among many observers of the rapid growth of Gestalt psychology that in spite of a broad range of researches in the animal and abnormal regions of the subject most of the positive contributions center about the old—some would say hackneyed—theme of perception. To some extent this tendency has been inevitable since the revolutionary character of any new doctrine can best be exhibited in the extension and re-interpretation of old problems, just as the Einstein theory acquired significance because of its novel mode of dealing with such classic problems as velocity, time and space coördinates, etc. Moreover, the defenders of the Gestalt position assert that while configurationist principles are most easily derived from an examination of perceptual behavior their studies in this area should never be considered as narrow researches in perception as such. For them, the principle is the important thing, and the particular type of organismic activity in which it is revealed is a secondary concern. Nevertheless, toward the end of the 'twenties, a definite increase in experimental productivity in the fields of the emotions and the will occurred, partly as an answer to the implied suggestion of neglect of the more complex activities, and partly to prevent the topic from being pre-empted by the dominant *Geisteswissenschaft* school.

Lewin's Theory of Psychic Tensions

The leader in this distinct but fundamentally related division of Gestalt psychology is Kurt Lewin. Like most of his group.

he was a pupil of Stumpf at Berlin. His academic career was interrupted by service as captain in the German army during the war, during which he maintained sufficient composure to prepare a unique article on the figure-ground phenomena present in the camouflaged scenery of trench warfare! Lewin's early papers indicate his growing interest in the problem of the relation of the will to the memory functions, but his theoretical position was not mature until the publication in 1926 of a brilliant programmatic essay entitled, "Purpose, will and need: With a preliminary account of psychic forces and energies and the structure of the mind." [1] To other than German eyes much of his discussion is irrelevant to the main problem of the title, but since many of these digressions are illuminating and interesting in their own right they will be included in the following exposition.

For Lewin, the difficulties in the way of psychological research result less often from obstacles of an experimental and technical nature than from a failure to develop the appropriate theories. Primarily *the psychologist must be guided by his theory for without it all his investigational activity is blind and meaningless.* On the other hand, the experimentalist must prove the correctness of his hypothesis by an appeal to a psychic event occurring in a perfectly concrete situation and at a definite moment of time within a certain individual and a prescribed environment. However, every step forward depends first upon progress in the sphere of theory. In both theorizing and experimenting the tension between the striving after comprehensive views and the grasping of concrete events in all their variety may be considered the basic phenomenon of the scientific life. The omnipresence of this tension allows us to say that experiment and theory are the poles of a single dynamic whole.

It is Lewin's opinion that most experimental inadequacies are due either to errors in theory or to failures to carry the theory through in a sufficiently *radical* manner, i.e., to select extreme instances in which the theory must apply if at all. This last defect is the commoner and more serious one. Certain basic assumptions of science, too, must never be surrendered in the face of apparent obstacles, such as one's faith in the reign of law

[1] "Vorsatz, Wille und Bedürfnis," *Psychol. Forsch.*, 1926, 7, 330–385.

among mental events or the infinite possibilities of experimentation. The first postulate has often been limited quantitatively or qualitatively by good authorities; e.g., rejected for the higher mental processes or excluded during headache; and even uncompromising natural scientists denied the possibility of an experimental psychology of will on the ground that one cannot artificially evoke vital decisions, since the investigator cannot interfere with the occupational and family life of the subject. To this Lewin retorts that one could just as well have held this objection against the early studies of electrical phenomena, on the ground that it was impossible to produce a genuine thunderstorm with the weak replicas of the laboratory! This is a wholly false conception of the nature of experiment which is not at all designed to recreate the natural world any more than art aims at photographic fidelity to the objective original. In fact, it is not the rare or the extraordinary which presents the valuable or even severe challenges to research, but rather the commonplace and the banal.

The first clear-cut indication of Lewin's affinities with configurationism appear in his conception of an "action-total," which he proposes to substitute for the microscopic reductions of emotions to blends of feeling-tone and sensation-masses, or the equivalent treatment of choice and other volitional phenomena. An action-total occurs in a field (note the kinship with the figure-ground contrast in perception) and typically has a beginning and end, which serve as "contours" of the event. The termination is marked by such unit-actions as making a period, sighing in relief, or emphasizing dropping of the finished task, all of which serves to isolate it as a relatively distinct whole from its temporal "field." The reality of these action-totals may be seen from the differential effect of "imbedding" the same action in a different setting; e.g., the man who is too tired to talk before an audience may use the same number and kind of words in a conversational group with surprising ease. Similar cases may be found in the old pedagogical tricks for getting a child to do something which it does not like (such as eating a certain food, taking medicine), or for arousing interest in certain things.

The all important topic of the causes of mental events is approached by employing the notion of psychic energies in place of the theories which associationism has built upon an *adhesion* basis. These energies or tensions result from some want or need, consequently *a "tense" psychic system is the condition precedent to all mental activity,* regardless of what course it runs, or the magnitude of the energy involved. The unfortunate tendency to thrust into the foreground an objection based upon pure *intensity* is a caricature of the method of inductive science. Just as little as one investigates the laws of falling bodies with volcanic eruptions or tiles which have been blown from the roof by the wind, or the principles of hydraulics with brooks and rivers, so likewise is it futile to consider as scientifically meaningful only those psychological experiments which are simple replicas of reality. The practicality of an experiment does not rest upon such a foundation but upon the successful production of those dynamic structural systems whose laws are to be investigated. Neural connections can never be the "causes" of mental events. In order that anything conjoined can move and give rise to a happening or process, kinetic energy must be released—a fact which holds even for purely mechanical systems. Hence, for every mental occurrence one must inquire: Where do the causative energies originate? However, this change of accent does not deny that associative couplings exist or that they are important when they do occur as in verbal groups. It is simply denied that association as such can ever be a *motor* of mental activity.

Lewin's use of familiar scientific terms like energy, tension, and system does not imply a reduction of mental phenomena to the data of physics, but simply results from the general requirements of a dynamic logic whether employed in economics or elsewhere. The forces of which he speaks occur in the *psychic* field and not in the physical. To clarify their nature one needs to examine the circumstances of their operation. At the very start, it is obvious from many facts that the amount of energy involved in a given psychic process does not flow from the momentary perception. The *Umweg* or indirect and roundabout means, which even an animal or young child uses to reach a goal, is a case in point, since the objective may be literally hidden or obscured during much of the solving process. What the perception of an object or event does to the organism is best stated in terms of four propositions:

1. It may produce a definite tension in a psychic system which immediately evokes a wish or intention which was previously non-existent.

2. An already existing state of tension, traceable to some need or purpose or an interrupted activity, attaches itself to a distinct object or occurrence in such a manner that this tension regains the dominance over the motor system. Such objects possess what one may term a "demand or compulsive character" or *valence* (*Aufforderungscharakter*), i.e., certain things call upon us to perform specific acts with them: steps lure the two-year old to go up and down them; doors stimulate the opening or closing act; a dog's furry coat evokes a desire to stroke him, etc.[2]

3. These "demand characters" function as field forces in the sense that they influence, i.e., guide or steer other psychic processes, especially the motor factors.

4. Certain actions, partially initiated by "demand characters" lead to satiation processes or the attainment of desired goals, after which a condition of equilibrium of the basic system on a lower level of tension ensues.

Stresses always remain within the perceptual field and, therefore, the most frequent way of transforming this organization is through action. If one sees an "attractive" object, one is actually attracted by it and tends to approach it, i.e., the organization of the psychophysical field contains a pull which is relieved by the movement of the body. Thus, action is directly adapted to experience because it is regulated by it in a perfectly natural way.

---

[2] Note the kinship to the dynamics of "closure" as observed in other perceptual situations. An uncontrollable impulse to do something is simply a strong or tightly-organized gestalt in which the gap "demands" tc be closed. One can watch this "mechanism" in persons with a strong sense of duty or, most clearly, with psychasthenics and hysteric patients.

With children, Fajans found that the amount of attention given to a desirable object varied inversely as its distance. See her "Die Bedeutung der Entfernung für die Stärke eines Aufforderungscharakters beim Säugling und Kleinkind," *Psychol. Forsch.*, 1933, *17*, 215–267.

Successful operation with these concepts is subject to at least one major caution—one must not work with vague totals but always with specific concrete sub-totals. When this is done, mind becomes divided into natural structures such as layers, spheres, and complexes; however, on all such occasions the primary problem is to determine where wholes are present and where they are absent. When found, action-wholes exist coextensively with the presence of some sort of tension.[3] This tension confers upon these totals whatever internal unity they possess and they are not held together by any associative "cement" as the older theories would have it. Lewin's favorite illustration of the significance of the former, and the futility of the latter, explanation runs as follows: Suppose one leaves home in the morning with a letter in one's coat-pocket which one plans to drop into the nearest mail-box. As soon as the first mail-box comes into sight, the "demand-character" which it possesses for the organism (by virtue of the existing tension set up by the mailing purpose) leads to the proper insertion of the letter. Thereafter, one may pass a dozen letter-boxes without experiencing any impulse to repeat the act. On associationist principles, having performed the act once should make one more likely to do it again. As a matter of fact, the release of tension seems to be the principal determinant of the action since it is obvious that one is really less likely to repeat the act upon seeing a second mail-box because the necessary inner condition is now absent. Such "determining tendencies" had already been recognized by Ach as a necessary supplement to simpler associationism, but Lewin goes one step further in tracing their origin to a purposive act, itself not reducible to any forms of association.

In this system of ideas, the volitional life develops from more primary needs. The obvious parallelism between the operation of a genuine want and the after-effects of an intention or purpose justifies Lewin in speaking of the latter as *quasi*-needs. These quasi-needs are far more numerous and flexible than the original and primitive needs and substitute satisfactions arise much more frequently in conjunction with them. The young-

[3] It is interesting that the words which we use to express inner conditions, such as "tense," "oppressed," "upset," etc., are largely drawn from descriptions of external objects.

ster, e.g., who dares not announce the departure of the train can at least mimic the "All aboard!" cry of the station officials. Or a boy is attracted to a puppy, wishes to pet it, but is uncertain and afraid. An older girl takes the puppy in her lap and the same conflict ensues; suddenly, the boy turns around and strokes the girl's head instead of the dog's!

In general, one may say that instinctive acts [4] (needs) are those which function directly in accordance with the field forces as typified by the presence of natural "demand-characters" whereas "willed" acts (quasi-needs) are those which require a purpose or intention in advance. Most, if not all, laboratory studies fall in this class because of the necessity of inducing the subject to agree to obey directions. It is of more than passing interest to notice that phenomenally, the understanding of instructions can hardly be distinguished from the intent to execute them!

A major pre-supposition of Lewin's investigations is the necessity of surrendering finally any attempt to deal with *"the* will" as a unitary psychic datum or area of research to be contrasted with, and sharply delimited from, "intelligence," "instinct," "memory," etc. Actually the term "will" embraces many very distinct kinds of problems such as decision, intention, self-control, separation from the environment, concentration, persistence, unified or inharmonious organization of volitional goals, and many others. Lest, however, the word sink into the disrepute which has befallen the designation "instinct," he proposes to substitute the conception of "need" to cover both problems—a step which compels him to make his peace with the reigning theories of native behavior. Typically, the theory of "drives" views them as permanent urges which confer upon the organism a tendency to respond in certain directions. However, Lewin maintains that the effectiveness of these drives

[4] Lewin's position is different from McDougall's on this point. Instead of championing the reality of a limited number of inner "drives," he merely holds that the organism has definite possibilities of reacting when certain conditions are present. We attribute different capacities to iron—it can fall, be electrified, etc.—without assuming the presence of mysterious impulses in these directions. For Lewin there is no independent source of energy inherent in a purpose any more than there is weight *in* a rock or *in* a table. Instead, purpose is a field property or a *structured* field of energy. A high energy potential exists in a field in reference to a low. The goal and the line of resolution are both simultaneously conditioned by the immediate situation.

hinges upon the presence of *acute* states of tension, to explain which the notion of "need" is more serviceable.[5]

Value and Meaning

Psychologically, any discussion of human "values" is impossible without reference to the affections.[6] Some percepts possess "initial" character, i.e., that which is perceived is "bad"; others have an "end" character, i.e., the perceived item is good. It is these dynamic features which we normally call "values." These affective qualities of perceptual structures are just as fundamental as any, and it is an error to consider them as purely subjective creations which we "project" into other objects. The upward urge of a Gothic cathedral is a property of the cathedral and not of my ego, much as it may provoke in the ego a similar urge. A thing is equally as "weird" as it is "black," in fact, even more so, since the first influence is stronger. "Weird" simply means that the thing serves as an "initial" phenomenon, from which one must move *away* rather than toward. Conversely, a desirable object is one which is felt as a goal to be striven for, the goal having a quasi-physical meaning of closing a gap. For this reason, every process directed toward some end can be termed "valuational" or meaningful, the two being inseparable. Value and being, consequently, are equally real and objective. Ideals of all sorts are simply end-goals of dynamic activity, i.e., figures or situations which are maximally *prägnant*, symmetrical, and stable. With this recognition, Dilthey's cleavage between an explaining and an understanding psychology disappears. Value and meaning are not creations of pure reason but are rooted in the nature of the world itself. It is through this avenue of reflection that Gestalt aims to break down the

[5] Gestalt theory could be much clearer on the subject of instinct than it is. It rejects flatly McDougall's classification and yet acknowledges the reality of native urges. If by instincts we mean the systems which the organism has at birth, configurationism certainly has a place for them, because the organism at any time is made up of physiological systems that are responsible for its conduct. These systems are functions of what they were at birth or as a consequence of maturation, *and* of the changes that may have been produced in them by use (changes commonly referred to as learning). If this approach be correct, then instead of two sharply divided classes, instincts and habits, we really have a continuum from maximally modified systems to those which have remained relatively unaltered. See the exceptionally intelligent discussion of this hotly-contested issue of the past decade by Miss Drury, "Can Gestalt Theory Save Instinct?" in *J. General Psychol.*, 1931, 5, 88–94.

[6] This paragraph is based upon Koffka's discussion in the *Lehrbuch der Philosophie*, ed. Dessoir, Berlin, 1925, p. 600.

venerable opposition between judgments of fact and judgments of value, which seemed so final to our immediate forbears.[7] The normative sciences—logic, aesthetics, ethics—which are impossible on mosaic principles thus win a sanction which theoretically places them on an equal footing with the descriptive ones.

In order to appreciate this conclusion, we must realize that from the configurational point of view, perception and action cannot be separated; the one flows over into the other. Consequently, there is no break in continuity between the phenomenal and behavior patterns. This is the standpoint of isomorphism, i.e., the view that the *form* of mental events is the *same* as physical. It is the fundamental thesis of Köhler's "Physische Gestalten." From the Gestalt view on methodology and experimentation, it is first necessary to understand the effect of the world upon the organism; hence, an introspective report may throw light upon explicit behavior. Since the configurational concepts are not limited to static events in the nervous system, perception may be regarded as a stage preparatory to action. If an object appears "friendly," this appearance implies my reaction to it as well as my perception of it.

Reward and Punishment

In the last decade or so, Lewin and his pupils have been engaged in extending the conquests of configurationism to those deeper and less accessible areas of organismic conduct represented by the topics of action, emotions, and the will.[8] A superficial view of their work is apt to leave the impression that the characteristic procedures which Wertheimer and Köhler have so successfully applied to the fields of perception and learning are abandoned in favor of a novel and less convincing approach in the more complex functions. As a matter of fact, the ideology is preserved essentially unaltered but merely extended ingeniously to newer enterprises.

---

[7] Husserl's dictum, "Alles was ist hat Sinn" (All that exists has meaning), was probably influential in establishing this view of Gestalt.

[8] In the original, the series of about two dozen papers which Lewin has edited with his pupils' aid is termed *Untersuchungen zur Handlungs-und Affektpsychologie.* Presumably this union indicates a belief in the essential identity of the problems of action and affection.

Since Lewin implies that the psychologist's task is exhausted as soon as he has fully described the dynamic processes occurring in every concrete individual situation, it is only inevitable that he should depend largely upon pictorial diagrams to clarify

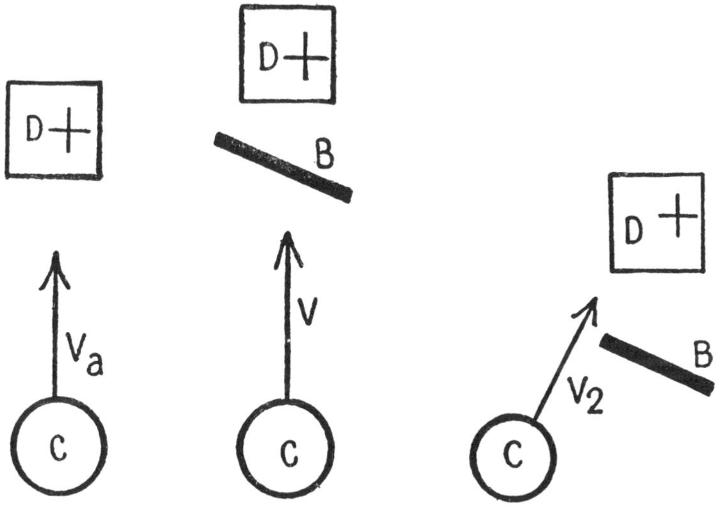

(29) (30) (31)

Figure 29. Lewin's Method of Depicting the Action of Field Forces in Conduct

The topology of the situation is: A child (C) is attracted by a doll (the plus indicating positive pull; the resulting tension is represented by the vector (arrow V_a).

Figure 30. Same as Figure 29 but Complicated by the Introduction of a Barrier (B)

The doll e.g., may be within the child's vision but out of its reach.

Figure 31. Same as Figure 30 but with a New Vector toward the Goal Circumventing the Obstacle

When a direct attack upon a problem becomes impossible, a roundabout solution (détour or "Umweg") is undertaken.

his position. Perhaps the best introduction to the specific uniqueness of his thought is found in a recent monograph [9] on reward and punishment, which presents in simple and clear form

[9] *Die psychologische Situation bei Lohn und Strafe,* Leipzig, 1931. For a sympathetic criticism of Lewin's concept of vectors, see an article with that title by E. C. Tolman in *J. General Psychol.*, 1932, *7*, 3–15; Lewin's answer entitled, "Vectors, Cognitive Processes, and Mr. Tolman's Criticism," appears in *ibid.*, 1933, *8*, 318–345.

his matured views through the instrumentality of a qualitative mathematical topology.

The theme of this work is that the actual behavior of the organism depends in every case both upon the individual's char-

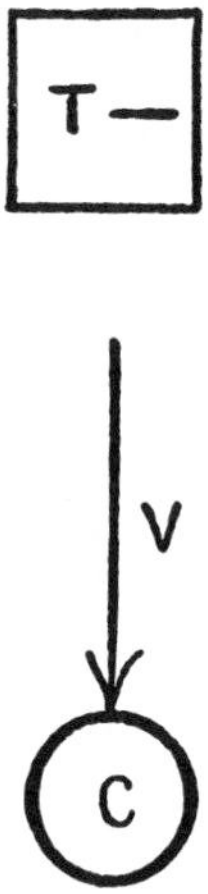

(32)

(33)

Figure 32. Introduction of a Negative Vector
An unpleasant task (T with a minus sign) repels the child, as shown by the reverse direction of the arrow.

Figure 33. Consequences of Introducing Disciplinary Measures
The negative "valence" of the threat of punishment pushes the child back in the direction of the task. He is now influenced by two vectors.

acteristics and upon the momentary structure of the existing situation. If we wish to portray what occurs when a child is led to perform a simple "interesting" act, such as playing with its doll, then Figure 29 results. The plus sign indicates that the doll has a positive appeal (*Aufforderungscharakter*) to the child, and if this attraction be sufficiently strong relative to the other psychic forces present in the field, an action of the child in this direction ensues (represented by the vector *a*). If, however, physical or social obstacles are placed in the way, a psychological *barrier* is established as in Figure 30. This alters the positional relationship between the child and the objective with the result that a new vector in the direction of the goal appears—the prototype of all *Umwege* or détours. Behavior of this kind has

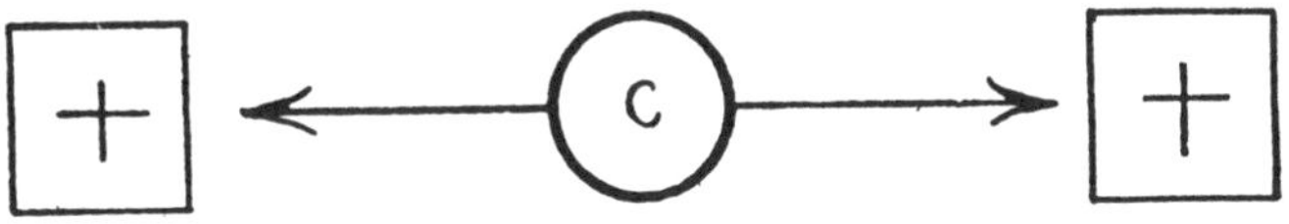

Figure 34. A Conflict Situation Provoked by Two Equally Attractive Goals
This is the classical dilemma of Buridan's ass.

a "purposive" cast and is dominated by a "natural teleology." Where a disagreeable task is imposed, such as performing a home assignment, a vector of rejection or repulsion becomes operative.

The application of reward and punishment, however, alters the total-situation by changing the "valence" of the goals or introducing a new vector. This means that in some way a field

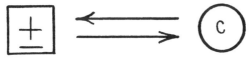

Figure 35. An Ambivalent Conflict Situation
The mental state of "temptation" with both positive and negative vectors operative.

force of sufficient strength to counteract it must be set up in opposition to the vector of repulsion. Topologically, then, a threat of punishment evokes the situation of Figure 33.

The "negative appeal" of the task is dynamically akin to a barrier since it blocks approach, and this, coupled with the presence of another negative character—the penalty—creates for the individual a situation involving conflict. Psychologically, conflict is distinguished by the presence of simultaneously antagonistic and approximately equally powerful forces. Where the vectors involved are both negative, Figure 33 applies; where they are both positive, as with Buridan's ass who starved between two equidistant bundles of hay, Figure 34 is pertinent; and if the situation is ambivalent (e.g., a child wishes to stroke a dog but is mildly afraid, or to eat "forbidden fruit"), then

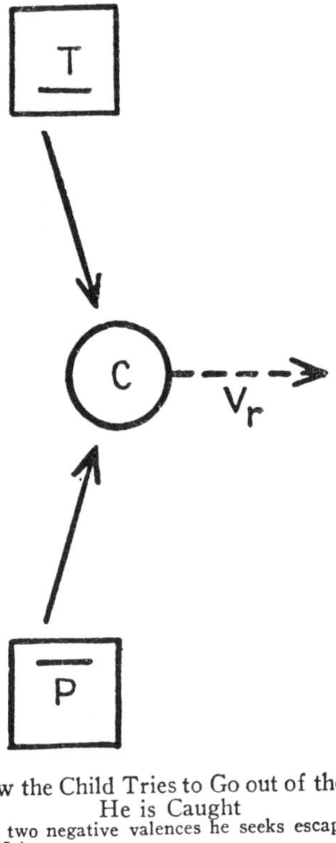

Figure 36. How the Child Tries to Go out of the Field in Which He is Caught

Torn between two negative valences he seeks escape by following the resultant vector (V_r).

Figure 35 offers the best symbolism. Obviously, a conflict situation tends toward resolution since it involves a labile equilibrium; hence, the slightest lateral displacement of C must produce a strong resultant V_r perpendicular to the direction: punishment—task (Figure 36). The child then seeks to "go out of the field," avoiding both the unpleasant duty and the penalty.

Going out of the field may involve literally running away or hiding, or busying one's self with a more agreeable but irrelevant occupation against which no one can legitimately protest. Such behavior is inevitable in accordance with the topology and the field-forces of the situation, *unless* special measures are taken to create an *outer barrier* which prevents flight. The function of the barrier is to forbid escape until either the task or the punishment is accepted. The simplest barriers are, of course, physical, as when one confines a youngster to his room until he obeys, but they are often of a sociological nature, such as the control

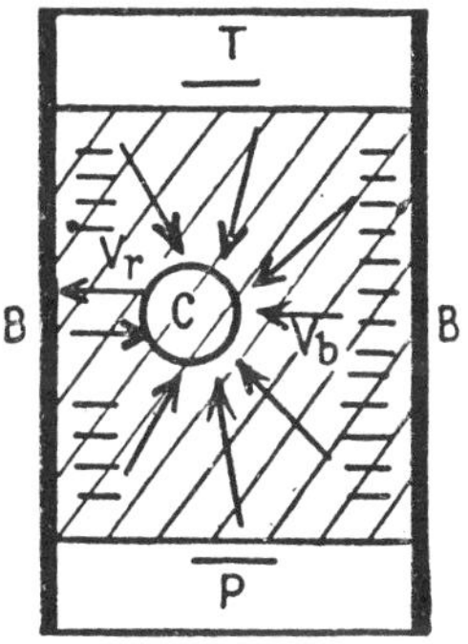

Figure 37. Tension at its Climax

The presence of the outer barrier (the heavy lines at B) forbids flight and the organism is completely encased by hostile forces. This is probably the origin of most prison psychoses. T and P still stand for task and punishment.

exercised through the "bad black man" or "God," from whose omniscience one cannot flee (cf. Francis Thompson's "Hound of Heaven" for an impressive poetic testimony of the strength of such "barriers"). At a more mature level, the appeal of group morality becomes effective ("unladylike!" "Be a man!") by virtue of a hierarchy of goals and values which the individual personally accepts. An appeal of this sort contains one of the most potent of threats—the danger of exclusion from the group.

When an outer barrier is rigorously held (represented by the heavy lines), "going out of the field" is impossible and a general *heightening of tension* is the consequence. (Figure 37). At every point in the field the child experiences an increase in pressure. A new negative vector V_b traceable to the barrier is now effective and tension, which is always due to the presence of opposed vectors, dominates the situation—(symbolized in the drawing by the cross-hatching throughout the field). Under these circumstances the child may execute the command, in which case the vector coming from the punishment proves itself stronger than the counter-forces; or he may accept the penalty should the reverse hold; or he may direct his energies against the barrier through temper tantrums, flattery, deception, or defiance, in the hope that it may be lifted through these means. Should the barrier be firmly maintained and a sufficiently strong tension throughout the entire field promises to endure, suicidal tendencies may arise since self-destruction appears to be the only way of "going out of the field." [10]

Whenever a child is threatened with punishment through adult intervention there necessarily results a situation in which the two are opposed as enemies. The child is normally caught within the net of more powerful field forces exerted by the adult, from which escape is often possible only through transference to a "plane of irreality." This region of psychic space (typified by dream and fantasy) is characterized dynamically by an unusual fluidity due to the absence of rigid barriers and the shifting nature of the boundaries between the self and the environment. If the plane of reality contradicts too sharply the wishes and needs of the child, substitute satisfaction will be found on the unreal level of play or daydream. This transition is simply an internal variety of "going out of the field." Revenge fancies and "conquering hero" episodes enable the actual weak field force of the defeated child to enlarge into the dominating influence on the level of imagination.[11]

The concrete resemblance of these situations to those treated by the psychoanalysts, especially Adler, is plain, but the Gestalt interpretation, as usual, is wholly different. It takes the following form: The solution of intellectual tasks admittedly always requires a certain tension, a vector in the direction of the problem. Now conflict situations with general tension, of the

---

[10] The suicide of the Russian commander when he realized that his army had been trapped in the Masurian marches by Hindenburg deserves to become a classic illustration of this outcome.

[11] Lewin illustrates this process at great length from an incident in the boyhood recollections of Tolstoi. His tutor, St. Jérôme, had locked him in a lumber room for some boyish prank. The story appears in Tolstoi's *Complete Works*, Vol. 1, "Boyhood," Chs. 14–15, translated by Wiener, Boston, 1904.

kind just described, are particularly unfavorable to rational solutions. The essence of problem-solving consists in a transformation of the structural relations of the situation so that a new organization or arrangement emerges. A prerequisite to the occurrence of such a shifting demands that the individual be able to *survey the field as a whole.* This decisive reconstruction of

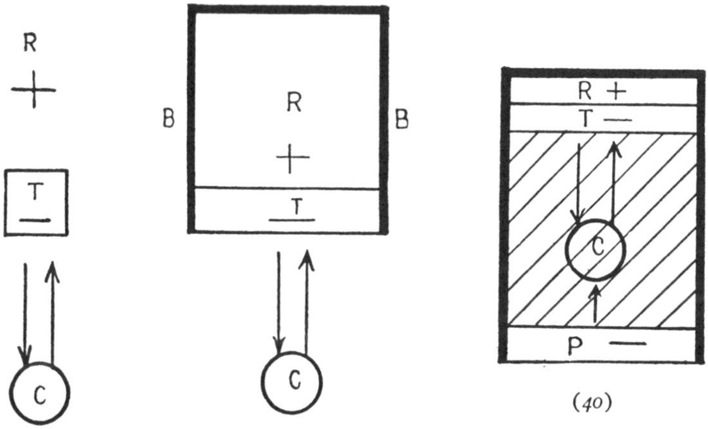

(38) (39) (40)

Figure 38. The Reward Situation
The reward (R) normally can be approached only by discharging the task.

Figure 39. Same as Figure 38 with a Barrier (heavy border at B) Added to Insure the Performance of the Task if the Reward is to be Gained
Note that in this situation the child stands outside the barrier rather than within it as in the punishment situation symbolized by Figure 37.

Figure 40. Combination of Reward and Punishment
The conflict situation here portrayed is typical of "examination fever" and is probably the cause of much pupil-teacher antagonism.

the field postulates the capacity to stand "above" the situation, to have a minimum amount of personal detachment, for only then does one see the general inter-connections and not just the specific details. However, if the child is in a conflict situation involving strong tension, it is bound to become submerged within or "under the situation, deprived of the possibility of survey and perspective—a circumstance decidedly unfavorable for quiet intellectual solutions."

In conditions involving reward rather than punishment, the subjective state gives less evidence of friction. Here it is the intention to create a positive vector of sufficient intensity to overcome the negative repulsion of the disagreeable task; hence, it is placed in the same direction but "behind" the problem (Figure 38). Functionally, the unpleasant requirement constitutes a *barrier* lying between the person and his goal (R). Since there is always the danger that the child will make a circuitous path to his goal and thereby avoid the problem, a barrier must be erected so that access to the reward can occur *via* the task only (Figure 39). The main difference between the punishment and reward set-ups is that in the former the barrier surrounds the child, while in the latter he stands *outside* of the circle constituted by the barrier and the duty (cf. Figures 37 and 39). Indeed, the reward situation never possesses the compulsive character so typical in the case of punishment.

The reward situation just described is usually complicated by the presence of a punishment factor. Normal motivation consists in the promise of satisfaction should a certain type of behavior be performed and of penalty if a different act takes place. This is the "sugar-bread and whip" combination in social control. The use of marks or grades in the school system is perhaps the simplest example of this sort. A good "report" has the character of a reward, a poor one that of punishment, and the total situation is such that either one or the other inevitably enters. If the child is confronted by an unpleasant school task which will be graded by the teacher, the tendency to do the job as well as possible is simultaneously traceable to the negative "valence" of an inferior mark and the positive attraction of a good one (Figure 40).

The usefulness of reward and punishment is most pronounced in those cases where no natural disposition toward a given kind of conduct exists, but a third possibility—the arousal of interest and creation of a tendency—must not be overlooked. Interest in a previously uninteresting object or activity can be awakened in many ways, e.g., through a model offered by a likeable teacher or through placing the task in another connection, as in computing in the form of a selling game. Fundamentally, interest of this sort is effective only when it is possible to modify the "valence" of the action under consideration. If one merely juxtaposes an undesired activity with something that the child does gladly—like decorating the "dry" primer with pretty pictures—the agreeable may co-exist as a summative conglomerate and yet be subjectively unrelated. It is possible, however, to *imbed* a task in other *contexts* in such a fashion that the meaning thereof and consequently its valence or appeal are completely altered. The youngster who refuses his food eats without further ado when the dwarf at the bottom of the plate is to be uncovered or if the spoon is declared to be a train running into the station (the mouth). In such instances, the original motor action of eating becomes a dependent part of a more comprehensive action-total. On both the receptor and effector sides of organismic behavior the whole primarily determines the psychological reality of these subsidiary parts. This circumstance is of especial importance for child psychology because *the greater dynamic unity of the infant makes the isolation of a single action more difficult than with the adult.*

Contributions of Lewin's Pupils

The first, and in many ways the most impressive, paper in the series of studies which may with undoubted appropriateness be called "the work of the Lewin school" was prepared by Zeigarnik [12] on the differences in retention between finished and unfinished actions. She approached this problem by administering to 164 subjects 18 to 22 simple tasks, such as match-stick puzzles, writing a series of cities whose names began with L, etc. One-half of these problems were interrupted by the experimenter before the subject had completed them, while the other half, of course, were allowed to be finished. Later the subjects were required to list *all* the tasks they could recall. If the finished and unfinished performances are equally likely to be retained, the ratio of the number unfinished recalled to the number fin-

[12] "Ueber das Behalten von erledigten und unerledigten Handlungen," *Psychol. Forsch.*, 1927, *9*, 1–85.

ished should approximate one. The deviation of the quotient $\frac{U}{F}$ from unity is, therefore, a measure of the degree to which one or the other type of problem is memorially at an advantage. The arithmetic mean of all quotients calculated in this manner was 1.9, indicating that the unfinished tasks were retained 90% better than the finished. It is significant, too, that the range of values was much higher upward than downward (6.00-0.75).

Other facts confirm this striking superiority of the unfinished performances. An incomplete task was *named first* in the free report three times as often as a finished. They also dominated second place. Apparently, the unfinished items were not only better retained but also pushed into the foreground! Moreover, the marked superiority of the incompleted tasks is all the more surprising in the light of the longer time spent upon the finished ones. The objection that the effect of the interruption varied with the nature of the problem was easily met by dividing them into two equal groups and rotating them among the subjects without changing the anticipated outcome.

The explanation of this interesting phenomenon is cleverly but perhaps too elaborately given in terms of Lewin's theory of tensions. At the moment that the subject plans to execute the task on the basis of the instructions given, a quasi-need arises which impels the organism toward the completion of the problem. Dynamically, this corresponds to the erection of a tense system which strives for "relaxation." The solution of the problem then signifies an "unloading" of the system, a release of the quasi-need. Where the task is interrupted, a residual tension inevitably remains, so that the quasi-need is unsatisfied. The urgency of these quasi-needs is expressed by many actions of the subject, such as his sharp defense against interruption and the strength of the drive to resume efforts at solution wherever the slightest opportunity is allowed.

Zeigarnik arranged to interrupt her subjects in their operations at different stages of the solution and found that the percent of retention for middle and "terminal" interruptions was 90% as compared with only 65% for work which was broken into at the beginning. A plausible explanation seems to be that the subject is more "in" the work toward the last. For instance, if we are interrupted in writing a letter at the start it is not nearly so disagreeable as when the interference occurs near the end. The need to finish the letter is then much stronger, partly because the developing tension has acquired a sort of momentum and partly because of the accelerating influence of the goal's proximity.

When those tasks in which the retention quotient approached unity as a value were analyzed, they were found to belong to the category of "continuous" activities as opposed to "final" acts. Examples of final actions are: painting a cube, solving a riddle, sketching a vase; continuous actions are represented by: stringing pearls on a thread, drawing innumerable crosses, etc. An end-action is, therefore, one with a *strictly definite and visible goal.* A continuous act, on the other hand, has no clearly defined end. Moreover, the separate divisions of the final action follow each other in such a fashion that each subsequent unit constitutes an organic *addition* to the preceding one, whereas the phases of a continuous act are merely drawn up in series, with a "drop-like" addition of successive segments.

The preceding paragraphs contain the essence of what promises to be, if it has not already become, one of the major "classics" of Gestalt experimentation.[13] The origin of this curious problem may be of more than passing interest. According to the story which goes the rounds of the Berlin Institute, Lewin caught the idea by noticing that German waiters, who serve as cashiers, could remember the details of a guest's bill (even though serving many other customers during the night) for a considerable stretch until the bill was paid; but if questioned as to what one had had after payment had been made, they were unable to reply. Evidently, the payment of the bill had released an understandable tension and ended the matter, with the result that forgetting immediately set in!

An extension and verification of Zeigarnik's investigation

---

[13] Walter Schlote, a pupil of Ach, has re-checked Zeigarnik's study and in general confirmed her findings. However, he objects to an explanation in terms of quasi-need, claiming that the older concepts of determining tendency and perseveration offer a better solution. See "Ueber die Bevorzugung unvollendeter Handlungen," *Zsch. f. Psychol.*, 1930, *I.7*, 1–72.

was made by Ovsiankina [14] who analyzed in detail the problem of the resumption of an interrupted task. Using much the same material as her predecessors, she discovered that performances with a definite terminus were resumed in 70% of the cases where the subject was free to do so; but only 46% of the continuous actions were taken up again. Many illuminating forms of substitute-satisfaction emerged if the prohibition forbidding resumption was in effect; e.g., one subject whose task was to shade a chess square pattern short-circuited his response by hastily drawing wavy perpendiculars in alternate squares and leisurely returning to the cross-hatching. Subjectively, the problem had been discharged for him in all its essentials even though a *pars-pro-toto* performance had resulted. The outstanding point is that the lust to finish even a disagreeable and stupid task once it has been begun is so keen that devious subterfuges to accomplish this arise compulsively.

Birenbaum's research [15] on the forgetting of an intention represents an extension of Zeigarnik's problem and ingeniously assembles some evidence in favor of Lewin's doctrine of segregated psychic systems. Her subjects were presented with a number of miscellaneous tasks to solve, and after the general instructions had been given, the experimenter asked them to affix a signature (or the number of the page, the date, etc.) to each page. This constituted the "purpose" to be studied. The subjects understood this as a request to aid the experimenter in arranging his records. Obviously, it was important to conceal the real meaning of the experiment from the subjects, otherwise the intention would have acquired the weight of a major task. According to Lewin's hypothesis, no forgetting occurs when "purposes" which are deeply imbedded in the total motor action are used; it is only with relatively isolated intentions that forgetting takes place.

In one series of problems, Birenbaum gave five similar match-stick problems consecutively followed by a pause, and then another related set of five. During the five- or ten-minute

[14] "Die Wiederaufnahme unterbrochener Handlungen," *Psychol. Forsch.*, 1928, *11*, 302–379.

[15] "Das Vergessen einer Vornahme. Isolierte seelische Systeme und dynamische Gesamtbereiche," *Psychol. Forsch.*, 1930, *13*, 218–284.

pause, other simple tricks were indulged in. The sequence of correct executions of the original instructions was: 80%, 100, 100, 100, 100; pause; 20%, 90, 100, 100, 100. The item of interest, of course, is the unusual degree of forgetting in the first problem following the hiatus. That this was far from accidental was indicated by the fact that in a control group, in which no temporal gap occurred, no failures to remember appeared.

In another series, five similar puzzles of the match-stick type were first given, while the sixth was a critical or new task followed by further different ones. The per cent of correct performance of the "intent" was as follows: First five problems, 100%; No. 6 (writing city names), only 40%; in order thereafter: (7) guessing name, 20%; (8) writing favorite poem, 40%; (9) word-building, 40%; (10) copying pentagon, 40%; (11) tracing figure, 0%; (12) sketching own monogram, 0%. The drop is the more pronounced the greater the difference between the new "psychic area" and the old. Presumably, the reason for the complete loss of memory in the case of the monogram lies in the fact that it was a sort of "substitute" for actually writing one's full name.

Throughout all these data one sees the evidence which can be used to buttress the theory of action-totals. This in itself is simply the general Gestalt view as expressed in the dynamics of motor performances. A *purpose* is forgotten when it is merely an independent system of tensions, but it is smoothly and inevitably executed when it is a dependent moment in a larger unified sequence of activities.[16]

One of Lewin's pupils, Schwarz,[17] worked on the problem of habit and reached conclusions which seem to be pertinent to many issues in clinical medicine, criminology, and psychotherapeutics. He was primarily concerned with an examination of the causes leading to backsliding, recidivism, and the performance of "automatic" actions against the broader will and inten-

[16] Perhaps man's extraordinary forgetfulness of his own dreams can be accounted for by their "isolated" character. Since they normally are unintegrated with the rest of our affairs they are readily lost. Dreams belong to the plane of irreality which is more fluid and less compactly organized than the plane of reality.

[17] "Ueber Rückfälligkeit bei Umgewöhnung," *Psychol. Forsch.*, 1927, *9*, 86–158; 1933, *18*, 143–190.

tion of the subject himself. These regressive phenomena fall into two classes: In the first type, the old "habit" appears because of the presence of a definite stimulus (such as a glass of whisky for the drunkard) which had previously been effective in the satisfaction of a given need. This need, however, is the decisive motive force behind the mental event. Upon the basis of this need the "stimulus" or the means of satisfaction will be *sought*. Genuine breaking of a habit cannot take place merely through the spatial elimination of the stimulus, but must consist in the removal or inner transformation of the need itself. If the need be absent, then the stimulus is indifferent. The second group of reversions consists in those cases of relapse which occur with fixed forms of motor execution attached to relatively neutral actions (such as the grasping of a doorknob, reaching for one's watch, etc.).

In his experiment, Schwarz operated with a situation of the latter variety. His objective was to construct a setting in which the habitual action was built into a larger framework of actions, within which it occupied a relatively secondary rôle. This was accomplished by means of a contrivance permitting a ball to run down a gutter and pipe and to drop into a concealed box, from which it could be obtained only by depressing (or, in the confusion situation, elevating!) a lever. Whether lifting or pushing the lever was to be effective in securing this result depended upon a minor internal alteration of the mechanism. The task could be complicated by using variously colored balls, requiring the formation of a pattern, etc. The subject then practiced the total action (involving *pressing* the lever) until a dependable sequence had been produced which normally occurred after 90 trials. What Schwarz terms "framework-action" was protected from mechanization by the periodic imparting of new instructions of increasing difficulty.

The situation was now altered and the subject told to roll the colored balls in a different order, *raise* the lever, and place the balls in different receptacles. This general intention, however, miscarried regularly from the very start; even when the handle was correctly used, muscular evidence of a *false start* was always plainly observable. Upon the basis of this and related findings,

Schwarz concludes that *the tendency toward a relapse is effective if the lever task is executed as a subsidiary process, but remains barren if the service of the lever is performed as the principal action.* Change of "accent" and emphasis among the different parts of the total act are the means by which this aim is accomplished. This gravitational shift is the only agency by which the reversion can be overcome; subjectively it is experienced as a sort of "counter-pressure."

The list of conditions necessary for the arousal of a "regressive tendency" is interesting enough to be reproduced here:

1. The change must concern a *dependent part of a larger total action.* A chain of relatively autonomous, thinly-connected partial acts must not be involved, but a smoothly running action-unit. If the change is introduced before the appearance of this broader action-total, no relapse occurs.
2. The part affected by the change in either instructions or the operating device *must not be the major performance.*
3. The larger action-total must have a "one-track" structure with respect to the part modified. It must not, e.g., be be mastered originally as one of two alternative variants.
4. The changed action must not be performed with too great a temporal gap between it and the old procedure.

A related motor study, free from Lewin's special terminology but belonging within the borders of configurationism, is Szymanski's sober analysis [18] of the ludicrous scratching function. He found that the scratching act normally obeyed the principle of least effort because the shortest path to the irritated area was chosen. Practically every part of the body with the exception of the upper extremities can be reached by both hands and as a rule that hand does the scratching which can most readily and conveniently reach the affected region. If, however, a part is stimulated which both hands can touch with equal mechanical freedom, then it is a matter of chance which one will execute the scratching act.

---

[18] "Untersuchungen über eine einfache natürliche Reaktionstätigkeit," *Psychol. Forsch.*, 1922, *2*, 298–316.

Comical as it may appear, the principle of least work is still obeyed even where the shortest path is not chosen, e.g., if one hand is hindered and the other free, then the free hand does the scratching. Szymanski watched people in libraries busily engaged in serious reading and noticed that whatever scratching occurred was done in such a way as to interrupt least the main business of the subject. This functional difference between main and auxiliary actions is easily demonstrated by a little experiment which any one can perform: A man with a hat on his head is asked to approach the experimenter and, having first removed his hat (a *conditio sine qua non!*) to write a given word on a sheet of paper with the pencil lying upon it. Even though normally right-handed, the subject generally removes his hat with his left hand and then grasps the pencil with his right hand—indicating that the important act dominates the subsidiary one. A clear and simple case of pattern regulation has occurred.

The Russian investigator, Luria, has independently developed a motor and affective theory which bears an extraordinary resemblance to Lewin's position. He considers it an excellent heuristic device to view the organism as a unity of many subsystems held in inner equilibrium, whereby changes in one of these systems produces alterations in another. That this is not a rash assumption neurologically is evident in the brain changes accompanying aphasia, which are known to be connected with manual activities and thus offer a possibility for re-establishing speech through the exercise of the hands. Conversely, cases of hemiplegia are often aided by speech instruction. Adler's thesis of organic inferiority and the consequent compensatory functions similarly suggest a notable reciprocal dynamic connection between the individual organs and the central nervous system.

According to Luria,[19] the feelings and the emotions are temporary disturbances of the equilibrium of these sub-systems, whereas the neuroses and psychoses represent more permanent

[19] Cf. "Die Methode der abbildenden Motorik bei Kommunikation der Systeme und ihre Anwendung auf die Affektpsychologie," *Psychol. Forsch.*, 1929, *12*, 127–179. A verbose English translation of Luria's *Nature of Human Conflicts* was published by Liveright in 1932.

alterations of the same nature. In a minor way, a method of studying these concealed central processes is provided as soon as we find a voluntary motor act which is tied up with them. On configurationist principles a disturbance of a higher order should be reflected in the modifications of a related finger reaction such as pressing a pneumatic key. Using an adaptation of Jung's diagnostic association method, Luria had his subjects depress the key whenever the stimulus word was given but to keep the hand resting there constantly. Indifferent or neutral terms gave highly regular graphic curves of response with even pressure peaks at periodic intervals and smooth valleys between, whereas the emotionally-toned items yielded peaks of varying heights with rough jagged intervening spaces due to variant trembling. The reason for this effect is found in the fact that the motor component is a dependent part of a larger unitary system. Apparently this is all that occurs in cases of hypnosis.

Using a modification of Ach's method of measuring "will," Luria was able to unearth objective evidence of the reality of "unconscious" impulses. He trained one subject to depress the pneumatic key simultaneously with the correct associative agent-action response, thus: lamp-lights. Then he changed instructions, requiring not the learned word but a wholly new one. The graphic record revealed the hidden and inhibited member in the form of a double peak with many approaches, indicating that the practiced word had first come to mind and only later, after some overt signs of inhibition, was the correct response "fire" accompanied by a "true" peak. Curiously enough, when the right hand does not betray the central disturbance, a displacement of the effect occurs either to the left hand or even to the feet! What this suggests for an understanding of hysteric symptoms is obvious.

The work of Anitra Karsten [20] is an excellent contribution to the theory of mental fatigue and incidentally throws much needed light upon the pronouncedly subjective character of monotony, boredom, and allied phenomena. Every observer knows that the satiation effects of repetition are highly elastic

[20] "Psychische Sättigung," *Psychol. Forsch.*, 1928, *10*, 142–254.

because of their dependence upon a broad complex of conditions: Karsten even reports that one child enjoyed opening and closing a door so much that it did so 82 times!

In studying the "saturation-process" by which an originally neutral task becomes a revolting performance, the author directed her subjects to make "fence-pickets" (////////) on sheets of paper until they lost all desire to continue the work. The qualitative analysis revealed the following features: At the beginning, the side of a page constitutes a unit of effort. Later a dissolution of the original configuration occurs, variability in performance being prominent in the final stages. Concurrently, errors and loss in quality appear and eventually the task loses its meaning. The work becomes not only disorderly and loosely-connected, devoid of definite boundaries and termini, but breaks up into little independent fragments. A larger whole has disintegrated.

It is easy to show that this simple act of making uniform pencil strokes can be continued after satiation, provided the act is imbedded in a new totality. That person who maintains he can no longer lift his arm for sheer weariness, has little trouble in passing his hands through his hair if it has become disarranged during the sitting. Changing the significance of the figural act is another method of eliminating the "apparent ennui." One subject had written *ababab* . . . until he was ready to run away from the scene in sheer nervous exhaustion, but yielded to the experimenter's plea that he was gathering autographs and readily wrote his name and address, for which several *a*'s and *b*'s were required! That which was impossible to accomplish by direct will force became attainable when the action was included in another complex system. Often the disagreeable act can be continued better if one views it as an auxiliary affair, in which case the accompanying singing or whistling becomes the main action.

In a section dealing with the spread of "satiation" from one activity to another, Karsten observed that in no subject did making strokes in the rhythm 3–5 (/// /////) "saturate" the action if the rhythm were changed to 4–4 (//// ////), since the "endurance limit" of the second function was reached on the average in 84% of the time required for the first. Evidently, the fatigue effect is highly specific and contingent upon the pattern of activity involved. The implication is that repetition alone is not the cause of monotony and boredom, since the same performance can be continued *ad libitum* in another configuration. It has long been known that varying the action makes repetition work more endurable, but to be efficacious this variation must extend to the total setting and not remain confined to the isolated behavior-unit.

Independently of Lewin's schema, as developed by Karsten, Hoche [21] showed that the experience of monotony is related to the perception of time, i.e., the subjective sense of the passage of time rather than objective or absolute time. The German word for monotony (*Langeweile*) is the only term in the major languages which suggests this relation. Monotonous conditions normally provoke a strong tendency to "go out of the field" as exhibited either by actual flight or its numerous substitutes, such as ill-humor, motor restlessness, frequent shifting of posture, finger-tapping, counting of irrelevant details, daydreaming, and escape in sleep. Externally there is a situation from which one cannot withdraw for physical, moral, sentimental, or other reasons, plus a mental content which is poor and unsatisfactory. The crux of the monotonous condition lies in this *disproportion between the temporal duration and the actual content offered.*[22] That is why smoking is often a refuge from boredom, not because of the mild nicotine narcosis, which would also serve as a protection, but because the mechanical occupation requires a certain amount of pseudo-activity and the smoke rings give a minimum of meaningful content. This theory Hoche believes is supported by the fact that we may have numerous mental experiences while dreaming, but monotony is never one of them, neither do we have any adequate apprehension of time relations; it is the absence of the latter which explains the absence of the former. Susceptibility to monotony is an excellent test

[21] "Langeweile," *Psychol. Forsch.*, 1923, *3*, 258–271.

[22] Among the Eskimos, the term "thinking" has the connotation of monotony. Perhaps that is why many scholarly university lectures and learned books are considered dry and sleep-provoking!

of normality and its re-appearance among inmates of hospitals for the insane is a welcome symptom.

Freund [23] applied the technique which Karsten had developed to the old problem of female ability during the menstrual period. His subjects were required to continue simple ornamental patterns such as borders until "psychic satiation" ensued. Using fourteen subjects he found that this point was reached in one-third to one-quarter less time during catamenia than during the intermenstrual period. Neither speed nor quality of work as such suffered, although the output, of course, was less because the tendency to "quit" appeared sooner. Freund maintains that if menstruation has any direct influence on the abilities it is not of such a nature that it cannot be compensated for by extra effort. Its undesirable influence consists in the increase in individual tension popularly known as "nervousness." The characteristic feature here is the tendency to take all events not as peripheral influences but as closely related to the ego and the central core of personality, just the condition which Karsten had previously found was most favorable to rapid satiation.

Hoppe's monograph [24] on success and failure is a continuation of the Lewinian method of experimentation in connection with a topic full of pedagogical and human interest. He had each subject carry out one act each day to the point of *satiation* (cf. Karsten) and another until *satisfaction.* After each performance, the subject was left alone in the testing room while the experimenter observed through a secret peep-hole whether the subject returned to his task or avoided resumption. Satisfaction was assumed to be present when success had been reached in some objective (like hanging sixteen rings on hooks) and satiation as soon as the subject spontaneously broke off an act and could not be induced to resume it. Using this criterion Hoppe found that all ten of his subjects began to work again after the satisfaction point, but only three following satiation.

[23] Psychische Sättigung im Menstruum und Intermenstruum," *Psychol. Forsch.*, 1930, *13*, 198–219.

[24] "Erfolg und Misserfolg," *Psychol. Forsch.*, 1931, *14*, 1–62. In a similar study with children, Fajans found that failure led to passivity or to an increased tendency to go out of the field, and success led to stronger action and greater endurance. See "Erfolg, Ausdauer und Aktivität beim Säugling und Kleinkind," *ibid.*, 1933, *17*, 268–305.

This preliminary analysis showed that experiences of success and failure even in the same person are not attached to a fixed and definite performance, but at different stages in the total development, the value of the same achievement is differently appraised. From this fact results the conception of the displacement of the *level of pretension, aspiration, or demand* (*Anspruchsniveau*), and the generalization that this plane rises after success and sinks after failure. The following tabular matter (*op. cit.*, p. 18) supports this thesis:

TABLE VI. NATURE OF CHANGES IN CHARACTER OF TASKS ATTEMPTED AFTER EXPERIENCES OF VICTORY OR DEFEAT. (HOPPE)

Displacement of the Level of Pretense	Raised	Lowered	Unaltered	Reproduction of Earlier Successes	Interrupted
After Success....	32%	0%	3%	0%	11%
After Failure....	0%	27%	12%	1%	15%

A shift in the level of aspiration occurs less often in those tasks where a sort of all-or-none principle of solution holds (as in some difficult match-stick puzzles) than in those problems like hole-shooting where quantitative variations are easier, with the result that the "pretension" level oscillates more upward than downward. The latter situation allows the subject more free play between his maximum and minimum demands than the former so that he can adjust his aspiration to the realities confronting him. There is a general tendency to hold the "ego-plane" as high as possible, and it is of considerable characterological significance that the level of success which different persons select for the same task lies at different heights.

If tasks which are too hard or too easy are presented, the experiences of success or failure remain entirely absent. It is only when the goal lies just within the boundary limits of the subject's performance that genuine experiences of this kind can occur. No sane adult is depressed by his inability to jump over a skyscraper or elated because he can tie his shoe-strings. To generalize: Feelings of successful accomplishment are possible only when there is adequate probability that failures can be expected, and conversely, failure reactions can enter only within the zone of possible successes. Educationally, this suggests that the learner's enthusiasm will grow best on challenges which are severe without being insuperable.

The relation of this study to the interpretation of many personality-patterns deserves a little comment. There are some natures whose demands upon life are so high as to run dangerously near the unattainable. Where ambition is keyed to such a high pitch, the possibility of disappointment, of course, is greatly increased. The cynicism born of disillusioned idealism (involving a lowering of the *Anspruchsniveau*), may have found here its first experimental demonstration! Also, it is of interest to note that the emotional outburst which accompanied the news of the prematurely-announced and actually-signed Armistice in November, 1918, may in part be accounted for by the silent realization that a mere twist of fate had brought victory out of defeat. Had the Allies triumphed over Siam instead of the mighty German Empire, it is unlikely that the jubilation would have been as intense.

The typical emotion of anger has been made the subject of an exhaustive analytical treatment by Dembo.[25] Like most of Lewin's research interests, the problem is approached from the *dynamic* point of view with the *genesis* of the affect at the center of attention. Quantitative exactness is out of place in such an endeavor, but significant qualitative observations are still possible.

At the outset, Dembo rejects the familiar plausible generalization that anger occurs whenever one is trying to reach a goal but is thwarted in the process. This is far from being universally valid, for a mother who wishes to hasten from the house, but is detained by her child does not always become angry; neither does one invariably react with irritation to interruption whilst engaged in some important occupation. The true explanation is a good deal more complex than this hypothesis allows.

---

[25] "Der Aerger als dynamisches Problem," *Psychol. Forsch.*, 1931. *15*, 1–144.

In constructing her experimental situations, Dembo's first procedure was to present tasks which were *impossible* to perform, but which were not obviously beyond the apparent range of the subject's capacities. Thus, on one procedure the subjects were directed to practice throwing wooden rings about the necks of bottles from a distance of fifteen feet until ten consecutive successes occurred—a feat which was practically impossible at this distance, but the subject was unaware of this. In a second "stunt," a square area was mapped off in a room with a flower placed upon a saw-buck four feet outside the square. A chair for the subject's convenience was placed within the square. His problem was to obtain the flower without permitting his feet to leave the square area. Objectively only two possible solutions exist:

1. One can place the subject's chair between the square and the buck and reach for the flower while supporting one's self with the other hand upon the chair.
2. One can kneel and still keep the feet within the square, thus easily grasping the flower.

Most subjects find both solutions after a little effort, but the experimenter unrelentingly demands a third which does not exist. The subject, not knowing this, zealously continues to hunt for a third solution. His efforts, of course, lead only to minor variations which are rejected. Occasionally, the subject demonstrates the logical impossibility of a third solution, but the simple insistence of the experimenter (who lies unblushingly) suffices to motivate new efforts.

Topologically, both the ring and flower situations are characterized by the presence of a vector toward the goal which may be produced by: (1) the request of the experimenter; (2) the attractiveness of the task itself; or (3) the difficulty of the task which arouses the self-assertion of the subject. Failure to reach the objective is caused by the *inner barrier,* i.e., the prescribed conditions of solution, and the *outer barrier*—the desire to follow the experimenter's instructions, etc.—hinders escape; consequently, the tension within the entire field is increased and the affective ground for an explosion is prepared. This may lead to unreal solutions or substitute ones. One subject saw himself floating in the air over the flower, another expressed a wish to hypnotize it, and a third planned to fill the room with water and swim toward it! On the unreal plane, both inner and outer barriers lose their rigidity and the subject acquires a greater freedom of movement.

Substitute solutions consisted in throwing the rings about a nearer stick or boldly leaving the square to fetch the flower. All such surrogates are merely compromise forms of "going-out-of-the-field" and a tendency to withdraw from the original goal. In all cases, the substitute goals are marked by the fact that they are more readily obtainable than the main objective. Especially significant is the fact that the substitute action in no case served to release the tension established by the main goal, suggesting that the two must lie in dynamically distinct systems.

Noteworthy as a support of the growing conviction that all psychological experiments have a social component is Dembo's account of the influence of the presence of the experimenter upon the subject's course of action. With different subjects, or on different occasions during the situation for the same subject, the experimenter may be: (1) the driving force behind all efforts to reach a solution; (2) a fellow-human, who knows more than you do; (3) an inner-barrier, since he simultaneously indicates the goal and blocks access to it; (4) an outer-barrier, who hinders escape; (5) a possible tool; (6) a provocative "stone of offense," who actively projects himself into the field and reveals himself as an enemy. At the beginning of the experiment, the social situation is that of intercourse between equals, but as the action proceeds a shift conferring superior status upon the experimenter occurs. This transformation of a "task-situation" into a social battlefield [26] is especially significant for the arousal of a strong affective state.

The ground affectivity having thus been established, a little "supplementary pressure" is all that is needed to bring about an outburst. Dembo explains this as a result of a breakdown of the walls or boundaries of the inner psychic systems. The ground affectivity is represented by a state of tension between

[26] Note how this throws some light upon the traditional pupil-teacher antagonism.

the superficial and deeper layers of the personality, which are normally well-insulated. A little added tension breaks these confines so that in a state of anger a dynamic unity of the total field is established and the organism changes in the direction of a less differentiated but "stronger" gestalt, i. e., toward a more primitive, homogeneous, single tense whole.[27] In the pure or extreme case, only the border layer between the inner psychic systems and the environment—the motor or action level—is preserved, but it, too, is in a state of extraordinary tension.

In Brown's study [28] one finds a most precise analysis of the problem of "reality," a concept frequently encountered in the writings of Lewin's school. He holds that all psychic processes have degrees of reality, that this reality is a special dimension in the environment, and that these differences in reality rest upon a definite structure of the life-space or region within which events occur. Taking his stand upon Dembo's claim that processes of low reality occur in a medium that is dynamically softer and more fluid, Brown argues that *tense* psychic systems should discharge more readily in a less real plane than in a more real one.

To test this, he employed a modification of Zeigarnik's "interruption" technique with two groups of university students. Group A (the "real" group) was given an alleged "intelligence" test or university entrance examination of ten problems. The reality of this set-up was intensified by the carefully printed and bound booklet and the emphasized solemnity of the situation. Group B (the "unreal" set) was given material similar to that taken by A, but the items were used to fill out a rest pause ostensibly needed for experimental purposes. The "irreality" of this situation was heightened by the oral instructions, the use of scratch paper, etc. In neither case were any of the items brought to completion. In a control series consisting of different individuals, the items presented in groups A and B were interchanged.

---

[27] Compare this with the familiar introspective reduction to minor feelings and sensations. Since anger may be manifested in laughter as well as tears, in mock politeness as well as rudeness, the impossibility of any uniform *content* seems clear.

[28] "Ueber die dynamische Eigenschaften der Realitäts- und Irrealitätsschichten," *Psychol. Forsch.*, 1933, *18*, 4–26.

In Table VII appear the results of the memory test given to four subdivisions of each group. RR means the per cent retained for *real* items;-RI, the percent of retention for "unreal" elements; the RR/RI quotient is of course the ratio between these two values.

TABLE VII—RELATIVE MEMORY FOR "REAL" AND "IRREAL" ITEMS OF EXPERIENCE (BROWN)

Interval of Delay	RR/RI Ratio
5 minutes	1.34
30 "	1.75
36 hours	2.53
One week	3.79

From an examination of the original data one gathers that the change in the size of the ratios with time is caused by a drop in the absolute number of irreal items retained. The real figures remain approximately constant. The variability is also much greater with the irreal items. Apparently, there is a greater stability of recall in the reality plane which is not just due to the greater *tension* of the real items. In a special check on his findings, Brown introduced an arrangement declaring the rest-pause problems the real ones, and the "intelligence" test items spurious. The "irreality" of the mental examination was accentuated by throwing the booklet into the waste-basket and having them plainly removed by a cleaning woman, while the coarse yellow sheets of the "rest-pause" session were carefully sorted and treasured. Confirmatory results heavily in favor of the "real" situation were also secured here. In general, the more real an experience, the better it is preserved.

Closely related to the question of the degrees of reality is the problem of substitute behavior and satisfactions. This has been studied in a series of three papers by Mahler, Lissner, and Sliosberg.[29] Mahler was concerned to know whether an unreal substitute action could lead to a genuine discharge of the

[29] The references are: Mahler, "Ersatzhandlungen verschiedenen Realitätsgrades," *Psychol. Forsch.*, 1933, *18*, 27–89; Lissner, "Die Entspannungen von Bedürfnissen durch Ersatzhandlungen," 1933, *18*, 218–250; Sliosberg, "Zur Dynamik des Ersatzes in Spiel- und Ernstsituationen," 1934, *19*, 122–181.

tension produced by a primary need. She recognized four degrees of reality (in diminishing order): (1) action; (2) speech; (3) thought; (4) magical solutions. The basic task would normally be started in the first degree of reality, interrupted, and brought to completion by a substitute belonging to a lesser order of reality. Thus, the subject started to use a needle for thrusting out the pattern of a word in a paper sheet; he was stopped (usually somewhere between the middle and end of a point where his absorption in the task was maximal) and directed to finish by writing the rest of the word with a pencil.

Using Ovsiankina's criterion of the "spontaneous resumption" of the original task, Mahler found that such resumption occurred about twice as often with *unfinished* acts as with those in which some kind of substitute completion was directed. Overt action had a higher substitute value than speech, for when used as a surrogate it was followed by fewer spontaneous resumptions of interest in the original task. Words, in turn, have a higher substitute value (as measured by this method) than mere uncommunicated thought. Generally speaking, "irreal" substitute acts do not result in a discharge of systems which belong to the plane of reality.

The most valuable part of Lissner's work consists in an extension of the theory of substitute gratification. She observes that apart from acts patently directed toward the attainment of a goal, the effect of tension may also appear in:

1. Diffuse action in the direction of the original goal.
2. Goal actions through fundamentally-modified procedures.
3. Irreal (fantastic) solutions.
4. Actions toward other goals.
5. General unrest behavior.
6. Emotional behavior.

Dynamically, the problem of substitute satisfaction may be expressed thus: Under what conditions will the discharge of a (substitute) system S simultaneously release another (= the original) system O? The general answer is: when the two psychic systems are dependent parts of a total system. This presupposes some degree of communication between the two systems. In cases where no substitute gratification occurs, one is confronted with two separate tension systems, i.e., two dynamically independent totals. Where full substitution takes place, the two systems are true dependent parts of a larger entity. Between these two extremes occur transition instances with varying degrees of communication between partially separated systems.

In Sliosberg's investigation appears a further development of the notion of substitute action, derived from play and serious situations in child behavior. In play situations, such as feeding chocolates to a doll, the substitution of grey cardboard wafers for the edible sweet is almost 100% acceptable. With a "sober setting," such as is present when an adult gives a child some chocolates and later offers him cardboard substitutes, the proportion of rejections is high.

As a rule, the more unreal the level of action, the broader the range of possibilities of handling an object. However, play and seriousness do not correspond precisely to irreality and reality; instead, the play situation appears to be a special area within the reality plane, but possessing more fluid dynamic properties.

It is significant that with an increase in the intensity of a need, the possibilities of substitution diminish. In making articles for a competitive kindergarten display toward which the youngsters were strongly motivated, substitute tools were uniformly rejected. Apparently in such a situation the real thing was none too good! However, when the child is no longer vitally concerned with doing anything (as in behavior after "satiation") it tends to accept substitutes more easily, i.e., the area of things which it considers "identical" broadens.

The perceptual properties of the object also influence its substitutability. When building with blocks was the original activity, the children found plastilin, sugar cubes, and chocolate wafers highly acceptable substitutes for the initial building materials; gravel was somewhat less acceptable; wooden animals were distracting and led to an altogether different game; but the sawed-up colored parts of these same wooden animals met with full acceptance because phenomenologically they were not "animal parts" but "blocks of wood." Repeated observations of this sort showed that "determinate" or unambiguous substitutes were never acceptable for "determinate" originals of a different nature; only 8% of determinate substitutes could be used for "indeterminate" or ambiguous originals; 63% of indeterminate substitutes took the place of determinate originals; and 94% of indeterminate surrogates were accepted for indeterminate originals. "Definites" do not go well in the place of the other definites, but "vagues" easily play the rôle of other "vagues."

From these samples of the work of Lewin's school one gathers that its major concern is with problems which would ordinarily be classified under the older rubrics of feeling and emotion, will and action. The Gestalt position, however, has dealt the deathblow to a system of categories which has been steadily disintegrating for decades under the impact of newer facts and theories. Configurationism holds that originally mental activity is undifferentiated in nature. The neonate's experiences are simultaneously cognitive, conative, and affective and the distinctions which are later justified are readily explained by the figure-ground individuation process. The ancient and medieval opposition of the voluntarists and rationalists; the heart *versus* the head debates of the Enlightenment and the Romantic Era;—are all swallowed up in this larger unity of organismic response, in which a controversy respecting the primacy of any part becomes absurd. Every sense-perception has a motor component and a feeling of some kind associated with it, and the converse combination is equally true. If the skeleton of nineteenth century subsumptions is still retained, it is purely because an acceptable new system of labels has not yet emerged and because academic necessity demands some pigeon-holes for its intellectual constructions and accumulations.

To maintain simultaneously the volitional character of emotion and the emotional nature of volition appears at first glance like some untenable Chestertonian paradox, but further analysis tends to confirm its reasonableness. If we adopt Wheeler's superb definition that "The will is the total human system consciously conditioning the activities of its parts" the functional resemblance to the emotional state becomes clearer; in both forms of behavior, we are dealing with a complex performance in which all the organism's resources are being vigorously employed to attain a distinct goal.[30] Tension, in Lewin's terminology, is involved in either case. To cite Wheeler (*Principles of Mental Development,* p. 207) again, "Emotion is not a special discrete kind of behavior. . . . *It is an aspect of whatever the person is doing at the time, when, in the approach to a given goal, the tension is increased and maintained through intraorganic stimulation.* . . . Emotive behavior is any intentional, intelligent behavior, *energized.*" The excitement of football spectators when the team is nearing a touchdown, the stirred-up condition of the salesman about to "land" a big order, the enhancement of lust as the copulatory embrace approaches culmination—are all illustrations of this uniformity.

[30] It is interesting to compare this with an earlier statement of Bergson's, "We are free when our acts spring from our whole personality, when they express it, when they have that indefinable resemblance to it which one sometimes finds between the artist and his work."—*Time and Free Will* (Eng. trans.), Macmillan, 1913, p. 173.

PART IV—PRACTICAL

CHAPTER 14

MENTAL PATHOLOGY

If the laws of Gestalt are valid laws, they must, of course, apply with equal rigor to both normal and pathological experiences. This test, which many psychiatric critics would consider decisive, is brilliantly borne by the configurationist hypothesis; in fact, some of its most substantial confirmation is derived from the behavior of disordered or injured organisms. Irrespective of the final decision, an examination of a number of representative observations made from this standpoint cannot fail to be of interest.

The Work of Gelb and Goldstein and Their Associates

The high frequency of head injuries among the wounded soldiers of the World War offered an excellent opportunity to study the adequacy of the established theories of cerebral function. In Frankfurt at the close of the hostilities, a research institute for the investigation of the sequelæ of brain injuries was established, in connection with which Gelb, the psychologist, and Goldstein, the neurologist, were able to carry out a classic series of coöperative studies.[1] It would take us too far afield to report upon all their unusual clinical cases, but an acquaintance with some of their most prized analyses is desirable because the principal pathological support of the Gestalt theory comes

[1] The series which began in 1920 has been issued as separately numbered monographs under the grand theme, "Psychologische Analysen hirnpathologischer Fälle." They are an attractive illustration of the position that a clinical symptom is to the disease pattern as the part to the whole and that diagnosis and therapy must aim at the latter rather than the former. It is a commonplace that identical symptoms (headache, e.g.) may appear in widely separated and complex maladies.

from them. For instance, one person with an injury to the occipital lobe was able to read his name written upon a blackboard if he first traced part of the letter outlines with his forefinger, but when a few parallel lines were drawn obliquely through the name he failed entirely, although to a normal person this was a negligible obstacle. In this case the perception of the figure was plainly affected by the organization of the ground.

In one investigation, Gelb and Goldstein [2] studied a patient suffering from amnesia for color names which is significant for its contribution to the understanding of aphasia as well as to the comprehension of normal speech and thought. The patient was a young man who had suffered a hand grenade wound in the left half of the skull in 1918, but who recovered with a curious complex of minor disorders. The most peculiar of these occurred with respect to color names when the Holmgren wools, or any irregular mass of colored papers, were placed before him. If asked, "What is this color called?" he would rarely answer correctly and even then the reply was given slowly and deliberately. He was not, however, color-blind in the ordinary retinal sense for he would use correctly such concrete designations as "like a cherry" for a certain shade of red, "like grass" for a definite green, and "like a forget-me-not" for a given blue. This, of course, is similar to our use of terms in the matter of smell sensations where general class names have not as yet been developed. Moreover, his matchings of colored pairs with the Nagel anomaloscope were perfectly normal as was his ability to select a *specific* hue from a mass of mingled colors corresponding to some indicated object. Where the color phenomenon had a concrete coherence with other experiences, as orange with a piece of fruit, the patient was successful, but failed wholly in sorting according to any principle of arrangement, i.e., he saw *a* blue thing but not *blueness* as a common attribute of numerous items. He was evidently permanently in the state of a normal person surveying a mass of colored materials, each of which could be individually perceived, but who had still to wait for the perception to organize itself on the basis of characteristic hues.

[2] "Ueber Farbennamenamnesie," *Psychol Forsch.*, 1925, *6*, 127–186.

Gelb and Goldstein claim he was deficient just in this respect alone, which they call "categorical" or "conceptual" behavior. When we name a color we do not give it a "singular" designation; instead, we designate the category to which the given color belongs. The patient in question could pronounce color-names correctly but they had become empty sounds to him and had ceased to be symbols for concepts. Categorical behavior and speech in its significative form are expressions of the same thing, for the same limitations of the subject appeared when he sorted metal and wooden objects as well as when he sorted colors.

The authors report a curious confirming case of a patient who was unable to confer correct color names immediately, but who, in the presence of any hue, recited the major color names in order; when the correct one was pronounced the object took on the hue of that color, but the utterance of the false name did not change the color at all. Apparently, the set toward redness or blueness made the simultaneous red or blue process supraliminal.

In another experiment [3] Gelb and Goldstein dealt with the question of the mutual functional interrelation of the injured and the intact visual sphere in cases of hemianopsia. A patient, who had received a bullet wound above the left ear, was afflicted with almost total inability to recognize forms which were projected upon the right half of either eye. If the patient was presented binocularly with a simple object projected upon the injured right region by means of an exposure apparatus, and an identical figure simultaneously cast upon the healthy left side, he reported seeing only the left object. This is a typical symptom of hemianopic attentive weakness and had already been reported by Poppelreuter. If, however, the subject was shown simple geometrical figures (e.g., a rectangle, square, circle, or straight line) in such a way that the midpoint lay at the fixation spot, be reported *seeing the entire figure on the right side as well as the left.* Ordinarily, the patient saw all objects which struck the right field as diminished in size, but those falling upon the healthy half were normal. If the object was equally

[3] "Zur Frage nach der gegenseitigen funktionellen Beziehung der geschädigten und der ungeschädigten Sehsphäre bei Hemianopsie," *Psychol. Forsch.*, 1925, *6*, 187–199.

projected upon both areas, the entire thing seemed smaller, but of a magnitude midway between the sizes when seen exclusively on the right or left! If the projections were more on one side or the other, the apparent size was conditioned by the visual half in which the major part of the figure fell.

The totalization effect reported above is of high theoretical significance because it indicates the *general* manner in which the organism attempts to preserve its threatened integrity. For instance, Hughlings Jackson somewhere analyzes the case of a man with an amputated hand who tried to use this spectral extremity or phantom to reach for the reins while riding and as a result was injured by a fall. In this instance, the bodily consciousness tried to maintain its "wholeness" or integrity in spite of the defect. The curious sensory experiences of individuals with amputated limbs can be understood better in the light of the principle of "closure," for the sensations resulting from stimulation of the stump are referred to the wooden appendage.[4]

Fuchs [5] reports some odd cases of pseudofoveæ among hemianopic patients. In clinical experience, one occasionally encounters a new center of clearest vision, in which the true anatomical fovea has sunk to the level of peripheral clarity. This new point is not fixed, but varies with the size and form of the seen object. The significance of this lies in the fact that *normally the fovea is the center of gravity of the patterned visual field;* consequently, an eccentric fovea must operate to produce a new equilibrium. In one patient, the functional character of the pseudofovea and its dependence upon the stimulus-complex was revealed by his ability to see letters of 1.5 units in size most clearly at a distance of 1.2 cm. from the fixation-point, whereas letters 18 units in size were best seen at a lateral distance of six centimeters!

To test his view that visual clearness rises and falls with the structure of the gestalt and that active or passive attention are irrelevant, Fuchs first found that a given small letter which

---

[4] That loss of bodily awareness is the last stage in the destruction of self-consciousness is nicely supported by some unusual observations of Pick. Cf. "Störung der Orientierung am eigenen Körper," *Psychol. Forsch.*, 1922, *1*, 303–318.

[5] "Eine Pseudofovea bei Hemianopikern," *Psychol. Forsch.*, 1922, *4*, 157–186.

had its center of clearness 1.5 cm. from the fovea appeared blurred at three centimeters, but that for the same letter somewhat larger the 3-cm. distance was optimal.

When an arrangement like Figure 41a was presented, the large letter was clearly seen, but the small one was foggy. Similarly, in Figure 41b, the L which is identical in both items, was practically invisible alone, but very plain when it formed part of the E-gestalt.

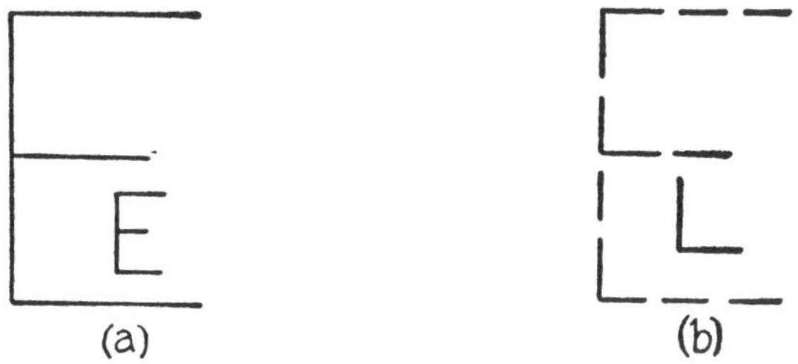

Figure 41. Pseudofoveal Vision of Fuchs's Patient

It is significant that the man could not perceive the L in the lower right-hand region of the b-figure, but could trace it perfectly when it appeared as a component part of the larger E-pattern (observe that it appears twice).

Gelb [6] has recorded the analyses of several patients suffering what he has termed *dysmorphopsia* or the distorted vision of optical forms. One subject saw a circle as an erect oval at four centimeters! In real life, he had already noticed the unusually thin factory chimneys which looked like telegraph poles, and pedestrians struck him as thin and gaunt. Strangely enough the patient did not see the objects deformed in the dark, but the dysmorphopsia immediately appeared in daylight. The existence of the same peculiar distortion in various after-images, led Gelb to maintain that the disorder must be conditioned by purely cerebral factors. What these central causes are is purely hypothetical but the deformation apparently must be due to some constant influence mis-shaping the visual patterns in a characteristic way. Presumably this distorting factor possesses broad generality, for all kinds of geometrical forms were thus affected.

[6] "Ueber eine eigenartige Sehstörung infolge von Gesichtsfeldeinengung," *Psychol Forsch.*, 1923, *4*, 38–63.

Another illuminating case involving so-called psychic blindness was studied by Benary.[7] The disorganization of pattern relations in this patient was illustrated by his inability to tell promptly which was the greater, 3 or 7? Accurate observation showed that in order to answer this question, he had to begin counting at one, but as soon as he reached three he knew the answer; the fact that seven occurred "later in the series" was to him equivalent to "greater." This suggests a theory as to why a normal person immediately attaches a definite meaning to 7 or 78 or 364. Apparently every number has its definite "place" with respect to other numbers in a "number-space" or series, especially with reference to certain prominent quantities; e.g., 364 is not only connected to numbers one greater or less than itself, but lies betwen 300 and 400, nearer the latter than the former, close to 350 (the middle), within the first five hundreds, etc. Getting acquainted with numbers means learning their interconnections or serial attributes as well as their individual features; in fact, a number *is* a number only by virtue of the order it occupies.

Mäki[8] prepared a supplementary study of Benary's patient with respect to his motor performance. This subject, who was "psychically blind" was able to grasp the meaning of a letter of the alphabet or of any simple figural outline only when he made "tracing" head movements of the contours which were often accompanied by a similar action of the right and left hands. It was noticed that when a man's head in profile or an animal sketch was placed facing the left of the observer the patient "recognized" them only by tracing with the right hand; with the left hand they were meaningless blotches. The converse situation was noticed when the picture was oriented to the observer's right. Generally, his right hand began its outlining sweep at the left of the picture, whereas the left member started at the right. This *abducent* motion of both hands was altered only when the final pathway occasionally made an adducent movement more in keeping with the rhythm of the whole.

---

[7] "Studien zur Untersuchungen der Intelligenz bei einem Fall von Seelenblindheit," *Psychol. Forsch.*, 1922, *2*, 209–297.

[8] "Natürliche Bewegungstendenzen der rechten und der linken Hand und ihr Einfluss auf das Zeichnen und den Erkennensvorgang," *Psychol. Forsch.*, 1928, *10*, 1–19.

This mirror-type symmetry was characteristic of all the patient's motor performances, e.g., if he were asked to trace a certain pattern in the air with his right finger and then to do the same with the left, the latter was always the mirror projection of the former, i.e., a U would be swung one way in one case and in the opposite direction in the other. If asked to draw a face in profile, the right hand drew one with features directed to the observer's left, while the converse occurred with the right. This is of more general significance for normal handedness, since it is known that right-handed school children draw most of their profiles facing the left while persons with sinistral preference do the opposite. The cave drawings of pre-historic man thus throw light upon the handedness of the primitive artist; and the problem of the direction of the line of writing in Oriental tongues is also illuminated by these observations.

Of considerable interest from the Gestalt standpoint was the patient's method of drawing symmetrical figures such as a rectangle, circle, or letter M. To produce these he drew two halves, the left side, of course, being the mirror duplicate of the right. This peculiarity the author believes to be related to the bilateral symmetrical nature of the human organism and accountable for the frequency of abducent mirror writing among left-handed persons, which is not at all pathological.

Contributions to Psychiatry

Turning to the more strictly psychiatric possibilities of Gestalt, we find a number of speculative hypotheses which merit examination. Schulte[9] has sketched the outlines of a configurationist theory of paranoia which is both novel and plausible. Taking a clue from Bleuler's assertion that paranoia is essentially an "hypertrophy of the ego," Schulte maintains that there are certain situations represented by groups of workmen and soldiers in which the individual is not typically present as a "self" but as a characteristic part of a "we." For some natures this *we*-contact is simple, whereas others may exhibit a de-

[9] "Versuch einer Theorie der paranoischen Eigenbeziehung und Wahnbildung," *Psychol. Forsch.*, 1924, *5*, 1–23. Nietzsche somewhere remarks that the "thou" is older than the "I." Katz also considers it probable that the "we-consciousness" precedes both the "you" and the "I."

ficiency therein. Where the "we" is not realizable, a gap appears between the individual and his group, and a new relation results: I am no longer "with the others" in a community, but I am now *between* them or *beside* them. Inevitably tension arises. If intelligence and energy are present, one flees for salvation to another circle of associates. With the ground thus prepared, new traumatic events may only be assimilated as part of the constellation; or in serious cases where they do not fit, the whole cosmology or delusional system is altered to take care of the partial fact. One reason why the prognoses for paranoid conditions have usually been bad is that they have been explained too much on an individual and not enough on a social basis. Freud's error in particular lay in making the unconscious too personal a matter.

Schulte cites a number of cases which conform to the etiology which his theory of a "we-sickness" demands. A Tartar soldier confined in an Austrian military hospital developed the persecution delusions of one linguistically isolated. When he found some one with whom he could talk his psychotic symptoms vanished! This is one reason why travelling in foreign countries is just as likely to encourage national hostility as an international spirit. Persons hard of hearing and mutes also tend to show misapprehensions because of their diminished powers of communication. The persecutory delusions of prisoners follow from the mechanically enforced isolation and generally disappear with a change of milieu. Even the paranoid maladies of senescence may be traced to arteriosclerotic changes evoking new peripheral sensations not understood. Finally, the reason this form of insanity does not develop until maturity is that a really isolated ego does not occur in early childhood, hence paranoid mechanisms are excluded.

Despite the provisional character of this theory its persuasiveness must be acknowledged. It establishes the "functional" disorders of mind upon a solid social base, a conclusion which many thinkers have more or less dimly foreshadowed. And, of course, if it does that it renders the search for organic lesions as the provoking cause of certain psychoses a good deal less hopeful than many neurologists of the old school would have us believe.[10]

Should one claim that *self*-consciousness and consciousness of external objects are mediated by different agencies, one will find that the Gestalt position has been well fortified at that point. Despite Descartes' famous dictum, the fact that "I think" or "I doubt" is no surer foundation for reality than "I see" or "I feel." Köhler[11] justly observes that no one marvels that the concrete object "pencil" lies outside the equally concrete thing "inkwell," and that there is just as little reason for being astounded over the fact that one's hand is a third object *beside* the other two. Awareness of one's physical frame must involve the same brain processes as awareness of extra-cutaneous data. This unquestionably occurs in special laboratory situations when a pronounced turning of the visual field leads to a convincing impression that the self is moving in a direction opposed thereto, despite the stability of one's physical organism upon a chair. If the observed ego is based upon one such set of processes, the physical environment upon another *like* it, and the relative localization of both is based upon the same functional disparateness found in distinguishing one outer object from another, then this old pseudo-problem disappears. All phenomenal events have equal standing within the brain-field which is the common frame of reference for all experience.

Bender[12] studied the ability of amentia and dementia cases in drawing ten of Wertheimer's figures illustrating configurationist concepts. The original drawings were placed on separate cards and the patient was told to reproduce them without any

---

[10] Köhler has made some general suggestions concerning man's social tendencies which appear to have been developed from Schulte's ideas. Thus, "After being alone for some weeks most persons will feel an all but insuperable 'drive' toward social contact, even with strangers. It is difficult to understand, at the present time, how this directed attitude should depend upon the physiological situation of the organism as, for instance, hunger depends upon it. Nevertheless, for the most part, this attitude is quite similar to the need for food, and I do not hesitate to interpret it as a stress in the field between the self and those particular surrounding processes which are the physiological correlate of our experience of other persons." *Gestalt Psychology,* New York, 1929, p. 326.

The sociological implications of Gestalt are poorly developed at present despite the rich possibilities it appears to possess. The growing trend toward a "collectivist" social order affords an inviting opportunity to apply configurationist thinking to politics and economic institutions. The revolutionist's advocacy of fairly quick change appears to be even more defensible psychologically than the doctrine of "gradualism."

[11] "Ein altes Scheinproblem," *Die Naturwissenschaften,* 1929, *17,* 395–401.

[12] "The Principles of Gestalt in Copied Form in Mentally Defective and Schizophrenic Persons," *Arch. of Neurol. and Psychiatry,* 1932, *27,* 661–686.

time limit. The quality of the reproductions improved in clear-cut organization with the increase in the mental age (from one to ten years) of the feebleminded. It was of considerable interest that many schizophrenics who had apparently been out of contact and incommunicative for years, and who did not speak or make any spontaneous productions by writing were still willing to copy these impersonal forms. In both groups sinistrad writing, counterclockwise motions, loops instead of dots were characteristic. From her examination, Bender believes that the more primitive sensori-motor patterns are whirling nebular movements in a vortex. Internally organized gestalten arise from it genetically by a progressive organization in connection with the integrated intellectual functions, and in schizophrenia there is a dissociation due to a reversion back to the genetically more primitive tendencies.

Speech Deficiency

Such a first-rate clinical problem as stuttering has benefited by Gestalt ideas and Travis [13] has built an elaborate system of speech pathology upon this conception. To the statistical evidence showing that the incidence of speech defect is greater among persons whose native handedness preference (generally left) has been tampered with by home or school influences, Travis adds his view that the imperfectly established cortical dominance or gradient of one half of the brain is the causal factor. "In the stutterer, instead of nervous energy being mobilized by one center of greatest potential, it is mobilized by two centers of comparable potential. Because both of these centers when operating singly function in reaction patterns of opposite motor orientation and configuration, there is produced in the peripheral speech organ an undesirable competition in the resulting muscular movements. The symptoms of stuttering are then mainly the peripheral signs of the rivalry between the two sides of the brain." (*Op. cit.*, p. 96.)

This failure of the cortex to function as a coordinated whole can be overcome only by building up an adequately dominant

---

[13] *Speech-Pathology*, New York, 1931.

speech gradient in the central nervous system. This is accomplished by first determining which hand or eye is naturally in the lead and then providing manual exercises for increasing directly the dominance of one hemisphere over the other and lower levels. Although his theory of lateral dominance requires confirmation by the neurologists, it marks a step ahead of the notion of well-insulated arcs and the Broca area type of localization. In addition, there is the usual gratifying record of therapeutic success, although, as Freudism, Christian Science, and many other cults have shown, the ability to make cures is uncertain testimony to the correctness of either the method or theory employed.

CHAPTER 15

INDUSTRIAL AND PERSONNEL SUGGESTIONS

Business Possibilities

The serviceability of the Gestalt viewpoint in applied psychology and psychotechnics is still to be demonstrated, but a beginning has been made, particularly under the leadership of Hans Rupp.[1] One of his first efforts in this direction consisted in the construction of apitude tests for textile workers on the basis of their ability to continue certain pattern designs, such as the following "beehive" model:

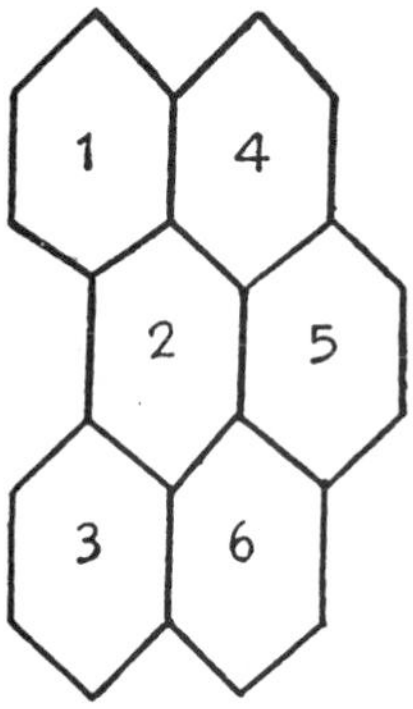

Figure 42. Rupp's Beehive Pattern

The ability to complete figures is indicated by the success with which the hexagons are built on to each other.

He found that persons poor in completing one type of pattern were also poor in others, irrespective of the particular nature of the design, a fact of considerable vocational importance. When presented with a cross-pattern (involving simple X's) many of the younger subjects drew plus signs instead, since these are easier and more *prägnant* figures. A marked correlation between this type of performance and scores on general intelligence tests leads Rupp to the view that *intelligence is the capacity to apprehend pattern-relations,* an opinion already implicit in the earlier animal experiments involving insight. The necessary analysis which these tasks require can occur only when a sense of the total construction has preceded it.

Of course, there are bound to be a good many experiments developing independently of his approach which are grist to the

---

[1] "Ueber optische Analyse," *Psychol. Forsch.*, 1923, *4*, 262–300.

Gestaltist's mill, for unwittingly or not, they contribute some support to his interpretation. An example of such studies is found in the investigation of Newhall and Heim on the memory value of absolute size in advertising.[2] Their problem grew out of the existence in the commercial world of two types of magazines—the common small so-called standard-sized periodical and the larger flat-sized variety. Most printed matter in the latter form, especially the advertising section, is merely scaled upward, and since more ink and paper are consumed by this policy the question arises as to whether a corresponding gain in appeal is secured. According to Newhall and Heim no such advantage can be demonstrated, for their data suggest that *contrasting* (or relative) size is an important condition of memory while mere magnitude is not—a conclusion perfectly in harmony with the Gestalt prediction.

Estimating Personality

The fields of character-judging, graphology, and physiognomy, which are still largely the exclusive province of pseudo-scientists, admirably illustrate the wide range and fructifying possibilities of Gestalt theory. Most American psychologists smile in conscious superiority when it is suggested that static bodily characteristics may conceivably reveal personality traits, for they will point to dozens of recent careful studies by workers in the applied and personnel divisions which appear to have given the *coup de grace* to all such claims, since their obtained correlations between highly exact measures rarely exceed chance values.[3] However, the configurationists are not readily daunted, for they will immediately point out that these statistical inquiries are excellent examples of a bad technique. The old errors of false analysis and atomism have obscured relations even in researches which seem to possess maximal certainty. Their point is that facial expression must be studied on Gestalt principles, and such variables as length of nose, curve of chin, etc., should be considered as dependent parts of a larger whole.

---

[2] *J. Applied Psychol.*, 1929, *13*, 62–75.

[3] For a most convenient recent summary, see Paterson, *Physique and Intellect*, New York, 1931.

Again, in graphology it is a mistake to make micrometric surveys of letter height, slant, and the like, for this is the old evil of unreal elements. It is only in the light of the Gestalt approach that we are able to understand the oft-noticed fact that character estimates made by judges are usually more correct than the detailed systems upon which these judgments presumably are based. The estimates have been given in terms of total impressions of unique wholes, whereas the measures have all been fragmentary.[4] Even where ratios have been employed, such as eye-width divided by facial length, the inner dynamics of the situation has been overlooked.

A recognition of this sort does not mean that a relapse to the intuitive nonsense of Lavater's day is in order, as Arnheim's [5] thoughtfully executed experiment shows. In one division of his work, he projected simultaneously for 20 seconds three handwriting specimens of the great artists of the Italian Renaissance—Leonardo da Vinci, Raphael, and Michelangelo—before a large audience which almost certainly had never seen any of these rare treasures. The subjects were then instructed to match the names and samples as best they could from their general knowledge of the men and their works, but to use spontaneous impressions whenever possible and not to speculate wildly. More than one-half of Arnheim's subjects responded with the correct arrangement of all three pairs, a result which is all the more striking when one recalls that only one-sixth would have been correct had chance alone been functioning. What was responsible for this 40% difference?

In his search for an answer, Arnheim constructed other objective situations in which the relations were made as *characteristic* as possible, on the principle that if we are investigating brightness discrimination, we first take greys which are readily distinguished before proceeding to less distinct cases. In addition, he always exposed his stimuli-patterns in groups, because only in this wise could significant relations be discerned. For example, in one experiment he projected simultaneously full portraits of

[4] The newer graphologists like Saudek and particularly Klages adhere more to the principle of *Ganzheit.*

[5] "Experimentell-psychologische Untersuchungen zum Ausdrucks-problem," *Psychol. Forsch.*, 1928, *II*, 1–132. His problem is one phase of the more general perceptual inquiry: How is one to explain the different functions of "l" in "life" and in "1935."?

six historically eminent poets and philosophers (without titles, of course) and then inquired, "Who wrote in classic hexameters?" "Who composed delicate little verses?" etc. In another, Arnheim exhibited six photographs of university professors at another remote institution and then read character sketches of each which had been agreed upon by acquaintances as faithful accounts: the task of the subjects was to mate the descriptions and the faces. In a third, three pictures of women were shown together with such questions as "Who is a forceful, independent widow?" "Who is a typical *Hausfrau?*" "Who is musical?" A fourth series called for judgments based upon the profiles of four psychopaths; a fifth, the interpretation of the personalities of the writers of envelope addresses; a sixth involved matching of handwriting samples from Schiller, Wagner, and Freytag; and a seventh, interpretations of silhouettes.

In 44 out of 48 experiments, the value of the completely correct judgments was greater than the sum of all the wrong guesses, which is statistically of high significance. On the average, there were two-and-one-half times as many right replies as mere probability would allow. The results were far from accidental, since all sorts of groups showed parallel answers. Many of the errors Arnheim found were caused by a faulty analysis of parts (which in itself was contrary to the original instructions); e.g., many mistakes with da Vinci's handwriting resulted from a stereotype as to what a typical engineer—a part-property of the man—was like. In this way the naïve total effect, which would have led to a correct judgment, was destroyed.

The Piderit models with their interchangeable facial parts commonly found in psychological laboratories are constructed on the assumption that the complication of expression by mere addition leads to a total expression which is intelligible as a complex of the correlated meanings. But this view neglects the fact that the aspect of a part like the eye or mouth is conditioned by the larger whole containing it. In one experiment, Arnheim presented a partly shielded pair of pictures of a girl and a baby with only the upper facial areas showing. Descriptions of the eye quality obtained under the circumstances differed markedly from those obtained when the rest of the portrait was suddenly exposed. A reversal of effect, analogous to that secured with ambiguous figure-ground patterns took place. The face as a whole determines what the eyes [6] shall seem to say. The same rule holds for other features, for in his silhouette experiments, Arnheim demonstrated that identical parts, such as the chin and nose, had not only different figural but also distinctly different characterological properties if the general structure were altered.[7] Hence, the absurdity of taking the single feature as one's point of departure—a fact which follows from the rejection of the constancy hypothesis in the sensory realm.[8]

Although most American students of personality are at present far from favorably inclined toward the *Ganzheit* approach, there is an active minority represented by Gordon Allport which has been seeking theoretical inspiration from European sources.[9] Their opposition to the "specificitarian" view of personality is partly methodological and partly interpretive, two points already noticed in our discussion of Arnheim's investigation. Concerning the first point, Allport writes:

> The methods of current research upon which the doctrine of specificity[10] rests are quite unsuited to the discovery of fundamental consistencies within personality. Until adequate methods are devised for the study of the *complex* correspondences which lie within *complex* unities of personality, an exaggerated faith in specificity will prevail. Cleeton and Knight measure the length of noses but not the cast of countenance as a whole, Hull and Montgomery measure microscopically the width of pen-strokes but not the form-quality of the total script,

[6] An illustrative parlor game consists in exposing only the eyes of close friends through slits in hangings; recognition is extraordinarily difficult under these circumstances.

[7] Knight Dunlap simultaneously and independently of Arnheim made some first-rate photographic studies of a somewhat more restricted scope but which led to approximately similar conclusions. Cf. "The Rôle of Eye-Muscles and Mouth-Muscles in the Expression of the Emotions," *Genet. Psychol. Monographs*, 1927, *2*, No. 3.

[8] Arnheim's general thesis was later confirmed by Theiss, who found that lay Europeans unacquainted with Oriental languages nevertheless made decidedly better-than-chance records in identifying personality traits with handwriting specimens. A "vain" and a "modest" Hebrew were thus distinguished as well as an "intelligent," an "energetic," and an "optimistic" Chinese. See "Die Erfassung des handschriftlichen Ausdrucks durch Laien," *Psychol. Forsch.*, 1931, *15*, 276–358.

[9] The conflict between the two groups is clearly exhibited in Allport's review of Symonds' *Diagnosing Personality and Conduct* in the *J. Social Psychol.*, 1932, *3*, 391–397. An excellent demonstration of the conclusion that a Gestalt theory of personality must be a *type* theory is found in Murphy and Jensen, *Approaches to Personality*, Coward-McCann, 1932.

[10] The doctrine that there are no common features in human conduct, i.e., a man may be *accurate* in his use of numbers but slovenly with words. For a sample of this type of study see the author's monograph *Precision and Accuracy*, Archives of Psychology, No. 100, New York, 1928.

Rich considers the hydrogen-ion concentration in saliva, but not the endocrine pattern or type, and Hartshorne and May deal with a psycho-social-ethical *mélange* called "character" which gives little opportunity for the discovery of consistent *psychological* dispositions in personality.

If it is objected that one cannot *measure* pattern, form-quality, or style, the proper answer is, so much the worse for measurement. It is still in these complexities that one must seek congruence and integration, and any two variables arbitrarily isolated from the total structure for purposes of correlation will result only in an illusion of specificity.

With respect to the interpretation of the quantitative researches in the sphere of personality executed by means of "exact" statistical calculations, Allport argues that no specificist who tries to be guided by his theory can believe it in the routine of his own daily life. Logically a specificist should never allow himself to use an adjective to describe a person, but only to describe a single act at a certain time. While it is true that "honesty" as measured by recent character scales seems to be a clear-cut case of specificity, there are other traits or true psychological dispositions which indicate, if they do not demonstrate, that an individual may be consistent in his own way. To cite again,

As ill-adapted as most of the current methods are to the discovery of consistency, they themselves yield copious evidence that the doctrine of specificity has been too hastily embraced. What else than personal consistency can the reliability of the scale signify? If a questionnaire contains a large number of items drawn from many representative fields of daily action, as most of them do, and if the subject answers these items consistently, which is what reliability means, where then is the "outstanding" specificity . . . in the results? There are scales whose split-half reliability and internal consistency reach +.75 or even +.85. These figures signify that most people respond to practically all the items in a consistent way. They are *characteristically* ascendant, extroverted, neurotic, or fair-minded. Their conduct is not specific.[11]

[11] For a brilliant and complete statement of this position see *Studies in Expressive Movement* by G. W. Allport and P. E. Vernon, New York, 1933.

CHAPTER 16

APPLICATION TO EDUCATIONAL PROBLEMS

Changes in Policy and Teaching Method

Educational theory and practice have always looked to psychology to provide the working principles which an auxiliary discipline must inevitably borrow from the more fundamental science. While it is undoubtedly true that teachers and administrators have been less affected by the positive results of psychological research than workers in the latter field would like to believe (just as governmental affairs are often conducted in sublime disregard of the existence of the social sciences), it is still true that the broader movements ultimately come to influence pedagogical activity in many subtle ways. Homogeneous grouping is directly traceable to the rise of mental tests, the growth of specific teaching methods and vocationalized curricula has been encouraged by the dominance of the Thorndikian interpretation of transfer of training, and the spread of nursery schools probably owes more to Freudian views about infancy than many sponsors of such organizations realize. With such a live tradition, it is small wonder that the psychologist is constantly asked, "What are the educational implications of the doctrine of Gestalt?"

Several writers have tried to answer this question. Ogden was one of the earliest to address himself to this task, and, of course, his remarks had to be rather broad in nature. It has long been observed that a child's first language efforts really have a sentence character rather than the traits of isolated words. Thus, the utterance "dolly" often means "Please, mother, give me the doll"—a form of telescoping which is truly representative of infant speech. That Swiss child who responded properly to the form and cadence of "Où est la fenêtre?" when formerly he had heard only "Wo ist das Fenster?" shows that the precise order and sound of single words is less important than the general "contours" of the phraseology.[1]

This same priority of wholes which should be of service in guiding a child's intellectual growth assists also in defining the objectives of training. As long as associationism in its various disguises was accepted as the reigning principle of mental life, the goals of training had to be expressed in terms of habit formation. The development of good habits of varying degrees of complexity was the lodestar of educational enterprise. However, as soon as one is convinced that the instinct (i.e., the larger unit) is more typical of original nature than the reflex, and that voluntary action (= the deliberate control of performance by the *entire* organism) is broader than myriad specific habits, new ends and new procedures for realizing these ends must be established. A neo-formalism results. "From this point of view the emphasis placed by Greeks upon music and gymnastics as the true basis of an education is highly illuminating; because it suggests that the Greeks were less concerned with the habituation of the contents of study than they were with the dynamics of form, both in mind and body. Indeed, one can discover in the writings of Plato and Aristotle a method of education which to us at this late day has all the features of a novelty: an education in which rhythm, melody, and design replace to a very large extent the arid coining of words, and the exercise of hand and voice in the production of school results which have a significance only to the teacher." (*Op. cit.*, p. 347.)

With even greater precision has Humphrey [2] endeavored to describe the possible relations between the two fields. It may well be that the Gestalt position will have performed a valuable corrective service to education if it only succeeds in focusing our attention once more, in these days of "additive" tests and "unit"

[1] The fact that a little child can correctly locate the thigh on its own person after having had it pointed out upon the body of an adult shows that the "frame" containing an item must be perceived as well as the item itself. The child does not see and note just a certain bodily region as such, but one "between the knee and hip."—The examples in the main body of the text above are taken from Ogden's article on "The Need of Some New Conceptions in Educational Theory and Practice," *Sch. & Soc.*, 1923, *18*, 343–348.

[2] "The Psychology of Gestalt, Some Educational Implications," *J. Educ. Psychol.*, 1924, *15*, 401–412. Students of arithmetic have long been puzzled by the fact that it is easier to add a small quantity to a larger one than *vice versa*. "Closure" may explain this phenomenon. A circle with three-fourths of its circumference exposed exerts a greater compulsion to see a full circle than one with only one-fourth exposed.

courses, on the primary interdependence of mental processes. Specifically, informed experts recognize that such a test as the Army Alpha does not discriminate in the higher reaches of intelligence. Configurationism would explain this as due in part to the fact that this measure, like many others, make the erroneous assumption that a simple operation of the mind is not altered by being divorced from its context as part of a complexity, and also that a complex action can be expressed as the sum of a number of simple ones. The same kind of criticism should be introduced into our conception of the curriculum. The Gestalt notion of cerebral "potentials" would involve a different hypothesis of the effect of any single school subject, with a more organic relation between the different branches of study than previous theory has accounted for.

The educationist has rarely concerned himself with most of the more technical issues faced in the psychological laboratory, but the analysis of the learning process has usually been followed in great detail because of its obviously more immediate bearing upon school problems. Even many pyschologists would agree that one of the most fundamental questions before them to-day is the method of elimination of useless movements in learning. The new "structuralism" holds that the selection of a new mode of response involves a transformation of the situation and the act thus acquired integrates with the learner's desire and with his achievement, whereas the "abortive" acts which do not accomplish this end are eliminated, because they do not participate in this integration. It may be wise to quote Humphrey at some length on this crucial point:

> It is claimed by Koffka that we can apply the term gestalt to series of actions directed towards a definite end, such as the movements of an animal acting instinctively or those of a chimpanzee striving to reach a banana. Now there seems good reason for applying the word gestalt to what is generally known as a purposive action (since they satisfy all the criteria of von Ehrenfels). . . If twenty dogs each made a motion corresponding to one of the motions a dog goes through while he is chasing a cat, the result is not the same thing as if all these movements took place in the same animal. The movements, when they are out of "functional relation" are different from the same movements in such a relation. In the same way, the same general act can take place under

different conditions. A dog can chase a cat through a swamp, down a street, up a stairway. The act of chasing a cat is "transposable." Further, if one of the component actions of the dog is taken away, or a fresh one put in, the other acts have to be altered. If the dog meets an obstacle during the chase, he must go round it or otherwise surmount it, which will mean that he will have to change the character of the rest of his hunt. . . .

If one will allow the term gestalt to a "purposive" series of actions, the problem is at once raised as to whether the Köhlerian theory of pregnancy does not apply, according to which the elimination of useless movements would be considered as a process of gestalt consolidation. On this view it would be expected that, after an organism has once responded in a certain way to a certain outside situation, there will be a subtle change in the organism which will make itself felt when a similar situation is again experienced, corresponding to the change which took place in "memory" in Wulf's experiment. It is possible, too, that those stimuli which harmonized with the new changed gestalt would be "satisfiers," the inharmonious ones "annoyers," and if this is the case we have a working hypothesis for experimentation upon that standing puzzle, the fact that a satisfying act can affect actions that come considerably before it in the series. Each member of the gestalt series is in close functional relations with other members and with the whole. . . . If one adopts the Gestalt idea, one should think of different phases of a single attack on the problem, each phase being influenced by the fact that it is, with other phases, part of a unitary attempt at solution. (*Op. cit.* pp. 409-410.)

There have been a number of other efforts to familiarize the teaching profession with the significance of Gestalt psychology for its problems, but most of these have merely been amateurish sketches of the movement with little evidence that the possibilities of application were clear even in the authors' minds. Perhaps the most competent minor attempt in this direction has been made by an Englishwoman, Marjorie Hammond.[3] With pardonable national pride, she points out that Ward and Stout a generation ago were preaching the doctrine that the act of apprehending the whole is other than that of apprehending parts. Nevertheless, the contemporary debate on configurationism has brought the issue to a head, and it would be a dull pedagogue who failed to find in it something useful for his teaching. In fact, much of enlightened practice is already in line with the

[3] "Gestalttheorie: Its Significance for Teaching," *Brit. J. Ed. Psychol.*, 1932, 2, 153–171.

theory, having developed in the direction of "wholeness" on purely empirical and pragmatic grounds.

In the old days, the boy was taught to make joints, plane and saw, put on hinges, etc., before he was allowed to make the rabbit hutch that required these skills. On "whole" methods, he is now usually allowed to start on the hutch and to achieve the minor skills with that end in view. Children were once set to draw vertical and horizontal lines, and to play five-finger exercises; now children may draw pictures and play melodies from the outset, acquiring the necessary skills in service of the whole. The same tendency is seen in the teaching of the academic subjects. The direct method of teaching languages, for instance, is more in line with "whole" methods than was the method used in the writer's school days, when first nouns and their declensions had to be mastered, then lists of exceptions, then adjectives, then verbs, and finally sentences. In those days, history was taught by the reign and plays of Shakespeare by the scene. Now, often, attempts are made to help the pupils to grasp the general purport of the period or the play, before proceeding to analysis.

This general conception is applicable to most of the concrete processes of instruction. In such a standard school subject as American history, the teacher will find it advantageous to present the story of Lincoln's Administration and the Civil War in broad outline first and then to develop the various phases. This is because the pupil who is properly oriented as to the general area will master the details more completely and correctly. That the whole determines the properties of its parts may well become the basic pedagogical maxim of the future. A clear definite general picture of the whole problem as a starting point for the work on a larger unit of subject matter serves as a convenient filing case with compartments properly labelled to store away a wealth of interesting material in a systematic way, keeping its organization intact and avoiding all confusion. When a child is properly guided in organizing subject-matter in the light of the whole, he will not only learn the facts more economically, but he will be able to unify facts and to generalize, since the items are learned in their right relationships in the first place.[4]

[4] For a further development of this theme, see *Studies in the Psychology of Learning* by G. N. Norem and M. F. Wiederaenders, University of Iowa Publications, 1933. The filing cabinet illustration used above is probably satisfactory if it conveys the suggestion of "orderliness," but a bit unfortunate if it implies arbitrary classification. The Gestalt viewpoint in educational psychology is better typified by the arrangement of words in Roget's *Thesaurus* than by the mere alphabetical sequence of the usual dictionary and encyclopaedia.

A sample of the experimentally verified benefits which may be expected to accrue to teaching procedure from an adoption of the Gestalt standpoint is found in a study by Clark and Worcester.[5] These authors made an investigation of the relative merits of the word unit method and the sentence unit method of teaching shorthand, in which five schools employed the word unit method and six the sentence unit method; and the latter proved superior in every test, despite the fact that four of the six teachers using the sentence method had been trained only in the word method. As in other related circumstances, the "whole" or sentence procedure was more difficult at the start but its superior ease became evident with time.

On a more elementary plane, the "global" method of teaching reading, spelling, and even writing has long had the sanction and active encouragement of educational psychologists whose theoretical views are otherwise often grossly inconsistent with this recommendation. Larger units such as sentences, phrases, and words are understood by the child long before it is able to segregate individual letters and syllables. Even then it is a trite observation that the same letter "a" has to do different duty when it appears in the words *ale, senate, ask, sofa,* etc. The Gestalt thesis of the genetic and logical priority of the whole configuration over the part elements has in practice often been adopted, and there is plenty of reason for believing that if raised to the level of a consciously applied principle it will modify beneficially the course of teaching procedure in all subjects. In most instruction, it seems desirable to offer the pupil a broad sketch of its general outlines before concentrating upon special details, a fact which accounts for the success of orientation and survey courses when wisely given. An integrated course in general mathematics appears to yield a greater increment of understanding than a series of separate courses in algebra, geometry, trigonometry, etc. Most students, too, would profit by reading books or other material as a whole first in order to

[5] *J. Educ. Psychol.*, 1932, *23*, 122–131. Comenius had advocated teaching reading by the sentence method as early as 1631. The Belgian educational psychologist, Decroly, has been a prominent advocate since 1927 of the "globalization" technique in the instruction of both normal and defective children. The probability that he was influenced in this position by the German view is very strong. For a convenient exposition of his ideas on this point, see his monograph *La fonction de globalisation et son application a l'enseignement*, Brussels, 1929.

seize the plan or "structure" of the volume, and then examining more carefully its subdivisions.

Teachers of speech in particular have been drawn to Gestalt theory in the hope that their own practice might be guided by a better light than that offered by behaviorism, which most professors have been compelled to adopt for want of a better system. Philologists have long known that syntax is the heart of human language and that individual words can be comprehended only in connection with the whole. The famous classical scholar, August Boeckh, is said to have formulated something like a *Gestalttheorie* a century ago, and Grimm's law may be but a statement of the transformations which typical configurations undergo.

Parrish [6] has seen some of the obvious relations between instruction in oral effectiveness and the Gestalt system of psychology. Some of his hints are a bit forced when they are not purely superficial, but in one paragraph at least he has driven home a good point.

> Mere repeated practice of a separate sound will not insure its correct pronunciation in the context of a word or phrase. That is, foreigners who are able to make the sound of *th* as in *with,* but who habitually substitute a *t* for it, will never learn to use the correct sound by practicing it alone. They must practice it in its context in a word or phrase. The situation is like that of the boy who was required to stay after school and write fifty times the form, "I have gone," in order to fix it in memory. At the end of the exercise, the teacher being absent from the room, he wrote on his paper, "Dear Teacher, I have went home." The practiced phrase remained for him an isolated and meaningless fragment, unincorporated into any meaningful configuration. The isolation of any phase of experience may vitiate its value because properly it belongs in a whole. (*Op. cit.,* p. 15.)

Effective oral and written composition both illustrate this point. First there is the general idea as expressed by the title or theme topic. Then one plans an outline showing the scheme

---

[6] "Implications of Gestalt Psychology," *Quarterly J. of Speech,* 1928, *14,* 8–29. There are a few other relevant articles in this same journal of a later date to which the interested reader may turn, but since they are largely low-grade controversial papers with a vanishing amount of genuine content, they may be disregarded here. There are some writers, for instance, who hold that Gestalt is not fundamentally different from behaviorism, because both schools of thought use the words pattern, whole, integration, etc.! According to this reasoning, the style of Walter Pater and the newest cub-reporter are identical, because both make use of "if" and "but."

of organization. This is further differentiated into paragraphs and sentences and finally the exact phraseology is formulated. The great masters of style and creative writing all emphasize having something to say, planning the composition as a whole, and eventually coming down to the mechanical details.

Intelligence Testing

Just as Spearman has tried to explain certain Gestalt principles in terms of his alleged fundamental laws of "eduction," so some configurationists have seen that his theory of ability and performance—that an individual's achievement is due to a general factor of intelligence (G), together with a variety of specific factors (S's)—is equally amenable to the whole-part brand of interpretation. Wheeler has showed how Coghill's work on the embryo suggests a conversion of Spearman's famous theory into the language of Gestalt.[7] His account is sufficiently interesting and provocative to extract in full:

> Every form of behavior is a pattern response, the most obvious features of which are its specialized aspects, but the total pattern is always functioning. Hold out your hand and bend your wrist. The wrist motion is merely a local specialization or individuation of the whole act of holding out the arm. *Whatever the wrist is doing at any time is part of something the arm is doing.* In like manner, when a person is solving an arithmetic problem he is exhibiting a specialized intellectual performance comparable to the wrist movement. There is a total intellectual pattern from which the arithmetical reasoning individuates. This pattern is the insightful aspect of the individual's total mental life and corresponds to what the arm is doing in the wrist illustration. This means that Spearman's S's are not factors separate from G. G and S are abstractions, and in reality, artifacts. When the wrist is bent we have an arm-act as much as a wrist-act. If the arm were moved without bending the wrist, the wrist would move also. The only difference between the two is differentiation of the arm movement itself in the one case and not in the other. In this sense, so-called "special" abilities are merely differentiations of so-called "general" ability.
>
> The intercorrelations between certain tests are higher than for others only because the differentiations of insight with respect to certain problems have gone on at the expense of others. There is apparently

---

[7] *Principles of Mental Development,* New York, 1932, pp. 193–194.

no reason for believing that a person could not undergo the maturation processes necessary for equivalent scores in every test he took. It is well known that the brilliant individual is especially good in everything he does, all things considered. Lack of opportunity, interest, and proper stimulation should account for all exceptions.

The law of "closure" has been of interest to the mental-test psychologists because of its obvious relation to many of the

Figure 43. One of Street's More Difficult Gestalt Completion Tests

What is this? See accompanying text for explanation.

conventional means of measuring intellectual capacity. Ebbinghaus believed that the power of synthesis was the essence of intelligence and his language completion test still survives as one of the most serviceable instruments in clinical practice. Binet's dissected sentences test and Healy's picture completion forms also represent efforts to measure the ability of the subject to "fill in" an organization whose total structure is only hinted at by the incomplete contours.

Street [8] has recently standardized a Gestalt completion test composed of fifteen items, each of which is a peculiar type of picture puzzle. By deletion, parts of a simply-sketched picture are made to form the "ground," so that in order to perceive the picture, it is necessary to complete the structure, i.e., to bring about a "closure" which causes the figure to emerge from the ground. Figure 43 represents one of Street's more difficult "tests," a man taking a picture with a camera. Only three-tenths of one percent of grammar-school children succeed in seeing this pattern. Apparently, if the figure field becomes broken so that the point of probable fixation is shifted to the ground field, it is harder to see the picture; in other words, as the density of energy is shifted from the figure field to the ground field, the perceiving of the picture becomes more and more difficult. The point of fixation is determined by the arrangement of the lines and by the relative size of the interspersed ground. According to Street, the subject's ability to supply the missing parts and to perceive in his own mind the figure in its entirety rests partly upon these external conditions and partly upon the maturity and social experience of the observer.

Theory of Experimentation

In this connection it will not be amiss to point out that Gestalt theory may ultimately alter profoundly many current ideas as to what constitutes legitimate educational research.[9] While the scientific character of its best examples is no longer doubted, there is still considerable uncertainty concerning its guiding principles. All the social sciences suffer from the practical dif-

[8] *A Gestalt Completion Test,* Teachers College, Columbia University Contributions to Education, No. 481, 1931.

[9] This section is introduced because of a conviction that Ragsdale has misrepresented the case in the following declaration: "Gestalt psychology is so new that its meaning is theoretical rather than immediately practical. It may develop a new attitude toward human nature and human behavior which will help us to determine the kind of experiment we should like to set up; but it will not introduce any new principle for conducting educational experiments."—*Modern Psychologies and Education,* New York, 1932, p. 382. For a fuller discussion and illustration of the point of view here represented, see the author's *Measuring Teaching Efficiency Among College Instructors,* Archives of Psychology, No. 154, New York, 1933.

ficulties which forbid the strict use of the experimental technique of the single variable and multiple constants and prevent the realization of the ideals of isolation and control of component factors. For this reason, many conscientious positivists, whose notions of scientific method and procedure were established by Mill's logic and the practice of Mid-Victorian physics, despair of ever placing the human "sciences" upon an acceptable foundation. The configurationist, however, has made a virtue of necessity and cautions us against the blind acceptance of older standards and the use of analytic thinking in fields where it is unwarranted.

Specifically, the chief limitation of those educational researches which have been executed according to the single-variable plan is their disregard of the probability that a change in any part of a life situation not only influences other parts but has marked repercussive effects upon the total in which they are comprised. The major analytical error which one is likely to commit is the silent assumption that the merits of any teaching method, e.g., are independent of the caliber of the persons using it. So far is this from being true that there is strong reason for believing that a "poor" method (i.e., one inferior on psychological and statistical grounds) in the hands of a "good" instructor is a better teaching risk than a demonstrated "good" method employed by a "poor" instructor. Failure to appreciate the significance of this nice organic adaptation of the workman to his tool has resulted in much futile criticism of the lecture procedure on the college level. When used by a person to whom it is ill-suited—e.g., some shy scholar with a feeble voice and an unimpressive physique—then, of course, it is a torment which no one can sanction. But when wielded by a master of expository skill with an appropriate "platform manner," it is a powerful pedagogical instrument, as the distinguished record of many lecturers in the German universities testifies. Educationists who have been blind to this fact are reproducing the persistent and pardonable error of the early vocational counsellors when they thought in terms of the evils of "square pegs in round holes," a view which we now know to be faulty because it posited a static relationship between the man and the job which never obtains. Instead, a reciprocal modification occurs. One may say that square pegs become a bit roundish and the round holes assume squarish outlines; at any rate, the worker-in-his-work [10] becomes the true indissoluble functional unit with which vocational guidance must operate. Similarly, the teacher-and-his-method may be the new dynamic organization to be introduced into our studies of classroom technique.

There are other considerations which make it plain that excessive concern with pure method as such is an artificial and unprofitable occupation. The "master method" has not yet been found because the relative merit of any procedure appears to vary not only with the teacher as indicated above, but with the subject of instruction, and the mental level and other pertinent traits of the pupils as well. In fact, there is reason for suspecting that the teacher-method unit just mentioned is still too atomistic to reflect the actual degree of integration which may be better represented by the *teacher-method-subject-pupil* configuration. It is highly probable that the typical parallel-group experiment is engaged in comparing such unified wholes or gestalten rather than the single variables which we have constructed mentally.

Kinship with Progressive Education

The historical link between Gestalt psychology and the progressive education or "activity" movement of contemporary America is undoubtedly to be found in the person and philosophy of John Dewey. The "enriched" curricula of present-day public schools are in large measure derivatives of Dewey's insistence that formal education and "life" (i.e., participation in significant political, social and economic enterprises) are essentially the same process. An interesting exposition of this relation has been made by Carr [11] in terms of four propositions common to both progressive education and Gestalt theory:

1. *The concept of education as a process of continuous growth is supported by the Gestalt hypothesis of the nature of*

[10] For a persuasive exposition of this point of view, see W. D. Scott, R. C. Clothier, and S. B. Mathewson, *Personnel Management* (rev. ed.), McGraw-Hill, New York, 1931, pp. 8–18.

[11] "The Relationship between the Theories of Gestalt Psychology and Those of a Progressive Science of Education," *J. Ed. Psychol.*, 1934, *25*, 192–202.

learning. This is evident in the tendency to integrate subject-matter around normal or "natural" child activities, particularly during the first few years of schooling. To the little child, experience is general and undifferentiated, but the various sorts of "learnings" in which he engages eventually grow into organized bodies which one may legitimately call "subjects."

2. *Progressive educators have stressed the necessity of enriching the environment in order that the child might attain complete development.* Gestalt writers likewise insist that mental processes do not merely bridge a gap between stimulus and response; they are part of an all-inclusive, dynamic field and have no meaning except in terms of that field. Altering the "field" alters the mind; modifying the environment (in essentials) modifies the child.

3. (a) *Learning takes place in response to a need;* (b) *conscious learning is guided by the purpose or intention of the learner;* (c) *learning is a creative process, depending upon creation and discovery;* (d) *learning enters into life to the extent that it is meaningful to the learner.* These pedagogical commonplaces rest upon an extensive body of experimental fact. Thus, (a) the problem-project method of teaching is the correlate of the theory that learning is the reorganization of perceptual and motor patterns; (b) Raup's "complacency" hypothesis as to the ultimate goal of educational endeavor is identical with the Gestalt closure concept even with regard to the illustrations of equilibrium employed; (c) the establishment of conditions favorable for the emergence of insight is the progressive substitute for repetitive drill; and (d) the largest gestalt which the child is able to assimilate is the best learning material for that child.

4. *The socially-integrated personality is the goal of education.* It is also the aim of the mental hygiene movement because the individual and society, conceived in an ideal sense, are simply phases of one whole. Functional defects come into existence as the individual, in conflict with the repressions of the social environment, fights to maintain the unity of his personality. An "insane" society obviously produces insane members. Just as bodily "health" (Anglo-Saxon origin) etymologically

means "wholeness," so mental "integrity" (Latin derivative) or completeness demands harmony in the totality of psychic functions.

Athletics

The field of sport, which will probably always offer a useful set of examples for motor psychology, has not been overlooked by Gestalt writers. Hartgenbusch [12] has offered a number of interesting observations drawn from athletics. The goal of physical activity in some events like the hundred-yard dash is definite and distinct and has the great advantage of prescribing the *exact* performance to be accomplished; but in others, like the broad jump, the objective is prescribed only within certain narrow limits. The pattern of activity in the former case is, therefore, easier to establish and execute than in the latter instance.

Most games and physical events, too, can only be considered in terms of the whole. The dynamics of pole-vaulting is illustrated in the smooth and continuous unitary action required for its performances. To view the process in the light of fragmentary analysis would be to destroy its fundamental nature. Group contests of various sorts are better apprehended in terms of configurational transformations: two opposing football or basketball squads, e.g., aim to penetrate each other's defense by attacking the most vulnerable "hole" in the formation. Effective use of the tactics of deception hinges upon the ability of one player to create a partially-closed gestalt which inevitably lures the opponent into it but which the deceiver fails to complete in the anticipated way. This constant reconstruction of a shifting field is the major feature in a hotly-contested game.

Aesthetics

The contributions of the Gestalt position to art criticism are far from distinct, but they may at least be said to be suggestive. Von Allesch, who has tried to show the connections more than

[12] "Beobachtungen und Bemerkungen zur Psychologie des Sports," *Psychol. Forsch.*, 1926, *7*, 386–397.

The author has found that the accuracy of basketball aiming is definitely greater when the usual net is suspended below the hoop than when the bare iron ring is the sole objective. Apparently a larger "mass" is more readily hit than a mere contour.

any other writer of the school, claims that much of modern criticism is faulty because the analysis to which it is addicted leads to a destruction of the meaning of the whole work of art. The essence of any artistic achievement, whether literary or plastic in nature, lies in its *style,* which is not a characteristic of any individual fragment but is inseparable from the total. From the standpoint of appreciation, this is clearly shown in the effect which changes in mental set have upon one's apprehension of any production: the transformations of this type affect every detail and are often so profound as to change the once beautiful into the unutterably ugly.

According to von Allesch, configurationism provides one with a stable canon of taste based upon the organic completeness or integration of the material structure represented.[13] A fine work of art is comprised of dependent members, a thesis which holds in classic or Renaissance architecture where one can come to rest at any point, or in baroque and, to some extent Gothic, where the feeling of dynamic incompleteness and simultaneous forward and backward reference creates an impression of movement. In any event, art is essentially construction, and the major business of aesthetics is to comprehend the resulting structures.

In a later article,[14] von Allesch has tried to specify the nature of the essential structural features which characterize good art, no matter what its content or the *Weltanschauung* of its creator. He holds that there are four main indices of excellence—*unity, compactness, breadth,* and *intensity.* None of these qualities are satisfactorily definable and all require concrete exemplification. The Apollo of the east gable at Olympia is a sculpture which reveals in every detail the noble, the heroic, the god-like, and the sublime. The effect, being one of unbelievable power, is possible only because intentional unity is at its maximum here. Compactness, or condensation, (= art of omission?) appears

[13] Psychologische Bemerkungen zu zwei Werken der neueren Kunstgeschichte, *Psychol. Forsch.,* 1922, *2,* 366–381. Cf. this view with Van Doren's remark that "Art must have its periods. It cannot be put off with a mere semicolon."

[14] "Ueber Künstlerischen Wert," *Psychol. Forsch.,* 1923, *4,* 23–32.

Those readers who take delight in the belief that there is nothing new under the sun will enjoy this pertinent citation from Renan's introduction to his famous *Life of Jesus:* "The essential condition of the creations of art is, that they shall form a living system of which all the parts are mutually dependent and related."

when the essence of an experience, or the typical symbol thereof is represented, as in Giotto's paintings. The best examples of modern architecture with their decisive rejection of all superficial ornament also illustrate this factor of *Prägnanz.* The third earmark of high art is its breadth and earnestness. This is what is so appealing in the work of Van Gogh, Rembrandt, and Michelangelo, who somehow add to the observer's comprehension of man and the world. Some early nineteenth-century pictures may satisfy the first two criteria of excellence, but fail just at this point: the house and garden scenes, the horse-races, etc., may be charming but they are unimpressive. Intensity is a general quality shared by all fine art, the trait which is responsible for its forceful and penetrating effect. All these criteria can be successfully applied only when one understands that they are *Gestaltqualitäten.*

Impressionism is too shifting a basis for artistic criticism to rest upon and it is conceivable that the Gestalt position will supply critics with a permanently valid set of standards by which to judge new productions. Maier and Reninger[15] have made the first tentative endeavors to operate constructively in this difficult and elusive task. They state:

> Once the artist has made his interpretation, he may find it desirable to communicate it to others for their understanding and examination. He therefore transfers stone, or wood, or rhythm and melody, or words. For the artist's own experience no concrete medium is necessary: the work of art, for him, is already in his mind. If we are to experience his configuration, he must communicate it to us. That is, he must set up certain concrete symbols, or substitute objects, which will act as stimuli, which will in turn produce in us approximately the same interpretation experienced by the artist. . . . Therefore, criticism has three questions to answer: (1) What is the artist's configuration? (2) How valuable is it? (3) How effectively has he communicated it? (pp. 14-19.)

This suggests that the criterion of *transposability* may also serve as the touchstone of the adequacy of aesthetic experience. In the field of literature, the writer's configuration (Coleridge's, e.g.) comes from a response to a situation (the events leading up to the composition of *The Ancient Mariner*); the reader's

[15] *A Psychological Approach to Literary Criticism,* Appleton, 1933.

configuration comes from a response to language (the word pattern and "swing" of this lyrical ballad). These configurations must be nearly identical if the writing is to be successful.

Ethics

The domain of morality has so long been associated with religious instruction that any effort to deal objectively with it is still greeted with suspicion. Even highly scientific minds view ethical conduct as an expression of human irrationality and consider it a hopelessly subjective matter; yet strangely enough, from the Gestalt point of view, it may represent the culmination of man's rational nature.

The latter position is made tenable by a simple extension of the notion of insight to an appreciation of the social consequences of one's actions. A "good" act is one which takes into consideration all the immediate and long-distance effects which it may draw after it, and is performed only if it leads to a better group organization (in the sense of Wertheimer's "good" gestalt). A "bad" act, on the other hand, is one executed out of relation to the setting in which it occurs and thereby inevitably creates tension or conflict between the offender and the society of which he is a "member." Society, however, is not absolved of at least partial responsibility, for there must be something "wrong" with it that one of its parts should react in a way which defeats its own integration.

Certain advantages which inhere in this interpretation are:

1. It is optimistic, for by identifying goodness with the operation of *Prägnanz* it suggests a steady evolution toward improved and more harmonious behavior. Symmetry as an end-state in memory and perception is matched by an equivalent drive toward "balance" in action. The possibilities which this conception holds for a scientific basis for happiness are obvious.

2. It is rational and supports the Socratic view that the wise man is also the virtuous one. A young child or a mentally deficient adult are incapable of ethical conduct because the structures which must be apprehended exceed the limitations of their insight. It is for the opposite reason that Arnold's praise of

Sophocles may be considered the height of esteem—"He saw life steadily and he *saw it whole!*" The ethical significance of the mental hygienist's emphasis upon an "integrated personality" is likewise revealed in a new light.

3. It is just and humane. "Society and the individual share in the ethical responsibility for the deeds of man; society because *it* is the whole from which man derives his moral standards, and the individual, because *he* is the immediate agent of the deed, executed in terms of his judgment." [16] The individual is simply the figure, subject to all the field-forces [17] which the ground exerts upon him.

---

[16] Wheeler, *Laws of Human Nature,* New York, 1932, p. 116.

[17] The *mores* and social pressure?—The reader should be cautioned that Wheeler's "physicalism" at times approaches the extreme limit of plausibility. In a minor article on "The Crisis in Educational Objectives" (*Journal of Educational Administration and Supervision,* 1934, *20,* 19–25), he writes: "Nature's processes are progressions toward states of perfection of some kind under laws of unity and balance. The laws of equilibrium pertaining to energy systems become laws of peace and harmony when applied to social systems. They become ethical laws when applied to systems of value." Recent advances in thermodynamics indicate that the end-result of anorganic evolution may be chaos or the complete dissipation of all energy within a given "universe."

PART V—CRITICAL

CHAPTER 17

CRITICISMS OF GESTALT THEORY BY OTHER SCHOOLS OF THOUGHT

No matter in what field of human interest they may arise, new ideas of fundamental theoretical significance inevitably provoke intellectual warfare. Protestantism, democracy, evolution, communism, have all had their academic champions and adversaries; and in its lesser way, psychology has grown so accustomed to the din of combat around such themes as behaviorism and psychoanalysis, that it appears to move forward by a succession of polemics which amaze the layman. Many intolerant representatives of the natural sciences have viewed this situation with a scorn which has aggravated the understandable "inferiority complex" of the workers in the younger discipline. It is too often forgotten that, in general, these controversies, however unlovely the personal animosities which mar them may be, are symptoms of expanding horizons and energetic enterprise. Even if psychology be a black pot in this respect there are plenty of other kettles equally dark. It happens that in psychology (as in most human or social sciences) the points of major difference lie nearer the surface and must be encountered by the beginner early in the learning stage, whereas in other areas only the advanced student discerns the reasons for many profound oppositions. It is only the narrowly-trained specialist who is ignorant of the fact that theories of cosmic rays, subatomic behavior, and the nature of light divide physicists into hostile camps, that much of organic chemistry is a bundle of hypotheses, and that architecture is now in the throes of a "modernistic" and "functional" debate—all of which should be proudly acclaimed as signs of progress rather than apologetically concealed.

Like other important concepts, Gestalt has had its devoted friends, its bitter critics, and its dispassionate judges. To be found in the ranks of the third group is probably the safest position for a narrator who is only incidentally a commentator. Such an attitude in addition promotes that detachment and perspective which are needed for the proper understanding of this section of our survey.

The Müller-Köhler Debate

One of the earliest and severest negative critiques of configurationism was prepared by G. E. Müller,[1] after Wundt the high captain of that elementarism against which the Gestalt writers rebelled. Müller prefers to call gestalten "complexes" and to account for their acknowledged unitary character by the action of *collective attention* upon the elements, a process which results in the "composition" of the whole. Müller rests his argument upon the facts of prior experience, memory, and association, and insists that most of the Gestalt phenomena must be interpreted in this light. He admits the existence of "coherence factors" in sensory experience which condition the outcome of an act of collective attention, but it is to the latter that the psychological existence and reality of totals are primarily due.

Since this attack is so typical of those generally leveled at configurationism, Köhler has prepared an elaborate defense[2] of the unique Gestalt approach. A few decades ago, a rejection of the empirical psychology of the time occurred because thoughtful people were repelled by the meaningless and accidental character of the psychic events which they saw it implied. To an extent this older point of view had its legitimate ethos, since it was a reaction against the romantic nature philosophy of a century ago. However, it is absurd to deny organization

[1] See his brochure entitled, *Komplextheorie und Gestalttheorie*, Göttingen, 1923. The tone of Müller's writing on this theme is one of hearty invective.

[2] Written under the same title as Müller's and published in *Psychol. Forsch.*, 1925, *6*, 358–416.

to our experiences or to make their structure a product of attention. The following example reveals the issues:

> Before me are some papers with a stone paperweight. The stone is optically one thing and the mass of papers another. Suppose I now produce a condition of intense observation of one corner of the stone and a neighboring bit of paper surface. The optical space in which these two things are found becomes thereby more lively and a kind of connection between them arises; but the unity of the stone and paper as a whole remains preserved. *If collective apprehension produces the boundaries and compactness of figures, then one should find the most stable complexes at points where attention is at a maximum.* The contrary is actually the case. (*Op. cit.*, p. 368.)

If one declares that experience has made the paper weight a unity, one finds difficulty in accounting for the effect of an ink spot which one has never seen, but which is just as much a whole. Everything one sees would demand deliberate attentive effort, a view which is contradicted by the fact that reversible figures undergo their characteristic alterations despite one's efforts, indicating that gestalten are in a certain sense autonomous. If one retreats and acknowledges that the collective apprehension may be thrust back into physiological formative stages and results from the color, contours, and field-properties of the stone, then conditions of a Gestalt nature are being satisfied. In this way Gestalt theorists make the concept of attention superfluous by denying to it the three grand functions which it was traditionally supposed to discharge, viz., that of synthesizer, for it is not justifiable by observation; that of threshold-determiner, for it is the gestalt which establishes the threshold; and that of a term denoting clearness, for changes of clearness also involve changes of the gestalt.

Configurationism explains the disintegration of patterns in the same terms which account for their formation. Müller's example of a "10" in which the 1 and the 0 can be seen as parts as a consequence of attentive isolation, is better explained, Köhler believes, as the inevitable sundering of "natural" sub-wholes; but other arbitrary sub-parts like ı ı ı which are also objectively present in the 10 are not seen. It is hard to segregate other than *genuine* components. Similarly, not all parts of a visual gestalt are equally capable of reproducing the whole, but only those which form "natural" units within the complex.[3] It is false to assert that attention builds a complex out of parts or elements as a mason makes a wall out of bricks, because the whole is just as perceptually immediate and direct as its parts. We do not normally see the D or the P in the letter R or the F in the E and consequently no reproductive link of the type P ⟶ R appears. The autochthonous nature of Gestalt forces, if recognized, makes superfluous accounts based on vague empiristic reasoning. The influence of experience as such is always secondary, and even then generally overestimated.

In a youthful article[4] published before the war, Köhler already anticipated some of Müller's arguments which he claims rest mainly upon the erroneous "constancy hypothesis," viz., that there is a constant relation between local stimulation and local experience.[5] Helmholtz was largely responsible for this view and he and his successors employed a number of auxiliary aids to prop up a weak hypothesis, such as the assumption that attention alters nothing about the sensory content, and that false "judgments" lead us to believe that we have other sensations than those actually present! Concerning the first point, Köhler alleges that when an overtone is isolated and heard, where before it was not perceived, that "attention" had really made it arise, i.e., it was previously not an "unnoticed" experience but psychologically non-existent. One can hardly say that a grey resulting from mixing red and green contains "unnoticed" red and green sensations! With respect to the second assumption, it is absurd to attribute complicated logical "inferences" to children who are "deceived" by apparent magnitude, memory colors, and other "illusions" just as we are.

---

[3] This point can be amplified by the following neat observation: Normally, the more of the original experience one retains, the easier it is to reproduce the whole. However, in the case of the 10 just mentioned, the reproduction occurs more readily with the 1 alone than with 1 | |. Only those processes are in contact which have an *inner* relation. Apparently, whatever is the rule in perception is also a law in memory.

[4] "Ueber unbemerkte Empfindungen und Urteilstäuschungen," *Zsch. f. Psychol.*, 1913, 66, 51–80.

[5] Not to be confused with the phrase or fact, "constancy of visual magnitude," etc.

Rignano-Köhler Controversy

Another eminent international authority who has entered the lists against Gestalt is Rignano.[6] Although far more sympathetic with the spirit of the new movement than Müller, he nevertheless roundly condemns it as the extreme of subjectivity. If all part-properties are determined by the whole, then such extraordinary variability is introduced that one would find recognition of any older specific object impossible since no two total-situations are alike. According to Rignano, a gestalt is really nothing other than a unification of perceptual elements together with the significance of the object thus constituted. A "thing" is built up teleologically on affective and utilitarian grounds. The question, "What is that?" is equivalent to the question, "What use does it serve?"

Rignano's method of attacking the configurationists consists in recognizing the validity of their special problems, but in offering a different hypothesis for dealing with them. He accuses Wertheimer and his disciples of mixing things up by confounding the term "gestalt" with the older and better term "concept." Once we understand how concepts arise the added notion of a gestalt in the thought-process becomes unnecessary. Applying his affective or utilitarian theory of their origin, Rignano holds that the first quantitative idea of length or distance arose from the comparison of two or more continuous stretches, which, however different in other respects, were nevertheless "equivalent" from the affective standpoint of fatigue as represented by the effort necessary to traverse a path from one spot to another. It is a familiar historical fact that the necessity for re-distributing the agricultural land bordering the Nile after its periodic floods led to the concept of surface area: each section of land held before and after the flood had to be "equivalent," i. e., equally capable of bringing forth the same amount of wheat, irrespective of the precise configuration of the allotted field. Presumably, too, it was the equivalence of various ves-

[6] The original Italian and the French paraphrase appeared in *Scientia*, September, October, and November, 1927, and May, 1928. The Berlin editors accepted a German translation for the *Forschung*, 1928, *II*, 172–187, and Professor Warren prepared an English version for the *Psychol. Review*, 1928, *35*, 118–135, under the title, "The Psychological Theory of Form."

sels of different form to hold water in amounts adequate to allay the thirst of a certain group of persons for an identical number of days which led to the concept of volume. Similarly, it is probable that it was the "equivalence" existing between the work accomplished by a powerful man as compared with several younger folk in lifting a heavy stone, felling a tree, etc., which marked the origin of the idea of energy.

To the charge of confusion, Köhler [7] (who as usual is in the front ranks of the defenders, largely, one may suppose, because of his multilingualism and his pitiless debating skill) retorts that the terms "form" and "shape" in other tongues adequately represent only the abstract connotation of gestalt, which in German since Goethe's day may also designate the concrete unity or group as such. Rignano's hypothesis of the affective or directly utilitarian origin of gestalten is refuted by the examples of the constellations, a knowledge of which constitutes the purest case of all "pure" science, cloud shapes, dimly-seen objects, etc. Visual tests, made immediately after an operation has conferred sight upon persons born blind, generally show that the patients do not *recognize* objects which they may have touched often before, but more significant is the fact that they comprehend the question, "What is *that* there?" which indicates that some kind of *extended unity* must exist in their field of view. If the immediate perception of these entities be acknowledged—as it must be—the absurdity of an affective origin becomes clear, because the patients could not have built up the units they perceived by such means. Whenever we say to ourselves or others: "Now look here! What may that something there be, at the foot of that hill, just to the right of the next tree, between those two houses, and so on?"—we ask about the meaning or the use of that something, demonstrating by that very question that segregation is independent of knowledge and meaning. Moreover, the utilitarian view collapses altogether when one recalls that crows and other animals, whose interests and preferences are certainly quite other than our own, still react to gestalten in the way which the configurationist theory demands.

[7] "Bemerkungen zur Gestalttheorie," *Psychol. Forsch.*, 1928, *11*, 188–234.

The laws of physical chemistry must be employed to help in accounting for the presence of segregated items in sensory experience. There is no reason to think of a "pre-established harmony" between external physical configurations and those within the organism. The interior of a homogeneous solution is known to contain a respectable amount of intrinsic energies; at the border other types of forces arise which under certain conditions maintain the contour; electromotive effects create a potential difference between the inner and outer areas, and the surface tension encloses the inner region like a cloak, embracing it as a unity and even simplifying its form. This is the source of whatever "independence" a natural thing possesses. Often a color difference is sufficient to establish the segregation as in the contrast between a tree and the surrounding grass, or even in the case of a stone upon the ground. Rough is distinguished from smooth, and clear from dull, on much the same basis.

Scheerer's Judgment

The reactions to any new scientific standpoint are invariably reflections of the theoretical prepossessions of the critics as one sees so clearly in the behaviorist's and elementarist's rejection of the claims of configurationism. This same feature characterizes a scholarly and exhaustive examination of the Gestalt doctrine by Scheerer,[8] a pupil of Stern at Hamburg. Like his master, he judges the Gestaltists in the light of the personalist position, a philosophical view holding that all mental science is concerned with an enduring ego, and akin to the self-psychology of the late Miss Calkins. As he sees it, configurationism attempts to solve the problem of subjectivity by objectifying it, and its claim that the self and consciousness are merely parts of an all-embracing natural process—an approach which endears it to many otherwise hostile judges—is alleged to be its major weakness. If psychology be the study of the outer and inner conduct of living creatures, then Scheerer holds that Gestalt is inadequate for dealing with the inner aspect. There is no "warmth" to configurationism for it fails to touch the deeds and sufferings of an active self.

[8] *Die Lehre von der Gestalt*, Berlin and Leipig, 1931.

But the main limitation of Gestalt from the standpoint of metaphysics is its false solution of the problem of meaning. It is simply not true that sensory atoms are meaningless and perceptual patterns are intrinsically meaningful. Employing Stern's dictum that there can be no gestalt without a *gestalt-er,* Scheerer believes that configurationists belittle the active modifications of the self which occur whenever a thing transforms its meaning. A curve drawn on a sheet of paper is a physical process, a symbol of some trigonometric function, an æsthetic ornament, or a religious symbol. These variations clearly are not traceable to the objective datum or thing, *(Sache)* but must result from the history of the individual self *(Person).* The locus of the problem of significance is to be sought here and not in the physical stimulus-constellation.

Brunswik's Interpretation

The attitude of Bühler and the Vienna school in general to the late developments of the Gestalt idea is typified by the competent monograph of Egon Brunswik.[9] It is his view that the Berlin school has been unduly insistent in stretching its physical interpretation and that its "structural monism" has blinded it to the fact that psychology needs other categories in addition to those of configuration. Especially has it failed in its neglect of sensation. It has tried to construct a mental world of form without content, making form the only ontologically real factor in experience. Instead, both the gestalt and the field-filling sensory quality must be present as correlates of the same total experience; sensation is not a dependent attribute of the structure but both are dependent aspects of an original whole. The gestalt is a moment of an experience, i. e., the concrete experience is not a configuration but is itself configured or *possesses* gestalt without being identical with it.

To simplify this terminological disquisition, we reproduce here Brunswik's relational table *(op. cit.* p. 94) which is representative of the views of the more conservative German psychologists who are trying to assimilate the Gestalt concepts to

[9] *Prinzipienfrage der Gestalttheorie,* in Beiträge zur Problemgeschichte der Psychologie, Jena, 1929, 78–149.

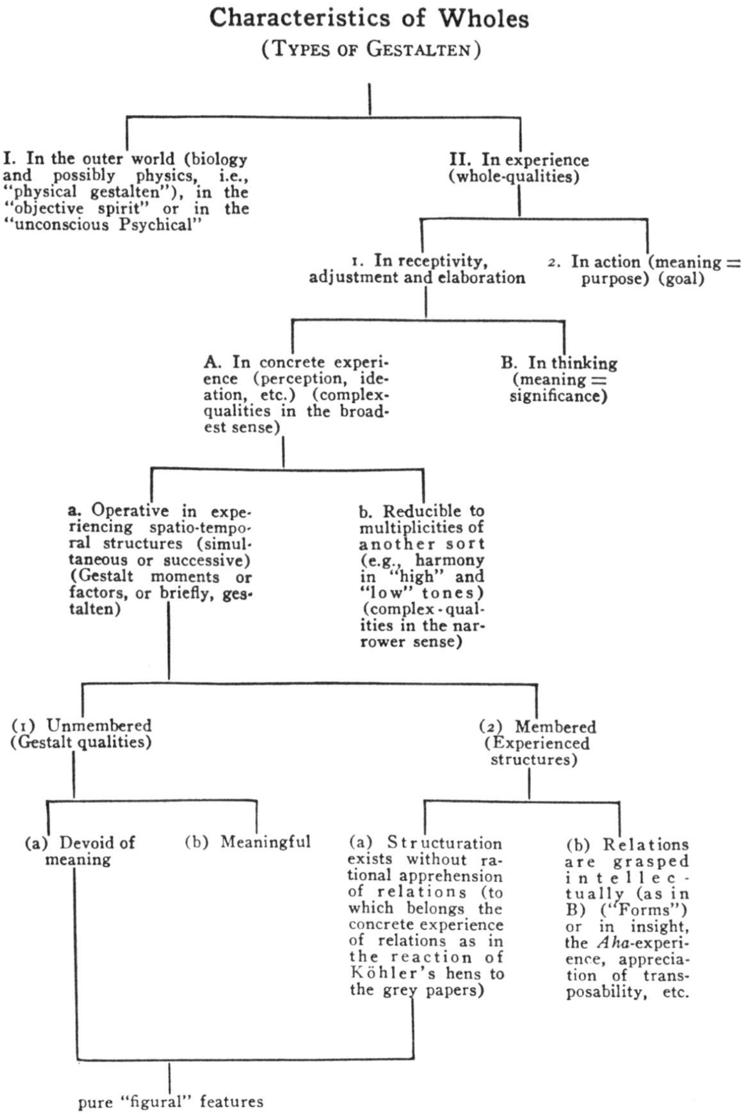

Figure 44. Brunswik's Survey of Gestalt Phraseology

the standard theoretical systems. Although the jargon is still distressing, the interrelation of the Berlin, Leipzig, Hamburg, Marburg, and Vienna groups—to mention only the leading schools—is implicit in this survey of the phraseology. Small wonder that in the absence of such a verbal guide each coterie should accuse the other of conceptual confusion!

Petermann's Analysis

Petermann's examination of the validity of Gestalt principles ranks as the leading ambitious and thorough endeavor to assess their significance for modern psychology,[10] and it is known to represent the point of view of a large body of continental workers.[11] He has nothing but praise for its proclamation of the anti-synthetic standpoint as the only adequate means of studying the problem of totality and the imposing range of applicability which this has revealed. On the other hand, it is doubtful if sufficient evidence has been brought forward to compel one to give up the old distinction between sensory processes and higher processes, since the entire theory is weak in its failure to recognize the primary influence of subjective factors, i. e., the modes of apprehension in determining the character of the perceived configuration. The means by which it seeks to adapt itself to the facts of subjective variability of phenomenal figural structures are far from satisfactory; the endeavor to fill the gaps met at this point ends in a purely verbal solution.

Certain Gestalt ideas, especially its key one of *Prägnanz,* exhibit a suspicious and remarkable teleology—none other than that which impelled the Greeks, and Kepler in his more mystic moods, to regard the sphere as the most perfect body and circular movement as the ideal movement. The freedom with which it is used shows the dangers of all attempts to explain the known by the unknown, for the greater number of such interpretations are purely *ad hoc* constructions without meaning outside the special circumstances they are called upon to explain. A very serious defect of configurationist theory has been its implied

---

[10] *The Gestalt Theory and the Problem of Configuration* (English trans.), New York, 1932. This edition creates a much more clumsy and labored effect than the original.

[11] Ach has personally put his stamp of approval upon Petermann's work, considering it the "definitive" statement.

belief that it is possible to solve research problems by the introduction of a few new categories. "In so far as the catchwords gestalt, gestalt completion, gestalt conformance to laws, create the illusion of a solution where in fact unsolved problems are still involved, we must regard the introduction of these categories as outrightly detrimental. The transition to gestalt dogmatism of this sort spells the end of psychological research."

So many new psychologies have sought to win popular favor by maintaining that they were closer to the realities of life than the views they wished to supplant that the Gestaltists may be pardoned for having stooped to this sort of appeal. Its falsehood is apparent to any one who cares to inspect the record of the topics with which they have busied themselves. They do not touch the ordinary man's concerns any more intimately than Fechner's foibles or Hering's color theory. It is really amazing that any brand of psychology should feel it necessary to publicize itself in this way, for certainly the superiority of the Einsteinian view of the universe to the Newtonian does not lie in its greater intelligibility or nearer approach to the central life interests of man. Petermann is unqualifiedly right in refusing to admit this pretentious claim of configurationism. To quote:

> The Gestalt theory's claim that its enunciations link up especially closely with life, rests upon the fact that it seemingly has the means of forthwith mastering, unequivocally, the problems of the meaning, of the purposiveness, and of the internal organization of our stream of consciousness, in terms of its basic doctrine. But how does this mastery of these problems develop? Once more, very simply: both the facts of meaningfulness, and those of purposefulness, as well as those of organization, are without exception correlated to the "structure" or gestalt concept. The concept of meaning, as well as that of purpose, is unhesitatingly identified with the gestalt concept, as conceived by the Gestalt theory—and this settles the whole matter. The fact that thought sequences have meaning, that reactions "leap forward" meaningfully out of what is given in the outside world, is simply due to the fact that gestalt coherences are present, which, as befits their essential nature, from the outset far transcend the "intrinsic arbitrariness" of atomistic coordination, in their inner closure and complete organization. (*Op. cit.*, pp. 300-301.)

But what has been achieved by this recognition? Since this is a point on which both Scheerer and Petermann are in complete agreement, we may in all fairness condemn the Gestalt protagonists for having overreached themselves in this respect. Perhaps it was merely an exaggeration made in the first blush of evangelical zeal, but since it has been allowed to stand without correction, we may assume that its proponents have not budged from their original position. So much the worse for them!

Helson's Verdict

Among the first and most competent appraisals of the Gestalt system is a treatment coming from the sympathetic hands of Helson.[12] Strongly attracted by the theoretical and experimental accomplishments of the movement, he has nevertheless been able to appreciate the weaknesses of many of its claims. In this citation he has shrewdly placed his finger upon one of the main limitations of the doctrine: "Questions and problems which have been the bugbear of other schools of psychology receive short shrift from the configurationists, who act upon the maxim given by Goethe to a friend, 'The greatest art in theoretical and practical life consists in changing the *problems* into a *postulate.*' The problem of complexes and relations is turned by the configurationists into a postulate and the riddle is solved" (Helson, p. 359). Despite the high authority of Goethe and the impossibility of research devoid of postulates, this method of attack is of dubious legitimacy. The great question for psychology, "How does organization occur in mental life?" is answered by saying that there never was a time when it was unorganized. Organization is coextensive and coexistent with mind. This may be the case but the reply comes dangerously near to begging the question.[13] How can there be organization with nothing to organize? Moreover, there seems to be some justification for

[12] "The Psychology of Gestalt," a series of four papers in the *Amer. J. Psychol.*, 1925, *36*, 342–370; 494–526; 1926, *37*, 25–62; 189–223. An excellent digest of the work available at that time.

[13] Allport, whose early article did much to introduce the English literati to configurationism, offers this same point as his most devastating criticism, "After the reader has grasped the issues he can perhaps decide for himself whether the experimentalists of the Gestalt school are justified in their refusal to reduce to simpler terms the experience of the structural complex; whether in their insistence upon the apprehension of the form of the whole independent of the apprehension of the constituent parts they are not dwelling in wonderland where grins may exist apart from cats; and whether, after all, the problems of content, attention-levels, relationship, and synthesis, association and attitude, are solved (or whether the question is begged) by postulating structural units as the ultimate facts of mental life." *Psyche*, 1924, 354–361.

the view that the Gestaltists find wholes in experience because they restrict their search to them.

If this be an outstanding deficiency, it is all but balanced by another excellent feature of this far-reaching program. Among members of the new school the emphasis upon physical and physiological hypotheses, while not peculiar to this brand of psychology, indicates a tendency to seek objective explanations of phenomenal facts, or at least to employ principles common to the natural or so-called "objective" sciences. As Helson remarks, the mind thus becomes a phenomenon within a larger system of phenomena and amenable to precisely the same laws, with no peculiar status or properties; but it does not lead to behaviorism which was a narrowly-conceived and amateurish endeavor to do the same thing. Instead, configurationism hopes to make the transition from brain process to conscious process without any break in theory. To do this, however, the concept of configuration becomes almost universal in application. It is to be expected that what it gains in universality it loses in specificity and uniqueness; hence the variety of meanings of the term "gestalt." We cannot be sure in any given case whether the facts referred to are psychological, biological, physical, or logical.[14] A single concept for all psychology is both a strength and a weakness. Clear thinking suffers thereby, although an advocate could defend this elasticity of meaning by pointing to its fundamental character, gestalt being a basic concept of *all* science like substance, energy, quantity, etc. Nevertheless, so many variables must be included within the configuration that, in its broadest sense, it means no more—and no less—than the totality of conditions both within and without the organism;—the nov-

[14] The following statement is representative of the irritation which many persons rightly or wrongly feel when the new terminology is brought into action, "The term insight functions as a most convenient maid-of-all-work for the configurationists. When search is made for the definition of insight, it at once appears that insight may assume so many forms, is so distinctly protean, that one is sometimes forced to wonder at the magical powers attached to this word." Squires, "A Criticism of the Configurationist's Interpretation of Structuralism," *Amer. J. Psychol.*, 1930, *42*, 134–140. Incidentally, Rubin himself acknowledges that a satisfactory definition of Gestalt is not easy to find. Some persons prefer the term "organic unit" to gestalt because of the latter's visual connotation. It is this fact, too, which may be responsible for the complaint that Gestalt literature does not distinguish adequately between laws which hold for all gestalten and those which are valid only for a special sense-modality. There is little doubt that psychology is constantly waging a battle with language and never quite expressing that which it intends. Tolman's *Purposive Behavior in Animals and Men* is a recent illustration of this. His sign-gestalt doctrine is a diluted and clumsy variety of configurationism. However, his distinction between behavior as a "molar" phenomenon and the "molecular" phenomena which constitute the underlying physiology is a useful one.

elty and significance of which is, comprehensively enough, not clear to many psychologists. If we assert that a given phenomenon is due to the configuration, we are merely uttering tautologies, for we are only saying that the total state of affairs is responsible for something in the total state of affairs, or that the total situation is what it is by virtue of being what it is!

Woodworth and the Critique of the Eclectics

One of the soberest and most effective criticisms of the Gestalt system has been made by Woodworth, whose theoretical views are fundamentally eclectic,[15] in the best sense of that much abused label, and hence so representative of a large body of nonpartisan psychologists. He believes that it shares in common the major defect of the introspectionists, behaviorists, and hormic psychologists, which consists in taking the particular stage of the total reaction in which they are most interested and interpreting the whole reaction in terms of that one stage. One group concentrates upon the sensation, the other upon the muscular reaction, and so on. The perceptionists or Gestaltists are able to oppose an enlightened "dynamic" conception only because in their general theory they "ignore the all-or-none law, intraorganic thresholds, synapse resistance, and everything that bespeaks that relative discontinuity which is implied in the notion of stimulus and response. They wish to think of the physiological mechanism as a complete continuum, similar to a network of charged wires."

Woodworth acknowledges that the Gestalt investigators have proved their case to the extent of demonstrating that perception (as well as intention and thinking) involves configuration, and

[15] The Gestalt writers are guilty of fostering a needless metaphysical uncertainty by their occasional implication that sensations do not "exist" and are "unreal." What they appear to mean is that sensations are the end-products of cognitive activity which can indeed be "found" but which are not present at the beginning of individual mental life or of any separate mental process. If pressed, most configurationists would probably follow Koffka's statement on this point: "The concept of sensation is the outcome of the analytic attitude. Sensations are real, but are not equivalent to the realities of our everyday phenomenal world. Being a reality, being a process producible under certain well-established conditions, sensation is worthy of study. The investigation of sensation may even help us to understand and better the laws of other and more natural phenomena but it will not do so if the sensation is treated according to the teaching of traditional psychology, as a mental element."—"Introspection and the Method of Psychology," *Brit. J. Psychol.* 1924, *15*, p. 158.

that the configuration is not to be described as the aggregation of elements. But unfortunately they are not content with this concession and in an access of extremism they contend that there is no unfigured activity of the organism, denying the reality of sensation because it is an unfigured stage in the total response.[16] To the conservative judge, however, there is no reason for considering any one stage of the complete reaction as more or less "real" than another.

A further doctrine to which Woodworth objects is the implication that a physical gestalt is necessary or sufficient to insure a perceived gestalt.[17]

> The "phi-phenomenon" is an instance of a perceived gestalt without any physical gestalt. The apparent movement in the motion-pictures is another example, since there is no physical motion on the screen. The constellations which we so readily see in the sky are not astronomical systems, but simply aggregations of luminous points that happen to lie in nearly the same direction from the earth. On the other hand, the solar system, which is a physical gestalt, is not readily perceived as such, but the conception of its dynamic unity has to be built up by piecing together discrete facts. The rolling ball we do not readily see as a unitary process (in which the motion of every particle in the ball is determined by the motion of the whole ball), but we do not see, and entirely overlook, the friction of the ball on the ground, which is essential to the physical gestalt, as without it the ball would not roll. It would seem, then, that the presence of physical gestalten in the environment is irrelevant to the perception of gestalt, and that we are still free to believe in an unfigured sensory stage in the total response of the organism. (*Op. cit.*, p. 68.)

Configurationists would acknowledge the correctness of many of these points, and Köhler himself employed them effectively in his polemic with Rignano (*vide supra*), but they deny that its consequences are in any way damaging to their scheme. A perceptual gestalt is dependent upon conditions, some internal and some external, and the major business of experimentation

---

[16] "Gestalt Psychology and the Concept of Reaction Stages," *Amer. J. Psychol.*, 1927, *39*, 62–92 (Washburn commemorative volume).

[17] Woodworth later generously retracted his assertion that "Finding configuration to exist outside the organism, they suggest that it passes by some continuous flux into the organism, so that there need be no unfigured stage in the organism's response." Nevertheless, the present writer confesses that there is much in Köhler's *Physische Gestalten* which could justifiably lead to this reading even though no specific passage can be found. Cf. *Psychologies of 1930*, p. 334.

is to establish what these are in detail, irrespective of the kind of organization involved.[18]

What is probably Woodworth's strongest concrete argument is presented in the following passage:

> The Gestalt conception seems especially inadequate to deal with the effects of a plurality of stimuli. Consider the case of two simultaneous stimuli. Let two bright lights suddenly appear in the field of view, one to the right and one to the left of the present fixation point. If either light were alone, "equilibrium" would be reëstablished by a turning of the eyes toward that light. Since both lights act at once, the principle of a continuum of forces would require us to conclude that the two forces would balance each other according to the parallelogram of forces, so that the eyes would remain staring straight forward, or come to rest at some intermediate position, according to the relative intensity of the two lights. Nothing of this sort occurs, however, but the eyes fixate one or the other of the two lights, and later, very likely, shift to the other. This principle of alternative responses, or of reciprocal inhibition, is illustrated also in spinal reflexes, in binocular rivalry, in the staircase and other ambiguous figures, in selective attention and selective motor response, and is absolutely characteristic of the behavior of the organism. Plurality of simultaneous stimuli is universal, and selective response is equally universal. The physiological Gestalt theory simply does not take care of this line of facts. (*Op. cit.*, p. 65.)

No one has replied to this specific stricture but it is not difficult to imagine how the objection would be met. The Gestalt position does not maintain that the *entire* visual field, e.g., is organized into a *single* pattern, but that whenever we open our eyes we observe a number of structures set off from each other. These structures characteristically behave as totals and even in

[18] The phenomena of camouflage, made familiar by the devices of the last war, show how shifting the relations between a physical and a perceptual gestalt can be made by modifying the figure-ground pattern. It is an interesting biological speculation as to how the two ever were aligned originally. Cf. a curious paper by Keen on "Protective Coloration in the Light of Gestalt Theory" in the *J. General Psychol.*, 1932, *6*, 200–203. In general, as Helson has shown, the fact that phenomenal and physical configurations do not always coincide is not cause for attributing all forms to a mental creation as the Grazers did or making the *reductio ad absurdum* of the idealistic logic—solipsism. The number of possibilities for correspondence or lack of correspondence between phenomenal and physical structures is finite (just four in fact) and we are beginning to know something of the laws governing them: a physical aggregate may be truly structured and arouse a phenomenal structure; physical structures may be paralleled by phenomenal fields lacking structuration; an unordered physical aggregate may be paralleled by either phenomenal structures or phenomenal fields lacking structuration. Correspondence depends upon a number of conditions both within and without the organism. See his discussion in "The Psychology of Gestalt," *Amer. J. Psychol.*, 1926, *37*, p. 61. Again, Köhler claims that stimulation as such is completely unorganized and that organization in a sensory field is something which originates as a characteristic achievement of the nervous system; certainly gestalten are not brought ready-made into the organism. *Gestalt Psychology*, New York, 1929, pp. 174–177.

the moot case of reversible figures, the sudden transformation when it comes affects the pattern as a whole, for we do not see first this line and then that "invert" its function—instead the entire arrangement moves together. One gestalt has been displaced by another. No organism behaves like Buridan's ass—although it may find itself in the "conflict" situation Woodworth describes—because neither the outer nor the inner situation remains exactly alike long enough to produce the theoretical stalemate indicated above.

Lund's attack [19] upon the "phantom of the Gestalt," as he entitles his paper, is representative of the logical difficulty which many psychologists feel in appraising the theoretical, as distinct from the admittedly valuable experimental, contributions of configurationism. To declare that experience is not a composite of sensational or behavior units but a composite of "wholes," "units and sub-units" called gestalten, is merely to substitute one form of atomism for another, i. e., large "chunks" of experience instead of small ones. The retort of the configurationists would be that if their patterns are atoms then it makes a big difference whether these are functional or structural entities, a distinction which the chemist tries to make when he uses the term molecule. A similar difficulty appears in the following question: "How can we have 'wholes' without 'parts,' unities without elements, experiences in which sensory and reaction elements have, at best, pseudo-existence? If I have witnessed a street accident and endeavor to give an accurate account of the experience, is my recall of the automobiles, the people, and the place *real,* my recall of the color and brightness of the objects *unreal?*" The Gestalt adherent would find little fault with this inquiry save that dynamic logic and not analysis would have asked, "How can we have 'parts' without 'wholes' or elements without unity?" If we wish to study organization as found in mental life, this inevitable dual reference must be considered.

There appear to be a good many competent scholars to whom the Gestalt system is in some respects baffling and who have yet to be convinced that their perplexities are due to their own want

---

[19] In the *J. General Psychol.*, 1929, *2*, 307–323.

of insight or comprehension rather than to some inherent deficiencies of the doctrine itself. Undoubtedly, one of the main obstacles to an appreciation of the configurationist approach has been the difficulty in discriminating its new interpretations from the older facts which it has often employed. As Wyatt [20] has pointed out, "traditional" psychology had already taught that it is a function of mind to discriminate and select from its data (the concept of figure and ground), to unify experience (the concept of wholeness), to be ever reaching a higher discrimination level (*Prägnanz,* precision, or definition), to anticipate or preperceive (closure) and to interrelate presented data *(Innigkeit).* It is an open question how much one gains by this new terminology, even though one may freely admit that the Gestalt system organizes these items of experience with less of the omnium gatherum style so typical of the older schools. Wyatt has also uncovered one of the weakest spots in the configurationist scheme: Unless we know the principles upon which in any individual case gestalt A passes on to gestalt B rather than to gestalt C, D, or E, or any of an indefinite number of possible gestalten, we can neither as theoretical psychologists explain, nor as practical psychologists (educationists, for instance), direct, the development of individual intellect, personality, or character. It is not wholly convincing to use such terms as differentiation and individuation to designate this process, for however justifiable these terms may be as *names,* they fail to advance noticeably our comprehension of *what* actually occurs or how and why it takes place.

The Configurationist's Defense

The two most devastating critical judgments which have been passed upon Gestalt theory have been: (1) the notion is far from new, all that is essential in the scheme having been put forth as early as 1890 by the various writers which have been considered in the first section of this book, and (2) no reputable psychologist ever adhered to psychic atomism of the element-

[20] "The Gestalt Enigma," *Psychol. Rev.,* 1928, *35,* 298–310.

aristic and mosaic type which configurationists continually attack, so that they are guilty of the oratorical trick of setting up a thing of straw for the purpose of tearing it down again and then boasting of this easy achievement. To these is often added a third condemnation that whatever may be true in the principal Gestalt contention is couched in such vague and general terms as to be scientifically and philosophically useless. Historical fairness compels one to acknowledge at once a certain justice in these remarks and it is small wonder that Köhler felt constrained to answer them in an article [21] primarily addressed to the lay reader.

Replying to the second point above, he readily admits that no *explicit* statements embodying the tradition which he and his associates have satirized exist, but insists that this confession does not invalidate their point. "In science, it is often much more important to ask what people are doing rather than what they are formulating. And psychologists in general ought to know that the main task of a new generation is to discover the *hidden* presuppositions of their fathers. It is these hidden presuppositions which usually have the most general and far-reaching effect, and this precisely because no one is aware of them at the time they are operative." In fact, a clearly-formulated *wrong* hypothesis would have been less pernicious than the unformulated assumptions which dominated practice.

Again, responding to the retort that the configurationists have a very deficient historical sense, Köhler maintains that the predecessors of Wertheimer were largely negative in their criticisms of the prevailing "analytical" psychology.[22] Gestalt writers can still use their contributions with telling effect, but

[21] "Some Notes on Gestalt Psychology," *International Forum*, 1931, *1*, 16–20.

[22] "Analysis" and "analytical" as used by the Gestalt psychologists have been much misunderstood. They would have created less confusion and objection in the minds of many had they not felt a literary necessity for some synonyms of "atomistic" and "mosaic." Every psychologist must *know* that the Gestaltists in their experiments inevitably "analyze" in the ordinary sense of the word, i.e., break up a broad problem into minor ones which can be more readily attacked. No research can be conducted in any other way. But they are irrevocably opposed to what may be called "analyticism," i.e., the tendency to consider parts as qualitatively unchanged by the organizations to which they belong. Failure to see this difference spoils an otherwise merry satire by E. S. Robinson, "A Little German Band," *The New Republic*, November 27, 1929, *61*, 10–14.

Bergson, in his *Introduction to Metaphysics*, states that "to analyze is to express a thing as a function of something other than itself." Leibnitz, too, had remarked that if one reduces the analysis of a piece of flint beyond a certain point it loses all flint-like characteristics.

the characteristic positive contributions are wholly different. Thus,

> Bergson seems to have been aware of the seriousness of the problem. But he goes from one extreme to the other. Denying atomism, he declares all boundaries, limits and segregations in mental life to be secondary effects of the intellect, the primary continuum of mental life being inaccessible to scientific treatment. It is obvious that Gestalt psychology does not hold with this romantic reaction against atomism. Almost the same may be said of James' criticism of atomistic psychology. He was indeed quite conscious of its inadequacy. But then a similar way out of it occurs to him as to Bergson. He declares that the field of perception, for instance, is an original continuum out of which we cut separate entities only on pragmatic grounds. This attitude definitely blocked the way to Gestalt psychology and there is in the teachings of James no indication of other explanations but this empiristic or pragmatistic one. And the empiristic principle is strictly opposed to dynamic autochthonous organization, which forms the central notion of Gestalt psychology.

If configurationism can be said to have gotten its ideas anywhere, they were suggested not by nineteenth-century philosophers, psychologists, or biologists, but by the most up-to-date physicists. Köhler especially mentions Planck's lecture on the "Present System of Theoretical Physics" in 1910 as the first clear-cut recognition of the Gestalt principle in natural science.[23]

To the charge of vagueness in the concepts of the new school, Köhler answers that this is inevitable in the initial stages of any scientific movement and that it is only with the progress of research that definite ideas could be centered about such terms as force, energy, entropy, and quantum. Advance in fundamentals will be retarded if final definitions are insisted upon at the beginning. Nothing is more pertinent to this issue than Lashley's dictum, "We seem to have no choice but to be vague or to be wrong."

---

[23] Whitehead is responsible for the following statements which show the often inarticulate common trend of natural science as a whole: "Science is taking on a new aspect which is neither purely physical, nor purely biological. It is becoming the study of organisms. Biology is the study of the larger organisms; whereas physics is the study of the smaller organisms." . . "An electron within a living body is different from an electron outside it, by reason of the plan of the body; but it runs within the body in accordance with its character within the body; that is to say, in accordance with the general plan of the body, and this plan includes the mental state." *Science and the Modern World,* Cambridge, 1926, pp. 145 and 111, respectively.

Wheeler, Perkins, and Bartley[24] have prepared four useful papers on the errors in recent critiques of Gestalt psychology which should serve to eliminate some of the most annoying sources of confusion. They admit the presence of inconsistencies in the literature of configurationism but claim that it has changed much since 1925, whereas most of the unfavorable verdicts are based on material available before that date. The existence of inconsistencies within a systematic theoretical structure may simply be a sign of rapid growth rather than of an irreconcilable opposition. One of their subtlest defenses is based upon the claim that the great majority of psychologists have an inadequate conception of the history of their subject. This notion, sanctified by the foremost historians of science, is that progress comes through unnoticeable increments. As soon as one holds that progress by spurts is an illusion one is committed to "machinism" as a theory of intellectual growth, both in individual and in group life.

It is also a fallacy to regard a new system from an old standpoint. The mere fact that Aristotle's *Poetics* and a host of antetwentieth-century writings contain vague references to the nature of wholes does not mean that the Gestalt principle had been "anticipated" long ago—it merely shows that the problem to which it refers had been struggled with but not *solved*. Nor will it do to dismiss configurationism with the gesture that it has simply put a lot of shiny labels upon ancient concepts;[25] instead, "Man uses the same words so long as his ideas do not change, and a change of words is a sign of a change in ideas."

Many persons insist that the prestige of Gestalt would be more secure if it thrust its experimentally-verified facts into the foreground and "soft-pedalled" its nebulous theories. However, Sir Arthur Eddington has recently suggested that we add this maxim to the rules for the guidance of science, "Never believe an experiment until it is checked by theory!" Wheeler and his associates therefore maintain that atomistic logic leads to the

[24] *Psychol. Rev.*, 1931, *38*, 109–136; 1933, *40*, 221–245; 303–323; 412–433.

[25] Here one may have recourse to a clever two-way argument: "If Gestalt is just the venerable, respectable psychology all over again in new clothes, then the targets of all this indifference, sarcasm, dogmatism, even contempt, are, in terms of the critics' own positions, the critics themselves, and the very psychologies which they are defending. The myth, the ghost, the straw man, comes home to roost!"

false supposition that a fact can be stated without also stating implicitly a theory. Even the apparently bald and non-committal description, "A piece of chalk fell to the floor," fairly reeks with assumptions pertaining to the law of falling bodies. There are no purely objective scientific facts, facts which do not contain or depend upon an assumption or inference. Experimental observations are not self-interpreting. In the Gestalt scheme, the function of theory is to serve as a framework to which facts are referred and the facts themselves are altered by being placed within one or the other system. Darwin's discovery of natural selection and of organic evolution is an interesting case in point. He had the facts from his study of plants and animals well in hand but they were unorganized and therefore without meaning because he had no theory to account for the facts. While reading Malthus' essay on population, Darwin suddenly formulated the theory which integrated all his facts into a single system.

To the frequently repeated charge that they are not historically-minded and hence do not recognize the origin of their ideas, the configurationists retort that the validity of this indictment depends upon the manner in which one interprets the history of scientific thought. It is perfectly true that the famous problem of "The Many and the One" goes back to the Ionian and Eleatic nature-philosophers of pre-Socratic Greece, but to have raised or stated a problem is something altogether different from solving it. Moreover, one must not mistake superficial resemblance for true identity. What Aristotle called "form" was disembodiable; Gestalt form is not. Aristotle's form and matter were not interchangeable; Gestalt form and content are interchangeable. The same sharp difference appears in the notion of "common sense"—to Aquinas this was the *result* of pooling of the data from discrete senses, but to the configurationist it is the origin of them.

To the charge of intolerance and unwillingness to compromise, the Gestalt exponents simply reply that one cannot reconcile irreconcilable standpoints. Opposing psychological theories must eventually come to a show-down. Wheeler insists, "The mechanistic and organismic systems are both all-or-none systems. They begin on opposite sides of the part-whole dichotomy. The assumptions necessary for the one are precluded by the other. There is no carrying of water on both shoulders. Eclecticism cannot be a legitimate goal for science when the price paid for it is self-contradiction. An eclectic or middle-of-the-road position is impossible. One or the other is totally wrong. It is a choice between them." (*Op. cit.*, p. 433.) Evidently, Wheeler holds with Morris Cohen that the mushiness of eclecticism is typified by those soapy minds, who, when confronted by the choice between heaven and hell, hope to combine the good points of each!

CHAPTER 18

CONCLUSION: THE PRESENT STATUS OF THE GESTALT SCHOOL

Our task is done. The survey of the new movement has revealed the impact of its ideas upon other systems of thought and the nature of the transformation thus established within an experimental science. Are its claims justified, or not? Frankly, no one knows at present. Perhaps by 1950 we shall be in a position to answer with greater confidence. The safest guess would probably be that the Gestalt theory is at least partly correct, and with even more certainty we can say that some of it must be wrong. One of the major tasks of the coming decade will be to help specify this judgment and to refine the process of sifting the chaff from the wheat.

There is some reason, too, for believing that configurationism as an ardent pioneering movement may have passed its peak and that it will now have to content itself with consolidating its gains. Convinced Gestaltists smile at this pronouncement and are persuaded that they have merely begun their march of conquest. The hostility which they have everywhere aroused is not just caused by a familiar resistance to new views or a rationalization of private philosophies, but has been intensified by the aggressive manner of the advocates. An air of superiority and intolerance in exposition, an unshakable conviction of the rightness of the chosen position, and a subtle implication that failure to agree whole-heartedly is symptomatic of dullness or incompetence, are hardly calculated to win adherents or even the esteem of an enemy—especially in the light of configurationism's neglect of the healthy practice of self-criticism. They have too often interpreted an attack upon their ideas as an assault upon their own personalities, whereas the desirability of dispassionate detachment and "perspective" is plain to every mental hygienist.

Gestalt theorists appear to be guilty of a lack of insight(!) into the defects of their doctrine, as their unwillingness to modify even minor features indicates. Surely not all wit and wisdom in the psychological world are arrayed on their side. In a laudable effort at originality they have blinded themselves to all ideas akin to their own which antedated their coming and to all uncomfortable facts thereafter, thus violating one of the first canons of exact scholarship. In making this decision, we are merely following the finding of Boring,[1] who knows the archives of psychology's development as well as any man living: "The virtue of Gestalt psychology is that it is simply psychology and as old as experimental psychology. . . . The eclectic who waits upon the course of history need not fear it because it is new; the new thing about it is that it has made explicit much that often remained only implicit before."

[1] In the *Psychologies of 1930*, Worcester, pp. 123–124. Darwin's practice of jotting down in his notebook all observations and data which conflicted with his pet theories apparently never made any impression upon the more ardent members of the Gestalt group.

A NOTE ON BIBLIOGRAPHIES

The books and articles referred to throughout this text are intended to serve as a selected list of the more significant publications in the field of Gestalt psychology.

Matthaei's monograph (*supra,* page 121) contains the most thorough and inclusive list of the older references up to 1927. He segregates the theoretical from the experimental papers—a dubious procedure in this new area of research—and provides a useful classification of titles under such topics as "illusions," "tactile gestalten," etc. The only difficulty with Matthaei's alphabetization is that it may be too inclusive, for even works which touch ever so lightly upon the problem are listed. It is an extension of Sander's earlier bibliography (*supra,* page 85), so that the latter is now out of date. The same comment holds for Helson's excellent compilation (*supra,* page 288).

For literature since 1927, it is best to consult the *Psychological Abstracts,* which fortunately began publication in that year. The problem of adequate cross-references has not yet been solved, although the most important titles eventually appear under the index labels of "Gestalt," "configuration," "insight," "figure-ground," etc.

Serviceable bibliographies which are reasonably up-to-date may be found in the books by Brunswik (*supra,* page 284), Petermann (page 285) and Scheerer (page 283). The references at the ends of Wheeler's chapters in his recent volumes are also good.

The current volumes of the *Psychologische Forschung* should always be examined for forthcoming researches. There is now hardly a number of the *Zeitschrift für Psychologie, British Journal of Psychology,* and *Journal of General Psychology,* which does not contain one or more articles obviously inspired by the Gestalt standpoint.

BIOGRAPHIES

Max Wertheimer was born in Prague in 1880, attended the universities of that city and Berlin, and received his degree *summa cum laude* at Würzburg in 1904. He was not particularly successful in his early academic progress, oscillating between Frankfurt and Berlin for about twenty years before his final call to a professorial chair at Frankfurt in 1928, from which he was expelled by the Hitler government in 1933. Wertheimer is not a prolific writer nor a fluent lecturer, but his economical and cryptic expressions suggest a wider variety of ideas than actually come to light. He is now connected with the "University in Exile" at the New School for Social Research, New York.

Wolfgang Köhler was born in Reval on the Baltic in 1887, and after a year each at Tübingen and Bonn, took his degree at Berlin in 1909. Thereafter, he was an assistant and *Privatdozent* at Frankfurt until the extraordinary opportunity to work at the Tenerife Anthropoid Station presented itself during the fateful war period (1913-1920). This experience influenced his scientific career in much the same way that the *Voyage of the Beagle* determined the future course of Darwin's researches. He was made director of the *Psychologisches Institut* at the University of Berlin in 1922, after an uncertain year or two at Göttingen. His first American visit was made possible by a visiting professorship at Clark in 1925-1926; he reappeared again during 1929, and was at Harvard late in 1934. He has lectured and traveled extensively in Europe and the two Americas, and is undoubtedly the propagandist par excellence of the Gestalt school. As an Aryan he relinquished his Berlin post only after the complete disorganization of the local Psychological Institute resulting from the German political upheaval had shifted the center of Gestalt activities to the United States. He has been lecturing at Swarthmore since 1935.

Kurt Koffka was born in Berlin in 1886 and educated at the

local university. A long term of service at the provincial university of Giessen followed (1911-1927). Visiting America about the same time that Köhler did (1924-1926), he held temporary academic appointments at Cornell and Wisconsin, and since 1927 has established himself at Smith College with an energetic group of European disciples. His strongest researches are in the field of visual perception, and he has distinguished himself as a careful and precise experimenter in all the traditional problems of laboratory psychology.

Kurt Lewin was born in Mogilno, Province of Posen (now a part of Poland), in 1890 and received his degree at Berlin in 1914, after a few semesters at Freiburg and Munich. Buffeted about by his military and inflation experiences, he led a free-lance career until established in an associate professorship at Berlin in 1927. Lewin's work is a bit divergent from the main line of configurationism and motivated by a highly personal brand of natural philosophy. His repute as a child psychologist is largely fortuitous, being attributable to his clever and extensive use of motion picture films, and his recognition that children's actions exhibit Gestalt laws in greater simplicity and purity than the adult's. He, too, has had an American sojourn and held an attractive academic appointment at Stanford University during the period 1932-1933. A victim of the "Aryan" policy of the Hitler administration, he held a lectureship at Cornell during 1934-35 and has since been connected with the Iowa Child Welfare Research Station.

Erich von Hornbostel was born in Vienna in 1877 and trained at the local institution, Heidelberg, and Berlin, where he obtained his Ph.D. in 1900. Following the path of his teacher, Stumpf, his main interest has been in the psychology of sound. Hornbostel is a gifted but somewhat erratic and exotic writer and experimenter. His acceptance of the Gestalt theory seems to have been a natural and gradual evolution, and probably dates from a *Mitarbeit* with Wertheimer on auditory localization, conducted at the request of the German Ministry of War during the last years of the conflict. He, too, was a member of the faculty of the "University in Exile," but left to return to Europe.

CHRONOLOGY OF SIGNIFICANT DATES AND EVENTS IN THE DEVELOPMENT OF GESTALT PSYCHOLOGY

1877 Hornbostel born.
1880 Wertheimer born.
1885 Mach's "Analysis of Sensations."
1886 Koffka born.
1887 Köhler born.
1890 Lewin born. Ehrenfels' paper on "Gestaltqualitäten." William James' "Principles of Psychology."
1891 Meinong and the founding of the Graz school of psychology.
1892 Cornelius' identification of gestalt and feeling: the whole as primary not only in perception but in all mental life.
1893 Külpe's *Outlines of Psychology.*
1894 Dilthey's paper on descriptive *versus* analytical psychology. Beginnings of the Geisteswissenschaft movement.
1895 Von Frey on cutaneous localization.
1896 Stout's "Analytical Psychology." Dewey's criticism of the reflex arc concept.
1897 Witasek and the production-hypothesis.
1898 Monograph by Erdmann and Dodge on eye movement in reading.
1899 Thorndike and the trial-and-error version of animal learning.
1900 Schumann's papers on space-perception.
1901 Beginnings of the Würzburg school.
1902 Bentley's summary of the work of the Graz and related schools.
1906 William Stern's *Person und Sache.*
1909 Köhler's dissertation analyzing tonal attributes.
1911 Katz's monograph on the phenomenal appearances of colors.
1912 Wertheimer's article on apparent movement.
1913 Bühler's monograph on the perception of visual patterns.
1915 Original Danish edition of Rubin's volume on visually-perceived figures. Krueger's "developmental" psychology.
1917 Köhler's report to the Prussian Academy on the adaptive behavior of anthropoids establishes the concept of insight.
1920 Köhler's philosophical application of the new theory to physics and biology.
1921 Koffka's *Growth of the Mind* (first German edition).

1922 Appearance of the first number of the "Psychologische Forschung," official organ of the Gestalt movement.

1923 Müller's attack upon the Gestalt theory from the standpoint of his "complex" theory.

1924 Spranger's *Lebensformen.*

1925 Lecture-tours of Köhler and Koffka in America.

1926 *Neue Psychologische Studien,* a series from from the Leipzig laboratory under the editorship of Felix Krueger.

1927 Koffka's appointment as research professor at Smith College.

1928 Polemic with Rignano.

1929 Köhler's *Gestalt Psychology.*

1932 Lewin's academic appointment in America.

1933 Advent of Hitler; expulsion of Wertheimer, Lewin, von Hornbostel, Stern, Werner, and other scholars.

1934 Köhler at Harvard again.

1935 Koffka's *Principles of Gestalt Psychology.* Lewin's major articles translated by Adams and Zener under the title, *Dynamic Theory of Personality.*

1936 Academic seats of German psychologists in America: Wertheimer at the New School for Social Research in New York; Köhler at Swarthmore; Koffka at Smith; Lewin at the State University of Iowa; Stern at Duke; Werner at Michigan; etc.

GLOSSARY

Of the More Important Terms Encountered in Gestalt Literature

(For general definitions of technical words not listed here, consult Warren's *Dictionary of Psychology,* Houghton Mifflin Co., 1934.)

action current—an electric current observable in nerves, muscles, or glands during stimulation.

acuity—ability to respond to faint sense-impressions or to distinguish slight differences between stimuli.

all-or-none law—a biological principle applicable to single nerve or muscle cells, which states that the intensity of a response to a stimulus is causally related solely to the temporary condition of the cell and not to the intensity of the stimulus. When tissue reacts, it either does so maximally or not at all.

analysis—a scientific procedure for dividing a complex experience into simpler constituents. *Functional analysis* is a method of influencing the conditions under which an event occurs for the sake of determining the factors essential to the event.

annoyer—Thorndike's term for a stimulus causing an unpleasant feeling with consequent activity directed toward the removal of the stimulus.

aphasia—a name applied to a complex set of brain disorders in which the ability to use connected speech and to understand spoken words is impaired.

apparent magnitude—the subjective or relative size of an object as seen in visual perception; it may be either larger or smaller than the objectively real magnitude.

apparent movement—the perception of motion when non-moving stimuli are rapidly exposed with short intervals between exposures. Several kinds have been distinguished: *alpha* movement occurs when parts of standard laboratory illusions or ambiguous figures are projected on the screen; *beta* movement is the apparent change in size by way of expansion or contraction due to a real difference in the size of the alternately-exposed items; *gamma* movement is the apparent contraction or expansion when a single object is exposed or extinguished, or when the illumination is suddenly raised or lowered; *delta* movement (a rare and debated phenomenon) appears when the second stimulus is more intense than the first, the second object returning to and "picking up" the first, which is not actually observed until the second is perceived. See **phi-phenomenon** and **short-circuit theory.**

arpeggio—sounding the notes of a chord in quick succession rather than simultaneously.

associationism—a theory of mental life which holds that the presence or succession of all behavior and experience is due to connections or links between separate movements or perceptions occurring in the history of the organism. The nature of these "bonds" and the way they are produced has been variously interpreted.

atomism—the assumption that any whole is a derivative of pre-existing parts. This more general logical position becomes in psychology the view that mental life is explainable in terms of elementary psychic units.

Aufgabe—a German word meaning task or assignment, now generally implying a subject's orientation or mental set toward a problem. This attitude is usually determined by the directions given to the subject or by some decisive factors implicit in the experimental set-up. See ***Einstellung.***

Aussage—German for testimony; ordinarily refers to the accuracy with which simple observations can be reported, and hence important in appraising witnesses' statements.

backward association—Ebbinghaus' term for the weak regressive connections existing between nonsense syllables presented toward the end of a series and those occurring earlier. Gestalt theory claims that these associations can be detected only when the related items are "parts" or "moments" of a larger whole.

belongingness—Thorndike's term for that attribute of an item in a larger response which stamps it as an integral part of other items in the same set. See **membership-character.**

blind spot—a small region in the retina that is insensitive to certain kinds of light-stimulation. It marks the entry of the large optic nerve into the retinal layer and is located a few degrees toward the nose half of each retina near the horizontal plane.

bond—Thorndike's term for "whatever in the organization of the individual is responsible for his making, more or less regularly, a certain response to a given stimulus or situation." What anatomical or physiological reality corresponds to this "connection" is left undetermined in the concept.

brightness—a qualitative property often attributed to eye, ear, skin and muscle perceptions. According to Hornbostel, brightness (like intensity) is a common property of all sensory response, regardless of the receptor involved.

cerebral dominance—a brain state presumably reached through the establishment of transcortical gradients and general maturation, whereby one hemisphere controls the other in initiating and guiding action, particularly with respect to handedness. The cerebral dominance theory claims that speech and the higher mental functions are regulated by the hemisphere which controls the most used hand. Incoordination resulting from the absence of this dominance is held responsible for speech and reading defects, personality difficulties, etc.

closure—a term introduced by Wertheimer to designate one of the basic principles of mental organization, in which certain segregated but imperfect wholes (such as perceptions, memories, thoughts and actions) tend toward complete or closed forms. The word also refers to the way in which changing, incomplete systems eventually attain equilibrium. Closure seems to be a special dynamic variant of the more general principle of *Prägnanz* (or precision), which see below. The close relation between the two concepts is best seen by the fact that closure is rendered in French by the word *prégnance.*

coincidence point—a term employed in English by Koffka and Harrower (after the German original by Ackermann) whenever two adjoining fields of different hue have the same brightness index.

common sense—an older historical term used by Aristotle and the Scholastics to indicate the capacity to combine experiences derived from the separate senses. Not to be confused with intelligence or reason.

configuration—any organized whole in which there is reciprocal influence among the members and the whole, so that "the totality contains more than a mere sum of what analysis would call its *parts* and their relations." In his article in the *Psychologies of 1925,* Köhler objects to translating gestalt by the word configuration (for which Titchener seems to have been responsible), because it implies elements put together in a certain manner; its connotations are also too geometrical. Since gestalt has the advantage of being a shorter word and bearing the stamp of its special origin, it would be desirable if it eventually (as now seems likely) supplants the term configuration altogether.

constancy—refers to the fact that items of perception seem to retain their "normal" appearance despite sharp changes in local stimulus conditions. *Color constancy* means that ordinary chroma and brightness are partly independent of the surrounding illumination; *constancy of form* means that the outlines of an object are preserved when, on purely optical or geometrical grounds, a change ought to be observed; *constancy of magnitude* means the "preservation of apparent size in spite of differences in the retinal image." These facts should not be confused with the presumably false "constancy hypothesis" which maintained that the relation between a specific local stimulus and sensation persisted unaltered, provided that the condition of the receptor did not change. This view is incompatible with the dynamic character of figure-ground functions.

constellation—"the sum of all reproductive or other tendencies which operate, in accordance with the laws of association, to determine (by mutual reinforcement or inhibition) the actual course of ideas." Propounded by Selz and G. E. Müller.

content, founded or funded—psychic processes that have emerged from the stage of mental organization and consequently placed on a higher synthetic plane (Meinong).

context—in psychology this refers to the totality of conditions influencing an organism at any given moment and constituting the setting or background for some fact or event.

contiguity, law of—a principle of mental association which states that if two experiences have occurred together in space or time, the presence of one will cause the appearance of the other.

contour—the outline or boundary of a plane figure.

creative synthesis—an active mental process which produces outcomes that are not a sheer summation of the constituent elements. The phrase "creative resultants" is an alternative but less commonly used designation for the same idea.

culture—the integrated acts, beliefs, customs and social patterns displayed by a given group or tribe.

determining tendency—a mental set voluntarily aroused by means of which a desired response is insured. First brought into prominence by Ach and the Würzburg school generally. Normally it results from the acceptance of an *Aufgabe*. See ***Einstellung***.

dynamic—"pertaining to the behavior of unified energy fields in accordance with the principles of balance, wherein activities occur in consequence of differentials."

dynamic theory—a view suggested by Wertheimer and developed by Köhler that physiological events are regulated by forces in the central nervous field as a whole rather than by specific neural structures and connections. See **machine theory.**

eclecticism—the organization of compatible (and presumably the best) features of various incompatible systems of ideas into a new theory. Eclectic schemes have rarely been favored by philosophers and logicians because of the difficulty of securing a harmoniously-integrated structure.

effect, law of—a satisfying or successful result of an action tends to strengthen its connection with preceding stimuli, and an unsuccessful one tends to weaken it.

Einstellung—a set, either temporary or permanent, which predisposes one to react in a given way. See ***Aufgabe,*** which is usually assumed to involve a larger measure of awareness.

element—the simplest component of any phenomenal datum. Elementarism is any systematic psychological position which describes mental life in terms of such constituents.

emergent evolution—Lloyd Morgan's name for the doctrine that successive stages of evolution lead to wholly new products which are not predictable, instead of being mere recombinations of existing items. The term "emergent" refers broadly to the gross or *molar* properties of any kind of "higher unit," as distinct from the specific or *molecular* attributes of its components.

empiricism—the theory that all knowledge is derived from experience through the learning process. See **nativism.**

entelechy—first used by Aristotle to mean the process of self-realization. To Driesch it is identical with the "vital principle." The Gestalt concept of *Prägnanz* is probably a more matter-of-fact statement of the same idea.

exercise, law of—the frequent repetition or use of a connection between a situation and a response is said to strengthen the connection. The physiological basis of this law is obscure.

figure-ground—a general dual characteristic of perception first emphasized by Rubin. When a total field is so structured that different portions exhibit varying degrees of integration, the most highly articulated ones are called "figures" while the simpler and more homogeneous areas are "grounds." In ordinary perception, what is ground for one figure will be a figure on another ground.

form—a basic attribute of organized wholes, depending not only upon the structure of the object or event (i. e., the figure), but also upon its setting or ground.

form-quality—a word coined by Ehrenfels to refer to the conscious content occurring in complex-patterns. It is of a higher order than the separable elements or sensations and confers the special properties that such wholes possess. The word should be sharply distinguished from gestalt, but is identical with ***Gestaltqualität.***

founding (funding) process—Meinong's phrase for a mental process whereby conscious contents are organized to form patterns of a higher degree called complexes. See **production-theory.**

gestalt—the uncapitalized noun refers to all those organized units of experience and behavior which have definite properties not traceable to parts and their relations. There are many kinds of gestalten in nature, such as physical, physiological, psychological or phenomenal, and logical gestalten. Gestalten always involve formed, patterned or structured processes whether they occur within or without the organism. (Pronounce gay-shtollt′, the "a" in gestalt having approximately the quality of the "o" in doll.)

Gestalt—the capitalized noun refers to the theory that all mental experience comes organized in the form of structures which, when relatively incomplete, possess an immanent tendency toward their own completion. It rejects the assumption that isolated local determination of psychic processes ever occurs and maintains that all organic and inorganic stresses tend toward an end—the state of equilibrium. In its broadest sense, the doctrine of Gestalt is a philosophy of nature and holds for all the sciences and not just for psychology. The external universe, life and mind are composed of gestalten.

Gestaltqualität—see ***form-quality.***

gradient—any quantity which slopes from a high to a low value by minute intervals.

Heymans' law—when an inhibiting stimulus is applied, the threshold value of a given stimulus is raised in proportion to the intensity of the inhibitor.

identical elements—an educational theory stating that the results of practice in one situation are carried over to another to the extent that the two cases involve the same or similar mental processes. See **transfer of training.**

imageless thought—a theory represented by Külpe and his pupils of the Würzburg school (1900-1909) which maintained that mental processes existed that were wholly lacking in sensory content.

individuation—the emergence or differentiation of a local and specific activity from grosser mass-actions.

insight—appropriate or meaningful behavior and experience in the presence of any life-situation. The suddenness of perceptual or imaginal reconstruction of the field is the most characteristic, but not necessarily essential, feature of the process.

Korte's laws—a series of qualitative and quantitative formulations of the optimal conditions for producing apparent movement. The properties of the two stationary stimuli which are exposed in rapid succession, the time of presentation, the nature of the spatial interval, etc., are among the relations involved.

learning—in Gestalt theory, this is equivalent to the process of acquiring insight into a situation; or more generally, the process of establishing new organized wholes.

machine theory—the view that physiological processes are determined by constant conditions like neural topography rather than by dynamic forces of a self-distributing nature such as electrical stresses. See **dynamic theory.**

membership-character—that quality of a part which influences its individuality when it is a constituent of a whole.

monad—in Leibnitz's philosophical system an individual, independent unit possessing the properties of both matter and mind.

motion, illusion of—a perception of movement in a resting object.

need—a condition of the tissues or system which provokes searching or striving behavior.

organism—a complex cellular structure capable of maintaining its existence as a unitary system.

organization—whenever psychophysical forces produce integrated and stable groups, organization is said to occur. The name may refer to either the process or the product.

part—anything that is the result of division, either real or imaginary.

pattern—"a functional integration of discriminable parts, which operates or responds as a unitary whole." Considered to occur in the nervous system, in thought, and in social behavior.

personality—from the Gestalt standpoint, this is a field-property of an individual's total behavior pattern.

phi-phenomenon—Wertheimer's designation for the impression of apparent movement (which see). First demonstrated to occur in vision, but known to apply to auditory (H. E. Burtt) and tactual phenomena (Benussi). See **apparent movement** and **short-circuit theory.**

Prägnanz—Wertheimer's term for the most typical form an organization can assume and toward which every such structure tends. It is the most general law of configurations and states that all experienced fields tend to become as well articulated as possible. The best English equivalent is "precision." See also **closure.**

precision—see ***Prägnanz.***

production-theory—the view of Meinong and his disciples in the Graz school that a special intellectual activity must supervene before sensations can be fused into complex spatial and temporal patterns and relations.

pure phi—that variety of the phi-phenomenon in which no trace of an object or its color, or of anything save sheer motion can be perceived. It is a kind of "disembodied" motion.

quantum theory—refers to the conception of discontinuous or discrete changes in physical phenomena, the quantum itself being a determinate quantity. Opposed to the continuity principle that nature reveals no breaks in substance.

redintegration—a term coined by Sir William Hamilton and reinterpreted by Hollingworth to mean the arousal of a response by a fraction of the stimuli whose combination originally evoked it.

relativity, law of—in psychology, this principle holds that every experienced item is affected by every other co-existing phase of experience. Commonly refers to the limitations placed upon scientific generalizations by their pertinence only to a restricted frame of reference or "universe of discourse."

satisfier—Thorndike's term for "any stimulus or situation which fulfills or extinguishes the fundamental wants or desires" of the organism.

segregation—Köhler's term for that psychophysical product of dynamic self-distribution which results in the demarcation of definite wholes from their surroundings. The process occurs independently of prior knowledge and experience of the constitution of the field.

sensory organization—that arrangement of the stimulus pattern on the receptor surfaces which initiates and maintains the neural excitations, the organization presumably being conditioned by the properties of the original stimulus pattern.

short-circuit theory—Wertheimer's tentative hypothesis that the phi-phenomenon is caused by a short circuit between the parts of the brain excited by each stimulus, thus producing a new integrated unit. See **apparent movement.**

step-wise phenomenon—special cases of configurational patterns and responses in which the reaction is made to the differential aspects of the stimulus-complex. The structure present reveals a directional tendency of some sort, i. e., an ascending or descending series.

structure—a quality of an organized whole presumably related to the positional interdependence of its parts. Physical, physiological and phenomenal structures are all "real" existences. It is distinguished from *constellation,* for the units of the latter are assumed to have no functional relation.

structure-function—an attribute of response resulting from reaction to a total stimulus-complex rather than to its components or their relations *per se.*

system—any totality all the aspects of which are interrelated members of the whole.

tension—a state of strain or disbalance in an organism which leads to behavior in the direction of restored equilibrium.

transfer of training—the improvement of any organismic function without direct practice by virtue of the training given to some kindred function. See **identical elements.**

valence—a translation of Lewin's *Aufforderungscharakter* which signifies the attracting or repelling power of objects or actions. Where the valence is positive, the subject approaches the field; where it is negative, he tends to go away.

vector—in physics and mathematics, this has long denoted any directed magnitude, such as a velocity or force. Lewin employs an adaptation of the idea in his system of action-totals.

whole—anything that has members or phases and yet possesses attributes which distinguish it as a unit from its parts or aspects. See **part** and **membership-character.**

INDEX